W9-CAJ-303

Flame of Faith, Lamp of Learning

Flame of Faith, Lamp of Learning

A History of Valparaiso University

RICHARD BAEPLER

Cover photography: Aran Kessler
Cover design: Todd O. Earley
Internal photographs and illustrations digitized by Robert Sirko

Illustrations on pages 113–28 are taken from the Valparaiso University Archives and are used with permission.

All Scripture quotations are from the King James or Authorized Version of the Bible.

Published by Concordia Publishing House
3558 S. Jefferson Ave., St. Louis, MO 63118-3968

Manufactured in the United States of America

Library of Congress Cataloging-in-Publication Data
Baepler, Richard, 1930–
Flame of faith, lamp of learning : a history of Valparaiso University / Richard Baepler.
p. cm.
Includes bibliographical references (p.).
ISBN 0-5786-0108-5
1. Valparaiso University—History. I. Title.
LD5565.V42 B34 2001
378.772'98—dc21 2001006194

1 2 3 4 5 6 7 8 9 10 10 09 08 07 06 05 04 03 02 01

Contents

Foreword

PRESIDENT ALAN F. HARRE

No two colleges or universities are alike. Each is distinctive. Each is unique. The special qualities of an institution are forged by its particular history. Each college is shaped in some sense by the characteristics of its graduates, the generations of administrations that have managed it, the personalities and skills of its presidents, the commitments of the members of its boards of directors, and the quality and perspectives of its generations of faculty and professional staff.

The written histories of colleges and universities often address matters of curriculum, faculty, student life, the larger issues of local and national environment, tenures of presidents, the construction of buildings, and the work of outstanding persons who have had a profound impact on the college or university.

Dr. Richard Baepler has produced a readable and highly interesting review of many of the realities that have made Valparaiso University what it is in the year 2000 A.D. He tells the story well. His work reminds us of much that has been forgotten, clarifies matters of historical significance, reviews the various historical contexts in which the university has had to labor, interprets choices that it made, and gives expression to its developing mission. He provides thematic treatment of six elements:

1. The various relevant broad contexts: cultural, educational, and religious.
2. The development of the physical campus.
3. The academic life of the campus: colleges, curricula, and faculty.
4. Valparaiso student life: extracurriculum, customs, sports, Greek life, and violence.
5. Governance of the University: board, administration, and financing the university.

6. Issues of identity: church, Christian character, relationship to major constituencies, and theory of Christian education.

Yet none of these elements stands alone; they are interrelated. The story of erecting the chapel, for example, is not simply a narrative of creating the physical base of the University. It also touches on each of the five other themes. These elements collectively provide continuity and unity as the story of Valparaiso University unfolds generation after generation.

Read the pages that follow carefully. While many of your questions about Valparaiso University will be answered, I suspect the narrative will provoke in the critical reader a host of new questions to ask and subjects to explore. The complexity that surrounds Valparaiso University is great. The personalities that influenced it are numerous and diverse. The social, demographic, and economic factors changed many times, sometimes radically, during the past 140 years. Concentrate your attention on understanding the big picture by giving consideration to important specifics that helped to create that larger perspective.

Perhaps an illustration will help place this assignment into a useful context for the reader of this book. The president of a large national company once told me that he thought private college presidents confronted one of the most difficult managerial tasks, and fulfilled one of the most demanding leadership responsibilities, that anyone could have. He said that his job was easy in comparison to that of the typical private college president. When I asked him to explain what he meant, he proceeded to articulate a long list of constituents of colleges and universities that often diametrically disagree with one another in their perceptions of reality and in their hopes for a specific beloved institution of higher education. He included in his list alumni, friends, donors, parents, members of the state and national legislative bodies, state boards of higher education, governors, multiple accrediting agencies, various federal and state regulatory agencies, local officials, NCAA enforcement officials, church leaders, parish clergy, laypeople of the denomination with which the college may be affiliated, students, faculty, staff, employers of graduates of the institution, admissions committees for graduate and professional schools, and the list continued from there.

I cite these constituent dynamics not to call attention to my role as president of Valparaiso University, but to suggest that all these individuals, in their public and private roles and in the responsibilities they carry, affect the day-to-day life of the typical college and university. Their perceptions and convictions give rise to the hundreds of countervailing forces that, over the course of time, help to form the culture and shape the mission of a particular institution. By giving or withholding funds, developing and enforcing accreditation standards, passing legislation, imposing service fees, imposing renovation of residence halls through building codes, legislating accommodations for handicapped individuals, recruiting future employees on a given college campus, etc., individuals, governments, and corporations "guide" colleges and universities to accommodate themselves to these forces in subtle—and sometimes less subtle—ways.

The content of this book provides the reader with a bird's-eye view of the impact a particular faith group has on the shaping of a university. Historically, ethnic church-related colleges and universities usually were founded by particular ethnic faith groups that wanted to prepare their young people for service as clergy and for other leadership roles in the church, to protect their ethnic and linguistic heritage, and to assist the children of fellow ethnics to make the transition into the mainstream of the United States. Who those original immigrants were, what caused them to leave the homeland, the particular era in which they came to the United States, and the length of time it took them to become part of popular culture are another set of important historical variables that often have not been considered carefully enough—if at all—when the histories of denominational colleges and universities are written. These factors usually are not weighed when historians make sweeping generalizations about denominational colleges and universities.

For example, in recent years much has been made of what some observers perceive to be the drifting away of church-related colleges and universities from their denominational heritage as those colleges have sought to achieve academic excellence. The implication, if not the conclusion, usually is drawn that there is a cause-and-effect relationship between the pursuit of academic excellence and enhanced reputation of the college or university and the loosening of ties between that particular academic community and a given denominational entity.

What specific causes produce changes in social organizations are difficult to identify, much less prove conclusively. All that really may be present are interesting correlations that call attention to similarities in trends. By definition, correlations are not causes. It may well be that a number of factors are identified as taking place in a given era, and those that correlate with one another may be caused by one or more factors not yet perceived by the historian.

Thus, one would have to be blind not to see that there is often a correlation between a college's pursuit of academic excellence and decreasing loyalty to denominational entities. But at the same time, there are other correlations that need to be noted. Correlations also can be seen between movement of a college away from denominational loyalties and the degree to which important laity, clergy, and leaders of that particular denomination are committed to the proposition that Christian higher education is a compelling component of the mission of the denomination.

The diminishing faithfulness to the religious or ethnic heritage of given colleges and universities also can be correlated with a diminishing of ethnic identity among the primary founding constituents of the institution and/or the increasing number of generations that have been born in the United States to that ethnic group; the increased affluence of the denomination itself and its laity; and the reduced birthrate among ethnic groups as they become more affluent, more Americanized, and more upwardly mobile in the social class structure of the United States. The loss of denominational identity and loyalty among and within congregations of the founding group and a host of other factors also correlate with diminishing loyalties of colleges and universities to their denomination.

I believe that the list of potential correlations would become quite lengthy if we reflected carefully upon the many possibilities present in the historical record. However, as stated above, correlations do not necessarily mean cause-and-effect relationships. They are simply elements that seem to move in the same direction at the same time. The real causes of trends suggested by the observed correlations may not yet be identified. As you read these pages, make distinguishing between correlations and causes one of your objectives.

Dr. Baepler offers two potential futures for VU in the final pages of this book. Obviously, each is possible, and other alternatives may become evident at some future time. The wide diversity of thinking concerning what Lutherans in the United States believe, teach, and confess; the forces unleashed by pursuing the divergent paths of ecumenical commitment or sectarian isolation among Lutherans; and the limited concern most U.S. citizens have for what will happen 50 or 100 years from now in respect to matters of faith and life will have profound effects on VU and every other Lutheran college and university. I personally believe that the degree to which VU remains a Lutheran university will depend far more heavily upon whether Lutheranism remains a viable option in the mix of American denominationalism than upon any other factor.

In the face of all the forces that would diminish VU's relationship to its Lutheran heritage, we at Valparaiso University say of ourselves that Valpo is "intentionally Lutheran." We value what Dr. Martin Luther bequeathed to the world through his theological perspectives and the content of the Lutheran Confessions as they are set forth in the *Book of Concord*. We believe that the Lutheran Confessions are a correct understanding of the Holy Scriptures. As Lutherans, we believe with Martin Luther that councils, church leaders, and others are capable of erring and subverting the Gospel while professing commitment to that Gospel. Only rigorous study, informed and open debate, a willingness to have all confessional commitments normed by the content of Holy Scripture, and life lived in the freedom assured by the Gospel can motivate and enable the church to be both reformed and in a continuing state of reformation. Failure of the church to be in a constant state of reformation causes one generation's fire and verve to be the next generation's dead orthodoxy. And failure to be in a constant state of reformation means that believers are subjected to the twin deterrents of vibrant faith: irrelevance and stagnation—in the life of the mind, in expressions of the faith, and in fulfilling the mission of the church.

In God's Light We See Light

Preface

In the fall of 1994, Provost Roy Austensen asked me to consider updating the history of Valparaiso University as a contribution to the planned celebration in 2000 of the institution's 75th anniversary under Lutheran auspices. His overriding concern was that the voices that brought the institution to life as a Lutheran university and animated it for nearly three-quarters of a century continue to be heard by the new generations of men and women who care for this university today and tomorrow. About six weeks later, I agreed to undertake the project in the fall of 1995 and to finish it in about two years.

It soon became evident that a mere updating was out of the question. A whole subdiscipline of American historical writing had developed that addressed the history of American higher education. There were relatively new journals—the *History of Education Quarterly*, the *History of Higher Education Annual*—and an entirely new approach to this work being conducted under the inspiration of leading scholars. So my work necessarily expanded backward to 1859 and outward to the various contexts into which the institutional story should be placed. Provost Austensen understood the necessity of undertaking a more thorough and academic treatment of VU's history and gave me the freedom to recast the assignment.

I am indebted to John Strietelmeier, who first shaped the story of the University, and to James Albers, who added subsequent chapters. I am grateful to a number of institutions for access to materials in their archives and libraries: the Indiana State Historical Society, the Chicago Historical Society, the Ohio State Historical Society, the Concordia Historical Institute, the University of Chicago, the University of Notre Dame, the Porter County Historical Society, and the Porter County Public Library. I especially acknowledge the help of the staff of Moellering Memorial Library at Valparaiso University, in particular Archivist Melvin Doering, whose mastery of VU's records and lore is thorough and who gave generously of his time.

Many members of the faculty helped me through conversation and by reading various portions of the work in progress. Dr. Albert Huegli, Dr. Robert Schnabel, and Dr. Alan Harre also gave me hours of time in interviews and comments on drafts of the manuscript. John Strietelmeier's hospitable home was the site of many discussions with various guests, including Donald Mundinger, now president emeritus of Illinois College. Lillian Reiser, Walter Buescher, and Robert Springsteen provided insight into the student life of an earlier era. Springsteen also composed the index. Dorothy Smith analyzed budgets for critical periods in VU's history and provided comments. Student Steven Gjerde researched the late 1960s for me; Dorothea Nuechterlein contributed both research and editorial work. James Nuechterlein took time from his own editorial duties to comment on the manuscript. I also affectionately acknowledge the support and assistance of my own family members.

Above all, I owe an immense debt to Professor Mel Piehl. When the first draft seemed too large and cumbersome, Provost Austensen had the good sense to suggest that Piehl, an accomplished historian and writer, be enlisted to solve some organizational problems and propose what should go and what should be retained. Unfortunately, much material of interest to a student of VU's history had to go, such as, for example, much new material on Henry Baker Brown and details of the context of professional education important for understanding Valparaiso's law, engineering, medical, and dental schools. Then, when budgetary problems required cutting the manuscript by another 25 percent, Piehl consented to help once again.

At the beginning of the project, I was tempted to make this work essentially a contribution to the new scholarship on higher education. It became clear, however, that the primary readership would be members of VU's broader family and that, therefore, a more popular presentation would be required. While not a scholarly work in the technical sense, the book is based on scholarship. Such notes as were included are designed to help readers pursue whatever interests in Valparaiso's history they may have. The notes and bibliography are not exhaustive, but suggest the many sources upon which the story relies. The title of the book is taken from the University hymn, composed by Philip and Martin Gehring.

What is most distinctive about Valparaiso University are the amazing people who have been drawn to this place: its faculty and staff, its student body, its alumni, and its key supporters. Some of them are mentioned in this book. Most could not be, such as Martha (Fritz) Baepler, Arthur Hallerberg, Jane Looman, Sharon Hersemann, William Seeber, Bette Galow, Paul Strasen, Barbara (Jutzi) Kehe—and many more. Without them, VU would be only an ordinary, good university. To them this book is dedicated.

—Richard Baepler

PART I

The First Two Valparaiso Colleges (1859–1925)

1

A Methodist College in the Vale of Paradise

Origins

Valparaiso University traces its origins to the founding of the Valparaiso Male and Female College in 1859. That same year, the abolitionist John Brown raided Harper's Ferry, setting the stage for Abraham Lincoln's election, the secession of the South, and the horrific Civil War that followed. The previous year, the newly ambitious University of Michigan in Ann Arbor offered graduate degrees for the first time, a first small sign pointing to the future overshadowing of the "old-time college" that dominated American higher education in the antebellum years.

Neither the academic world nor the nation at large took notice as one more new "collegiate foundation" appeared on the midwestern landscape. Even if they had, few people beyond the pioneer-era Indiana town and local circles of Methodist clergy would have held out any high hopes for its future. Yet the larger history of American higher education, and indeed of American society, was to be strikingly registered in the subsequent history of that small Methodist college and its two successors. Eventually, through many surprising twists and turns, near-death experiences, and dramatic resurrections, the "collegiate institution" in Valparaiso began to make its own distinct contribution to those greater stories as well.

The first of three quite different incarnations of the institution now called Valparaiso University, the Methodist Valparaiso Male and Female College lasted for only 12 years beyond its founding. During this period, the small college touched the lives of nearly 2,000 students, most of them in its preparatory division. A common curriculum, common texts, and a shared approach to education linked the VMFC to a network of more than

200 mostly Protestant colleges then scattered across the landscape of the United States.

Despite its short history, the story of this school on a hill opens a window on the larger story of the early search for a uniquely American form of education. "Old-time colleges" such as Valparaiso helped to shape the values, public discourse, and institutions of a youthful society at a time when the nation was torn by political antagonisms and eventually bloodshed. One of the last "antebellum colleges" to appear on the scene, the VMFC weathered the stormy campaign that put Lincoln and the new, aggressive Republican Party in power. It survived the competition of a rival Presbyterian Valparaiso Collegiate Institute. It suffered successfully through the grim days of a prolonged Civil War. But it finally succumbed when it lost its supporting preparatory division to the new politics of public education.

The Valparaiso Male and Female College, like many similar institutions, emerged from the closely paired impulses of American republicanism and religious faith. Faced with building a new nation, the Revolutionary generation declared education for character essential to the future of a free people. The grandest law reflecting this commitment was the Northwest Ordinance of 1787, passed by Congress under the Articles of Confederation. This ordinance set aside land grants for schooling in every township in the future territories of Ohio, Michigan, Indiana, Illinois, and Wisconsin. Linking patriotism, religion, and learning, the ordinance proclaimed: "Religion, Morality and Knowledge being necessary to good government and the happiness of mankind, schools and the means of education shall forever be encouraged."

Amid the raw frontier conditions that still prevailed in the Great Lakes region in the first decades of the nineteenth century, the newly admitted states proved incapable of establishing public education on their own. Into this vacuum of public policy stepped the Protestant churches. Demoralized by low membership and loss of state tax support immediately after the Revolutionary War, the churches had emerged fresh and self-confident from the Second Great Awakening that swept across the country after 1800. By the 1830s, evangelical Protestant Christianity had become the largest single subculture in the United States. Merging Christian tenets with democratic popular culture and employing the method of explosive revivals, the popular churches such as the Methodists and Baptists exhibited a passion to convert the rough-and-ready frontier population and create the moral commitments necessary to build civilized communities.

A whole network of voluntary organizations helped mobilize the evangelical crusade, both on the Atlantic seaboard and among the people pouring into the West. Prominent among their many causes were the common school, the academies, and the colleges, all considered heralds of the kingdom of God and strongholds of what many called "the Christian Republic." Church leaders clearly understood that whoever controlled the nation's educational institutions controlled the future. In addition, the suddenly swarming Catholic immigration of the 1830s and after, thought to be antirepublican and absolutist, gave urgency to the Protestants' rush to build institutions to stem the tide.

Indiana's constitution initially envisioned a network of public county "seminaries," or secondary schools. When the state's counties failed to fund them, religious and other private groups jumped in to create their own secondary academies. By 1850, there were 175 privately run academies in Indiana, three times as many as the county seminaries.

Closely related to the academy movement, and often developing from it, was the Protestant impulse to found colleges. Across the new nation, hundreds of colleges were founded, though some of them existed only on paper. More than 200 survived by mid-century, up from 20 in 1800. These were sponsored mostly by religious groups, though the states were beginning to found colleges and universities as well.

METHODISTS IN THE "VALE OF PARADISE"

The particular branch of evangelical Christianity that founded the college in Valparaiso was the amazing American Methodists. Under the leadership of the remarkable Bishop Francis Asbury, by the mid-nineteenth century, the Methodists had become by far the largest United States church body, a full 38 percent of the churched population. Methodists could muster a preaching force of 4,000 itinerant and nearly 8,000 local preachers. Instead of learned sermons read from the pulpit, Methodists preached to the common people with a new look-them-in-the-eye rhetoric. The audiences, empowered, received their salvation with tears, joy, and sometimes ecstatic behavior, eager to *do* something in response. Methodists effectively marshaled the new popular press, enlisted folk music in the worship of the Lord, and cultivated the intense spirituality of small groups led by active lay leaders.

Although well-educated Methodists were uncommon, the leadership, skilled at adaptation, soon sensed that a new generation would need schools to advance their standing. In 1820, the national General Conference urged the establishment of "literary institutions," thus launching decades of college-building that eventually would include universities such as Northwestern, Vanderbilt, Duke, Emory, Boston University, Southern California, all the Wesleyans, and many more. At its first meeting in 1832, the Indiana Methodist Conference declared that "next to the salvation of Christ," learning would bring the greatest benefit to humanity. Compared with the Presbyterians and Congregationalists, heirs of the Puritan tradition of a learned clergy and custodians of the venerable colonial colleges, Methodists came late on the scene of higher education in the Midwest. In Indiana, the Presbyterians already had established Hanover College (1830), then Wabash College (1832). Indeed, every faculty member in the state institutions at Bloomington and Vincennes was Presbyterian. One politician met the Methodist protest over this monopoly with the observation that there was "not a Methodist in America with sufficient learning to fill a professor's chair." He reportedly paid for this remark in the next election at the hands of the much more numerous Methodists.

Undiscouraged by such disparagement, the Indiana Methodists countered by creating their own institution in 1837: Indiana Asbury University (later DePauw University) at Greencastle. Numerous other institutions followed. The newly created Northwest Indiana Conference of the Methodist Church, stretching from Indianapolis to South Bend and west to the Illinois border, soon took up the church's educational mandate with typical elan. By the Civil War, it had opened 15 institutions, mainly academies. But two of these academies included colleges as well. Northern Indiana College at South Bend was established specifically to counter the perceived "Catholic threat" created by the founding of the University of Notre Dame (1842) in the north. Valparaiso Male and Female College eventually occupied a campus in the seat of Porter County, seen as the key to the future of the Calumet region. Asbury University was the mother of many of these institutions in the sense that its graduates staffed and directed them, while trustees and presidents of all the schools seemed to be interchangeable parts of an influential network of Methodist educators.

Although religion was the primary motive for college-founding in the antebellum era, local boosterism also played a part. Fortunes were quickly made and lost as the nation systematically moved across and carved up the

Old Northwest. Only scattered settlers and a few resilient American Indians inhabited Indiana's new Porter County when a small group of land speculators made a deal with the government in 1836 to locate the county seat on property they owned at the geographic center of the county. Originally called Porter, the town's name was changed to Valparaiso ("Vale of Paradise") to honor Commodore David Porter's famous battle off the coast of Valparaiso, Chile, in the War of 1812.

After two railroads bypassed the isolated town, the announcement that the new Chicago, Fort Wayne, and Pittsburgh line also might skirt Valparaiso galvanized the town's boosters. They were determined to make certain that at least one train would pass through the town, even if they had to build some of the tracks themselves—which they did. That was in 1858, a year when the Northwest Conference of the Methodist Episcopal Church also was scheduled to meet in Valparaiso. This was the biggest event in the town's brief history, and the citizens strained to accommodate the visitors.

That regional Methodist meeting was crucial in advancing the "college idea" in Valparaiso. The belief that a college would enhance the spiritual and cultural life of a town, while also raising property values, was partly responsible for the college movement that swept the Midwest in the three decades before the Civil War. In Europe and colonial America, colleges or universities had been few in number, offering an educational capstone for well-prepared students who would likely enter the elite professions. Just the opposite was happening in democratic America. Now colleges were being established to stimulate popular education, to create leadership cadres that would perpetuate established values, and to enhance property values. Denominations eagerly joined with local boosters to direct and staff these institutions as part of their mission to create a Christian America.

Spiritual and economic interests thus mingled comfortably in the story of nearly every college founding. Reaching out for broad public support also guaranteed that no matter which denomination sponsored the college, the institution would not be "sectarian" in its teaching or policies. It would simultaneously serve a major public and economic interest along with the cause of religion.

The Northwest Indiana Methodist Conference's decision to launch a college in Valparaiso was no light undertaking because it committed the conference to the supervision and moral support of the school, though financial support was expected to come mainly from local sources. The legal Articles of Association, dated March 14, 1859, bore the signatures of five trustees. Three were prominent and experienced Methodist pastors from the region: the Revs. John L. Smith, Benjamin Winans, and Samuel L. Cooper. The other two were prominent Valparaiso Methodist laymen and strong boosters of the town: John Skinner and Azariah Freeman. Skinner was a public-spirited merchant, the Methodist Sunday school superintendent, and later a mayor of Valparaiso. Freeman, a former New Yorker, had joined the California gold rush but had returned to settle in Valparaiso, where he speculated in land and promoted education.

Toward the end of March, the local paper carried an announcement that a meeting would be held on March 29 at the courthouse to enlist public support for the new college. Several pledges of a thousand dollars each already had been made toward the goal of raising $15,000 to $20,000. At the meeting, prominent citizens pledged an additional $11,000, guaranteeing that the college would be launched.

Azariah Freeman, one of the $1,000 donors, offered to sell the board a large plot of hilly land a mile southeast of the town's center. It was an undeveloped, wooded tract connected to the town center by a winding trail. It was bounded on the south by a bluff overlooking the newly laid railroad. The board envisioned the expansion of the town toward that site, and after setting aside five acres for the campus, it began the sale of lots between the campus and the town as an additional source of college revenue.

The board of trustees of the private American college developed as a uniquely American institution. In Europe, most of the vital academic governance duties were vested in venerable faculties or in state educational bureaucracies. But in the United States, the colleges had a special relationship to their supporting constituencies that was expressed in the selection of a private board of trustees that nevertheless bore significant public responsibility. That board had the authority to run the college as a private, nonprofit corporation, a power established in law by the famous *Dartmouth College* Supreme Court case of 1819, the legal charter for all private higher education in the United States.

That first Valparaiso College Board of Trustees was elected by the Methodist Societies of Northwest Indiana and approved at the Quarterly Conference. The board was all-powerful. It held the property, elected the president and set his salary, filled vacancies, created the rules for regulating the school, settled difficulties between teachers and students, determined the course of studies and the calendar, and conferred degrees.

Although all five founders were Methodists, board membership was not limited to members of the denomination.

The new VMFC board was soon enlarged by several new members and then elected its officers, choosing the Rev. John L. Smith as its first president. The Northwest Conference also added two "visitors," annual appointees who also served as voting members of the board. Their duties were to visit the school regularly and report their findings to both the board and the wider Methodist constituency through *The Western Christian Advocate*, a widely read Methodist paper published in Cincinnati.

A key officer of any college of the time was its "agent," a kind of primitive admissions and fund-raising operative whose task was to canvass the region to solicit both students and funds—all for a fee. His assignment included the formidable task of persuading families to consider higher education as an option in an era when the income foregone by attending college was a significant cost. At Valparaiso, the college president frequently joined the agent in that work during the summer months.

The board moved quickly to turn what was soon called "College Hill" into a viable campus, despite the political unrest gripping the nation and the impending 1860 presidential campaign, which promised to be bitter and divisive. The board quickly erected a temporary wooden building to be ready for a September 1859 opening. Tuition would be $8 for each of three terms, while boarding at private homes ranged from $1.50 to $2.25 per week.

By mid-August, the board had appointed the VMFC's first president plus a faculty of five—one man and four women. As the first president, the board selected the young principal of the prosperous Methodist Thorntown Academy, the Rev. Charles N Sims, who also was named professor of ancient languages and literature. (The initial "N" stood for nothing.) When it turned out that Sims had to delay his arrival at Valparaiso for a term, Francis D. Carley, professor of mathematics and natural philosophy (natural science), assumed the acting presidency. Neither Carley nor anyone else could predict what the response to the college would be. When the institution officially opened its doors on September 21, 1859, however, 75 students crammed into the lone wooden structure. Before the year was over, the enrollment had risen to 175, complete with literary societies and a "literary paper," the *Echo*.

These gratifying numbers justified the founders' larger plans. Board member John Skinner, a builder, determined to construct a permanent building as soon as possible. Rather than wait for the necessary funds, he persuaded the board to allow him to start building in time for use in the fall of 1860. The financial drive went well, so in April 1860, the village band marched to College Hill, followed by a crowd in festive spirits. The Methodist authorities made speeches and laid the cornerstone that would not be disturbed until the venerable Main College Building was destroyed by fire in 1923.

Meanwhile, President Sims had arrived on campus and assumed his office. In the fall, the new building was ready for use. A simple but handsome three-story brick structure, it was built in neoclassical style with a wide, low-pitched, triangular pediment surmounting the facade and brick pilasters on the front wall. Inside were rooms for teaching, for public assembly, and for the literary societies, as well as spaces for a small library and offices.

By the fall of 1860, enrollment at the fledgling college had risen to 327. But this hopeful start was threatened by events that changed everyone's lives. In the hard-fought national election in November, the Republicans won both the presidency and a majority of the congressional seats. Although the new Republican Party's antislavery program focused for the most part on containing the spread of slavery, not abolishing it, Democrats depicted party members as radical pro-black abolitionists, Within a few months, seven southern states had seceded.

The northern part of Indiana was preponderantly Republican, and when the South fired on Fort Sumter in April 1861, people in the region were euphoric over the prospect of a short, vigorous "police action." When news of the Fort Sumter engagement reached Valparaiso, students gathered in the town center and noisily followed a band playing patriotic songs to College Hill, where several students hoisted the Stars and Stripes to the peak of the college building. The college choir sang patriotic songs; President Sims and the mayor orated. After this patriotic outburst, a number of southern sympathizers in the student body withdrew, while some male students began to leave for war.

Most people thought the war would be brief and painless. Instead, it was long and appallingly bloody. Indiana sent almost 200,000 men into battle, second among the northern states in proportion to its population. Twenty-five thousand Indiana soldiers died, and numerous disabled veterans could be seen everywhere for years afterward.

While the Union and Confederacy fought on the battlefield, other lesser rivalries continued in the North. The Presbyterians chose this moment to renew denominational competition by creating a rival institution, the Valparaiso Collegiate Institute. It occupied a building near the center of town on Institute Street, the present site of Valparaiso's Central Elementary School. This location was an advantage because the unpaved roads to College Hill became hard to negotiate during the winters and long, reluctant spring thaws of the region.

The VMFC suffered another setback when President Sims, his health uncertain, resigned his position in early 1862. The Rev. Erastus Herman Staley, another young Asbury graduate, was quickly appointed the college's second president. The loss of students because of the war constituted a serious threat to the young school, and the benevolence of the civilian population was completely absorbed in relieving the hardship of soldiers through gifts of clothing and food. President Staley countered by expanding the board to 18 members, thereby reaching out to surrounding counties in an attempt to expand the influence and support of the school. He introduced flexibility into the curriculum, especially by allowing students to substitute other courses for some of the classics, thus creating a "scientific" program. After less than a year, however, Staley, too, resigned to take up the presidency of Indiana Northern College in South Bend.

In hopes of stabilizing the college's leadership, the board now turned to its classics professor, the Rev. Benjamin William Smith, for leadership. Dynamic and energetic, Smith scoured the region for students, oversaw improvements to the property, and gave scholarships to war orphans and veterans. For three years, he attempted innovations in the curriculum, adding courses such as commerce and telegraphy that would appeal to the practical-minded returning veterans. Then Smith, too, left to pursue a career as pastor, postmaster, and activist state legislator. In a history of the VMFC that he later wrote, Smith referred to the growing financial troubles of the school.

The college's accumulating debt deepened after Smith's successor, the Rev. Thomas Bond Wood, a young man who would become the most eminent of the young presidents to serve the VMFC, added a new wing to the college building. Highly talented and personable, Wood led a campaign for funds to build the new wing during the "Methodist Centennial." This handsome addition stretched eastward from the main unit and featured a high tower visible in all directions for long distances. A promotional lithograph confidently illustrating the projected building shows another wing to the west with a twin tower, but Wood succeeded in completing only the east wing and tower. Female students lived in the new wing, meeting a desperate need for college housing because only a few boardinghouses had been built in the College Hill area.

" ... AND FEMALE COLLEGE"

The very presence of "coeds" at the fledgling college was notable. While nineteenth-century American society and higher education were still male-dominated, the growing aspirations of women were vividly present in the Valparaiso school's beginnings. By choosing the name "The Valparaiso Male and Female College" and specifically inviting women to enroll, the new board consciously entered the vanguard of a national controversy over women's educational and social opportunities.

The road to college admission had been difficult for women. After the Revolutionary War, few had questioned the dominant social image of "True Womanhood," which was characterized by piety, purity, obedience, and domesticity. This ideal image was reinforced by the rapid rise of a rough-and-tumble entrepreneurial capitalism that became the "proper domain" of aggressive males. The home became a haven from these stresses, the "proper domain" of women. This "dual sphere" ideology defined Victorian gender relationships and extended into after-dinner conversation and social clubs as well.

This same ideology, however, also laid a strong burden of moral education on the home. Mothers especially were assigned the republican and Christian tasks of raising virtuous and God-fearing young citizens. No one, therefore, objected when newly established women's academies, or "seminaries," set out to prepare women for these crucial domestic roles through a restricted curriculum that was focused on teaching the domestic and ornamental arts and "moral" literature. But mathematics and classical languages were considered beyond women's capacities, and physicians commonly insisted that intellectually demanding work would forever damage a woman's health.

Thus in its proclamation and practice of coeducation, Valparaiso was taking a progressive step ahead of most of its sister colleges. Indiana Asbury University was at that time contemplating the creation of a "Female Department" as soon as funds were available. But it was not until after the Civil War, nearly a decade later, that the first five women were admitted to Asbury. Everyone remembered the day when five female students entered the Asbury chapel for the first time and marched defiantly to the front row amid hostile stares. Thereafter, every day at chapel, the young men would block the women from the chapel door until the president entered, creating an opening for the coeds.

As a new foundation, the college in Valparaiso did not face this kind of entrenched hostility. At least one of the new professors at the VMFC, Helen E. Houghton, was identified as coming from a "New York teachers' seminary," which may well have been the "female seminary" founded by Emma Willard in Troy, New York. Pioneer educators such as Willard, Mary Lyons in South Hadley, Massachusetts, and Catharine Beecher in Hartford, Connecticut, created women's seminaries that, well ahead of their times, prepared women to become highly qualified teachers.

But it was in the academies and colleges of the western states, led by Charles Grandison Finney's Oberlin College in Ohio, that the idea of collegiate coeducation took hold. While scholars now point out the limits of Finney's egalitarian vision—for example, women initially were channeled into a less demanding course of studies—the rise of coeducation was clearly a major step in enabling women to compete on equal terms with men in intellectual achievements.

The precise mix of religious conviction, idealism, and practical calculation in the VMFC's founding as a coeducational Methodist college is difficult to discern. In the beginning, the school sent out mixed signals. To reassure parents who might worry about coeducation, the college bulletin declared that the campus was carefully divided into a "male and female area." But this announcement in the catalog disappeared after the first year, and evidently the gender segregation disappeared along with it, if indeed it was ever practiced. A decade later, the VMFC students recalled the initial controversy over coeducation with amusement, noting the strong support for it that quickly developed within the college and the constituency. In a critique of a public oration given by a woman on campus, one student critic attributed the occasional reticence in women's public oratorical style to the lingering but "silly" convention against women being able to speak in public at all.

CURRICULUM: BETWEEN PAST AND FUTURE

For both men and women, the board of the VMFC established a comprehensive educational program that included a large precollege division, a feature almost universal in the West. As a practical matter, this arrangement prepared students for college at a time when secondary education was scarce, and it also supplied needed revenue for the college. The VMFC eventually established four divisions: primary, intermediate or preparatory, academic, and collegiate. Students ideally would spend two years in the primary and intermediate departments, three in the academy, and three or four in the college, depending on whether the baccalaureate was classical (four years) or "scientific" (three years). In addition, the VMFC offered prospective teachers a course in which they reviewed the primary curriculum for seven or eight weeks before teaching the long winter term in the local elementary schools.

Although only a few students completed the entire degree program during the college's brief history, its curriculum reveals the character of the old-time American college and the experience of the students who passed through all or part of it. In the first VMFC College Bulletin of 1859–60, the following program was laid out. Subsequent programs varied only in detail.

FRESHMAN YEAR

First Term: Caesar, *Anabasis*, Algebra, American History
Second Term: Sallust, *Anabasis*, Algebra, Roman History
Third Term: Virgil, *Memorabilia*, Geometry, Grecian History

SOPHOMORE YEAR

First Term: Livy, *Odyssey*, Geometry and Plane Trigonometry, Anatomy and Physiology
Second Term: *Germania*, Natural Theology, Biblical Antiquities, Mensuration [Measurement] and Surveying
Third Term: Sophocles, Natural Philosophy, Philosophy of History, Analytical Geometry

JUNIOR YEAR

First Term: Logic, Chemistry, Differential Calculus, Political Economy
Second Term: Chemistry, Integral Calculus, Rhetoric
Third Term: Botany, Geology, Astronomy

SENIOR YEAR

First Term: Mental Philosophy, Plato's *Gorgias*, Physical Geography, History of English Literature
Second Term: Moral Science, Butler's *Analogy*, Mineralogy, Constitutional History of the United States
Third Term: Evidences of Christianity, Constitutional History of England, Biblical Literature, Elocution

In addition, there were "exercises" in composition and rhetoric throughout the curriculum.

This curriculum was naturally modeled on Asbury's, which in turn was part of a tradition of classical education dating back to the colonial colleges and to the Christian humanism of 16th-century Europe. In the old-time college, students studied the classics, composed declamations, and engaged in disputations, all of which prepared them well for public roles in one of the "learned professions"—the ministry, law, or medicine—or for membership in society's elite.

While the classics retained their prestige and core status in the curriculum, two sets of newcomers began to emerge during the pre-Civil War period. First, challenging the classics as bearers of the liberal arts was a rather broad group of courses just appearing in academe: modern languages and literature, history, and constitutional and international law. Some colleges began to allow substitution of some of these courses for part of the classics curriculum. In some colleges, including later the VMFC, this led to the degree of "Mistress of English Literature" for women. Many schools developed a program of studies called the "scientific course," which led to a Bachelor of Science degree ("science" referring to general learning as distinct from the classical Bachelor of Arts) and usually took only three years rather than four for the classical Bachelor of Arts. The classical course always carried the higher prestige, but throughout the nineteenth century in many colleges, including the one in Valparaiso, "classicals" and "scientifics" (as their respective student adherents were called) shared a history of rivalry.

The second challenge came from the emergent natural sciences. The study of science and its applications was tremendously popular throughout the nineteenth century. It was typically in the hands of devout Christians who saw scientific progress as revealing the hand of the Creator, which in turn was to lead the student to sing the Creator's praise. At the VMFC, the "Mensuration and Surveying" class represented a nascent civil engineering emphasis found in a number of colleges, one especially relevant to the new world of canals, roads, and railroads.

The American colleges also were self-consciously Christian, mainly Protestant, institutions. They aimed to build character and develop moral zeal through a holistic college experience, appealing to the entire person. Their curriculum bespoke an intellectual dimension of the evangelical Protestant faith, evident in courses on the Bible and others such as "Evidences of Christianity," which attempted to prove the "reasonableness" of Christianity and to reconcile Christian truth with new discoveries in geology and astronomy. These colleges and academies also sought to maintain a churchly hold on the leadership group that they produced.

The relevance of the Christian faith to the culture was especially expressed in the famous capstone course taught by the college president, usually titled "Moral Philosophy" or "Moral Science." Moral Philosophy was typically supported by two other courses, "Mental Philosophy" and "Political Economy." All of these courses were efforts to relate Christian faith and morality to the most important problems of American society and to instill an intelligent, evangelical zeal in students.

The curriculum and experience of the VMFC faithfully followed these well-trodden paths during its brief life. For most of its history, there was little or nothing original or distinctive about the college's offerings—which is what both faculty and students expected. Although a few traces of innovation are evident, anything really different would have been startling and probably unwelcome. The college's final integrative studies, especially, were part of a whole ecology of knowledge, unifying what was taught at the VMFC with the same lessons being taught in the more than 200 colleges dotting the land from the Atlantic westward. These campuses comprised a network of collegiate institutions teaching a common approach to current social and intellectual life and creating a widely shared—if not universal—vision of American culture.

LITERARY SOCIETIES AND STUDENT LIFE

In most cases, the classroom activity of the early American college was an ordeal marked by drill and recitation in a highly authoritarian setting. Amid this generally dreary routine, it was the student-controlled literary society that became for many students the true center of their social and intellectual education and a distinctive bridge between the official curriculum and the "real world." Meeting once a week, these organizations featured parliamentary discussion, debates, orations, and dramatic presentations. More than the classroom curriculum, the literary societies effectively prepared students for the public life of nineteenth-century America, in which careers and reputations were made by successful sermons, political speeches, trial arguments before juries, festival orations at holidays, or eulogies at the funerals of notables. Closely related to such displays of rhetoric was the general American fondness for public expositions, music, and melodrama that pervaded even the small towns and constituted much of the entertainment of the era.

The literary societies also served as the centers of student social life. Each society had its own hall, carefully fitted out as a combination lounge and library. The literary societies' libraries often rivaled the college's own formal library, which typically was open only a few hours a week to upper-class students. The private libraries of the societies were not only more accessible to students, but they also offered what the college library did not: contemporary literature and periodicals.

It was an important function of the literary societies to present public "exhibitions" of their forensic skills, especially at the close of each term. Debates and presentations constituted a weekly public social event, though visitors were ushered out when a "secret session" got under way. At the VMFC, as elsewhere, newspapers regularly reviewed the students' intense debates on contemporary affairs or moral problems such as these: Was the president justified in issuing his Proclamation of Freedom? Does war ultimately result in the good of mankind? Was the purchase of Alaska from Russia bad policy? Which is more pernicious, a bad book or a bad companion?

While several societies existed for short periods of time at the VMFC, two seem to have been most prominent and enduring. These were the Philological Society for men and the Calliopean Society for women, or, as they were known, the Philoes and the Callies. In addition to a president, secretary, librarian, and treasurer, the societies elected other special officers. The "critic" offered criticism of the rhetorical performances in the weekly meetings. The "censor" reported on the behavior of the members, ranging from minute infractions of the rules (spitting on the floor, moving chairs improperly, boisterous behavior) to scholastic deficiencies or general behavior that reflected badly on the whole society. Officers levied fines as the normal penalty for such failings.

Closely allied with the desire of the students in these literary societies to read modern literature—an option not available in the official curriculum—was the urge to write. Such compositions not only became part of public oral presentations, but also resulted in the VMFC societies publishing several journals.

Student behavior in early American colleges was notoriously unruly and often rebellious. Under the strict Calvinist doctrine of human depravity, the dominant Presbyterian colleges of the era typically exercised a stern discipline. In contrast, the Methodist emphasis on human freedom and voluntary "perfectionism" produced what the denomination's college catalogs called a "mild parental" approach to discipline, one that allegedly appealed to the students' "nobler qualities." Nevertheless, strict personal adherence to the Wesleyan code of behavior was written into the list of regulations for Methodist colleges: no drinking, dancing, card playing, or swearing, along with an emphasis on punctuality and industry. A system of demerits and public comments on behavior were the main sanctions; there was no reference to corporal punishment in any form.

The class days at a Methodist institution such as the VMFC began early in the morning with required chapel, probably around 8 A.M. Attendance was kept, and sympathetic janitors sometimes prolonged the bell-ringing for the sake of stragglers. At the VMFC, this required the student body, which at first lived exclusively at town boardinghouses or at home, to trek a long distance to arrive on time. Chapel was simple. The president would read Scripture, lead the singing of a hymn, and say the prayers. The ancient college student tradition of pranks often would focus on these solemn minutes, including such mild mischief as putting a rooster in the organ or spreading the floor with sulphur matches that exploded when stepped on. After chapel, classes commenced and continued until 4 o'clock in the afternoon, broken only by study hours that were subject to an exacting discipline of promptness and no whispering.

It was presumed that parents and boardinghouse mistresses would cooperate with the college in enforcing the behavior code. In the later years of the VMFC, its boarding wing housed young women at $60 per term under the supervision of a matron, Mrs. J. A. Woodson. The VMFC Bulletin described the living style as that of "one Christian family." It was also possible for students who lived off campus to pay for board alone, so gentlemen students could join the young ladies in the college dining hall for a weekly fee of $3.50.

The surviving issues of the Philological Society's journal, *The Monitor*, give some insight into the life of the VMFC collegians in 1867–68. The journal reported news from other colleges, suggesting a self-conscious collegiate mentality. Evidently the older students' lives were less regulated than those of the younger ones. One writer reported on a social outing—a sleigh ride to nearby Westville and back during the Christmas season. Four male students met four women at the boarding wing in the afternoon and headed off on an 11-mile trek over packed snow and hilly terrain to a prearranged meal at the Smith Hotel. There they were joined by another couple for the return trip. Both journeys were adventurous, with the four horses balking and finally, on the return trip, breaking away after throwing the passengers into a snowbank. Finally, around midnight, the whole party managed to return to campus.

From the same source, we have a detailed description of the class of 1868. There were six women and two men. The two men were veterans, the one having lost an arm at Gettysburg. One eventually became a lawyer, the other a minister. The oldest man was 27; the youngest woman was 18. Half the women became teachers; half became homemakers. Both men smoked, one chewed, neither indulged in games of chance, but one swore "under provocation." According to the writer, "The ladies are decidedly averse to keeping hours after 2 A.M. unless the occasion is unusually interesting." Such playful language, and other details of the account, presents an image not of a stern Methodism, but of a vital religion adapting to the changing mores of American life. No doubt the impact of the Civil War and the influence of veterans who had seen battle also were altering the more rigid ethos of antebellum college life.

The college's regulations did, however, strictly prohibit "promiscuous" relationships between the sexes. This was a common expression that required such relationships to be structured by custom: There were certain approved times and places for meetings and certain protocols to be followed in male-female encounters. Formal social activities following such guidelines afforded young men and women a time for proper acquaintance and conversation.

Especially important were the public exhibitions and meetings of the literary societies, as well as their fund-raising "socials" designed to raise money for room furnishings and society libraries. Such socials were public occasions that featured fairly standard fare, such as oyster soup or ice cream and strawberries. Organized trips to Lake Michigan, to visit a local farm, or casual group hikes and sleigh rides were common amusements. No intercollegiate sports competition existed, but various kinds of ball games were becoming popular among students.

Within this broad but restricted social context, young men and women occasionally broke through the stiffness of protocol. A few decades later, a senior citizen wrote of his earlier life as a student at a small college similar to the VMFC: "While it would be hard to get the old gray-haired men and women who attended this school in the fifties to admit it, they actually practiced campustry on this plat and spooned just like the boys and girls do now at college." While there is no proof, it is not unlikely some such "spooning" also occurred among the students of the Methodist college in Valparaiso.

The many religious activities conducted by the VMFC were also social occasions. Students were expected to attend worship services twice on Sunday. *The Monitor* provided commentary on the sermons and Bible classes. Revivals did not seem to be a part of campus life as they were at some evangelical colleges, but an optional Wednesday evening prayer meeting served as a more sedate equivalent. In the Methodists' widely popular *Western Christian Advocate*, Visitor W. Brokner reported that at the public examination he had witnessed, the religious tone of the college manifested itself in the majority of essays and other "exercises." He continued: "A number of the students have been converted this past winter, and are now happy in the love of God. On Sabbath morning we attended the students' class meeting in the college, where a number of the lately converted assembled to speak of their religious experience."

The end of each term, and especially the end of the spring term, which involved commencement, were special occasions. Public and festive, they lasted nearly a week. The literary societies gave public presentations to large crowds. The students endured a public report on their behavioral and academic performance, then were carefully questioned concerning their studies. The public, using copies of the college's textbooks, actively joined in the quizzing. Commencement week also included a baccalaureate service, at least one public lecture by a notable, and reunions of former students and teachers who feasted together and often joined in the public presentations. For a college town, this was one of the year's highlights.

THE FINAL CHAPTER

The VMFC Catalogue and Bulletin for 1867–68 displayed a variety of offerings that clearly shows the college attempting to adapt to the new needs of its constituency and potential students. In addition to the standard literary departments (collegiate, academic, preparatory, and primary), it listed several departments as "extra-literary." These included the musical, ornamental, commercial and telegraphing departments. The turn toward more "practical" subjects reflected the struggle to attract students. The last detailed enrollment figures show 226 students in attendance in 1867–68, most of them taking both literary and extra-literary courses.

The Monitor from the same year, however, exuded an optimistic tone, with no hint of the college being in trouble. It praised the faculty for strengthening the quality of the institution, particularly in the academy. During the war, it noted in a critical tone, the mostly female students, naturally impatient with tradition, went through the curriculum with little attention to sequence and prerequisites. Then the same thing happened with the equally impatient returning veterans. But the hope was that normality would return; the regular sequence of courses had been reestablished, and the quality of students was rising.

But outside forces plainly were having a negative impact on the college in Valparaiso. In 1867, the Indiana state legislature passed a bill that provided dramatic new support for public education. The rival Presbyterian-sponsored Valparaiso Collegiate Institute saw the handwriting on the wall and closed, selling its property to the city for use as a public school. The VMFC tried to endure, but the precollegiate enrollment eroded, and with it much of the institution's income. President Wood also left, embarking on a remarkable career as a missionary, educator, and developer of the school systems in several South American countries, especially Argentina.

In its final few years, a local clergyman, editor, and lawyer, the somewhat controversial Rev. Aaron Gurney, was asked to take charge of the college's fortunes. Despite newspaper appeals for students and endowment, the enrollment faded until only two programs, one in commerce and one in music, remained. Finally, in 1871 the board shut down the college and appointed a three-person committee to find new parties who would use the property, still officially owned by the Methodist Church, for educational purposes.

While external forces were probably too strong to resist, the college's sponsors also bore some responsibility for the college's failure. Methodists themselves recognized that in their zeal to achieve their goals, they had spread their resources and leadership too thin. The minutes of the 1869 Northwest Indiana Conference contained this self-critical passage:

> One of these mistakes is the creation of too many educational centers. We have acted under the law of diffusion, without having first brought into requisition the law of accumulation and consolidation, and as a result, we have within the conference nine schools and colleges claiming recognition and patronage of the church, and not one of them has acquired a self-sustaining power. A large sum of money has been virtually thrown away. We have cast our bread upon the waters that flow in the wrong direction, and give no promise of a future gathering.

Despite its early demise, the VMFC served many important purposes. It established the town of Valparaiso as the center of higher learning in northwest Indiana and educated many of its leading citizens. The VMFC's campus and physical structures provided the basis and incentive for a new college venture in Valparaiso. Within a decade of the original college's closing, the brick Main College Building would receive its new wing and twin tower. Memories of the Civil War-era Methodist college remained alive in Valparaiso and among its alumni.

In contrast to later eras, there are no physical remains of the first phase of the VMFC story and only a precious few documentary ones. The threads of continuity in Valparaiso University's history clearly reach back to the later Brown-Kinsey institution but only thinly to the original Methodist college. Some graduates of the VMFC did serve on the later Brown-Kinsey VU faculty, but perhaps the strongest connection was through the continuing links to the town of Valparaiso and its citizens. One James McGill, for instance, was in the first class of the VMFC, and numerous descendants of the McGill family have been staunch supporters of its successor institutions in Valparaiso for more than 125 years. While town-gown relations certainly have not been without their ups and downs, the fact that Valparaiso University and the city practically grew up together has made the ties exceptionally close and cordial.

In any case, it is significant that the modern Valparaiso University can claim an institutional heritage deriving from the classical era of American college-founding in the Midwest, as well as an origin as a Christian institution of higher learning. For many years, it was common for historians of American education to regard these "old-time colleges" as repressive, stultifying places. More recent studies have revealed their vitality, as well as their weaknesses. Most scholars now agree that, whatever their academic flaws, they contributed importantly to their times and places.

From the standpoint of later, more sophisticated, ideas of Christian higher education, it is clear that the evangelical Protestant cultural synthesis of religion, republicanism, and "commonsense philosophy" embodied in the old-time colleges was too narrow and uncritical of its own premises. Its static categories could not comprehend the dynamic and organic developmental qualities of a new age of scientific and historical thought. Nor could its individualistic ethic and optimistic view of human nature deal with the effects of the huge concentrations of wealth and power that resulted from the unleashed expansionism, acquisitiveness, and technological spirit of the post-Civil War industrial era.

Nevertheless, that original American educational outlook did not simply disappear. From the husk of the old courses in political economy and mental and moral philosophy would emerge the new disciplines of political science, economics, psychology, and sociology, with approaches to social reality more attuned to a world of rapid intellectual and economic change. Another scientific revolution and a more positivistic frame of mind would alter the very conceptions of knowledge and of the American university. Although some Christian thinkers initially were involved in these movements, the idea of a unifying Christian worldview faded further and further into the shadows of the past, no longer even remotely compelling. Christian thought and its role in culture would diminish within the new American research universities and even in many of the surviving liberal arts colleges. But the ideal of linking faith and higher education endured to inspire others in later years—including some who looked toward Valparaiso.

2

THE FIRM OF BROWN AND KINSEY

A NEW WORLD OF HIGHER EDUCATION

While certainly caused by many local factors, the closing of the Valparaiso Male and Female College in 1871 coincided with the disappearance of a whole social and educational world that had sustained the traditional classical-Christian liberal arts college as practically the only form of American higher education since the early days of the Republic. In the three decades after the Civil War, heavy industrialization, urbanization, mass immigration, and other pervasive social, economic, and political changes transformed the United States from a provincial and largely rural country into a powerful industrial nation. These changes opened the way for dramatic innovations in higher education as well.

Acquiring the physical remains of the VMFC, but little of its mission or practice, the remarkable educational entrepreneur Henry Baker Brown built Valparaiso College—later the first Valparaiso University—into one of the largest and best-known academic institutions in the United States. Providing a focused education to thousands of earnest, eager students—native and immigrant—who could not afford other colleges, Brown and his close associate Oliver P. Kinsey shrewdly applied some of the deepest impulses of nineteenth-century American popular democracy and entrepreneurship to higher education. Like its predecessor, then, the second Valparaiso College thoroughly reflected both its own era and the continuing search to create academic institutions suitable to the spirit of American life. Unlike the struggling and short-lived Methodist college, the Brown-Kinsey university proved to be a roaring success.

The growing sophistication of knowledge that accompanied the social changes of the late nineteenth century, and particularly the explosion of historical and scientific scholarship emanating from the new German universities, opened a vast terrain of learning for American academics, presenting challenges as exciting and daunting as the expansion of the North American frontier once had been. However, most of the students turning to colleges after the Civil War wanted not so much advanced knowledge as an education with immediate practical uses. In the face of this need, Congress passed the Morrill Act in 1862, which laid the cornerstones of the great American public land-grant universities such as Illinois, Wisconsin, and Purdue, especially after the act's expansion in 1890. Other public and private colleges expanded with the growth and movement of the population, and the number of colleges grew from 200 in 1860 to about 1,000 by 1890. Some of the older and better-funded liberal arts colleges remained, but they were increasingly overshadowed by the more utilitarian approaches to education that pervaded many of the newer institutions. Immigrant populations, especially Catholics and Lutherans, founded new colleges with a variety of purposes, but their institutions often retained European features in their organization and curriculum. Women's colleges and black colleges appeared to serve groups still largely excluded by other institutions. Bible schools, normal schools, and commercial colleges provided compressed programs of study to their constituencies, joining the proprietary medical and law schools that dotted the land.

Despite this diversity, the future belonged to one quite different type of institution that slowly grew up alongside the others—the modern research university. The research ideal took clear form with the founding in 1876 of The Johns Hopkins University as an explicitly graduate institution. Here the "German model" of professionalized scholarship with its Ph.D. was adapted to American education. Scholars trained in this way soon began organizing many of the new professional academic associations for natural scientists, economists, historians, literary scholars, sociologists, political scientists, and others. This development reflected the newly defined domains of knowledge and the new approach that understood advanced learning to involve not so much the transmission of a tradition as the generation of new knowledge by scientific methods.

In the two generations that followed Johns Hopkins' founding, the new research university model reshaped a number of the older colleges, including Harvard, Yale, Princeton, and Columbia. It was central to the major new private universities created with money from the industrial barons, notably the University of Chicago, Stanford, and, later, Vanderbilt, Duke, and Rice universities. And this model influenced the character and structure of the leading state universities, such as the University of Michigan and the University of California at Berkeley.

It is said that history is written by the winners. In retrospect, the triumph of the research university came to seem inevitable. As a consequence, most histories of American higher education present the story as if the conclusion were foreordained—and those who were shoved aside are left out. Yet in the late nineteenth century, there were many alternatives and competitors for control of American higher learning. The research universities eventually did triumph and assert their domination over American colleges in the twentieth century. But it should not be forgotten that for several decades they were only one alternative—and a relatively small one at that—among many remarkably diverse types of schools contending for the American public's attention, loyalty, dollars, and students.

BACKGROUND OF THE SECOND VALPARAISO COLLEGE

After Valparaiso University achieved success and national recognition for its distinctive approach to collegiate education, its founder, Henry Baker Brown, was widely hailed as a creative academic genius and pedagogical innovator. In truth, however, Brown was not so much an original educational thinker as a gifted collector and adapter of the ideas of others, a man who had a keen eye for anything that "worked." Like Henry Ford in the automobile world, Brown and his collaborator, Oliver Perry Kinsey, displayed a remarkable knack for translating the theories and inventions of others into institutional practice. They also were flexible enough to tap into some of the strongest educational and social currents of the times.

Brown and Kinsey's Valparaiso University grew out of a strong strand of American popular education that represented a major alternative to the rather fixed form of the traditional liberal arts college. The curricular innovations attempted in the final struggling years of the VMFC foreshadowed the academic changes that began to crop up in many colleges after the Civil War: offerings in science and modern literature, partial courses for part-time students, electives, coeducation, business programs, teacher education, and technical training.

One general predecessor for Henry Baker Brown's Valparaiso College idea was the popular "commercial school," designed to supply the pressing need for business instruction beyond elementary commercial skills in arithmetic and bookkeeping, which were provided by the common public schools. Another predecessor was the normal school, which began in New England and spread widely across the country after the Civil War as women, in particular, flocked to the teaching profession. Most normal schools focused exclusively on teacher training, but a few began broadening their curricula to extend far beyond instructing future pedagogues.

It was one of these institutions, the National Normal University in Lebanon, Ohio, that educated Henry Baker Brown and provided the actual model for Valparaiso College. Founded as a proprietary institution in 1855 by Alfred Holbrook, whose father, Josiah, earlier had developed the American Lyceum as a vehicle of popular education, the National Normal flourished by taking students from practically any background and income level and intensively educating them for a variety of occupations.

Holbrook and his brilliant son, Heber, liked to draw sarcastic comparisons between the work of the National Normal and that of traditional "elite" colleges:

1. Elite colleges required four expensive years, wasting much of that time (and student money) on frivolities such as recreation, athletics, and fraternities. The Normal cut that time in half by eliminating all such frills, including long vacations.

2. Elite colleges relied on entrance examinations for admission; the Normal took students from many backgrounds and admitted them to either the Preparatory [remedial] Department or the Scientific Division.

3. Elite college teaching methods relied on lecture, recitation, and memorization from textbooks. The Normal encouraged "vitalized recitation," with a teacher guiding discussion and encouraging debate and mutual criticism. Instead of textbooks, the Normal used a variety of readings and encouraged independent use of the library to enable students to work up topics for presentation.

4. Elite colleges hired faculty based on their academic degrees. The Normal valued knowledge of the subject matter and the ability to impart that knowledge enthusiastically.

5. Elite colleges evaluated by stiff examinations. The Normal deemphasized formal testing and relied on the cumulative judgment of professors in evaluating students.

6. Elite colleges were for the most part closed to women, or looked down on them. The Normal welcomed them. [The Holbrooks even suggested that all-male colleges refused to admit women because men did not want their sisters to witness their debauchery.]

7. Elite colleges governed student behavior through strict rules, which actually fostered rebellion. The Normal counted on encouragement, the positive influence of faculty, and the treatment of students as adults for prompting good behavior.

Despite its polemical and self-serving tone, this list does indicate that the Holbrooks were serious, imaginative educational reformers. They intuitively recognized the principle—perhaps understood by the wisest teachers in any age—that good education must involve the student in active rather than passive learning. Their student-centered pedagogy, with its emphasis on practice and empirical discovery, anticipated somewhat the reforms associated with Dewey and the progressives of the early twentieth century. This contrasted with the stern discipline and rote memorization that characterized much nineteenth-century education, whether at the elementary, secondary, or collegiate levels.

While hardly a competitor with Harvard or Yale, or even with other local Ohio colleges such as the College of Wooster or Ohio Wesleyan, the National Normal perhaps embodied more careful and active attention to the question of what a college education really should be than did more prestigious institutions. It was from this particular milieu, and from the Holbrooks' educational philosophy, that another young educator, Henry Baker Brown, conceived plans for a revived college in Valparaiso.

BROWN LAUNCHES "THE NORMAL"

Born on October 6, 1847, on a farm in northern Ohio, Henry Baker Brown left the farm in his teens to begin teaching in the common schools. For most young men of the time, the poorly paid teaching occupation was simply a stepping-stone to some other job. But Brown took an interest in teaching itself, and he sought further education to enable him to do it better. After briefly attending Ohio Wesleyan College in Delaware, Ohio, Brown entered Holbrook's National Normal University at Lebanon, graduating with a Bachelor of Science degree and a commitment to become a professional educator.

At Lebanon, Brown developed friendships with many peers, including Oliver Perry Kinsey, Sarah J. Porter, Samantha Baldwin, Martin Bogarte, J. Fraise Richards, and others. Shortly after graduation, Richards set out to start his own normal school: Northwestern Normal in Republic, Ohio. His friends Brown, Bogarte, and Baldwin followed him. Henry Baker Brown both studied and taught at Northwestern, completing the classics program and its Bachelor of Arts degree while teaching. Rather than work for someone else, Brown wanted to start his own normal school. In 1873, when he heard of a possible opportunity in Valparaiso, Indiana, where a Methodist college had failed, Brown made the 200-mile trip to investigate.

Henry Brown was 26 years old when he arrived in Valparaiso to meet one of the Methodist founders, Azariah Freeman, and to inspect the dilapidated and deserted college building that reportedly was available for educational purposes. Despite its abandoned condition, Brown saw the possibilities and made further plans. Upon his return to Republic, he conferred with a group of his friends and persuaded them to follow him to Valparaiso and undertake this adventure.

One by one, Brown and his band of ambitious young Ohioans converged on Valparaiso in the summer of 1873, with their arrival carefully reported by the local press. Brown was the oldest of the group and clearly its dominant figure. He already had sorted out the respective talents and academic strengths of his friends so they could constitute a faculty, though they all were just out of school themselves. The areas "covered" by Samantha Baldwin (always known as "Mantie") were literature, rhetoric, history, and geography. Benjamin Franklin (B. F.) Perrine shared Baldwin's interests, in addition to Latin and physics. The precocious Martin Bogarte, only 18 years old, was interested in both elocution and oratory and higher mathematics, especially its practical applications to surveying. He also taught commercial subjects.

When the press announced that the "Northern Indiana Normal School and Business Institute" would open on College Hill, the old booster spirit reignited. Speaking for the Methodists who still held title to the college property, Azariah Freeman enthusiastically offered Brown the building rent free on a trial basis and estimated that he could expect 30 students from the immediate region.

But Brown thought big and displayed his talent for recruitment and publicity from the start. Before leaving Ohio, he already had recruited 15 students to attend Valparaiso. In Indiana, he quickly kicked off a major advertising campaign that used newspapers, brochures, and personal appearances. Mantie Baldwin wrote the advertising copy and, according to one observer, "It was her clever and appealing ad-writing that made the school a success."

The advertising pounded away at a few themes. First, this college would provide the least expensive education found anywhere. The claim was based not only on low tuition ($7 a term) and room and board ($3 a week), but especially on the "no frills" education that would offer focused learning, enhanced by debates, in such a concentrated way that only half the usual time would be required to complete the courses. This was the real saving because most Americans of the time already were earning a living in their teens, and the cost of foregone earnings would be substantial in a regular academy or college. The school motto Brown adopted and incessantly reiterated was "Work, Not Wealth"—which nicely combined an appeal to the laboring class with a sense of discipline and virtue. This virtue was enhanced, and the previous Methodist owners were surely pleased, when the prospective students took a pledge of abstinence and promised not to patronize the local saloons.

Hard work by Brown, Perrine, and a few of the Ohio students restored the building and grounds to good condition. The lovely maples planted by the Methodists once again formed a beautiful grove when the Northern Indiana Normal School officially opened with 35 students on September 16, 1873. Within a few weeks, the numbers grew to 61, who were quickly sorted into classes. In the winter term, 90 students enrolled. By the spring term, the enrollment had shot up to 172 as Brown's advertising campaign took hold. So many students came from Ohio that Brown's promotion was considered a prime factor in the decline and eventual demise of the National Normal University. Brown also shrewdly discounted the tuition for all Porter County teachers who would take courses at the institution. NINS was launched successfully.

Over the summer, the furious pace continued: More property improvements were made on College Hill, and thousands more brochures were mailed. Brown himself was a whirlwind of activity, visiting one teachers institute after another in Indiana and beyond, speaking and promoting the school. For the fall term, 299 students were enrolled, and 30 more had to be turned away for lack of room. A student editor, urging the local citizenry to help out financially and otherwise in meeting the extreme student housing shortage, calculated that in its second year NINS impacted the Valparaiso economy by an astonishing $50,000. Recognizing the tremendous impact of this revival in the college's fortunes, local citizens provided financial help to build East Hall, a boarding hall for 200 women. The city council also appropriated $12,000 and gave it to Brown to amortize the college building over a 10-year period. The county government added $10,000 of its own for the college.

Prominent northwest Indiana citizens also rallied to provide aid. Several leading bankers and merchants helped finance Brown. Others built and operated rooming houses on College Hill as business ventures. With such backing, Brown was able to add the west wing and second tower to the Main College Building, which had been designed but never built by the Methodists. This structure was ready in February 1874, enabling enrollment to climb further. By the beginning of the school's third year, the Indianapolis *Sentinel* noted that "the Northern's" enrollment of 900 students made it the largest normal college in the nation.

This exploding enrollment went far beyond even the optimistic Brown's dreams. He initially had hoped for 300 students. With more than triple that number already overflowing the campus, the president and his faculty were kept scrambling. During the first year, instruction was offered through three "departments": preparatory, teaching, and business. Preparatory provided students with foundational courses needed to qualify for higher level studies, and the teaching department prepared them to teach in the elementary schools. The business department, modeled after the Ohio commercial schools, featured the simulation of business transactions in a large room that could be fitted out with a bank, an auction house, a railway station, a factory office, and a court of justice. Teaching students by simulating contemporary business or legal operations was known as the "actual business method."

Lessons in penmanship and vocal music were available to all students at no extra cost. All students also were assigned to debating clubs, which met frequently. A "Normal Congress" simulated the federal legislative branch. There was simulated electioneering, legislating, and similar activities, which created tremendous public attention as students took up the controversial issues of the day.

Whatever their areas of "expertise," the small faculty was forced to teach almost everything. The notion of strict academic disciplines was as yet largely unknown, and the philosophy of the school, as well as the can-do spirit of the young faculty, made the boundaries between fields open and unpatrolled. As the enrollment swelled, Brown announced that a classical curriculum would be added in the future. He also expanded music beyond voice to include piano and organ. The success of these programs owed much to Brown's adaptation of the Holbrooks' pedagogical methods and their implementation in the hands of several especially bright young professors.

The beginnings of longer-term Valparaiso programs in both elocution (or rhetoric) and engineering are intertwined with the career of Martin Bogarte. From 1875 to 1890, his course on "Elocution and Oratory" was mandatory for most NINS students. As many as 200 students gathered in one classroom to hear this compelling teacher, who also taught them how to deliver classical orations and debate their classmates. The activities of this class spilled over into the cocurriculum, as well as into mock trials, the mock federal Congress run by students, and similar activities. Bogarte was also something of an expert on Shakespeare. He incorporated the Bard into his public speaking courses and also promoted campus performances of Shakespeare's plays, often taking leading roles himself. Bogarte's popular courses and his own theatricality did much to nourish the ambience of public speaking and drama that became a hallmark of education at the Normal.

During the 1878–79 school year, Bogarte and Lillian Chamberlin, instructor in music, took a leave to pursue further studies in Boston, where they also were married. Chamberlin studied music at Boston University while Bogarte divided his time between studies at the Boston School of Elocution and Oratory and at the Massachusetts Institute of Technology. When he returned to Valparaiso, Bogarte brought together the course offerings in surveying, science, and mathematics, initiating a program in civil engineering at the college in 1883.

The full development of the "commercial course," which became the business college, was the achievement of Chauncey Watson Boucher, another National Normal graduate who arrived at NINS in 1876 and fashioned a business curriculum that remained for decades. The "theoretical stage" consisted of acquiring book knowledge of such things as mathematics, commercial correspondence, accounting, business forms, commissions, partnerships, shipping, banking, and railroading. All business students also took English grammar, taught in a huge class by President Brown himself at 6:45 A.M.

The second stage was a development of the "actual business method," with its simulated real estate and insurance offices, commercial trading operations, shipping and importing companies, merchants' emporium, railroad office, and bank. During a sojourn in each "business," the student learned the relevant commercial law as well. The business school printed and used its own money and business forms for this facsimile business world. The program expanded so rapidly that Brown had to build a new building for it. Commercial Hall, built in 1881 on the southwest corner of College and Union, held two complete sets of these simulated business operations.

The arrival in 1878 of Professor Richard Heritage inaugurated the strong musical tradition at the burgeoning college. When this Ohio educator began, there were only three pianos and a simple program of vocal instruction. Within a few years, Heritage dramatically expanded the music program. Highly entrepreneurial, he took over the oldest building on campus and refurbished it with a large practice room, 22 small practice rooms, 20 pianos, seven organs, and a set of band and orchestra instruments. Then he acquired Flint Hall, built by John Flint in 1875, which he renamed Heritage Hall, after himself. (Heritage Hall now stands as the only surviving structure from the nineteenth-century Valparaiso institution.) He also edited and published a journal, *The Musical Ideal*, and sold musical instruments to students. Heritage remained the musical director of NINS for 19 years.

In 1878, Brown enticed Harrison N. Carver, his former professor at the National Normal, to head the new classical program in the collegiate division. This polymath taught everything from Homer to Herbert Spencer in his courses on philosophy, Latin, and Greek. Carver became the resident intellectual at the college, good for speeches on any occasion that might be graced by classical allusions or references to the American Civil War, in which Carver had served. Not many students at this fiercely utilitarian institution naturally sought his offerings, though he made up for that by teaching a huge variety of subjects, including beginning legal studies.

EXPANDING "THE FIRM OF BROWN AND KINSEY"

In the first few years, President Brown, still in his late 20s, simply managed the school out of his vest pocket in his highly personal style. Soon, more formal institutional organization was required. In 1878, only five years after the school's beginning, Brown drew up new articles of incorporation and received from the state of Indiana a charter that certainly covered all the bases. It authorized the college to offer programs in "preparatory, teachers, business, collegiate, law, medical, engineering, music, fine arts, phonographic, telegraphic and teacher review." With more than 1,000 students enrolled, and no sign of leveling off, Brown realized he needed assistance in running things. He reached back again to Lebanon, Ohio, and invited his friend from National Normal days, Oliver Perry Kinsey, to join him in Valparaiso.

Kinsey's life and career closely resembled Brown's. Born on a farm near Freeport, Ohio, in 1849, Kinsey had taught in country schools before enrolling in the National Normal. After graduation, he joined the faculty as a professor of English literature. A few years later, he married a fellow alumna, Sarah Porter, who had been a school principal in Iowa.

Brown's offer to Kinsey was attractive because it invited him to acquire half of NINS and to share in the management as well. The Kinseys arrived in Valparaiso in 1881, and Kinsey quickly assumed direction of the scientific department, in addition to duties managing the dining and boarding facilities. There his task was to keep the cost of room and board low enough to undercut all competition from other schools, yet at a level where he could squeeze out a small profit for what students called "the firm of Brown and Kinsey." The low cost was an important promotional point in attracting students to the college, and Brown and Kinsey intended to keep it that way.

Sarah Porter Kinsey joined the faculty as well, teaching geography and grammar. She also became the matron of the school's flagship dormitory for women, East Hall. The Kinseys' civic spirit also made them at once leading citizens of Valparaiso. He served on the city council, the county council, and the library board. Kinsey spearheaded establishment of the city waterworks, especially for the sake of the thousands of residents on College Hill who always were threatened by fire. Also active in civic and cultural affairs, Sarah became a national leader in the growing women's club movement.

Much of O. P. Kinsey's later fame rested on his astute management of the business side of the university, especially his uncanny knowledge of the fluctuating grain and livestock markets in Chicago and throughout the Midwest. He developed an extensive campus work-study program, employing hundreds of students who could not stay at school without earning money. The Kinseys owned a large house on the corner of Greenwich and Monroe streets that featured a long, sweeping lawn. This house became a frequent site of campus social activities. Alumni remembered the familiar sight of Kinsey pedaling his bicycle down College Street to the Old Main College Building, a colorful figure with muttonchop whiskers and uncontrolled reddish-blond hair. Inevitably, the college's colors became Brown and Gold, brown for the founder and gold for Kinsey's hair.

The partnership was as closely matched as the school colors. Brown and Kinsey worked together in close harness for more than 30 years, though they had contrasting personalities and interests. They even managed to maintain their friendship despite the fact that they were active in opposing political parties, Brown a Democrat and Kinsey a Republican.

As their core programs flourished, Brown and Kinsey dared to venture into new educational territory. One of these was a school of law. During the first half of the 1800s, most American lawyers, like Abraham Lincoln, entered practice after "reading law" and serving a minimal apprenticeship. By mid-century, an elite group of eastern lawyers demanded that training for the law be upgraded. They also wanted to polish the tarnished image of the profession. In 1878, the American Bar Association was formed, and as the chosen instrument of improvement, it promoted a reconnection of law with academe. More law schools then appeared, some of them connected to colleges and universities.

With his finger to the breeze as always, Henry Baker Brown announced in 1879 that NINS would offer a complete two-year course in law, with Professors Boucher and Carver in charge. Neither was a lawyer, though Boucher in his commercial course dealt with the fundamentals of commercial law and Carver would teach anything. That spring, Carver began lectures on Blackstone's *Commentaries*, created a moot court, and arranged for close observation of the local courts.

Then Brown enlisted a prominent Valparaiso attorney, Mark DeMotte, to create a full law department. A Civil War officer and a former prosecutor for the six-county circuit in northwest Indiana, Colonel DeMotte had both the Bachelor of Arts and a law degree from Asbury—an unusual qualification for the day. The law school officially opened on November 11, 1879, with ceremonies before a large assembled crowd. Addressing the audience, DeMotte "showed how the profession of the law and the lawyers had been abused, and this on account of the ignorant quacks and pettifoggers who sometimes disgrace the profession." The remedy for this state of affairs, DeMotte asserted, was better legal education.

The school's original faculty consisted of DeMotte and another local lawyer, H. A. Gillett. Dr. W. A. Yohn, a physician and teacher of science and medicine, also was listed as "Lecturer in Medical Jurisprudence," a sign of the increase in industrial accidents and perhaps the prospects of a practice in tort law. When law classes began, there were nine students enrolled, including two women. By the time of commencement in the spring of 1880, there were 18 "juniors" (first-year law students) and one senior, John A. Whitmore, the first lawyer to graduate from Valparaiso.

DeMotte also organized a moot court, which met on Monday and Wednesday evenings. Student George Norris, who graduated in 1883 and later became a renowned United States senator from Nebraska, remembered that at first law courses were held "in town in the office of Judge Mark DeMotte. He was the instructor, and we used his library. At night we would hold our moot court there." The law school then moved for a time to the Old Main College Building, but eventually it settled into a remodeled house on Greenwich Street, where it stayed for 40 years. From its founding until 1906, the law department was owned and tightly run by DeMotte, though Brown was listed as the "chief administrative officer." DeMotte took the major financial risks, but he greatly benefited from the close association with NINS, to which the law school paid a percentage of its tuition income. Despite its separate proprietary status, the law school was fully integrated into the Normal as one of its departments.

Like law, medical education was undergoing a transformation from informal apprenticeship to more systematic education, especially after the revolution in scientific knowledge that emanated from European laboratories in the 1870s. Aware of the new European medical discoveries, and sensing another opportunity, Henry Baker Brown was eager to incorporate some kind of medical education into the college. Lacking the equipment and faculty for a full medical program, Brown began by establishing a "first year of studies." Dr. Yohn, another early NINS graduate, was placed in charge of this small program, which included basic physiology and work on cadavers imported from Chicago. It soon became apparent that the new directions in medical education required greater resources and large population centers for clinics. The program for "medics" at the Valparaiso institution thus remained incomplete and did not offer the M.D. degree. Not until two decades later would Brown make a bolder foray into medical education.

More successful was the program in pharmacy. Another NINS alumnus, Horace Evans, established the first program in pharmacy in 1892, beginning a long tradition of instruction in that field at Valparaiso. After taking leaves of absence during the winter term for three successive years to acquire an M.D. from Northwestern University, Evans returned to build the pharmacy department into one of the college's strongest programs. Because pharmaceutical and medical education overlapped, medical schools typically granted one year of advanced standing to "pharmics." About one half of the Valparaiso "pharmics" went on to medical school.

HARD WORK FOR A PRECIOUS EDUCATION

As advertising and word of mouth spread the news about NINS, students from all over the Midwest and beyond flocked to the college in northwest Indiana. They usually arrived at one of the two railroad stations in Valparaiso. There they were met by the horse-drawn school wagons, which took the students and their belongings directly to the Old Main College Building, where Henry Brown worked out their schedules, took their money, and gave them tuition cards to present to their instructors on the first day of classes. Then the students were turned over to an "agent," an older student who gave them a choice of rooms in several halls and at various prices, as well as a choice of places to eat, usually a hall or a boardinghouse with dining rooms.

Because most students were from rural or working-class backgrounds, the struggle to come up with tuition dollars was a perpetual concern. Often students had worked to save money before coming to NINS. Most worked during the summers, or they left school for a period of time to teach, harvest crops, work on riverboats, or shovel coal on the railroads. Many worked on campus as waiters, private tutors, book agents, or janitors. Others worked on area farms, especially at harvest or planting times, or in the town of Valparaiso.

Recognizing the difficulties most of his students faced, Brown did everything possible to cut costs. He arranged reduced student fares with the railroads for travel to and from Valparaiso. He provided texts at low rentals. Life in the boardinghouses was kept simple so students' limited dollars could be spent on tuition, books, and clothes. There was no running water; students had to haul water from the pumps that stood here and there on College Hill. Each student also had to buy his or her own wood for heat: boardinghouses, such as Stiles Hall on Greenwich Street, had their own woodsheds in back.

Coming from generally poor backgrounds, students expected to work hard for their precious education, and they demanded few luxuries. Harvey Hatch, who arrived in 1877 from a farm in Wisconsin and left letters recording his experiences at NINS, chopped wood for a Porter County farmer in return for a free supply. George Norris later remembered:

> Only once was I able to continue through an entire year. Every other year I had to stop school in order to raise money so that at least half the time I was out of the field at work. ... Intolerable, had it not been that nearly everyone else was in the same position. I bought a used

> overcoat for five dollars that lasted me for several years. ... I took my shirt, and perhaps a collar, to the washwoman; then at the end of the week brought them to my room, changed clothes, and carried the soiled clothes back to be done. In all of the boarding houses ... where the students lived I do not remember seeing one bathtub. Our baths were entirely sponge baths except in the summertime, when we would go to Sager's pond, a mile or two distant, for fine swimming, but we had to swim at night because none of us had a bathing suit.

When Norris first arrived in Valparaiso, he boarded at Flint Hall. Cheap as the place was, he could not afford it. He found even cheaper rooms with several other students in the "Octagon House" on Garfield Avenue across from the present site of Porter Memorial Hospital, a building still standing in 2000.

For students, academic life at NINS was arduous, reflecting the Brown philosophy of success through hard work. At 6 A.M. the bell rang for breakfast, at 6:45 for the first class, and again for each class thereafter. Chapel was at 8:30 A.M.; classes then resumed and continued throughout the day. Some classes were held in the evening, others on Saturday mornings. Students took their identities from their departments, being known as Scientifics, Teachers, Classics, Commercials, Junior or Senior Law, or Preps. The Old Main College Building housed most classrooms, the laboratory, the main office, the library, a bookstore, the chapel, a large room for art exhibitions, and a studio, in addition to halls for the two major literary societies, the Star and the Crescent.

STUDENT LIFE ON COLLEGE HILL

Initially, Brown wanted to govern the college in Valparaiso through the same easygoing, minimal rules that he had known at the National Normal, expressing what he called "self-governance." At first, this system worked. But as numbers increased and social backgrounds diversified, Brown had to change his approach. Student Harvey Hatch wrote home that Brown's discipline was becoming much stricter. Already, visiting a saloon, associating with people of questionable virtue, and gambling were grounds for instant dismissal. Now, said Hatch, unexcused absences from class were to meet the same fate. A tough new set of rules to that effect soon appeared.

Victorian manners prevailed. No matter how poor, students dressed formally: men in coats and hats, women in blouses and long skirts and often in gloves. This was true even when their studies led students into the fields, where the male students learned surveying or the young women found plants for botany and rocks for physical science. In the classrooms, men and women were seated separately, though in the laboratories they would mingle, with occasional explosions from mismanaged chemistry experiments adding to the excitement. Men and women did not speak casually with each other until they had been properly introduced. But once that essential formality was completed, they could visit each others' rooms without chaperones. Usually, however, "mixed" social activities were done in groups, with men and women pairing off within the group but rarely going off alone.

Taking walks was the leisure activity of choice. If they had time on a pleasant weekend, students could walk to Sager's Lake, about a mile south of campus, where there were boat rentals. They also could hire a horse and carriage and go even farther for boating on Flint Lake, where local residents sold snacks to students on such outings. From time to time, NINS organized a "reunion," a public social affair with musical and dramatic entertainment and much milling about eating ice cream and strawberries. During winter, there was sleigh-riding and ice-skating.

As for sports, baseball was becoming an American passion. The *Student*, the first campus newspaper published on College Hill, noted in 1874 that NINS students loved to play baseball on the commons east of the campus and challenged other teams in town. Croquet also was popular as a recreation that men and women could enjoy together. The student paper proposed to President Brown that he provide a gymnasium suitable for "physical culture," where "experts" could conduct extracurricular classes in the use of parallel bars, Indian clubs, and dumbbells.

Henry Brown loved music and thought everyone should study it. Voice lessons in music promoted skill in public speaking, for one thing. Harvey Hatch wrote home about his eagerness to start the voice lessons NINS provided. Musical presentations were part of the regular fare at the college. If George Norris was not debating in the evening, he was rehearsing musicals such as the popular Gilbert and Sullivan operettas, which he and his friends took on the road to nearby towns and crossroads venues.

Everyone attended church on Sundays. During his years at NINS, Hatch attended both morning and evening services, in addition to the "Normal Sunday School," which actually met on Thursday night and which he found to be "splendid." Couples seen sitting in church together were thought to be serious. The Normal YMCA (begun in 1879) and YWCA (begun in 1890) organized Bible studies, prayer meetings, and service projects and provided a general place of hospitality for the whole campus. Norris remembered that among the many democratic features of life at NINS, the easy mixing of often-rivalrous denominations on College Hill was an especially pleasant development.

Of extraordinary importance to students were the public performances sponsored by the two literary societies, the Star and the Crescent. The Star met on Friday and the Crescent on Saturday evenings for speeches, debates, and musical presentations in their well-furnished halls, which seated more than three hundred each. These programs were open to all students and to the general public, providing a valuable source of entertainment and enrichment.

The two major societies vied with each other for campus prominence. There also were factions within the societies that competed in elections and other contests. Campaigning for offices within literary societies and beyond was a major student activity, and these contests often reflected the fierce rivalries and occasional undertone of violence that operated beneath the well-managed surface of Brown's college. One such contest that occurred in the 1880s illustrates the fiercer underside of social relations among students of the time.

George Norris, well-liked and constantly active on campus, was a member of the Crescent Literary Society and a leader of one of its factions. Each year, students awaited with bated breath the showdown oratorical contest between the two rival societies. The Crescent and the Star could each choose two contestants, and in 1883, Norris vied with fellow member Charles Hyde to be one of the Crescent's representatives. Hyde's mother had traveled all the way from Illinois to see her son achieve this pinnacle, but he was "humiliated" when four of the five judges voted for Norris. Hissing and booing broke out from the Hyde faction, but the result stood.

Hyde's supporters got their revenge in the ensuing election for president of the Crescents, which Norris lost to his rival by one vote. Amid accusations of "dirty tricks" and fraud—not uncommon charges—Hyde's followers celebrated their victory all night.

Licking their wounds, the defeated Norris and eight of his loyal followers decided to form a secret society that would "celebrate the friendship" that had grown among them. They wrote a constitution that limited membership to the nine and committed each member to an annual meeting for the rest of their lives. The true name of the society was never to be revealed.

When word got out that a group mysteriously called the "L.U.N." would have their first meeting in August at the Merchants' Hotel in town, the Hyde faction vengefully pasted posters on trees, denouncing the meeting of "Lunatics Under Norris." Remembered Norris:

> One of our fellows found it out and rounded up the rest of us. We captured a culprit down an alley—with a revolver, shooting it off once in a while. We collared another who had a pastepot and was pasting up the trees on campus. We brought him to our headquarters and locked him up until one or two in the morning. In the end we made that poor devil tell everything. He had to go to all the places and tear off the circulars, and we got the supply, several hundred.

The opposition seems to have solidified Norris's comrades in their commitment to their pledge. The group of friends, whose "secret" initials probably stood for "Loyal United Nine," met annually for almost 60 years, from 1883 until 1941, when wartime conditions and advancing age made meetings impossible.

Other activities generated partisanship and conflict as well. Every Saturday morning was the "General Debate," and these verbal contests could sometimes be acrimonious affairs. The campus newspaper reported that one debate almost turned into a duel between the two participants. Boxing matches were also a way of settling disputes or establishing a reputation, and these were often bloody affairs. Fights between NINS students and tough town boys were not uncommon.

The prestigious president of the General Debate was elected in each term after hard-fought campaigns in which alliances, dirty tricks, and various political maneuvers produced enduring friendships or animosities. The president controlled the highly political General Debate agenda. Therefore, he could determine which public issues would shape campus discussion. Examples of debate topics included the following:

- "The jury system should be abolished."
- "The Navy is inadequate to the national defense."
- "The Negro should be disenfranchised."
- "Ethnological science conclusively demonstrates that man evolved from a lower species."

Debate and politics intermingled once again in the annual Mock National Convention held each August at the time of commencement. This series of events lasted more than a week. Again, heavy politics dominated the election of candidates for various offices. There were spies for each party, dirty deals to guard against, shifting allegiances, and a great deal of excitement. Women as well as men joined in these intense, exhausting contests marked by harsh words and injured feelings. Eventually, both the General Debate and the Mock National Convention were banned by the administration.

Nevertheless, the atmosphere of vigorous political and intellectual controversy that flourished in the late-nineteenth century NINS must have helped its students as they entered the equally rough-and-tumble world of United States political and business life. Certainly many NINS alumni, mostly from humble backgrounds, distinguished themselves in fields where their experiences at Valparaiso were an asset. Mary Abbe became president of the Chicago Teachers Federation, Robert Aley became president of Butler University, and Samuel Ralston became governor of Indiana and later a United States senator. George Norris, first elected senator from Nebraska in 1913, was an eloquent orator known for his rock-solid probity and his defense of the Muscle Shoals power site, later the foundation of the Tennessee Valley Authority. Across the aisle from Republican Norris during much of his tenure in the Senate sat NINS schoolmate and fellow Crescent member Democrat Andrieus A. Jones, senator from New Mexico. It was part of College Hill and Indiana political lore that O. P. Kinsey had predicted this particular future for the two men.

THE 1890S: BROWN TRIUMPHANT

By the 1890s, Brown and NINS were no longer struggling to make it. Both the man and the institution were confident, successful, and increasingly recognized for their achievements. Beginning with next to nothing in advantages or resources, Brown and his close collaborators had built a remarkable college through vision, energy, and a keen intuition of the needs and aspirations of the times.

In their character and career, both Brown and his academic creation reflected much of the open, democratic, upwardly mobile values of the nineteenth-century United States. While national economic hierarchies and class conflict were beginning to erode some of that earlier optimism in the 1890s, Brown had come to maturity when the United States consisted largely of what historian Robert Wiebe has called "island communities," primarily run through informal, personal arrangements. In such a society, the barriers to mobility were thin, and almost anyone could aspire to rise into a "profession."

Like many of his contemporaries, Brown believed that God had ordained the primary values in life to be thrift, sobriety, and hard work. Pursuit of these virtues inevitably would bring success to individuals, and individuals who rose through such means would create communities open to others as well. Committed to the importance of individual self-development, Brown was more dedicated than most to extending similar opportunities for self-improvement to others through his chosen vocation of education. Brown looked on teaching as craft and set out to practice it—and lead others to practice it—with the same dedication his father had brought to farming. Brown saw this personal mission as consistent with his belief in democratic, egalitarian, even populist, values.

From the time young Henry Brown arrived in Valparaiso, he impressed people with his hard work and sense of opportunity, while at the same time he identified the "influentials" in town and won their support. His success with the school was accompanied by social success as well. After a decade and a half as a most eligible bachelor, Brown married into the local establishment. Geneva (Neva) Axe was the daughter of one of Valparaiso's first citizens, Elias Axe. A student at NINS in the 1870s, she was active in the numerous musical productions. She became Henry Brown's secretary, and in 1886, they married.

The marriage created something of a crisis within the close-knit and hardworking founding group of educators. There is much evidence that one of Mantie Baldwin's motives for coming with Brown to Valparaiso was the hope of marriage to him. Baldwin was a highly capable and astute woman, and many people considered her the third founder of the college, along with Brown and Bogarte. It was Baldwin who wrote articles discussing the state of education and projecting a tremendous future for NINS, and she played a prominent behind-the-scenes role in making that happen. By the 1880s, Baldwin had become a major force in the school, beloved of alumni, an intellectually talented woman who was an inspiration to many other young women at NINS. Despite her feelings, she did not let Brown's marriage to someone else slow her down, and she continued to teach until a second broken hip forced her retirement in 1914. When she died in 1933, Mantie Baldwin's tombstone in Valparaiso's Graceland Cemetery was inscribed with the phrase "An Intellectual Leader"—a fitting epitaph for one of the founders of NINS whose personal disappointment did not inhibit her commitment to her work.

As Brown's social standing rose, he became a leading citizen of Valparaiso. An elder of the Christian Church (Disciples of Christ), he would stand at the door of the church and, according to the developing legend, greet each person, especially his students, by name. He moved from his boarding rooms at the college to a mansion built by the prominent Calkins family, a graceful white building set on a hill on Jefferson Street. Sitting on its grand front porch, Brown could look about a mile to the south and survey the twin towers on College Hill.

Like Henry Baker Brown, NINS was increasingly inclined to display its success in tangible ways. In May 1892, the college dedicated its magnificent new Chapel Hall, a fine statement in brick and Bedford stone that featured a huge auditorium that could seat 2,500. Indiana governor Ira Chase delivered a dedicatory oration—praising the institution to an overflow crowd. Chase was followed by Indiana superintendent of education H. O. Vorien, himself an NINS graduate and another sign of the school's success.

Chapel Hall became the scene of daily "exercises," of speeches by notables whom the administration regularly invited to NINS, and the stimulus for an enormously expanded music program. Richard Heritage's student and successor, William Wade Hinshaw, transformed the music department into a conservatory. Hinshaw eventually left Valparaiso to become a baritone with the Metropolitan Opera in New York, and later he created his own opera company in Boston. During his tenure at NINS, Hinshaw established a continuing tradition of high musical culture for the campus, featuring the performance of several operas each year, along with major choruses and ensembles.

Valparaiso's successful graduates spread its reputation throughout the region. In the early 1890s, Chicago-area alumni banded together into an association that began holding twice-annual dinners at a major downtown hotel. Brown always would appear and address these large gatherings. Each summer at commencement, alumni would trek to the campus from Chicago and elsewhere for banquets, entertainment, and reunions with old friends and former professors. A few years later, the alumni raised funds to present a great organ for the new auditorium.

The year 1898 was the silver anniversary of the Northern Indiana Normal School. For the celebration, a medal was cast that depicted Chapel Hall next to the original VMFC building in which NINS had gathered its first handful of students. Much praise was lavished on Henry Baker Brown, increasingly depicted as a great educator who, against all odds, had struggled and succeeded in realizing a dream.

Pride and boosterism reached new heights in the *Messenger's* editorial on the occasion. Boasting of NINS's 2,500 students and 19 departments, from preparatory to law, the writer declared that the 51 faculty were

> among the most able specialists in the land. Many of them are authors of works considered standards in their respective lines. President Brown and Vice President Kinsey have always believed in putting a premium upon original thought and research among the corps of instructors. The library is an exceptionally great one, and every department is lavishly supplied with all needed apparatus. ... Beside the graduates of Harvard and Heidelberg you will find the alumni of the Normal equally successful and equally armed for the conflict.

While exaggeration on such occasions is common and perhaps pardonable, the truth is that Harvard and Heidelberg had little to fear. Most of the faculty writings were textbooks, and the great library and lavish equipment existed primarily in the writer's imagination. But by invoking such grand standards, and suggesting that greater things were yet to come, the local press did reflect the large ambitions of Brown and Kinsey, even as they had to face an academic revolution that was beginning to take place around them.

3

Valparaiso Makes Its Mark

The Age of the Research University

In 1900, the Northern Indiana Normal School was rechartered as Valparaiso College. The change was a sign of the increased stature and high hopes that surrounded the enterprise as the new century began. Having built a college from scratch, Henry Baker Brown and his collaborators dreamed of even greater things, and the conditions of United States society had seldom been so favorable for such ambitions. Emerging from the depression of the 1890s, the United States was entering a long era of prosperity and progressive reform. In metropolitan areas, a substantial new middle class was emerging, and more of them were beginning to recognize—as Brown and Kinsey had long ago—that higher education should not be the preserve of a narrow elite.

For the first decade of the new century, Valparaiso College—soon renamed Valparaiso University—seemed to be riding the crest of the new educational wave. Reading trends and nimbly adapting to new opportunities as he always had, the now-venerable Henry Brown added ever more programs and buildings to his campus and began operating personally on a larger national stage. Valparaiso University also took advantage of the massive influx of immigrants to become a kind of academic agent of Americanization.

But there were troubles beneath the surface. Brown's vision and style were peculiarly suited to the freewheeling social and educational environment of the Gilded Age. The new forces in higher education, particularly the national universities and their standardized academic models, were in many ways inimical to the kind of open, quasi-populist impulses embodied in institutions such as Valparaiso. When the founder himself passed from the scene, the new challenges posed by World War I and a rapidly changing society proved too much for Brown's successors. The once-proud

Valparaiso University fell into decline and only narrowly escaped a fate worse than extinction.

The research university first appeared on the American scene in the late nineteenth century, but as previously noted, it did not immediately dominate its competitors. In the early twentieth century, however, the modern American research university did plainly triumph as the dominant institutional form of higher education in the United States. Some other types of institutions managed to survive, though on the lower rungs of an increasingly defined hierarchy. Others largely disappeared. In a famous metaphor, David Riesman and Christopher Jencks once described American higher education as a snake in which the middle and tail portions inevitably follow the head wherever it goes. That image was not true when the century began, but it became increasingly true with each passing decade.

While the older college focused on the student and character development, the research university focused on the faculty's discovery and dissemination of specialized new knowledge. It was only marginally concerned with the beliefs and character of the people who acquired such knowledge. Despite its claims to "objectivity," or perhaps because of them, the new education was also profoundly utilitarian, designed to find knowledge that seemed "useful" to society at large, rather than to convey a cultural and intellectual tradition or contemplate difficult moral or religious questions. This was part of its appeal to fabulously wealthy men such as Ezra Cornell, Johns Hopkins, Cornelius Vanderbilt, Leland Stanford, James Duke, and John D. Rockefeller, who financed the new universities and their research. Whether deliberately or not, such institutions also advanced a particular new vision of the "good life" that stressed freedom of choice, technological progress, and the pleasures of consumption.

The religious impulse was not dead, but increasingly the new knowledge experts in the universities assumed the role—once reserved for institutional religion—of guarding society's moral health. There were battles for control of both state and private universities. Usually these battles were not framed in overtly anti-Christian terms but were waged by the new type of academic professionals against what was referred to as "sectarian control of the colleges." Indeed, as historian George Marsden has shown, most of the new educational leaders in the first generation or two considered themselves Christian, though their Christianity was of the liberal Protestant sort that tended simply to identify the kingdom of God with the new intellectual forces advancing under the banner of science.

By the beginning of the twentieth century, a new structured organization of knowledge had appeared, represented by the basic professional associations of the various communities of inquiry. Within the universities, and eventually within the colleges, these associations appeared as departments that each laid claim to a specific field of knowledge. Between roughly 1890 and 1905, the department assumed its modern form as the local embodiment of a national organization of discipline-structured knowledge. Each discipline had its heroes and saints, its acceptable disputes and changing alliances. Its members guarded the gates to the community and the career possibilities of its novices. The community's discourse conditioned its members to regard their disciplinary structures as normal and self-evident, even as their inquiries were increasingly dominated by certain kinds of privileged, often positivistic, "scientific" models that ruled out other kinds of knowledge. Gradually, religion disappeared as a significant factor in the new social sciences and largely from history, philosophy, and literature as well. The "master narrative" in the academy became humanity's ascent from religious obscurantism to enlightened objective rationality and conquest of nature.

The future belonged to the great new universities built upon such assumptions and to the new communities of inquiry that shaped their scholarly life. Because the research universities trained the apprentice faculty for all the colleges, and because almost all young faculty with Ph.D.'s had internalized the research model of the academic life, it was only a matter of time until the "lower" levels of higher education largely fell into line in the parade.

The incredibly high costs of the new research universities quickly made fierce competition for resources and prestige part of the American academic way of life. Besides funding research, the two fabulously wealthy educational foundations established by Andrew Carnegie and John D. Rockefeller sought to bring order to the confused educational scene. The Carnegie Foundation for the Advancement of Teaching, with the weight of the steel magnate's hundreds of millions of dollars behind it, defined a "college" through largely quantified criteria, such as admission of only graduates of accredited high schools; 120 standardized "credit-hours" over four years of work; a minimum of eight departments with at least one full-time professor in each (prohibiting jack-of-all-trades faculty); a minimal productive endowment; and a conservative approach to giving honorary degrees. The Rockefeller General Education Board also endorsed these criteria, as did the new regional accrediting agencies, such as the North

Central Association of Schools and Colleges, which was formed in 1905. The Carnegie Foundation also required the severing of denominational ties as a condition for colleges to participate in the pension program (later TIAA-CREF) that it established for college faculty. Many formerly religious colleges proceeded to do so.

By 1908, the "standard American research university" was clearly identifiable and on its way to domination. Out of the chaos had come not only order, but also an interlocking system of education that, while voluntary and informal, was costly to those who resisted it or stood outside. The elite research universities, public and private, defined the domains and parameters of knowledge. Liberal arts colleges and other institutions continued to exist, but as subordinate enterprises. The Catholic colleges and some others fought what they saw as a model hostile to their religious tradition and vision, but theirs was a rearguard action that steadily lost ground in subsequent decades. Soon almost all colleges seeking academic respectability fell into line, adopting such standard features as departmental majors, survey courses, and distribution requirements to preserve an element of breadth. Most important, colleges began to accept the key principle that the Ph.D. degree granted by the research university was a plainly superior qualification for college teaching.

EXPANSION AND RECOGNITION

In the new century's first years, these powerful national forces were beginning to be felt at Valparaiso College, but they certainly were not perceived as a threat. Indeed, the college appeared to be going from strength to strength, with more students, new programs, and a growing reputation. More of the students who came were already prepared to do college-level work, and there was a general rise in academic aspirations. Terms were lengthened by two weeks to allow for more thorough coverage of subject matter.

In 1900, by far the largest proportion of the 2,500 students at Valparaiso College were those preparing to teach. Valparaiso still offered its basic education curriculum in the "Teachers Department," but it also was developing more specialized forms of training. A new kindergarten department focused on preparing teachers to work with young children. A Department of Domestic Economy (home economics) opened in 1914, responding to a state mandate to increase the numbers of teachers in that new area.

A major achievement for Valparaiso was the creation of a Department of Psychology and Pedagogy in 1898, reflecting the new developments in progressive education pioneered by John Dewey and G. Stanley Hall. Students who completed the scientific course (normally two years) would spend an additional year of studies in this new field, together with the writing of a thesis on an educational subject. This earned them the Bachelor of Pedagogy degree. An additional year of individualized study under the direction of a faculty member would lead to the first graduate degree offered at Valparaiso, the Master of Pedagogy.

Some teachers added the classical curriculum as well. Gradually, within the context of the scientific and classical "courses," new departments, offering more specialized study, began to appear: biology, geology and mineralogy, natural science, English, German, Spanish, French, Italian, and others. Eventually, the college's organizational structure did turn, somewhat grudgingly, toward the more standardized model of an umbrella College of Arts and Sciences, sheltering its separate departments with concentrations and standard degrees. The Department of Elocution and Oratory continued the strong tradition of public speaking and drama at Valparaiso, though with less of the flamboyance of the early days of NINS. There were both a fine arts department and a music department, the latter continuing on its quasi-conservatory path. The strong, scientifically oriented pharmacy department continued to attract students, some of whom became medical students elsewhere.

Reflecting its growing enrollments and aspirations, the campus's physical structure rapidly expanded, which in turn stimulated more growth. A new music building was erected across from Chapel Hall in 1906, contributing to a doubling of enrollment in music. By 1910, the music department housed 72 pianos for rehearsal and performance. The proud, new, well-equipped, three-story red brick and stone building with SCIENCE cut prominently in the stone of its front wall was another statement of Valparaiso's arrival. "Science" embodied the difference between old knowledge and new knowledge. Because Valparaiso stood for "up-to-date" education, Brown and Kinsey spared no expense in the Science Building's construction.

In 1906, the college built a companion biology building with MEDICAL carved on its front. By then, the southern perimeter of the campus was formed from east to west by East Hall, South Hall, the Old Main College Building, Science Hall, and the Biology/Medical Building. The Music Hall, Chapel Hall, and Heritage Hall were in the center. In 1912, two major student residences, Lembke Hall to the east and Altruria Hall to the north, were added. The Domestic Science Building, built in 1914 immediately north of Heritage Hall, completed the campus.

As its campus and enrollment grew, so did Valparaiso's reputation. Its unique features—open enrollment, low cost, work-study programs, and the ban on intercollegiate athletics and Greek organizations—attracted much favorable journalistic attention, especially in national magazines and major newspapers. One of the most significant evaluations came from A. E. Winship, editor of the prestigious *New England Journal of Education*. In an article dated March 31, 1904, and titled, "Valparaiso, A Revelation," Winship wrote:

> After knowing fifty-eight colleges and universities and sixty-three state normal schools, Valparaiso (Indiana) College is a revelation. It enrolls more than 3,000 students a year, has from 2,000 to 2,500 there at one time. Two-thirds of the students are men. ... They are every whit as brainy and well-poised as the students of other colleges, they know as much upon graduation as four-fifths of the graduates of the great universities. The cost of a four years course for tuition, board, and rooms is $560. The institution has never had a dollar's endowment or state aid, and asks for none, has bought and paid for some fifty acres of land, and has erected and equipped ten buildings, and all out of the profits of $1.00 a week's tuition. Isn't that a revelation? ... The tuition of $1.00 a week covers any and all courses one can take except in the law and medical schools, and private lessons in music and art.
>
> The equipment is all that could be desired by nineteen-twentieths of the students of any state university. The laboratory equipment for chemistry, physics, biology, and physiology is astonishingly complete and abundant. ... The professors and teachers are experts with good scholarly training.

Similar encomiums regularly appeared in the popular press from 1901 to 1914, including features in the *Chicago Sunday Herald* and the *New York Herald* newspapers. *McClure's* magazine and *Collier's* emphasized the incredibly low cost of living. Sometimes such features contained unflattering passages, as when William Forbush wrote in the *Boston Evening Transcript*, "College Hill, which is given up entirely to students, is a group of hideous square-shouldered wooden boarding houses. The fashions of dress are followed here at a respectful distance." Forbush's snobbish piece did, however, have a "diamond-in-the-rough" theme. Perhaps in response to such criticism, the Valparaiso University catalog soon included a paragraph stating that "many wealthy and fine families are now sending their sons and daughters to Valparaiso." While many writers, like Winship, focused on the low cost and "efficiency" of the college, several also pointed to the democratic spirit that Henry Baker Brown had infused into the faculty and students as one of its attractions. Such commentary, with its explicit or implied criticism of more restrictive colleges, made Valparaiso well known throughout the Midwest and beyond.

The decade of 1900–10 also saw renewed and expanded efforts in professional education. Unable to start a medical school in the 1880s, Brown was ready by 1902 to launch one, this time in Chicago. That year, Valparaiso College acquired the building and equipment formerly used by Northwestern University on Lincoln Avenue, near the 3,600-bed Cook County Hospital, one of the largest facilities in the country. First called the American College of Medicine and Surgery, Brown changed the name in 1907 to the Chicago College of Medicine and Surgery.

At first, students commuted by rail between Valparaiso and Chicago, using special low student fares that Brown had arranged with the railroads. But it quickly proved more advantageous for students to take two years of low-cost medical courses in Valparaiso, then move to Chicago for the final two clinically oriented years. Eventually, some freshman and sophomore medical students resided in Chicago from the start and never set foot on the home campus until graduation. A number of Valparaiso professors commuted to Chicago to teach basic science courses to these students. To round out the range of medical education, in 1903 Valparaiso acquired from Lake Forest College the highly regarded Chicago College of Dental Surgery, which was on West Harrison Street.

Law school enrollments nationwide doubled between 1900 and 1920 to nearly 25,000 students. Following the trend, Valparaiso's law school continued to grow and professionalize as well. Colonel Mark DeMotte, dean of the Valparaiso law school from its inception, retired in 1906, selling the school to the University. To replace him, Henry Baker Brown selected Milo Jesse Bowman, a Hanover College graduate who had learned the law through the older method of reading in law offices. Nevertheless, in the continuing dispute between those who wanted legal education to be the exclusive preserve of law schools and those who thought the bar itself the best educator, Bowman cast his lot with the academicians.

Throughout his two decades as dean, Bowman displayed a keen eye for hiring good faculty and introducing the most advanced developments in legal education. As soon as he assumed the deanship in 1907, Bowman proposed to the faculty a new curriculum based on the "case method," which would replace the older "Dwight recitation method." The faculty approved the basic change, though hemming it in with some cautionary and compromising language. In 1914, the ABA-commissioned Redlich Report strongly endorsed the case method as the most "scientific" approach to legal education, and Bowman could proudly claim that Valparaiso had anticipated this movement. At the end of his first decade in the deanship, Bowman looked back on the changes that he had implemented:

> The standard of admission [of the early law school] was low, but the faculty and student body were filled with the spirit of work. A very large percent of the graduates became successful practitioners. Many have served as governors, members of supreme courts, and senators and representatives in congress. Under the present management the law building has been remodeled, the library enlarged, the requirements for admission raised, the case method adopted, and the curriculum enriched by the addition of many subjects of instruction.

These developments continued to attract substantial numbers of prospective attorneys to the school. In the 1900s and 1910s, the Valparaiso University law school was the largest in Indiana.

Engineering was another professional field in which Valparaiso became more heavily involved in the pre-World War I era. A kind of proto-civil engineering program had been offered since the days of M. E. Bogarte, but in the early twentieth century, this program was expanded and increasingly professionalized, following the general recommendations for engineering preparation in the Mann Report sponsored by the Carnegie Foundation. Meanwhile, new fields of electrical and mechanical engineering, emerging from industry rather than academia, generated some tension between academics and industry-oriented professionals, though Valparaiso developed only small footholds in these areas.

The 1909–10 Valparaiso University catalog described an enhanced engineering curriculum, and for the first time, it printed a list of engineering students. It declared that "the field of the professional engineer has grown so broad, and the demand upon him so varied that it has been necessary to revise this course and adapt it to the present condition." The new three-year program, with four 12-week terms per year, lengthened the time of study for most engineering subjects and introduced new related requirements such as chemistry and bacteriology (for the new field of sanitary engineering). Throughout the program, there was a tremendous emphasis on design and on the scientific foundations of engineering. Engineering students made much use of the new laboratories in the Science and Medical buildings.

While Valparaiso was self-consciously "progressive" in its incorporation of new approaches to medical, legal, and engineering education, it was strikingly backward in its business education. Academic business training was exploding in the nation at large, with 33 new business departments founded between 1900 and 1915. In 1916, the American Assembly of Collegiate Schools of Business was formed to raise the standards of this new professional study. Given this climate, the near-total failure of Valparaiso University to recognize the beginnings of serious management studies in these prewar years was perhaps one of the first signs of the sleep that was descending upon the institution. It is astonishing that, despite its vaunted orientation to the practical, there was almost no recognition at Valparaiso of how rapidly business and management were changing or of the need to adapt to a world where work was increasingly located in very large organizations. Until 1919, the old "actual business method" continued almost unchanged from its origins 40 years earlier. Only in 1919 was the School of Commerce founded, focusing on accounting and commercial law. In 1920, courses in economics and some more modern work in management made their first appearance.

In 1905, Henry Baker Brown announced that Valparaiso College had become Valparaiso University. The change reflected the institution's rapidly expanding size, added complexity, and general upgrading in academic aspirations. The expanded curricula available on the Valparaiso campus, including an enhanced engineering program and law school, continued to draw increasing numbers of students from a wider range of backgrounds. Strong medical and dental school enrollments at the newly acquired VU programs in Chicago brought the total enrollment to around five thousand—an astonishing figure in an era when most colleges still numbered their students in the hundreds, if not dozens. By 1910, Valparaiso University was among the largest American universities, only a little lower in enrollment than Harvard. This parity in numbers, if not in academic rigor, contributed to the popular description of Valparaiso as "The Poor Man's Harvard."

The change in name from "college" to "university," which a number of other institutions of the time were making as well, also may have reflected some growing anxiety about the rapidly changing academic environment. While Valparaiso did exhibit some of the size and complexity of a "university" through its professional schools, there was also an awareness of the ways in which it had not, and could not, become anything like Stanford or the University of Chicago, Purdue or Michigan State. Universities that actually were committed to the new university movement featured graduate work, which Valparaiso did not. Nor did Valparaiso promote research as either a qualification for its faculty or an institutional aim. It was strictly a teaching institution. Moreover, it was a teaching institution that was totally dependent on its constituency of less affluent students rather than on wealthy donors or state government.

Nevertheless, the catalog announcing that Valparaiso was now a university did have a new tone of assertiveness. It declared a substantial 50 percent hike in tuition (from $10 to $15 a term), which it attributed to the general upgrading in equipment and programs. There was also a new 50-cent "library fee." The new VU plainly thought it was worth more to its students, and it probably was.

THE RISE OF "COLLEGE LIFE" AT VU

Valparaiso was also changing in its social character and clientele. The original Northern Indiana Normal School had been consciously hostile to the more frivolous and social side of nineteenth-century student life as practiced in the Ivy League colleges and their numerous imitators. The high-spirited rituals of "college life," including secret fraternities and sororities, had been created as a form of opposition to the authoritarianism of these schools. Its proponents claimed that students' most significant "education" occurred not in the boring recitations of the classroom, but in the rich social and athletic life fostered by this "state within a state."

Around the turn of the century, American college administrators moved to co-opt the tremendously popular collegiate life by maneuvering the "Greek" organizations to act for the sake of the institution rather than "underground." They appointed student deans whose task it was to implement the new order. Newly formed student governments channeled these energies and gave students a role in nonacademic governance processes of the campus, thus freeing faculty from disciplinary duties for their new professional roles.

At Valparaiso, the official stance of Brown and his administration remained hostile to the more frivolous side of "college life." Fraternities and sororities, the national purveyors of collegiate culture, remained illegal. Nevertheless, it was impossible to completely suppress the new trends, and Valparaiso gradually accommodated many of the tendencies associated with the increased influence, and perhaps slightly greater affluence, of its students. Some who promoted these changes were transfer students, who brought "college life" with them to VU.

The newer forms of social life at VU developed principally around the departments and their classes. Each school or department formed a major social unit for purposes of intramural sports and various social activities. The four largest departments at the turn of the century—the lawyers, the pharmic-medics, the scientifics, and the professionals (or educationals)—were soon joined by the engineers and the aggies as the prewar decades unfolded. Students in the smaller units, such as classics and the arts, often attached themselves to one of the larger groups for various activities, especially sports.

On the first day of each term, after Brown and later Kinsey met in the auditorium with all the students to explain the rules of the University, each department's students met to organize their classes, elect officers, and discuss plans for social activities. At the end of the year, a booklet was published with pictures and information about the graduating class of each department, its history, its class prophecy, and details about the final banquet. In 1911, several units combined their annuals and produced *The Record*, which became the all-university yearbook.

In the early prewar period, these student departmental organizations dominated student life. Each had its colors, its pennants, as well as its teams representing it in athletics and other contests. Rivalry was intense and often violent. The perpetual student question was, "Who runs the Hill?" There were various ways of staking claims to "rule" and defending it. Most common was the brazen attempt to take physical possession of another department's building and to run one's own flag up to its top. Sometimes "rule" was asserted by getting a departmental flag to fly from the highest point of College Hill, the top of the Old Main College Building itself. These efforts by groups of students to attack or defend departmental territory frequently were accompanied by violence, often leading to the intervention of Vice President Kinsey or the local police.

One yearbook tells of the halftime activities during a football game between the lawyers and the engineers. The tattered black and orange flag of the lawyers suddenly appeared in bits and pieces, strewn about the field. This meant the engineers had stolen the flag, mutilated it, and now would face retaliation and the need to defend their own blue and gold pennant, perhaps at that time flying from the law school's flagpole.

Other student traditions developed as well. Each spring the entire VU student body, led by the lawyers, would march from College Hill through the downtown streets of Valparaiso in the "Straw Hat Parade." The lawyers all wore straw hats, and many dressed in outrageous costumes representing mythical or comic figures. Pictures of these parades always show someone carrying a sign asking, "Who runs the Hill?"—both a claim and a taunt. Unlike some of the on-campus high jinks, these parades were initially orderly, always stopping at local theaters for yells or a few vaudeville skits, then returning to the Hill for a giant cleanup and bonfire, in which all the straw hats and other garbage would be burned. The parade was spectacular enough to draw both Pathe and Fox film crews one year, which allowed students to watch themselves later on the newsreels at the local movie houses.

Around 1910, however, a more pathological version of the Straw Hat Parade began to appear. For half a dozen years, newspapers headlined student "riots" at VU. The students called them "rampages." Beginning as efforts to let off steam at the end of winter term, these became destructive events in which students, some of them drunk, marched downtown singing and shouting, took over the local cinema with threats of violence, and actually destroyed property both in town and when they returned to College Hill. When a rampage approached downtown, police sometimes had to intervene, jailing ringleaders and even using the threat of weapons to rein in the menace.

While Brown accommodated the student departmental rivalries and a more intense social life than had ever existed in his "old" school, the increasingly uncontrollable and often rowdy student behavior led to growing conflicts with the rather old-fashioned administration. The departmental class books reveal something of the life of the students during this period of rapid change. In 1904, one lamented the loss of former classmates because of the "winecup, green-covered tables and music of the feet," referring to Valparaiso's ban on liquor, saloons (with their green pool tables), and dancing. Enforcement of such rules became harder and harder for Brown and Kinsey. They placed "spies" in the student body and attempted to suppress unauthorized organizations that promoted college life. But these steps could not prevent the formation of a secret society, the Alpha Epsilon fraternity, which managed to exist underground for more than a decade.

While the spirited departmental rivalries, punctuated by occasional riots, represented the most visible and intense form of student life, less competitive activities attracted some students as well. For many VU students, mundane social life revolved around clubs. Some of these represented students from various regions of the country: The Southern Club was the largest and most active. With the large influx of immigrants onto the campus, there were numerous clubs for foreign students, organized by nationality. Some groups, such as the English Club, were organized by disciplines. All of these organizations had regular meetings, social events, and some program of activities.

A minority of students was involved in political activities and organizations. Democrats and Republicans had their student adherents, but more radical ideas stirred some students as well. Many in the sizable contingent of Russian immigrant students wanted only to argue politics. Some U.S.-born students also were attracted to socialism, and a Socialist Club flourished. In 1909, the class orator for the professionals (teachers) spoke in favor of socialism. At the same time, Ira Tilton, a Valparaiso graduate, an attorney, and a part-time teacher at the law school, was publishing his paper *The Socialist Educator* and urging the doctrines of socialism on everyone who would hear. A large chapter of the International Socialist Club was able at one point to mount a 600-student rally against armaments. At least some Valparaiso graduates retained their radical beliefs after leaving Indiana. For example, Merton C. Willer (class of 1913) eventually became the Communist candidate for governor of Wyoming during the Depression.

Religion played a larger part than politics in the life of most students. Attendance at the college-sponsored chapel declined, but local churches began to take a more active role, offering social activities in addition to a religious home to students. General Protestant assumptions about "building the kingdom of God" still prevailed, and student publications did not hesitate to talk about a "Christian America." But the growing diversity of the students, including immigrants, meant that the campus was no longer a Protestant preserve. A Menorah Club gave Jewish students a presence, and the large number of Catholic students were active in the Catholic Club. Of all the religious organizations, the YMCA and the YWCA continued to be the most prominent. The YMCA had the most elaborate facilities and programs. Its building had a reading room, a large room fitted as a gymnasium, and showers available to all—a real benefit at a time when many students lived in boardinghouses. Perhaps a quarter of Valparaiso's male students bought a membership card, and female participation in the YWCA was comparable. Besides religious and recreational activities, "Y" members undertook service projects with young people in town or at the Gary YMCA, where they did such things as teach English to immigrants.

Sager's Lake had lost none of its attraction as VU students' prime recreation spot. Boats and bathhouses drew a large clientele, and when the lake froze, two or three hundred students could be found skating each day. The term "Sagerology" was used to refer to the romantic episodes that the casual hiker might stumble upon quite easily around the lake. The footbridge built over the railway on the route from the campus to the lake, soon known as "Kissing Bridge," began to figure regularly in student pictures and romantic poetry.

Musical and theatrical programs abounded, and Valparaiso students developed a strong reputation for their love of music and theater. The annual climax was the May Festival, which normally lasted for three days of performances and included presentations of the Valparaiso University Symphony Orchestra, with guest performers from Chicago.

THE "NEW WOMAN" AT VU

The changing social atmosphere at VU was especially reflected in new attitudes and opportunities affecting female students. On questions of gender, the decade of the 1890s had marked a clear transition to recognizably modern concerns. For women, there was a rapidly developing consciousness of new opportunities and roles, exemplified by the image of the "new woman." More expansive and spirited than the deferential Victorian "true woman," she was visually symbolized by the mentally and physically vigorous "Gibson girls," who appeared in magazines and posters playing tennis or riding bicycles. The loose-fitting clothing the Gibson girls wore while pursuing athletic activities symbolized emancipation, with skirts edging up every few years. By 1900, college women who especially identified with these changes appeared in a variety of new roles and types: the "lady scholar," the "curious thinker," the "cultivated dilettante," the "effervescent flirt," the "social butterfly," the "all-American girl," the earnest "dig," and the striving "outsider." At the same time, new media, especially the movies, introduced people in urban areas to a faster-paced lifestyle that included automobiles, changing fashions, dancing, and the availability of liquor and cigarettes for women.

The changing attitudes and social situation of women at Valparaiso were reflected in the pages of the *Current*, a campus journal that adopted a positive stance toward the "new woman." In 1893, it applauded when professional women turned up in large numbers at the "Woman's Congress" of the Chicago Columbian Exposition, signaling the end of the professions as an exclusively male preserve. At the same time, it reported with dismay the Chicago public school system's reaffirmation of its rule that female teachers had to resign upon marriage.

While female students at VU remained a decided minority, consistently outnumbered about two to one, there were indications that small but significant changes were occurring among them as well. In 1898, the *Current* reported that Northern alumna Florence Higgins, professor of rhetoric and public speaking, had been added to the faculty of the VU law school, "the only woman on record who occupies such a position." The cover of the April 29, 1899, issue of the *Current* featured a Mrs. C. M. Lane as "The Law Student." She was, evidently, the only female law student at NINS at that point and was favorably described as a "new woman," though she was not active in the suffrage movement.

By the first decade of the twentieth century, female students at VU reflected the range of possibilities regarding women's roles and some of the attendant tensions as well. Most women were in the teaching department and other female-oriented programs, but a small minority made their way into nontraditional areas such as pharmacy and business. Female students themselves were divided about political issues—like the vote. While some women became active and outspoken advocates of suffrage and other women's causes, others, such as Lane, were more reluctant to adopt that stance, even as they entered traditionally male domains. Other female students were still quite traditional and looked, in the long run, toward marriage and children as their major life goals.

The lives of two VU graduates, Petra Dahl and Beulah Bondi, while certainly not "typical," do demonstrate that the "new woman" was an active presence at Valparaiso University and that women's accomplishments in the face of still-formidable obstacles were considerable. Petra Dahl, born to Norwegian immigrants in Iowa, already had begun teaching school at the turn of the century when she decided to attend Valparaiso, where she obtained her Bachelor of Science in 1902. In a recommendation for her, Professor B. F. Williams wrote:

> Miss Petra Dahl has been in my classes in American and English Literature during the present school year, and her work throughout has been of exceptionally high grade. ... Miss Dahl is a young woman of strong personality, clear-headed, quick, with a strong fund of common sense and an inherent refinement of manner.

After serving for a time as a school administrator, Dahl returned to Valparaiso for a Bachelor of Arts in music and a Master of Arts in teaching. Then Dahl became a junior faculty member in the English department at the University, referred to by students as Professor Williams's "great big beautiful Dahl." Dahl was indeed a forceful personality, and she became known for her cleverness and verbal abilities. A reporter for *The Porter County Vidette* gave this account of a speech Dahl gave in the chapel-auditorium:

> She was the impersonation of the twentieth century woman, and then some. Her style was smooth, her humor rich, her wit incisive, her command of English admirable, and her logic markedly feminine. Her pleasant sallies of wit brought the house to laughter several times. President Brown, Professor Kinsey and B. F. Williams each in their turn experienced the effect of her mirth-provoking spirit. The subject matter of her talk was equality between man and woman, and incidentally "Woman's Suffrage." The following paragraph is typical: "While man won glories on the battlefield, devastated fruitful areas, marched in triumphal processions, tortured his victims, sang in immortal lines his glorious achievements, this other being, woman, conscious of a divine descent, was working out her salvation and has gained a place of recognition by persistently fighting every inch of the way, and that without bloodshed, destruction or cruelty, but by dint of that same spiritual strength that enabled her to accept and endure what seemed unbearable yet was unable to avoid in the so-called divine decrees; and has now attained to a place in the world and its affairs that need no longer be sneered at by members of the more fortunate, because divinely preferred sex!"

After an attack of rheumatic fever, Dahl decided to abandon teaching in favor of a medical degree. In 1912, she began the four-year course, spending the first two years in Valparaiso and moving to Chicago for the final two years, graduating with the M.D. in 1916 and going into practice. Dahl subsequently became a health officer for the city of Chicago and engaged in a lifelong political struggle to reform the city's health programs. She served in many capacities in the Medical Women's Club of Chicago, an activist group working on behalf of health issues and for which she wrote extensively.

In 1919, Dahl entered the race for alderman of the 41st ward of Chicago, perhaps the first of her gender ever to do so. One of her proposals was that each ward should have two aldermen, one man and one woman. Dahl's presidency of the Norwegian Women's Club of Chicago suggests another dimension of her many interests, which also included studying law as a "hobby."

Another notable Valparaiso student of the pre-World War I era was Valparaiso resident Beulah Bondy, who later changed her name to Bondi. Bondy's mother had attended the Normal in the 1880s and communicated her love of elocution to her daughter. Beulah enrolled at Valparaiso University in 1910 and quickly became a leader in campus performance activities. She participated in the lively theater program, and, as the class poet for the 1916 University *Record*, she wrote a parody of classical verse in which she assigned one of the nine muses to each of the nine oratory graduates of 1916. She received her bachelor's degree in 1914 and her master's two years later. Her classmate Lowell Thomas recalled that Bondy's residence was a center of campus social activity.

After much amateur theater and stock company work in Indianapolis, Beulah Bondi earned a part in a Broadway production and went on to numerous character roles in major plays. In 1929, she gained a role in *Street Scene*, which ran for more than 600 performances, then she did the film version as well. She went on to appear in 65 films, including *It's a Wonderful Life* as Ma Bailey, playing alongside numerous Hollywood stars. Later in her career, she turned to television, where she won an Emmy Award for her performance in *The Waltons*.

"A NEW PENTECOST"

Among the changes that the twentieth century brought to Valparaiso University was a substantial new constituency from the wave of southern and central European "New Immigrants" pouring into the United States. In the Midwest, Chicago was becoming a city of ethnics as hundreds of thousands of refugees from European politics or poverty crowded together in miserable slums, working to improve their lot. While most immigrants struggled merely to earn enough to survive, a few of the ambitious young newcomers looked eagerly to education as a way to succeed in the New World. One place to pursue the dream was a college in nearby northwest Indiana.

The attractions of Valparaiso University to many immigrant students were later stated by the writer Stoyan Christowe in his autobiography:

> I had read an advertisement in one of the Chicago papers stating that it was possible to enter Valparaiso in a state of complete illiteracy and come out an engineer, a lawyer, a pharmacist, Bachelor of the arts and

> sciences. … I was cheered when I found out how inexpensively one could live and study at Valparaiso. I was loath to leave Chicago, but tuition fees at the University of Chicago and Northwestern were too high. … Valparaiso was only forty miles east of Chicago and appeared the most logical place for me.

The advertisements for VU that Christowe and numerous other immigrants read were placed in Chicago newspapers by Brown and were specifically designed to attract students who knew little English and had even less money. Valparaiso's traditional ability to serve poor, hardworking American students was easily adaptable to these newcomers. The preparatory department began to specialize in teaching English to nonnative speakers. Once the first immigrant students succeeded, word of mouth about the college quickly spread in the highly networked ethnic communities of Chicago and Gary. The new electric railways made transportation cheap and easy. The substantial number of immigrants soon changed the face of Valparaiso and the character of its student body. In May 1912, the Indianapolis *Journal-Educator* reported that there were nearly 700 foreigners enrolled at Valparaiso, based on the official roll, including 100 students from Russia and more than 40 each from such places as Poland, Germany, Norway, Cuba, and Central America.

Along with campus life, the "Y" and local churches became centers of socialization and "Americanization" for many of these immigrant students. One student said the atmosphere at Valparaiso resembled "a new Pentecost," so great was the variety of languages actively spoken on College Hill. As with female students, there was a tremendous variety among the many immigrant students who passed through Valparaiso University in the early 1900s. Here, too, the profiles of a few students, such as Stanley Balzekas and Michael Borodin, though they may not be "typical," reveal something of the kind of students who attended VU in these years.

A study entitled *The Lithuanian Diaspora—Koenigsberg to Chicago* provides an account of one Chicago immigrant community, the Lithuanians, and explains their attraction to Valparaiso. It reported that Valparaiso's policy of accepting students "with little knowledge of spoken or written English" especially attracted immigrants and that its accessibility "acted as a magnet for ambitious young Lithuanians who were drawn there by word of mouth." As early as 1905, there already were 13 Lithuanian students at Valparaiso University. One of the students who came a few years later was Stanley Balzekas.

Balzekas arrived in Chicago in 1912 at the age of 20. After working in a butcher shop, he saved enough to buy his own store. Soon he created a chain of four more stores. After seven years of growing prosperity, Balzekas realized that further progress depended on education, so he enrolled at Valparaiso to study business administration and law.

While a student at the college, Balzekas made the acquaintance of Valparaiso businessman Al Heineman and quickly won his confidence. Heineman turned over to Balzekas the management of the three town cinemas he owned. A year later, Balzekas also began managing Heineman's new automobile dealership. Using these businesses as a source of income and as places of employment, Balzekas personally recruited 55 more Lithuanian students to Valparaiso and operated a kind of one-man financial aid/work-study operation for his fellow nationals. Many of the recipients of this aid eventually became prominent Chicago jurists, businessmen, bankers, and civil servants. When he returned to Chicago in 1923, Balzekas quickly became a leader in the Lithuanian-American community and the larger Chicago business world.

While Stanley Balzekas represents one path that immigrants who attended Valparaiso followed, a quite different career was that of a Russian immigrant named Michael Grutzenberg, known to history as the prominent revolutionary Bolshevik Michael Borodin (1884–1951). Grutzenberg (also known at various times as Berg, Altschuler, and Borodin) already was involved in revolutionary politics before he came to the United States. He was among the top one hundred young revolutionaries recruited by Lenin in 1903, and he became associated with Stalin in 1905. Arrested by Czarist police in 1906 and deported to Britain, Borodin eventually made his way to the United States and to Chicago.

By 1908, Borodin was attending Valparaiso University, studying rhetoric, elocution, and several business subjects for two terms. During his third term, Borodin enrolled in a "Civil Government" course, but after three weeks, he reported ill and never returned to the campus. During his time at Valparaiso, Borodin had become close friends with two other Russian Jews, Henry Krasnow and Hyman Bolotin. Krasnow was a medical student who earned an M.D. from Valparaiso's medical school in Chicago, and Bolotin studied pedagogy. Back in Chicago, Borodin and Bolotin joined their efforts in developing the Berg Progressive Preparatory School, which imitated VU's basic methods.

When Lenin's Bolshevik Revolution broke out in Russia, Borodin and many other politically active immigrants returned to join the cause.

Borodin became a substantial figure in the Soviet Communist Party. As Stalin's emissary to the Chinese revolutionaries, Borodin played a key role in fostering the Chinese Communist Party of Mao Tse-tung and Deng Hsiao-ping. Borodin later served as editor of the Communist *Moscow Daily News*.

ALUMS OF THE OLD VU

Women such as Dahl and Bondi or immigrants such as Balzekas and Borodin were only part of a student body that included many other types of young people as well. The experience of Stoyan Christowe and George Stimpson, two VU student leaders from quite different backgrounds, shows how the mix of immigrants and U.S.-born students created interesting relationships on the campus. Two other students, Lowell Thomas and Gerald L. K. Smith, were among the most famous alumni produced by Valparaiso University. Their profiles also indicate how varied the student body was in those years.

The close friendship and subsequent careers of students Stoyan Christowe and George Stimpson show the positive effects that the "mingling of cultures" among immigrants and U.S.-born students could have at VU. Arriving on the campus with little knowledge of English, Christowe received a large boost through a fortunate friendship with two remarkable fellow students. George Stimpson had arrived at Valparaiso from Iowa without a high school education but with a deep, self-taught love of the English language and English literature. Stimpson and another similarly word-intoxicated friend, Felix Cotten from Mississippi, helped teach English to Christowe and immersed him in the richness of its language and literature.

Christowe's success with English was not immediate, however. In a later book recalling his Valparaiso days, he remembered:

> For a long time I had been hearing about "Sagerology," "Cemetery Science," and "spooning." I knew "Sagerology" had something to do with Sager's Lake and the woods that surrounded it, as I also knew that the cemetery adjoining the campus, protected by high and thick hedges, was a safe place to take a girl in the moonlight, since no discreet person, unless it were a fellow student taking the same course, would ever think of walking through it. My ardent interest in philology, however, caused me to confuse "spooning" with "spoonerism." A coed cleared that up for me. It was all part of my American growth.

After mastering English, Christowe threw himself into writing on campus, introducing a new international sophistication to *The Torch*, the student newspaper. After graduation, Christowe became a Chicago journalist, then a foreign correspondent and the author of six popular books. He eventually settled in Vermont, where he served 12 years in the state legislature.

Like his friend Christowe, George Stimpson spent much of his five years at Valparaiso writing for campus publications, including *The Torch*. Stimpson believed deeply in the old "democratic traditions" of the University and defended them when they seemed under attack. After graduation, Stimpson and his friend Felix Cotten made their way to Washington, D.C. They were amazed to find a significant number of Valparaiso alumni playing key roles in the capital, including seven members of the House of Representatives. Senators Norris and Andrieus Jones expressed their love for the school and especially for Henry Baker Brown, the Kinseys, and Samantha Baldwin. Stimpson made his career as a journalist and writer in Washington, publishing a number of books that included a slender history of Valparaiso University. Cotten and Stimpson developed a wide acquaintance among Washington notables, and each was elected president of the National Press Club. When Stimpson died, his funeral was held in the U.S. Capitol.

When Beulah Bondi died in 1981, it was one of her closest lifelong friends, Lowell Thomas, who clipped her substantial obituary from *The New York Times* and sent it to mutual friends who had graduated from Valparaiso University in their era. Thomas, perhaps the old VU's best-known alumnus, arrived at the University in 1909 at the age of 17. In 1932, he remembered:

> I arrived there with about sixteen dollars, and my first job was taking care of a three-story dormitory. I poked up the fires at four A.M.; then fed the furnace at intervals all through the day; banked the fires at eleven P.M.; scrubbed the halls twice a week; ran a washing machine on Saturday; and acted as a valet to a cow. For this I received my board and room and $3 a week.

The dormitory was Stiles Hall, where Thomas roomed with law student George Washington Vilain, a Spanish-American War veteran who was hurrying to get his degree. Widow Stiles's "Amazon daughter" had eyes only for Vilain, which scared him into spending his whole day at the library or elsewhere, leaving Thomas without distraction.

The next year, Thomas boarded at Mead Hall, where he ran into the same luck, though for opposite reasons. His roommate had taken up with "Mabel, the Campus Widow," known for her generous favors to students. He spent day and night with her, again leaving Thomas alone. Although Thomas worked that year as a short-order cook at the Greenwich Cafe near the campus (later Greek's Pizza, then Maria Elena's), he was able to take a rigorous array of courses both years, including science, German, and Latin (Cicero, Horace, Tacitus). He did well in all of them. Thomas was active in Alpha Epsilon, the underground fraternity, and was generally a big man on campus. Although Thomas conceded that he took too many courses, he did well enough in them to earn a Bachelor of Science degree in 1910 and an A.B. in 1911.

After leaving Valparaiso, Thomas started a journalism career, where he quickly gained a substantial reputation as a writer. During World War I, Thomas achieved worldwide fame as the correspondent who discovered the mysterious Colonel T. E. Lawrence, "Lawrence of Arabia." His first book, *With Lawrence of Arabia*, made Thomas the toast of London. Fifty-four popular books on contemporary affairs followed. Thomas became the epitome of the globe-trotting journalist, visiting every continent many times. From 1930 to 1976, he did a nightly CBS News international report, and he also served for two decades as the narrative voice of "Movie Tone News."

Although Thomas also had connections with three other universities, he remained loyal to Valparaiso even after its acquisition by the Lutherans. In the 1930s, he would return to the campus to lecture, and afterward, he would delight students gathered in the Greenwich Inn with tales of his Valpo days. Sometimes Thomas would turn up unannounced for talks and end his impromptu remarks with his famous signature, "So long for now." He lent his famous name to VU fund-raising efforts whenever asked and continued to strongly support the University until his death.

Perhaps it was out of a superabundance of loyalty that Thomas introduced a fellow Valparaiso alumnus, Gerald L. K. Smith, to the elite Advertising Club of New York in 1936. Thomas was the kind of famous graduate that all universities enjoy pointing to with pride. Smith was the other kind. Smith grew up in Viroqua, Wisconsin, where he starred in high school athletics and oratory. Eager to attend college, Smith found that Valparaiso was the only one that such an indigent boy could afford. He worked in the fields all summer after high school graduation. In the fall of 1915, Smith bought two Sears Roebuck suits and a train ticket for

Valparaiso. After he arrived and paid the tuition at the University, he found he had only ten dollars left. A matron of one of the large boardinghouses offered him a cot in a large closet if he would wash dishes. Smith earned a promotion to waiter and took extra jobs working in gardens and mowing lawns.

Although he signed up for overloads, Smith became vice president of the campus YMCA and played many roles in the theater. A posed photo in the yearbook showed him orating on a tree stump with a Bible in one hand. The caption read, "Billy Sunday," a takeoff on the popular contemporary evangelist. Smith was active in the Valparaiso Christian Church, where the pastor got him part-time preaching jobs. His undoubted oratorical talent was nurtured by Professor Rollo A. Talcott, one of the faculty stars.

Smith's preaching so delighted congregations that even while a student he was offered permanent preaching positions at two churches, one just outside Valparaiso and one in Gary. After his graduation in 1917, he launched a flamboyant ministerial career. By the 1930s, Smith had become a prominent figure in Louisiana, closely linked to Senator Huey Long's demagogic "Share Our Wealth" scheme. After hearing Smith speak, H. L. Mencken called him "the gustiest and goriest, loudest and lustiest, deadliest and damndest orator ever heard on this or any other earth ... the champion boob-bumper of all epochs." After Long's assassination, Smith preached the funeral sermon on the grounds of Lousiana's capitol building to 150,000 mourners.

Until the mid-1930s, Smith's religious-political career was self-promoting but not particularly nasty. After Long's death, however, Smith developed delusions of grandeur and turned increasingly to an ugly politics of viciousness and smear. He became closely involved with Father Coughlin's fanatical anti-Roosevelt campaigns, then moved on to the America First movement, and finally led a series of anti-Semitic, anticommunist, and antiblack crusades that brought him notoriety, wealth, and a chapter in any book on right-wing American hate-mongers. The subtitle of a recent biography, *Minister of Hate*, captures Smith's place in the history of fanaticism. There is no evidence that he learned any of these doctrines at Valparaiso University, but such an alumnus is not the sort any institution wants to claim.

While these names constitute some of the most visible of the old VU's alumni, there were many more who made a mark on the public record. A sampling of such people would include: John A. Anderson, director of the

Mount Wilson Observatory and member of the National Academy of Science; Harold Butler, dean of the College of Fine Arts at Syracuse University; Russell Hendrickson, cellist for the Chicago Symphony Orchestra; David B. Johnson, dean of the School of Pharmacy at the University of Oklahoma and president of the American Pharmacy Association; Reuben Kahn, discoverer of the Kahn blood test for venereal disease; Wayne King, band leader; Fernandus Payne, Indiana University zoologist and dean of Arts and Sciences and Graduate Studies; Angus Ward, American diplomat; Gerald D. Timmons, dean of the Indiana University School of Dentistry and president of the American Dental Association; and Harry Stack Sullivan, the eminent American psychiatrist, who graduated from the VU medical school in Chicago.

Worth amused notice is Erle Stanley Gardner, the creator of Perry Mason, who studied law at VU for several weeks before fleeing after a fight with an instructor. Other well-known figures who passed through Valparaiso University, at least briefly, include oil multimillionaire H. L. Hunt and the extraordinary historian and writer W. J. Cash, author of *The Mind of the South*.

The sale of Valparaiso to the Lutherans in 1925 undoubtedly created a sense of loss for many of these alumni, whose memories and ties were to "Mr. Brown's School." There were some, however, whose loyalty was to Valparaiso University, no matter under whose auspices. Lowell Thomas was a faithful contributor and supporter of VU for many years. Benjamin Garman, a law graduate, left $2 million to Valparaiso and the state universities of the five states in which he practiced. The Lutheran institution was the beneficiary of this gift, one of the most generous donations from the alumni of the Brown and Kinsey school.

Considering the decidedly poor backgrounds from which most of the old VU's alumni came, there were a remarkable number of men and women who achieved distinction in their work and many more who served skillfully and well in classrooms, courthouses, state governments, medicine, and in the business world, both in the United States and in many other nations. Although Valparaiso University could hardly take sole credit for their achievements, the "poor man's Harvard" of that era did indeed distinguish itself in providing a unique educational opportunity to thousands of ambitious young people who dreamed of college and found a place that would accept and inspire them. It was a worthy contribution and a unique chapter in American higher education.

BROWN ON THE NATIONAL SCENE

Valparaiso University's success helped to catapult its founder and president into increasing national prominence. While Brown lacked the background and connections of the famous elite university presidents of the era, such as William Rainey Harper, David Starr Jordan, and Charles Eliot, he possessed the same instinct for turning his academic institutional position into a vehicle of public status and influence. Some of Brown's activities—and particularly the bitter battle for control of the National Education Association in which he became embroiled—reveal the ways in which he, and his institution, were part of an older social world that was being squeezed between new, powerful cultural forces.

As president of NINS and then Valparaiso University, Brown developed a strong political base in Indiana. In 1901, the state's teachers elected him president of the Indiana State Teachers Association. In August 1903, the *Vidette* reported that newspapers all across Indiana were "booming" Brown for governor and that his candidacy had strong support within the Democratic State Central Committee. But after accepting an appointment from the Republican governor to the board of a state institution for the deaf, Brown publicly withdrew his name from gubernatorial consideration.

While public office was not in Brown's future, office in the politically potent National Education Association was. In 1907, he was nominated for membership on the board of trustees, the most powerful unit of the NEA. The board was chaired by the autocratic Nicholas Murray Butler, president of Columbia University, who, among other things, excluded women from all leadership positions in the organization. At the NEA national assembly that year, the growing number of opposition "insurgents" revolted. Some simply were seeking more democracy in the organization; others, such as fiery Margaret Haley of the Chicago Teachers Federation, the nation's first teachers' union, were promoting an explicitly feminist agenda. With insurgent backing, Brown was elected to the board.

Brown thought of himself as a "progressive" but not an "insurgent." He recently had taken public positions in favor of improving teachers' pay, and Valparaiso was thought of as a bastion of democracy (though within his own institution, Brown could be as autocratic as Butler). Now in a position to help oust or retain Butler as chair, Brown engaged in an extensive correspondence with the powerful Columbia president that shows Brown to be solicitous but also clever in trying to turn the situation to his own—

and VU's—advantage. Perhaps feeling himself squeezed between the insurgents who had elected him and Butler, who exerted his own increasing pressure, Brown steered a difficult course, sometimes voting with Butler and sometimes against him.

A dramatic mobilization of insurgent forces at the 1910 NEA meeting in Boston featured the strong feminist leadership of Chicagoan Ella Flagg Young and NINS alumna Mary Abbe, who took advantage of Butler's absence in Europe and effectively seized control of the board. Young, the formidable first female superintendent of the Chicago public schools and a professor at the University of Chicago, was elected NEA president, though the result was disputed by the old guard. The insurgents also tried to elect Brown chairman of the trustees, but he would accept only the title of "acting chairman." In that position, however, Brown stood for several months at the pinnacle of the NEA's educational hierarchy.

In this role, Brown came under intense pressure from both the insurgents and Butler's allies. Under stress, Brown dragged his feet and tried to avoid a final showdown in the fierce contest of wills between Young and Butler. For a time, he appeared to be sympathetic to Young and rebuked one of Butler's allies for his charges of fraud. But by the time acting chairman Brown finally called a meeting of the board of trustees in New York on January 11, 1911, he proved unwilling to side with the insurgents. Citing a technicality, Young refused to attend the meeting, and the board majority ended up censuring her. S. Y. Gillan, an editor sympathetic to the insurgents, wrote critically in January that "the gentleman from Indiana has been won over by the Ring—or he may always have been with them." Another described the situation as "Brown and Greenwood jumping through the hoop whenever Butler's whip cracked."

There is no direct evidence as to what led the whipsawed Brown finally to act against what appeared to be his personal inclinations and join in censuring Young. But Margaret Haley, a woman who was deeply involved in the battle, later hinted in an early draft of her memoirs that Butler had threatened to use his power to destroy Valparaiso as a means of swaying Brown.

> Do you know how Brown was controlled? Nicholas Murray Butler even at that time was able to put his paw down and kill any of the private proprietary schools like the Valparaiso Normal. Brown was much beloved and revered by his students. ... People who were poor could go to that school and live cheaply. ... He made life easy and helped those people along. And he had a devotion that was beautiful to see

> from the students. When Miss Abbe found out what Nicholas Murray Butler was doing, she went to Indiana to see Brown and had a long talk with him and he wept like a child. He said, "Miss Abbe, you'll have to trust me. I can't tell you what the trouble is. I had to do what I did."

Whether or not this dramatic secondhand account represents the full story of this affair cannot be determined. Nevertheless, the essentially deferential and subordinating dynamics of Brown's relationship with the new educational establishment of the era are evident. The day of the self-made educational entrepreneur was passing, and the movement toward a single national standard of what constituted American higher education was irresistible. The president of Columbia University did not have to threaten to "kill" the old Valparaiso University, if in fact he did. VU already was beginning to suffer from a near-fatal illness of its own, caused in part by large cultural conditions of the time.

In April 1912, an unprecedented holiday was declared at Valparaiso University because the entire faculty went to Chicago to hear Henry Baker Brown, William Jennings Bryan, and the president of the University of Chicago speak on the same platform. It was the last public celebration of Brown's career. In the fall of 1912, Brown visited Boston again to be inducted as a thirty-third degree Mason. While there, he suffered a stroke that severely limited his participation in University affairs and from which he never fully recovered.

4

DECLINE AND CRISIS

CHANGING TIMES

After a period of attempted recuperation, it became apparent that Henry Baker Brown would have to withdraw from managing the University. The logical choice as his successor was O. P. Kinsey. But Kinsey was already in his mid-60s and would accept only the title of acting president, which he assumed in the fall of 1912. Meanwhile, Geneva Brown summoned her oldest son, Henry Kinsey Brown, to leave his banking work in California and return to represent the family's interests in the University.

Only 22 years old, Henry Kinsey Brown was an unlikely academic leader. As soon as he arrived, it was obvious that this young man would bring change to the campus. Some students continued to revere Acting President Kinsey, with his diligent Victorian ways, as an authority figure, but the younger Brown, called "HK" or "the Boy," was from the students' own generation and was immediately popular with many of them. He was handed the official title of treasurer of the University, and to all public appearances, he began work in harmony with Kinsey. But generational and policy differences soon produced strains.

For a decade or so, there had been open discussion concerning a post-Brown and post-Kinsey Valparaiso University. The general feeling was that the institution was so strong that its own momentum would carry it forward. Such optimism misread the strong new trends affecting U.S. higher education, which demanded structural change and increased financial backing for institutions to survive. The old hand-to-mouth methods of funding that Brown and Kinsey had followed were no longer adequate. On the surface, Valparaiso seemed to be a strong institution, but it was more fragile than almost anyone suspected.

Valparaiso University did not seem fragile when its enrollment reached an all-time high of 4,977 in the year 1914–15. VU kept adding new and somewhat poorly conceived programs, evidently without much concern over how to integrate or sustain them. When VMFC alumnus William Pinney donated a large farm to the University in 1915, an agricultural department was established. In 1916, a "School of Bible Study" was created, the result of another gift.

The first signs of serious trouble began to appear on the horizon, though few recognized them. The enrollment began to slide as some of the typical recruitment pools waned. The outbreak of World War I in Europe in August 1914 gradually drew some immigrants back to their homelands and prevented others from coming to America. The substantial new Domestic Science Building, built at a cost of $100,000, was financed through loans, the beginning of a financial burden that gradually took its toll on the University's operating budget.

Perhaps sensing the dangers, VU announced in June 1916 that it was reorganizing into a new legal entity with a board of trustees and the authority to accept gifts for a sustaining endowment. The reorganization was blocked at the last minute, however, when Geneva Brown intervened and refused to sign over the title to the VU property. One major change did occur in 1917. Facing costly requirements to upgrade its medical school in Chicago, VU sold it to Loyola University, which incorporated it into the Loyola School of Medicine. VU retained its dental school, however—another source of eventual trouble.

These small warnings of administrative difficulty went largely unnoticed on the campus in the immediate pre-World War I period. Along with the addition of new academic programs, the most noticeable development in the early 1910s was the intensified turn toward "collegiate life" at VU. The de facto retirement of Henry Baker Brown, who had retained his strong hostility to such developments, was undoubtedly a factor in the changing climate. The clearest sign of this transformation was an upsurge of interest in organized sports during the prewar years. The first hint had been the building by the engineers of a cinder track and a clubhouse for the athletic field, called University Park, in 1911. By 1914, Henry Kinsey Brown, serving as treasurer, was gaining popularity with students through his vigorous promotion of athletics, including providing uniforms and equipment for the intramural teams.

In 1914, a new monthly student publication, *The Torch*, made its first appearance. The next year it became a weekly student newspaper, bringing a new unity and morale to campus life. One of its primary policies was to "boost" VU athletics. In 1915, a student-run Board of Athletic Control appeared, followed the next year by a Student Council that integrated and controlled all student activities, beginning with athletics. The year 1916 saw the beginning of intercollegiate sports at Valparaiso. The first off-campus competitions apparently occurred during the winter term when an all-star basketball team drawn from intramural squads took on the Chicago YMCA Training School. This was followed in the spring term by the first series of intercollegiate baseball contests with nearby institutions. Track, basketball, and football soon followed.

By entering belatedly, but perhaps inevitably, into intercollegiate sports, Valparaiso was joining what is one of the most distinctive—if puzzling—forces in the history of American higher education. While its distant roots lay in the gentlemanly rivalries in rowing (crew) and track between Oxford and Cambridge, nothing in other nations' experience compares to the way U.S. universities became intensely identified with the mass popular entertainment of college sports. Beginning with baseball after the Civil War, then especially with football in the late nineteenth century, American colleges discovered that intercollegiate competition created a campus spirit and loyalty that nothing else could match. And they succeeded, too, in making U.S. colleges what they had never before been: popular institutions directly linked to the great democratic public.

A crisis over the brutality of football in 1905 led President Theodore Roosevelt to call representatives of Yale, Harvard, Princeton, and other colleges to the White House. Their efforts produced improved equipment, changed rules, and started other "reforms," notably the creation of the National Collegiate Athletic Association in 1908 to regulate intercollegiate sports. But these efforts barely contained the unconcealed institutional and commercial empire-building that made football and other sports tremendously popular with the American public. In contrast to the British amateur tradition, a "win-at-all-costs" mentality dominated big-time U.S. college sports and readily triumphed over the intermittent protests of reformers.

The academic year 1916–17 was a major turning point for the development of "college life" at VU and the demise of the older "poor students' school" outlook and values that had once pervaded the college. Breaking with the strong social organization of the campus by departments, the Student Council created an all-senior class organization to develop, as they called it, a "varsity spirit for the whole institution rather than for the separate departments." Simultaneously, green "beanie hats" for all entering freshmen appeared, together with the beginning of freshman hazing.

Campus-wide "school spirit" rapidly diminished the departmental identifications.

Sports were closely linked to the new outlook. The students pushed hard for the University to build a gymnasium, and when no response was forthcoming, they undertook the task themselves. They sponsored the project and began raising money, though the administration eventually loaned them most of the $7,000 construction cost. The gym quickly proved its worth as the most popular venue for both campus sports and social life. This was especially true for dancing, a pastime that was sweeping over the college population. On March 21, 1917, the Western Society sponsored the first dance in the new gym. In May, there was a senior prom, the first ever, for which O. P. and Sarah Porter Kinsey led the grand march.

The assertiveness of "the new woman" made itself felt in the campus sports arena as well. VU women played intramural basketball from early on, but the issue of whether or not they could play even intramurally before an audience was controversial. Female students evidently believed there was nothing improper in this, but after several women on the faculty demurred, the administration forbade it. Eventually, though, the objections melted away. After World War I, in 1919, not only was a women's physical education program developed, but a Girls Athletic Carnival in the spring featured contests, gymnastics, and plenty of spectators.

WORLD WAR I

The upbeat spirit of social and athletic life was rudely interrupted, however, when the United States entered World War I in April 1917. The American involvement in the war was a hard blow for many private colleges, including Valparaiso. While other factors already were affecting VU negatively, the effects of the war pushed it into a rapid downward spiral.

American students reacted strongly to the declaration of war, especially as the anti-German propaganda machine heated up. "Democracy versus Autocracy" was the theme repeated many times in *The Torch.* In January 1917, even before the formal entry into the war, nearly the entire student body, in a patriotic show of force, marched down Lincolnway, the main street, to a rally in downtown Valparaiso. They also sent a wire to President Wilson that declared, "We are ready!" As a similar mobilization frenzy spread over all the nation's campuses, the federal government urged restraint. *The Torch* of September 21, 1917, reported speeches by President

Wilson and the secretary of war urging college men to stay in school until drafted.

Nevertheless, the impact of the war on college enrollments and operations was severe. At Valparaiso, a steady stream of students left campus for the armed forces; eventually, well over a thousand men were drafted or enlisted. Hundreds of others, including women, abandoned their studies to work in war industries, especially the nearby steel mills. Furthermore, new students failed to arrive in anything close to their prewar numbers.

Financially weakened by the loss of students, Valparaiso University actively sought some revenue-producing connection with the war effort, despite the incongruity of turning the University into an army camp. Income from services offered to the military could, at least temporarily, replace lost tuition. In January 1918, two companies of students elected officers and began military drills in the gym. In May, the University formally became a training school, part of the massive Student Army Training Corps (SATC), which included numerous colleges and universities in the general mobilization. For the next seven months, through the end of hostilities in November 1918, about 8,000 soldiers came to the campus for periods of drilling and learning practical skills, such as caring for motor vehicles. Eight barracks were constructed near the gym. The athletic field became the parade and drill grounds. By late 1918, various service buildings also were going up, including a new YMCA facility and a canteen.

The town and University eagerly accommodated the soldiers. When the first batch arrived, Kinsey had coffee and donuts waiting. The town sponsored dances in the courthouse square, and the University sponsored them in the new gymnasium. VU women enthusiastically did their patriotic duty as dancing partners for the doughboys. In turn, the soldiers staged boxing matches for the public and joined with University students in putting on shows and plays for general entertainment.

The whole experience was such a success that when the war ended, Henry Kinsey Brown went to Washington to see if the arrangement could be continued, despite the demobilization. That request was denied, and by spring 1919, the burst of activity from the war had come to an end. The barracks were taken down and the lumber sold. The University did receive some continuing benefits by becoming a government-subsidized center for teaching technical skills to wounded veterans. This continued for a number of years and was extended into a vocational studies program for some nonveteran students. But the fact that the tuition income from the federal government generated by these programs became the major source of budgetary support for a number of years indicates the hard times that had befallen Valparaiso. For the standard operations of the University, the two academic years directly affected by the war, 1917 to 1919, plunged the school ever more deeply into a debt from which it never recovered.

Amid the general trauma of the war years, President Emeritus Henry Baker Brown died on September 16, 1917. He had not been active in administration since his stroke five years earlier and was seen on campus only at chapel and on ceremonial occasions. At his death, Valparaiso came to a standstill, and courts throughout the region, including the federal court in Hammond, paused in their proceedings. Eulogies poured in from many sources across the country, and the *Indianapolis Star* called Brown an "educational genius."

O. P. Kinsey, who had insisted on remaining "acting" president while his old friend was alive, was officially named president of VU in November 1917. But only a year and a half later, in May 1919, Kinsey retired to a home in Florida, sending news to various publics that "the firm of Brown and Kinsey has been dissolved."

"H. K." AND GROWING TROUBLES

Not yet 29 years old, Henry Kinsey Brown now became president of Valparaiso University. In taking over, Brown carried out the reorganization that had been proposed earlier. This officially put the University under the direction of a board of trustees made up largely of leading northwest Indiana citizens but also including businessmen and others from Chicago and as far away as New York.

Recognizing the severe financial difficulties now facing the college, the young "H. K." decided to go all out in using intercollegiate athletics as a way to reshape the institution and attract needed support. He declared that one weekend each fall would be designated to honor the University president with a special day devoted to rallying alumni and friends. This athletic highlight of the year was called "Brown Day," and University Park was renamed Brown Field, though there was some ambiguity about whether this was to honor the president or his father.

Asserting that he was trying to "modernize" Valparaiso, Brown and the board also moved in 1919 to hire a professional athletic coach. In earlier days, college sports teams had been managed by a student captain or a popular player. As intercollegiate athletics grew, however, the professional coach—hired first by students, then by the institution—appeared on the scene and soon became a popular and powerful figure on American campuses. As his coach, Brown was able to land one of the great early U.S. sports figures, George E. Keogan, a former dental student whose players called him "Doc." Keogan already had led a number of highly successful sports efforts at various colleges. At Valparaiso, he immediately began coaching football, which made its appearance on campus as a regular intercollegiate sport for the first time, along with basketball and baseball. By his second year, Keogan rather incredibly had Valparaiso's football team playing two of the leading national football powers of the day: Harvard and Notre Dame.

The 1920 Harvard game was played in Cambridge and went down in Valparaiso sports annals as a heartbreaking loss. VU held one of the nation's top teams scoreless for three quarters, only to run out of reserves and lose 21–0.

Shortly thereafter, 13 special cars on the Grand Trunk Railroad carried 800 VU students and more than 200 local and regional fans to South Bend, where a powerful, undefeated Notre Dame team thirsted for revenge—not against Valparaiso, but, vicariously, against Harvard. Shunned for conference membership in the Midwest's Western Conference (now the Big Ten) because of its reputation as an Irish football factory, Notre Dame also had been snubbed by Harvard, which declined to play the Catholic university. Notre Dame, therefore, was determined to defeat Valparaiso by a larger margin than Harvard had done.

That season, coach Knute Rockne had devised a new tactic of starting his second team, then bringing in his first team only after having reconnoitered the opponent's plays. After Valparaiso took the lead with a field goal, in came the crack first team, led by consensus All-American George Gipp, who proceeded to pass for two touchdowns and kick three extra points. The Irish finally won 28–3, fulfilling their goal of exceeding Harvard's margin of victory. A few months later, "the Gipper" died. Along with the 1924 "Four Horsemen," George Gipp entered the American sports pantheon—especially after Rockne's legendary locker-room exhortation to "win one for the Gipper."

Keogan also brought success and recognition to Valparaiso basketball. In this sport, even more than football, Coach Keogan displayed his coaching genius by inventing a new type of zone defense. By putting two men stationary under the basket and having the three forward defenders shift to match up with the offensive players on the perimeter, his team was able to stop larger opponents. It was a technique later copied by many coaches, including Ray Meyer at DePaul. After two years of highly successful coaching at VU, Keogan was lured to Notre Dame, where he spent 28 years as the masterful Fighting Irish athletic director. Although Brown's hopes that athletics would solve financial troubles were misguided, Keogan definitely had succeeded in giving Valparaiso a small spot on the map of big-time American college sports.

As another part of his campaign to "modernize" the University, while also appealing to a new kind of student, Henry Kinsey Brown gave official recognition to fraternities and sororities. Within a year of his appearance at a meeting of the Alpha Epsilon fraternity, the oldest of the formerly illegal secret organizations, seven other fraternities and five sororities, all local, had blossomed. They quickly assumed a prominent role in campus social life.

While highly popular with students, Henry Kinsey Brown's emphasis on athletics and Greek organizations could not arrest Valparaiso's quickening financial crisis and its slide into administrative chaos. Academically, Brown's only move had been to dissolve the old Bachelor of Science program that had been the backbone of the University, leaving a Bachelor of Arts that required only 12 credits in a major field, with the rest coming from electives.

Despite all the new measures, the University failed to attract enough new students, and the enrollment continued to slide. In a considerable understatement, H. K. declared in June 1920, "I am not an educator," and resigned the VU presidency. Brown's sharp break with his father's and Kinsey's traditions and spirit had alienated many alumni and split the university community into noisy pro- and anti-Brown factions—"boosters" and "knockers," as the pro-Brown *Torch* called them.

Adding to the growing turmoil, newspapers headlined an acrimonious legal action brought by Henry Baker Brown's widow, Geneva, against the former dean of the VU School of Pharmacy, J. Newton Roe, who had administered Brown's educational enterprises in Chicago. Claiming that Roe had wrongfully obtained a half-interest in the dental school and was trying to sell it, Geneva Brown sued him. In June 1920, the court found in her favor. But a continuing feud between Roe and H. K., including Brown's public charges that Roe was violating Prohibition, for which he was subsequently tried and convicted, added to the sense of crisis.

SOWING THE WIND

After H. K. Brown's resignation, it was up to the board of trustees to choose a new president. The board turned to Daniel Russel Hodgdon, formerly president of the Newark Institute of Technology and currently of the homeopathic Hahnemann Medical School in Chicago. Hodgdon, who presented sterling academic credentials that included an LL.D. and a doctorate from Columbia University, was appointed president of VU in the summer of 1920.

Hodgdon was an exceedingly curious individual. To the board and others, he appeared to be exactly the wonder-worker the University needed. He was full of grandiose visions, dreams, and schemes that seem to have convinced many people who heard him, no matter how fantastic they seemed. Among other things, Hodgdon envisioned a vast new VU campus to be built around Sager's Lake, a major university that would be a "School of Opportunity" (his phrase), purportedly a version of Henry Baker Brown's earlier principles translated into contemporary terms.

For promotional purposes, Hodgdon created a chart with more than two dozen circles representing a hierarchy of academic units, from training schools for the unlettered all the way up to a "school for advanced research." He indicated that his future VU would embrace all the departments of a "modern" university, including extension and home-study operations. He openly projected an enrollment of 10,000 students within the decade. Focusing on its geographic location on the edge of the booming Calumet industrial district, Hodgdon envisioned a Valparaiso University that would serve this economic center of the nation with the research and expertise to fuel progress. He was confident that men of wealth, especially those connected with the great industrial corporations of the region, would finance such a university. After all, that is how the major new research universities had come into existence.

As soon as he took over, Hodgdon quickly reorganized the existing university, requiring even more elaborate charts. The long string of departments became colleges and schools. Thus was born not only a College of Arts and Sciences, but a College of Applied Sciences that incorporated two "divisions": the School of Engineering (civil, architectural) and the School of Co-Industrial Engineering (chemical, mechanical, electrical). Altogether, then, there were three colleges and 10 schools, including home economics, music, commerce, pharmacy, law, premedical, medical, and nursing. With this elaborate reorganization came the need to employ a new administrative hierarchy of deans and directors, whom Hodgdon grandly assembled as his "Cabinet" and "Council of Deans." These administrators, many of them completely new to the campus, came to be known as Hodgdon's "satellites" in the divisive campaign against the president that developed later in the year.

The linchpin of Hodgdon's grand plan was an endowment campaign called the "Million Dollar Campaign." It was directed by promotional expert Frank Converse, also brought in by Hodgdon. The campaign was launched with an enthusiastic banquet held in East Hall, which rocked with songs and cheers from the participants, who then pledged more than $100,000 to the endowment fund. Henry Kinsey Brown, speaking for the family, announced that it would hand over the university to the public as a nonprofit institution. *Applause!* A telegram from O. P. Kinsey in Florida was read, supporting the whole idea. *Applause!* Hodgdon announced that an option on the Sager's Lake property had been secured. *Applause!* It was, wrote the local press, the greatest event of its kind ever held in the history of Porter County.

The successful seasons of the football, basketball, and debating teams generated even more enthusiasm for the new regime. The games with Harvard and Notre Dame, especially, seemed to evidence rebirth. In the November 1920 elections, VU alumni John J. Blaine and Len Small were elected governors of Wisconsin and Illinois, respectively. The pro-Hodgdon *Torch* suggested that people across the country were now looking to Valparaiso University for leadership.

What was not given public notice amid all the public relations was the North Central Association's refusal to accredit the university. An academic team had visited Valparaiso and found that, despite its great work in the past, the University violated key association standards, including the academic preparation of the faculty and their "ridiculous" work loads. There was a place for an institution such as Valparaiso, the team declared, with its practice of extreme flexibility in admissions and programs for nontraditional students; but NCA standards would have to be met. The days of educational free-lancing were over.

Even without this spear in the heart, VU was in dire straits. As time passed, little money actually came in for the "Million Dollar Campaign," despite the constant barrage of optimistic press announcements. Soon, several students began to investigate Hodgdon's background, specifically the source and validity of all those degrees that he pretentiously strung out after his name on all the University publications. Through determined and stubborn investigation, they determined that Hodgdon's Bachelor of Arts from Bates College was the only legitimate degree of the six he claimed to possess. His Master and Doctor of Science degrees were from "Potomac

University," which turned out to be a correspondence school unrecognized by any state educational authority or university. Hodgdon's LL.D. was honorary, having been conferred by Henry Kinsey Brown. The M.D. he had received was from the Hahnemann Medical School, where he was the president. The Ph.D. that he claimed to have earned from Columbia University was entirely a fiction.

Meanwhile, in March 1921, the Moline *Daily Dispatch* carried a report indicating that because the people of northwest Indiana had failed to support the University, the administration had decided to move it to a new location near Rock Island, Illinois. Later investigation showed that Hodgdon had indeed been negotiating privately with the Rock Island Chamber of Commerce on a possible sale of the University.

By this time, controversy over Hodgdon and the future of the University had created increasing tensions and divisions on the campus. On April 4, 1921, the VU Student Council met and unanimously requested Hodgdon's resignation. The next day, the Council of Deans, all Hodgdon appointees and supporters, met and administratively dissolved the Student Council. Outside the windows of the room where the Student Council continued meeting, its student supporters were cheering them when suddenly they were attacked by a mob of athletes and fraternity men, supporters of Hodgdon. The crowd eventually broke up and headed home. A few days later, while Hodgdon made another trip east in support of the endowment campaign, demonstrations and near-riots broke out between Student Council and Hodgdon supporters. The fraternity bullies attempted to kidnap two anti-Hodgdon student leaders and put them on a train leaving town. The student leaders were dramatically rescued by their friends.

Meanwhile, Hodgdon was in New York, supposedly raising money. In a speech before the New York chapter of the VU Alumni Association, he suddenly announced that President Warren G. Harding would be VU's commencement speaker the following May. Hodgdon invited the alumni to attend as his special guests. When word of this news leaked back to the campus, inquiries at the White House revealed that the President had absolutely no plans to visit Valparaiso.

On April 12, half the faculty sent a petition to the trustees requesting the reinstatement of the ousted student leaders and the resignation of President Hodgdon. Hodgdon's response was an immediate attempt to fire the faculty signatories.

Finally, the board voted to dismiss Hodgdon. Two days after his ouster, Hodgdon released to the Hearst Press a letter of resignation in which he blamed his troubles on bolshevism, communism, and other anti-American cults that, he said, were acting as "part of a deep-laid plan to make Valparaiso the center of radical teaching. It is possible that much of the unrest of college life today is due to these destructive outside influences, aimed to destroy the basic principles upon which this government is founded." He implied that Valparaiso already had become a center of leftist activity and that radical forces had taken over the campus.

This was the period of the Red Scare and other post-World War I hysterias, so these and other charges created a sensation in the national press. The charlatan Hodgdon finally left Valparaiso, but not before he was hung in effigy by the students. Eventually some of the uproar over his charges died down as the local post of the American Legion joined with the Valparaiso Chamber of Commerce and the veterans studying at Valparaiso to certify the University's ideological acceptability. But considerable damage had been done to an already beleaguered institution.

Reaping the Whirlwind

In desperation, the board turned to the highly respected alumnus and faculty member John E. Roessler, professor of German, appointing him first acting president, then, in the fall of 1921, president of VU. Roessler quickly achieved a remarkable reconciliation among the internal factions, retaining the new student social life that included a de-emphasized athletic program. With the help of his vice president, Alpheus Americus (A-Square) Williams, a mathematics professor who was also a campus character, Roessler balanced the books.

But Roessler's best efforts could make no progress on the accumulated debt. Fresh fund-raising initiatives, including a bond drive, made little headway, and Roessler soon decided to resign. His letter of resignation also reveals some bitterness over the board's frequent meetings without consulting him and over the continuing hostile influence of the Brown family and other unnamed forces. After doing his duty to the end of the spring term in 1922, Roessler and his wife left for permanent retirement in California.

Giving another spin to the revolving door, in fall 1922, the board appointed the law dean, Milo Jesse Bowman, interim president. Bowman served for only half a year until another new president, Horace M. Evans, arrived to take office in January 1923.

Compared to what had gone before, Evans seemed a solid choice. He was a VU alumnus and a University loyalist who had served on the faculty for 10 years, then worked in business, with experience in public and educational administration. But as the fifth president in four years, Evans faced an almost impossible challenge. The University verged on bankruptcy, and its faculty was demoralized, often waiting until the next term's tuition receipts for their previous term's salaries. Many of the better faculty simply left. The enrollment continued to decline. In the fall of 1922, there were still 1,200 students, but by the next fall (1923), that figure had dropped to about 800. The largest numbers were again in the school that catered to adult nontraditional students and the preparatory department that took on many academically deficient students.

Considering the dire straits of the University and the terrible morale of the faculty, student life at VU in the early 1920s remained remarkably upbeat. Or perhaps it was a matter of partying as an escape from all the troubles. This was the era of prosperity, Prohibition, and bootleg gin, and undergraduates everywhere were indulging in rampant frivolities. As historian Rod Geiger notes, the postwar period was one in which the U.S. four-year undergraduate college worked to attract students by stressing its difference from the research university model, with a significant component of its education being defined as the cultivation of the necessary social skills to go along with the knowledge needed for white collar positions.

At Valparaiso, *The Torch* and *The Record* for these years certainly reflected these collegiate social trends. Athletics, parties, and election of the "Smile Girl" and "Most Popular Boy" dominated their pages. As the school tottered on the brink of oblivion, the paper seemed unaware of its desperate condition. *The Torch's* editorial platform defined the "100 percent student: book-learning, athletics, social recreation, and high class entertainment." It conceded that book-learning was important, but so were the other aspects. Many students evidently made sure that they had a true "college experience," even as their college literally crumbled around them.

The nadir seemed to have been reached when the Old Main College Building, built by the Methodists in 1862, burned in the fall of 1923. The destruction was a fitting symbol for the collapse of the University itself. The VU board announced its determination to rebuild at once, and *The Torch* ran a picture of a newly designed college building, along with official plans for fund-raising. In actuality, the University did not have enough money even to clear away the burnt rubble from the fire scene.

SHAKING HANDS WITH THE DEVIL, ALMOST

President Evans, supported by influential citizens who rightly connected the University with the town's prosperity, was determined to save the school at all costs. He recognized that the University's problems were far deeper than a meddlesome board or the still demanding Brown family. There was a debt of around $375,000, a recently passed state mandate for colleges to have an endowment of $500,000, unaccredited status, the need for basic modernization, and a rapidly growing "image" problem.

The most immediate problem was the debt owed to the Valparaiso Realty Company, the Brown family's corporation, which also still held a lien on the physical campus and related properties, though it no longer owned and operated the University. The realty company had raised some of the funds for its loans to the University by selling stock to J. F. Wild and Company, an Indianapolis investment bank, pledging the campus as collateral. The Browns had further stipulated that any settlement of their claims against the University would have to include an annuity of $5,000 a year for Geneva Brown.

Evans knew that selling the University was the only option. Desperate to find a buyer to save the institution he cared about, he looked everywhere for help. He approached wealthy individuals, the Rockefeller Foundation, and the Indiana legislature, as well as several churches and fraternal organizations. None of the leads panned out. By the summer of 1923, he was turning to less reputable sources in hopes of saving VU from extinction. In the words of historian Lance Trusty, Evans "was willing to shake hands with the devil for his desperate school, and he very nearly did."

Evans did not have to look far to find a devil to deal with. The Invisible Empire of the Ku Klux Klan was omnipresent in Indiana in the early 1920s, and it nearly purchased Valparaiso University. While the idea now seems incredibly farfetched, it was not so at the time. The historical context is crucial to understanding what really happened.

The Ku Klux Klan of the 1920s was not a direct continuation of the militant antiblack organization of Reconstruction days in the South. Although the name, of course, suggests continuity, the "reorganized" Klan was a completely new organization founded in Georgia in 1915 by William J. Simmons, a circuit-riding minister, salesman, and fraternal society organizer. For Simmons and his followers, the enemies of true American life were there for all to see: heavy immigration, gyrating commodity prices, infidelity in religion, political corruption, and so on. The idea of an "education" in true Americanism as a way to attack these evils was actually part of the Klan approach from early on. Simmons, who called himself the "Grand Wizard" of the Klan—one of many bizarre titles the organization cultivated—in fact became associated with Lanier University, a Baptist institution in Atlanta, where he lectured on "Civil War and Reconstruction."

In 1920, the Klan took off when two unusually effective promoters, Elizabeth Tyler and Edward Clarke, began using modern methods of advertising and paid operatives, called Kleagles, to organize not only in the South, but also in the North. There, they discovered that many people were seeking someone on whom they could pin the blame for society's many ills. The Klan specialized in finding such scapegoats in Catholics, Jews, labor organizers, and Bolsheviks, as well as the African-Americans who had migrated north in large numbers during the war years.

A standard $10 initiation fee for new members quickly produced large sums of money that enabled further expansion. Within six months, 85,000 people had joined the Klan. Within a few more years, perhaps four million people had paid to become members, at least temporarily. Money flowed in from various fees and from the sale of regalia, literature, jewelry, and other items. Awash in success, Simmons saw the Klan's visionary task as rebuilding the United States to save it from foreigners and non-Protestants. His grandiose plans included creating Klan universities, publishing houses, banks, hospitals, and so on.

The common view today is that all Klan members were ignorant and violent, and there were certainly such people in the organization. But in fact, the "1920s Klan" in many places contained a substantial membership of "respectable" citizens. For example, the University of Wisconsin housed a Klan fraternity, and young people's Klan organizations presented themselves on a par with similar groups. Hundreds of thousands of women joined a parallel women's Klan organization with hierarchy, robes, and all. The rapid spread of the Klan among many white Protestants reflected their comfort with their racial and religious privilege, their rather narrow ethical point of view, and, above all, their anxieties about the future. Many members were fearful of the cultural, social, and ethnic changes overcoming American life and sought in the Klan a way to preserve what they regarded as the true "American way of life."

The Klan's relatively benign public face and its emphasis on preserving "morality" and "Americanism" drew in—at least temporarily—many fearful, well-meaning, ordinary citizens. But the organization always possessed an uglier, less visible, face as well. Meeting secretly, the Klan's lecturers and leaders spewed hatred for foreigners, blacks, Jews, and Catholics, together with bootleggers, dance hall operators, and movie theater owners—all of whom were lumped together as responsible for the decline of "purity" in America. Whispering campaigns and intimidation influenced local politics, ousting Catholic teachers from public schools and shattering many lives, while promoting patronage of Klan-operated businesses. There also were clandestine terrorist activities, especially in the rural areas of the country.

In 1923, the Klan was riding high, though its internal organization was increasingly riddled by strife and corruption. No Klan leader was more corrupt than the powerful Grand Dragon of the Realm of Indiana, D. C. Stephenson. Stephenson, whose mansion at the edge of Indianapolis became a notorious center of debauchery, had proclaimed, "I am the law." For a brief period of time, his boast was close to the truth. At least one governor of the state, Edward Jackson, was Stephenson's pawn.

One of the Klan's most active and popular campaigns was against parochial schools, identified as an insidious arm of the Catholic Church. Many "100-percent Americans," whether or not they were Klan members, joined in this campaign—an effort that also affected the German Lutheran community, which sponsored many such schools. In response to this threat, German Lutherans, under the leadership of laymen and laywomen in Fort Wayne, Indiana, founded and spread throughout the Midwest a vigorous new organization, the American Luther League, which collaborated politically with the Roman Catholics in defense of parochial schools and religious education.

After this unusual Catholic-Lutheran alliance successfully waged its political battle to preserve the right to maintain religious schools apart from the public school system, the triumphant American Luther League leaders turned to a new cause, the foundation of a national Lutheran university in America. Ironically, then, it was the defensive Lutheran reaction against the threat of the Ku Klux Klan that first set in motion the groups and forces that eventually led to the purchase of Valparaiso University.

In May 1924, the citizens of Valparaiso witnessed the supposedly benign public face of the Klan when the Invisible Empire's "Domain of Lake Michigan" advertised a public rally at the County Fairgrounds immediately north of the city. One of the estimated 10,000 spectators at that event noted that "a casual visitor might have mistaken this solemn occasion for a political rally, a county fair, a Fourth of July festival, or a circus."

As part of the publicity surrounding this event, the editor of the Chicago-based Klan paper, the *Dawn*, contacted the Valparaiso Klavern seeking information about the city. It was evidently an unnamed Valparaiso student serving as chairman of the Klavern's publicity committee who first presented the Klan with the idea of acquiring the well-known, but desperate, University as an educational center for a bargain price. The *Dawn* immediately seized on and puffed the idea and continued its campaign well after the hooded organization's rally.

Soon rumors abounded in the city of Valparaiso that a major announcement regarding the University's future was imminent. University denials did not quell the rising excitement; in fact, VU officials had embarked on talks with the Ku Klux Klan regarding sale of the institution. The precise details of those negotiations and of the actual offer itself were shrouded in secrecy and may never be known. Grand Dragon Stephenson was rumored to have made several trips to Valparaiso. Sometime in late June or early July, nameless hooded "friends of the institution" did meet with University officials and tentatively agreed on a purchase price of $340,000. As part of the bargain, the Klan evidently agreed to follow this with a million-dollar endowment fund to maintain and operate the institution. A single letter in the VU Archives from President Evans to a frightened Dean Hugh Muldoon seems to confirm, generally, that these were the terms of the agreement.

The Klan's principal spokesman during these negotiations was Milton Elrod, the editor of the *Fiery Cross*, the Indiana Klan's weekly propaganda sheet. President Evans and trustees Charles Jeffrey and Leonard Maxwell also met with several other Stephenson representatives at a huge Klan rally in Kokomo on July 4, 1923. The Klansmen agreed to deposit $30,000 of earnest money, pending completion of the sale. The trustees then traveled to Indianapolis to confer further with Elrod, where they were given more details on the deal, though no names of specific persons or organizations to be involved in the University were revealed.

On July 27, five hundred county Klan officials gathered in Indianapolis for another meeting. National Klan leaders in attendance apparently joined further talks with the VU leaders. Finally, it seemed that a firm agreement had been reached. The Valparaiso team settled back in relief, believing that it had acted in desperate circumstances on behalf of the University and a community that depended on it for its economic health.

To those who began to hear of the proposed sale, President Evans tried to present the best face. He naively imagined that the KKK would operate a standard university with only a few "added features," such as a chair in Bible studies and a new course in constitutional law. The academic community knew better. Throughout July and August, anxious rumors swirled about the VU campus. University Secretary Catherine Corboy, a devout Roman Catholic, warned prospective students that "hereafter Valparaiso will not be the place for the Kellys, Burkes, and Steins." On her advice, many Catholic students withdrew during the summer.

If there was hostility on the campus, some people in the town endorsed the idea. Many thought of the Klan as a group of nonthreatening folks, including local businessmen, who enjoyed putting on hoods and other regalia but had no serious agenda other than their "hyper-American boosterism."

Meanwhile, the national press had a field day with the idea of "Klan U." Editors sent scores of reporters to interview Valparaiso citizens, civic leaders, and businessmen. For more than a month that summer, the merciless glare of national publicity spotlighted Valparaiso and its struggling university with sarcasm and devastating mockery. *The New Republic*, the nation's leading liberal journal, took glee in imagining the scenes on the campus of KKK University:

> It is a warm spring afternoon in 1935. On the campus all is quiet, save for one corner where a group of seniors hang the dean to a lamp-post as a protest against probation. … From the red tassels on their hoods, the giant keys that hang around their shoulders on hemp rope, one might guess that they are able students, Phi Beta Ku Kluxa Kappa men.

And it envisioned a student lynching party returning to campus singing the alma mater:

> Land where the mob is boss,
> Land of the rope and toss,
> On every flaming cross,
> Let freedom ring.

For the somewhat naive leaders who had apparently believed that they could "save" the University by putting it into the hands of a group like the KKK, this kind of attention was a rude awakening.

To add to its cup of woes that summer, the University faced another threat: an aggressive move by Henry Kinsey Brown, who had just purchased Cook Laboratories, a Chicago manufacturer of surgical supplies.

When the University was late in making a payment on the school's debt, Brown announced that he would exercise his lien and turn the campus into a manufacturing center for his business. Evans and the trustees fought this new assault by making their overdue payment with funds hastily gathered from friends and from insurance money on the burned-out college building. Then they sued Brown. Brown attempted to move the suit from the Porter County Circuit Court to the friendlier federal court in Indianapolis. But in late July, Circuit Court Judge Loring denied Brown's request for a change of venue and confirmed the trustees's position.

On August 15, 1923, *The Porter County Vidette*'s headlines shouted: "EXTRA! EXTRA! KLAN TO BE HERE TOMORROW WITH $1,000,000 TO TAKE OVER V.U." Hundreds of rejoicing citizens poured into the streets to meet Evans and the returning Valparaiso University representatives at the train late that night. They were escorted to College Hill and showered with speeches of praise. Then nothing happened. The expected Klan emissaries did not appear. Neither did any cash. After an agonizing two weeks of silence, word came on September 6 that the deal was off because of "legal technicalities." Actually, as was not learned until later, the deal was off because there was simply no money in the Klan's treasury for the purchase of VU, at least nowhere near the amount needed.

In the recriminations that followed, Grand Dragon Stephenson blamed the Grand Wizard in Atlanta for holding back on promised funds. Elrod charged that the University was snarled in legal technicalities, making a deal impossible. And so on. The weak attempt of the Klan to save whatever face it could from the debacle only confirmed the increasing backbiting and tensions within the organization, as well as its fundamental moral rot.

Historian Lance Trusty has examined the record and concluded that greed and corruption was the probable real cause for the Klan's failure to follow through on the deal. No doubt the daydreams of the local Klan and Elrod had falsified reality. Access to sufficient money was not itself the problem. There was, for a period of time, a huge flow of cash within the Klan from membership fees and regalia purchased by middle-class Klan enthusiasts that could have been brought to bear on the purchase, if the Klan had been determined to follow through on the plan. Stephenson personally had gone through more than a million dollars in pursuit of women, cars, airplanes, and so on, until the Grand Dragon's viciousness and debauchery finally caught up with him. Despite his political influence,

Stephenson was convicted in 1925 of the rape and murder of his secretary, Marge Oberholzer, and sentenced to life in prison—the event that effectively ended the Klan's influence.

Meanwhile, the battered Valparaiso University, its enrollment fallen under 1,000 students and rapidly declining, now faced worse image and financial problems after this misbegotten flirtation with an organization that was the antithesis of a university. VU's feeble response was a new financial campaign, led by an alumnus who agreed to donate a year to the task. On November 9, 1923, the board issued a rather bland "Declaration of Principles" that purported to repudiate the Klan connection.

One of the most prominent VU alumni, Governor John J. Blaine of Wisconsin, wrote a steaming response to President Evans:

> I say all these things frankly because I am interested in seeing the great Poor Man's University continued, and on the other hand I am not very much interested in any declaration of principles that contains, to a large extent, a lot of clap-trap about co-operation of groups and Americanism, that omits frank specification and specific declarations.

He regarded the Klan episode as menacing, if not fatal, to the institution, if a stronger repudiation were not made.

Other unhappy alumni wrote in as well. Evans and the University evidently responded. A month later, the editor of the *South Bend Tribune*, a noted Klan fighter and VU alumnus, released a statement that was widely published across the country. Headlines in *The New York Times* of February 3, 1925, read:

> KLAN IS REPUDIATED BY INDIANA COLLEGE
>
> Valparaiso University Statement Denounces
> Principles of Ku Klux, Reputed Buyer
>
> *South Bend, Ind. Feb 2.* Speaking for a committee of former students of Valparaiso University, reported last summer to have been taken over by the Ku Klux Klan, F. A. Miller, editor of the *South Bend Tribune* issued a statement today, declaring the school to be "open to the education of all without thought of race, religion, social standing, wealth, politics or influence."
>
> " 'For the information of its 100,000 or more former students and graduates now scattered throughout the country and in foreign lands,' Mr. Miller said, 'the trustees have adopted a code of principles upon which the institution proposes to base its future operations. This code proclaims opposition to any individual group, lodge, church or so-

> ciety which intentionally endeavors to separate our people into class-conscious groups, setting one against the other in promotion of hatred. This pronouncement is taken as a vigorous stand against the Ku Klux Klan and to mean that henceforth, as heretofore, Valparaiso University cannot be named as an educational institution controlled by any class organization or any religious sect.' "
>
> The committee for whom Mr. Miller spoke includes Dr. Horace M. Evans, President of the university, Judges, Congressmen, United States Senators and other graduates of the school from virtually every state.

The Klan had not purchased VU. But something had to be done or the University would likely shut its doors within a matter of months. As a final desperate measure in the spring of 1925, Evans mobilized state political support for a bill in the Indiana legislature to purchase VU and turn it into a state school. Porter County sweetened the deal by offering to sell $250,000 in bonds to eliminate all existing debt. When the legislature passed the bill, the campus community and the good citizens of Valparaiso raised their hopes again. But they were once again let down when Klan-connected governor Ed Jackson pocket-vetoed the bill. Thus it appeared certain that Valparaiso University's 66-year history was about to come to an end.

Shortly thereafter, the Lutherans appeared on the scene.

SELECTIONS FROM THE VALPARAISO UNIVERSITY ARCHIVES

The original building of the Valparaiso Male and Female College when it opened its doors in 1859.

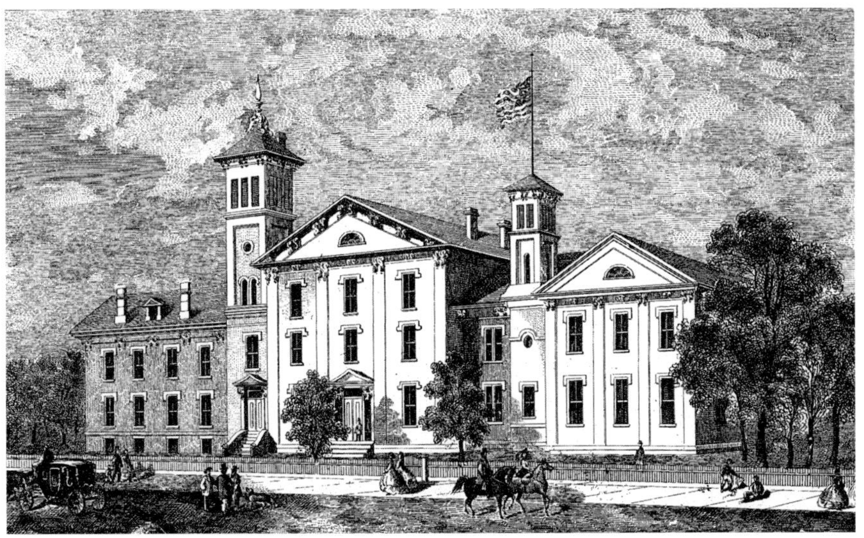

Architect G. P. Randall's 1866 drawing of the VMFC building. The center unit already had been constructed in 1860. The left tower wing was built in 1867, and the right tower wing, slightly revised, was added in 1880 after the college became the Northern Indiana Normal School. Until it burned down in 1923, the Old Main College Building, as it came to be known, was the focal point of the campus.

Henry Baker Brown revived the college in 1873 and served as its president until his de facto retirement in 1912. He built Valparaiso into the nation's second largest university in the early 1900s.

Oliver Perry Kinsey, Brown's friend and close collaborator, served as vice president from 1881 to 1917. Kinsey headed scientific studies and managed housing and dining facilities.

Samantha "Mantie" Baldwin, a member of President Brown's first faculty, was much beloved by students. Her epitaph reads: "An Intellectual Leader."

Noted orator and three-time presidential candidate William Jennings Bryan and Mrs. Bryan with President Brown and President George M. Dodge of Dodge Telegraphy School, 1902.

Sager's Lake, favorite site for student recreation and romance, gave rise to the informal course title "Sagerology."

George W. Norris, 1883 alumnus, seated on porch railing, and fellow "L.U.N" members held an annual reunion for 58 years to commemorate their student friendship. A renowned U.S. senator from Nebraska, Norris received an honorary degree from the Lutheran VU in 1943.

Lowell Thomas, as a VU student, escorts two professors' daughters on Student Bridge. The world-renowned pioneer radio journalist, Fox Movietone News narrator, author, and adventurer continued to be a strong supporter of VU until his death in 1981.

Students bustle between the auditorium and Science Hall, c. 1907. In 1959, VU's centennial year, Science Hall was renamed Baldwin Hall.

The attempt of the Ku Klux Klan to purchase VU in 1923 was lampooned in many national publications, including the *New York Call.*

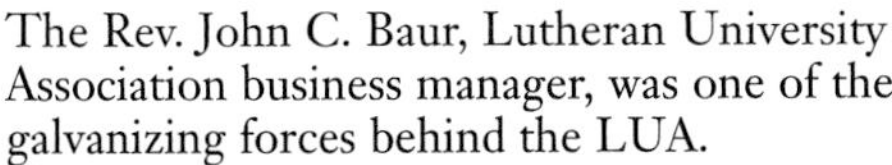

The Rev. John C. Baur, Lutheran University Association business manager, was one of the galvanizing forces behind the LUA.

Dr. William H. T. Dau, left, and the Rev. Oscar Carl Kreinheder, the first two Lutheran presidents of Valparaiso University.

The Valparaiso University Guild, organized in 1931 to promote the Lutheran university, meets annually on the campus to elect officers and adopt projects. Here, Guild members picnic on the West Campus lawn between sessions of their 1947 meeting.

Freshman students meet their new president, the Rev. O. P. Kretzmann, at a 1941 reception.

Looking over a 1940 issue of *The Torch*, VU's student newspaper since 1914, as it comes off the press are, left to right, Louis E. Lambert, faculty advisor; Alfred R. Looman, associate editor; John H. Strietelmeier, editor; and Richard R. Haratine, sports editor. Looman later served in several VU administrative positions, and Strietelmeier became a professor of geography, *Cresset* editor, and vice president for academic affairs.

In 1944, VU acquired more than 90 acres adjacent to its old campus, which was developed after World War II as the East Campus. This 1948 photo shows, top to bottom, the land acquisition along U.S. Hwy. 30, the new Guild and Memorial Halls, three surplus barracks hastily erected as temporary structures to accommodate the postwar flood of students, and the gymnasium. At top left is "Merlin," the large oak tree that still stands south of the Chapel of the Resurrection.

Heralded as the "world's tallest basketball team" in the wartime 1940s, Valparaiso competed against the nation's top teams in the premier arenas.

The dramatic story of VU student initiation, planning, and building of the Engineering Laboratories in 1948–49 inspired the Freedoms Foundation award-winning film "Venture of Faith." It was produced by the Lutheran Laymen's League and filmed on campus in 1951 with students and staff performing in minor roles alongside professional Hollywood actors. Here, President O. P. Kretzmann talks with one of the student builders.

The interior of the Chapel-Auditorium where daily worship services were held until the building was destroyed by a fire in 1956.

Dr. Willis Boyd, popular history professor, teaches a class in the "bullpen" on West Campus.

President Kretzmann views the ruins of the Chapel-Auditorium after the Nov. 27, 1956, fire.

The dedication on Sept. 27, 1959, of the new VU chapel, for which ground had been broken seven weeks before fire leveled the old Chapel-Auditorium.

In spring 1965, Valparaiso students traveled to Birmingham, Alabama, to join Miles College students in promoting black voter registration.

The Rev. Theodore Hesburgh, president of the University of Notre Dame, speaks after receiving a VU honorary doctorate on Reformation Day 1967.

Presidential candidate Senator Robert F. Kennedy addressed a packed VU gymnasium in May 1968, a month before he was assassinated in Los Angeles.

Dr. Albert G. Huegli distributes communion to students in the Chapel of the Resurrection. Worship in the chapel has been a constant feature of campus life for generations of VU students.

New construction was a constant, and noisy, feature of campus life throughout the 1960s and 1970s. Here, President Albert G. Huegli takes the bulldozer wheel in one of the many groundbreakings.

President Robert V. Schnabel listens with characteristic friendly attention.

President Alan F. Harre at his 1988 inauguration. Students lined the walks from the Union to the chapel, celebrating the induction of Valparaiso's sixth Lutheran president.

Teaching and mentoring students remains at the heart of VU's academic commitment to "Scholarship, Freedom, and Faith." Pictured is chemistry professor Dr. A. Gilbert Cook and a student.

"The Shot": Bryce Drew launches the last-second winning basket against Mississippi in the first round of the 1998 NCAA tournament.

The VU Jazz Trio and a guest saxophonist perform in the lobby of the Center for the Arts at its Sept. 16, 1995, dedication.

The scene at the Sept. 23, 2000, dedication of the Kade-Duesenberg German House.

PART II

THE MAKING OF A LUTHERAN UNIVERSITY (1925–40)

5

The Valparaiso Movement

Starting Over: The Missouri Synod

On a warm summer day in June 1925, a stocky, dark-haired visitor quietly slipped into Valparaiso, Indiana, and walked around the campus of the bankrupt university that was up for sale. The buildings he saw were unattractive and rundown, plainly showing the effects of years of neglect. In the middle of the campus lay an ugly pile of burned rubble, the remnants of a fire that had occurred two years before. Yet the man also saw great possibilities in the place and drove away eager to recommend its purchase.

That visitor was the Rev. Otto H. Pannkoke of New York, one of the most prominent Lutheran churchmen of the day and someone well versed in both finances and the cause of the Christian college. He was acting on behalf of a group of Lutheran laity and clergy, primarily from Fort Wayne, Indiana, who were determined to create a new Lutheran university in the United States. When Pannkoke reported back to the group, he could barely contain his excitement, urging them to act immediately to acquire the famous but bankrupt institution. Within a few months, the deal was done, and by early August, the newly incorporated "The Lutheran University Association" owned Valparaiso University.

The Lutherans who purchased Valparaiso University that summer of 1925 were members of a German immigrant church commonly known today as The Lutheran Chuch—Missouri Synod. The Lutheran University Association they had organized was a self-styled "progressive" group of clergy and laity who had often found themselves at odds with the leadership of the Synod on many matters related to the Americanization of their immigrant religious tradition and its Christian mission in a new land. The creation of the modern Valparaiso University involved not only the founding of a school, but it represented the centerpiece of a movement for social and intellectual change within this large subculture that constituted about one-third of American Lutheranism.

Throughout the nineteenth century, and well into the twentieth, the Missouri Synod was a cohesive, largely German-speaking immigrant community, a highly distinctive conservative subculture of American life. For much of its history, the reborn Valparaiso University represented a kind of counterculture within that subculture, with its student body, faculty, and supporters drawn from the people of the Synod who supported what was known as the "Valparaiso movement." That movement's institutional manifestation was The Lutheran University Association, but it had widespread connections and implications that reached considerably beyond simply running a college. It was a prime carrier of a new view of what American Lutheranism was and what it should become.

The Lutheran University Association was one of a number of voluntary groups that developed among people of the Missouri Synod to meet a wide variety of religious, social, and intellectual needs that the Synod itself chose not to meet. The Synod, well into the mid-twentieth century, defined its sole purposes as proclaiming the Gospel and preserving doctrine. Therefore, it strictly refused to undertake any activities that could not be linked directly to a narrow interpretation of those purposes. This self-constraining understanding left it to various self-generating groups of church members to undertake what seemed to be increasingly vital tasks.

Because these independent groups were not under the direct control of the Synod, they often were critical of the clerically controlled, inward-looking church body, which brought them periodically into tension with the synodical leadership, sometimes to the point of visible dissent. It was in these associations, especially, that the Missouri Synod laity found a voice often denied them within the parish or the church's official agencies.

This was especially true regarding education. By the 1920s, colleges and universities had become points of contention within many church circles. For many church people, these institutions were places of danger for the faithful. But more progressive laity and clergy recognized that they were becoming important portals to a larger future in American life.

Immigration to North America in the nineteenth and early twentieth centuries resulted in many Lutheran church bodies worshiping in more than a dozen languages, from German to Icelandic. At first, Lutherans settled in the Atlantic coastal cities, in Pennsylvania, and in the great river valleys of the Ohio and the Mississippi. As the railroads opened the rich farmlands of the upper Midwest in the late nineteenth century, Lutheran immigrants came in great waves to populate them.

By 1900, the overwhelming majority of American Lutherans lived in a swath stretching west from Pennsylvania (the center of the older Lutheran settlements) through Ohio, Indiana, Illinois, Missouri, Iowa, and Nebraska, and to the north in Wisconsin, Minnesota, and the Dakotas. (There also were smaller concentrations in the Carolina Piedmont and south central Texas.) German Lutherans were more heavily concentrated in the lower Midwest; Scandinavians were more heavily concentrated in the upper Midwest states. But the various ethnic groups and their numerous synods were everywhere intermingled.

The Missouri Synod arose from the experience of confessionalist German Lutheran emigres who had been opposed to the forced union of Reformed and Lutheran churches by the Prussian state in 1817 and were also dismayed at what they viewed as the doctrinal laxity of the Lutheran bodies they found in the United States of the 1830s and 1840s. The two primary settlement groups involved in the formation of the Synod had failed in achieving their respective original immigration goals of evangelizing American Indians (predominantly in Michigan) and creating a Lutheran "Zion on the Mississippi," first in Perry County, then in St. Louis, Missouri (hence the name "Missouri" Synod). So they turned to serving and incorporating into their midst the flood of German immigrants arriving throughout the nineteenth century, meeting them at immigration ports and seeking them out in the little Germanies of American cities and towns and the farmlands of the Midwest.

Amid the freewheeling New World atmosphere of religious revivalism and voluntarism, these sober, confessional Lutherans erected a remarkable institutional structure, bonding ethnicity and religion into a compact, clannish German-American subculture that was organized for self-perpetuation, the promotion of church doctrine, and what they understood to be biblical ways against the threat of the outside world. These Lutherans also offended their Protestant neighbors by drinking beer and enjoying themselves on the Sabbath.

These unassimilated Lutherans prospered within a tight matrix of congregation-school-family, a triad that actively reinforced the beliefs and roles of all members of the community. In the congregation, the pastor was a patriarch whose authority derived from his office, his education, and his presence at all the meaningful rites in the community: baptisms, confirmations, Holy Communion, weddings, and funerals.

Worship featured long doctrinal sermons reinforced by strong Germanic Lutheran hymns and chorales, vigorously sung to musical accompaniment and especially moving in the seasons of Christmas and Lent. There was regular doctrinal review, reinforced through the memorization of Luther's Small Catechism and the rite of confirmation of youth, usually around age 13 or 14. The poor, the sick, orphans, and widows were understood to be the community's responsibility as well. In the larger cities, hospitals, homes for the aged, and orphanages reflected the Lutheran community's concern to extend its nurturing protection as far as possible through all ages and conditions of life.

Throughout its first century, the Missouri Synod was thoroughly shaped by a clergy that afforded laypeople little freedom or voice. In the early 1840s, the attempt by 900 Saxon immigrants to build a Lutheran "Zion on the Mississippi" south of St. Louis had foundered on a lay revolt led by two attorneys who challenged the episcopal pretensions and personal morality of their leader, Bishop Martin Stephan. That crisis led to the deposition of the charismatic bishop. When the Missouri Synod was subsequently officially organized in 1847, congregations rather than the clergy alone were made "sovereign." Theoretically, this development should have given the laity a prominent role in church affairs, matching the lay leadership characteristic of much American Protestant church life.

However, the clergy soon reasserted control. This was not difficult. The pastor was the key leader in each congregation, and the laity were thought of as followers who quietly and obediently paid for and maintained facilities. At major church meetings, the clergy knew one another well because of common education and frequent intermarriage. Moreover, the clergy met frequently for pastoral conferences to discuss church doctrine and affairs. There was nothing comparable for laity, most of whom were farmers, artisans, or petty tradespeople. It would take time before educated or economically successful and confident laity began to appear in any numbers. It would take much more time before a theology of the laity would empower them.

Maintaining parochial schools was a matter of conscience with clergy and laity alike. Beyond the parish-sponsored elementary schools, a remarkable Synod-wide educational structure developed at higher educational levels to nourish the cohesion of these communities. There were nine schools modeled after the German *Gymnasium* (the equivalent of the American high school and junior college)—most named Concordia College. Two Concordia Seminaries, in St. Louis, Missouri, and

Springfield, Illinois, trained the clergy in Lutheran doctrine. Two Concordia Teachers Colleges—one originally in Addison, Illinois, and one in Seward, Nebraska—prepared teachers for the parochial schools. Concordia Publishing House produced a constant stream of German literature, including theological journals, school textbooks, hymnbooks, prayer books, and magazines. But almost alone among the larger Christian denominations in the United States, the Missouri Synod had no college for its lay members. The church had put all its resources and energy into teacher and clergy education.

Lutheranism was a faith with a high reverence for learning, and it was only the difficult social circumstances of immigration that had prevented members from doing more. Within their tradition, educated Missourians (which at first meant mainly the clergy) carried memories of the great German Lutheran universities where their predecessors had been educated and before that of the Wittenberg of Martin Luther and Philip Melanchthon. Dr. C. F. W. Walther (1811–87), the great nineteenth-century church leader of the Missouri Synod, had dreamed of building a large Lutheran university on the German model somewhere near Chicago, with the traditional European fourfold faculty of philosophy (liberal arts), theology, law, and medicine, but he was never able to mount such an ambitious enterprise.

STIRRINGS IN MISSOURI

In practice, the failure of the church to address the issues of cultural encounter and advanced education for its lay members meant there was an ever-widening gap between the narrow but intensely formative world of the congregation and school and the wider arenas of life in which the Missouri Synod's members grew up, especially in larger communities. This caused some members of the church to leave the Synod and others to recognize the importance of the issue. A few pioneering groups that began, in groping fashion, to address these broad problems helped create the precedents for the Valparaiso movement.

Each new generation of Missouri young people bore the increasing tensions associated with "Americanization." Most were faithful to the church and dutiful to their elders, but their hopes were American and the strictures of the parishes increasingly irrelevant to the actual way they lived or wanted to live. A first step in seeking some positive approach to these dilemmas occurred at the end of the nineteenth century when a number of young people's groups from urban congregations organized the "Walther

League." But such forward-looking activities quickly ran up against constraints. When the Walther League was formed in 1893, some of its local societies were not only mixed in gender, but had young women as presidents. Thus one Josie Ax, from a prominent lay Missouri Synod family in Dallas, Texas, presided over the young people's society of Zion Lutheran Church. Naturally, the young women spoke and voted in the organization's meetings.

This precipitated a heated controversy over the "ladies' question" at the next Missouri Synod convention. A Concordia Seminary faculty committee questioned the propriety of young men and women meeting together in convention away from home, and as for women voting, much less holding national office in any church-related organization, the answer was a loud "No!" Not for the last time, the new generation chose not to follow the Synod's dictates, though the League did dutifully compromise by granting female members suffrage but not national office. Such controversies over what traditionalists saw as "the subversion of youth" continued to recur, so though the Walther League was thoroughly pious and loyal, it took 30 years for the Synod to recognize it officially.

Other alert Missouri Synod groups began addressing social questions in the large cities that traditional synodical congregations found difficult to confront. Didn't the church have anything to say and do about the urgent human problems found in the streets and squalid slums: roving bands of children, crime, poor working conditions, and terrible public health problems? The vanguard of pastors and laity who tried to move beyond synodical constraints in dealing with such social problems often were stymied. But persistence was not a virtue lacking in Missourians, including the pious dissenters among them. An early picture of these forward-looking Missouri pioneers depicts them sitting for their portrait upright and formal in bewhiskered Victorian propriety. Behind them, on the wall blackboard, appear the initials "K.O.K."—for "Keep On Kicking," their unofficial motto.

These pious rebels organized another group threatening to traditionalists, the Associated Lutheran Charities. Its annual meetings vigorously addressed questions that ordinary pastoral conferences refused to face and involved the collaboration of lay experts in fields such as child welfare or public health, as when Dr. Albert G. Huegli, a Detroit physician and the father of a future Valparaiso University president, presented a paper on hospital policy. In 1919, the ALC's annual meeting in Fort Wayne spun off another organization to address unattended spiritual and social needs, the

Lutheran Deaconess Association, which offered Missouri's women a further opportunity for a public share in the church's ministry. The precedents, principles, and presence of many of the same people involved in the formation of groups such as the Walther League, the ALC, and the LDA provided the ferment and energy for the idea of creating a broader type of higher education for Lutheran young people.

It is ironic, though perhaps not surprising, that many of the social and cultural forces bringing change to the Missouri Synod came not from its midwestern centers of population and power, but from areas where Missouri Synod Lutherans were relatively few and far between. As early as the 1870s, some eastern businessmen, backed by their pastors, had challenged Walther's teaching forbidding the charging of interest on loans. After a decade of controversy, the easterners persuaded Walther to reverse his position. Like many changes in the Missouri Synod, which liked to imagine that its teachings had never changed, the matter simply disappeared from public discussion.

In New York, pastors and laymen together organized a Lutheran Education Society, which was chaired by layman Henry Ressmeyer. Noting the growing wealth of fellow eastern Lutherans, they purchased land in Bronxville, north of New York City, to which they transferred and expanded the Concordia Collegiate Institute. This same group also organized the American Lutheran Publicity Bureau in 1914, hoping to apply the newly developed techniques of advertising and public relations to a reshaping of the image of the Lutheran Church. The fierce anti-German sentiment during World War I, which included ugly attacks on German-American Lutherans, was a serious trauma for the Missouri Synod and gave added urgency to efforts to present the Lutheran faith to a wider public. In 1918, the bureau launched *The American Lutheran*, the only uncensored church magazine in the Missouri Synod.

There were similar stirrings in the Midwest, though the density of traditionalist clergy there made them less visible. In 1911, wealthy layman John Baden successfully insisted on coeducation when he created St. John's College in Winfield, Kansas. The institution was sponsored by the Synod's English District. In the Chicago area, the Lutheran Education Society moved Concordia Teachers College from rural Addison, Illinois, to the Chicago suburb of River Forest. Leaders of this society included powerful new laymen such as businessman William Tatge, who would later serve on Valparaiso's board, Chicago alderman William Beilfuss, and Theodore

Lamprecht, a successful woolens merchant who was fast becoming the leading layman in the Missouri Synod.

The year 1917 was the 400th anniversary of the Protestant Reformation. For years, Lutherans had planned massive national observances of this quadricentennial. In New York, a large group of clergy and laity from all synods formed the Lutheran Society of New York to present to the American public an account of the relevance of the Reformation to American life. The society chose as its director for this event a Missouri Synod urban missionary, the Reverend O. H. Pannkoke.

Less than a decade out of Concordia Seminary, Pannkoke had studied at Columbia University and Union Theological Seminary, a rare educational path for a Missouri clergyman. Pannkoke and his group generated a wide variety of materials for journals and the public press that highlighted the Reformation's impact on social and economic life, government, education, and music. There were major celebrations at Carnegie Hall and the Hotel Astor that featured the governors of New York and Pennsylvania. Pannkoke had organized what was, in effect, a giant religious and cultural coming-out party for all of Lutheranism in America. Its success was followed by the brilliant eastern tour of the St. Olaf College Choir, featuring sacred song rather than the traditional college glee club music. At the same time, Lutheran church organist Edward Rechlin rose to prominence in concert tours as a leading Bach interpreter.

The Missouri Synod leadership in the Midwest opposed the pan-Lutheran cooperation behind the Lutheran Society of New York and its related activities. Synodical leaders requested all Missouri Synod members to withdraw. But they did not. For Pannkoke, this was the beginning of adversarial relationships with leaders of his own church, including the controversial Concordia Seminary professor Theodore Graebner.

Historian Richard Solberg has called Pannkoke "Lutheranism's first promotional genius." Intuitively recognizing what almost no church leaders of the time did—the power of public action and public relations in democratic American society—Pannkoke appealed to all Lutherans beyond restrictive synodical boundaries and presented historic Lutheranism in positive terms to a wider American public. By the early 1920s, he had taken up another cause: Lutheran higher education. Although remaining in the Missouri Synod, Pannkoke was an independent operator who freely ranged across the intricate synodical and parochial divisions of American Lutheranism to serve its common interests. During his career, Pannkoke conducted promotional campaigns for more than 20

Lutheran institutions of higher education. His strongest personal involvement was in the founding of Valparaiso University.

The Missouri Synod leadership was slow to comprehend the new cultural forces at work, and most of what they did understand they resisted. Successful Americanized lay leaders, however loyal to the Synod, increasingly chafed at what they saw as clerical incompetence in organizational and financial matters. They were joined by dissatisfied clergy innovators, who often had quarrels with the restrictive ways that Synod traditionalists defined the church's teachings and mission. Historian Alan Graebner has identified some of these clergy whose work directly affected the origins of Valparaiso University.

Theodore Graebner was a brilliant polymath who wrote books on everything from science to business ethics. Witty and sarcastic, Graebner hammered away at every major issue of the day in his lively *Lutheran Witness*. He could change his positions under the force of argument or circumstances and was frequently a foil for those involved in founding VU. Walter A. Maier was a Harvard Ph.D. candidate who in 1920 became executive secretary of the Walther League. He later joined the Concordia Seminary faculty. In the 1930s, Maier became the speaker for the *Lutheran Hour* and quickly achieved fame as one of the nation's leading radio preachers. Paul Lindemann founded his journal, *The American Lutheran*, in New York, then moved to St. Paul. His eloquent writing gave voice to the vision of a progressive, Americanized, but deeply spiritual Lutheranism. He became the mentor of many younger clergy, including Otto Paul Kretzmann, third Lutheran president of Valparaiso University. John H. C. Fritz was the first synodical English-speaking missionary in Brooklyn. Fritz wrote the first manuals on urban missionary strategy and parish finances. He later moved to St. Louis, where, as seminary dean, Fritz championed lay activity—and, therefore, Valparaiso University.

These four leaders and others attempted to fashion new "home mission" policies for the Synod and to present a new face for Lutheranism to the wider world. They also wanted especially to increase dramatically lay involvement in the life of the church. Already in 1917, 12 prominent laymen gathered in the Milwaukee mansion of Fred Pritzlaff, the son of a Lutheran immigrant who had made a fortune in the hardware business. The group committed itself to raising $100,000 among themselves and their friends to liquidate the Synod's current debt. Forming the Lutheran Laymen's League, they next proposed a multimillion dollar campaign to create a new structured pension fund for retired pastors and their widows.

Such efforts suggested the still largely latent strength of lay leaders within the Missouri Synod.

THE IDEA OF A LUTHERAN UNIVERSITY

Besides these broad developments, a confluence of specific ideas, people, and organizations in the years immediately following World War I provided the direct background for the movement that led to the Lutheran acquisition of Valparaiso University. First, the idea of a Lutheran university for the laity began to be seriously debated in a few of the Missouri Synod's more advanced circles. Second, the National Lutheran Education Association, formed in 1918, represented the first organization to specifically call for lay education in Missouri. Finally, and most important, the American Luther League, which had been organized to fight the Ku Klux Klan and other organizations that threatened parochial schools, turned to the cause of Lutheran higher education as an essential way to further a strong, positive Lutheran presence in America.

World War I delivered a tremendous shock to many in the Missouri Synod. Besides forcing them almost overnight to abandon the suspect German language for English, it jolted many Missourians out of their isolation, forcing them to realize that further "Americanization" was a necessity. For the first time, progressive Missouri thinkers began to speak out and to find a sympathetic audience. Furthermore, after the war, more Missouri Synod young people were seeking a college education, and the Synod had little to offer them.

In 1919, the Rev. William Schoenfeld, a prominent eastern pastor, became the first voice to call for the expansion of the Synod's system of higher education to include the laity, which he envisioned leading to the creation of a Lutheran university in America. In a paper presented to the Synod's Atlantic District convention, Schoenfeld argued that World War I had been a judgment on the nation. A renewal of society was not the task of the organized church, he contended, but of Christians who are called to be salt and light to the world. Schoenfeld argued that Lutheran young people should be able to study for influential careers while at the same time becoming "strong in the Lord." He further insisted that as teachers, writers, editors, lawyers, and statesmen, Lutherans must become intent on "rendering that service which will secure to all men their rights and liberties, the nearest possible to equal justice, protection, and opportunity for all, without any discrimination because of race, creed, or color." Learning and practicing such principles was God's will, Schoenfeld declared, though they represented only "civic righteousness" in terms of Lutheran theology.

With respect to higher education, Schoenfeld called for the immediate transformation of several of the synodical schools into four-year colleges that would prepare both laity and future pastors for the modern world. He especially wanted such colleges to include courses on social and economic affairs. He endorsed full accreditation by the new regional accrediting agencies, even if the Synod had to reduce the number of its schools to improve academic quality. But such Lutheran colleges should not only keep pace with the advance of learning, they should contribute to it. Either through the addition to present institutions, or if necessary the creation of a new one, there eventually should come the establishment of a genuine Lutheran university.

Responding to Schoenfeld's proposal in the July 1919 *Theological Quarterly*, Concordia Seminary professor Theodore Graebner raised numerous questions and objections. He asserted that the Synod could not lay on its members the obligation to pay for colleges for the laity, much less a more comprehensive university. It had all it could handle supporting the church itself in its essential task of preaching the Gospel. Graebner warned that creating a real university would be prohibitively expensive. While one could establish a college for a million dollars, a true university would take $10 million, including endowment. Graebner also claimed that finding sufficient Lutheran faculty would be difficult and that academic freedom would be a "problem" for Lutheran scholars because Lutheran doctrine was at variance with the norms of knowledge in several fields.

Schoenfeld's paper was uniquely visionary and put the idea of a Lutheran university into general circulation. But it was true that he had not examined the obstacles. Although Graebner threw some dust, many of his objections were serious and real. He spoke from knowledge of the actual condition of American higher education, in which the new universities were spectacular but expensive propositions. Those who shared Schoenfeld's vision and hopes seldom reckoned with the difficulties.

While Schoenfeld was sparking discussion of founding a university, an actual association with large educational aspirations was forming in the midwestern heartland of the church. In 1918, a group of midwestern Lutheran laity, clergy, and parochial school teachers had organized the National Lutheran Education Association. In an article in *The Lutheran Witness* in 1920, one of the NLEA's principal leaders, an Iowa businessman named Byron Holst, informed the journal's readers that the organization already had nearly 6,000 members and a treasury in six figures. In its 1920 convention, the Synod recognized the association.

The stated purpose of the NLEA was to further the cause of Lutheran higher education for the laity. But the organization actually was searching for the particular form its mission should take. One of its projects was to establish a Lutheran student center at the University of Iowa, a model for similar campus ministries at other public colleges. But Holst wrote that its real hope was to establish one or more institutions of higher learning for the church's youth. "As a church we have failed to establish institutions of higher learning," Holst wrote. When Lutheran young people went to college, they too often failed to return to the church. "Shall this exodus of our young blood be permitted to continue?" he asked. "Or will we come to the rescue while yet the opportunities are ample and the future is rich with promise?"

With its grass-roots support, substantial funding, and status within the Synod, the NLEA was waiting to make a move. Unlike Schoenfeld and others, it was evidently not interested in the possible option of expanding the mission of the synodical Concordias. The NLEA appeared to be the most likely nexus for creating some kind of lay-oriented Missouri Synod college. But it proved to be another new organization, not the NLEA, that provided the actual impetus for such an institution. It was the activities of the American Luther League and its energetic leader, John C. Baur, that led to the Lutheran refounding of Valparaiso University.

By the early 1920s, the fierce patriotism of World War I had become the "100-percent Americanism" of the postwar period. Soon after the armistice, various hyper-patriots, including the Ku Klux Klan, turned against parochial schools in many states, seeking legislation requiring all children to attend only public schools. In Fort Wayne, Indiana, a major center of Missouri Synod Lutheranism, businessman H. D. Holterman reacted by writing a pamphlet entitled "LUTHERANS WAKE UP!" Declaring that several hundred Lutheran schools already had been closed by such pressure, Holterman announced that 3,000 Lutherans in the Fort Wayne area were banding together in a new organization: the American Luther League. It would mobilize to fight such threats, to defend constitutional liberties, and to promote the welfare of Lutheran schools.

The league quickly spread throughout the Midwest and beyond and took up a number of education-related causes. The American Luther League was an organization made up entirely of Lutheran laymen. Pastors were admitted in an advisory capacity only, ostensibly to avoid any church-state complications in the political struggle. A parallel Mothers League also involved Lutheran women nationally in the battle for the schools and the cause of Lutheran education. Together, these two leagues generated millions of pamphlets, newspaper articles, speakers' bureau activities, public rallies, and other forms of political action to promote their cause.

The Mothers League and the ALL made their most brilliant move by hiring a young Fort Wayne pastor to be their field secretary. The Rev. John C. Baur became the living, directing force of this highly successful effort. Born and raised in Connecticut and New York, Baur came to Fort Wayne's Trinity Lutheran Church after a stint as a city missionary in New York. Baur possessed boundless energy and was completely unafraid of crossing the boundaries of traditional formal organizations, not a typical trait of the Missouri Synod's clergy. He edited ALL's magazine, *The Lutheran Layman*, and wrote innumerable pamphlets and articles.

During Baur's eight years as ALL field secretary, he was often on loan to other closely connected projects and campaigns. Church leaders in Kansas, Oklahoma, and Oregon requested his help in similar antiparochial school battles in their states. The biggest battle in this nationwide contest took place in Michigan, where the Klan, leaders of the Scottish Rite Masons, and other groups formed the Wayne County Civic Association as their political vehicle in a public referendum. Baur and his close friend and schoolmate O. H. Pannkoke formed an alliance of Michigan Lutherans, Roman Catholics, Seventh-Day Adventists, and Christian Reformed. In the end, they succeeded in fashioning a state policy that permitted religiously sponsored education to survive with basic public standards.

The alliance with the Roman Catholic leadership in Michigan was completely out of character for a Missouri Synod pastor, and no one was more embarrassed than Baur when Archbishop Denis Dougherty of Detroit publicly embraced him after their political victory. All this made Baur a controversial figure. Crossing denominational boundaries provoked controversy in the Missouri Synod, and Baur's open disregard for many traditional Missouri cultural and intellectual restrictions was well known. He expressed exasperation, for example, at some Missouri Synod pastors who opposed the use of radio for the church's mission because radio would cross parish lines, thus invading another pastor's territory.

As the ALL's successful political campaign on behalf of parochial schools began to wind down, its leadership realized that they had tapped new energies within the Lutheran community. Considered by many to be a "meddling" organization because it did not adhere to synodical guidance, the ALL's talented laymen and their clergy friends, especially the core leaders in Indiana and Michigan where the hardest battles had been waged, were looking for another outlet for their energies and their cause. They soon found it.

THE LUTHERANS BUY A UNIVERSITY

Numbers of people in Indiana and elsewhere knew in early 1925 that Valparaiso University was up for sale and that the KKK deal to buy it had fallen through. But it was evidently the young pastor of Immanuel Lutheran Church in Valparaiso, Rev. George Schutes, who first broached the idea of a Lutheran purchase of the institution. Schutes was a progressive and pioneering leader who in 1925 was busy installing at his church a new radio station, WBRC, with the largest broadcast radius in Indiana. It so happened that VU President Horace Evans was Schutes' neighbor, and at some point that spring, Schutes became excited about the idea that the Lutherans might be able to buy the University.

When Schutes contacted John Baur in Fort Wayne, Baur first arranged for him to meet with the faculty of Concordia College in that city, where Schutes found little interest. But when Schutes was invited to present the idea to the laymen of the ALL, he discovered an excitement equal to his own. Ernest Gallmeier, one of the organization's younger members, later recalled how the whole group gathered in the upstairs dining hall at St. Paul's Lutheran Church and eagerly discussed the possibility of creating a Lutheran university. They had built a Lutheran high school, they had founded a Lutheran hospital, and they had beaten the Klan. They were eager to take on this new challenge.

Initially, Baur himself seems to have thought that the NLEA would be the most likely Lutheran group to become involved in the Valparaiso situation. He urged Schutes to contact Byron Holst of the NLEA, which had both substantial funds on hand and the official blessing of the Synod. Holst traveled to VU and subsequently issued invitations to people from Valparaiso to the upcoming NLEA convention in Mankato, Minnesota, to discuss the idea of selling the University.

Meanwhile, the Fort Wayne ALL group had contacted their widely experienced friend O. H. Pannkoke for advice on the matter. He listened to a plan they had devised to sell bonds to finance the purchase, then to run the University on current income. Pannkoke quickly disabused them of this idea. He explained the realities of financing a university, including the need for costly accreditation and an endowment of at least $500,000.

But their excitement and commitment was such that he agreed to make an inspection trip to determine if Valparaiso University was worth buying.

Despite the serious problems he saw on his site inspection, Pannkoke returned to Fort Wayne as enthused as the others about the prospects of Lutherans buying a university rather than starting one from scratch. The northwest Indiana location was in the center of the American Lutheran population, Pannkoke pointed out, and accessible by rail and auto. Pannkoke urged the group to move quickly on their own and not to wait for official church sanction. There never would be a Lutheran university if it were left to synodical debate. The Synod was a debating club! To seize the opportunity by swift action was the best way to go.

A few days later, the ALL held its annual banquet in Fort Wayne. At a special meeting of the city's pastors after the event, the president of the ALL, the prominent physician Dr. Herman Duemling, presented the possibility of a new direction for the organization: the purchase and operation of a university in Valparaiso. After a generally favorable reception, the clergy present agreed to send their own committee to Valparaiso. They, too, liked what they saw.

The Valparaiso enthusiasts wasted little time. The Central District convention of the Synod was scheduled for June 17–23 in Fort Wayne, shortly after the clergy committee's visit to Valparaiso. When the delegates arrived for the convention, they encountered a promotional display about Valparaiso University and an eager pack of pro-VU lobbyists. On June 19, delegates heard a presentation by the Valparaiso Chamber of Commerce on the University and the town.

The problem of how to organize themselves effectively to acquire the University on such short notice was a delicate one that the pro-Valparaiso leaders astutely solved. Knowing that the NLEA permitted any group of Lutherans interested in higher education to establish a chapter of that group, the ALL members moved to do so. On June 22, interested lay delegates and pastors met to organize as a "Central States Division of the NLEA," then to nominate members of an incorporating committee. The next day, they elected the committee, empowering it to act on their behalf. Meanwhile, the ALL leaders took to the floor of the convention, seeking an endorsement of their effort. This would put the large and influential district behind the movement, which they knew would be essential for any large-scale fund-raising.

There was lively debate for six hours. Opponents argued that the university project was not directly connected with the central mission of the church, preaching the Gospel. But powerful voices responded. The Rev. M. F. Kretzmann of Kendallville, Indiana, secretary of the Synod's board of directors, voiced his support. The Rev. Francis J. Lankenau of Napoleon, Ohio, a leader in reconceiving the church's mission in America, spoke of the many young people who went away to college and never returned to the church.

It was the highly respected Rev. Jacob Miller, the tall, bearded senior pastor of St. Paul's Lutheran Church in Fort Wayne and a vice president of the Synod, who gave the most eloquent address. He had given the matter much thought, he said. Many of the lay leaders behind the movement were his own parishioners and they already had become familiar with his arguments for their cause. Miller said:

> I'm for Valpo because I love my children and want to deepen their faith as they develop, which is why we built our schools. Secondly, the church cannot rise higher than the pew. Finally, Christians are supposed to be the salt of the earth. We must have Christian doctors, lawyers and others active as citizens for the sake of our society.

In the movement to purchase Valparaiso University, it was clear that something of a theology of the laity was struggling for expression.

The Valparaiso movement prevailed, and the convention endorsed the organizing committee's purchase of the University. The delegates also pledged themselves to support the institution, if there were "proper safeguards" to keep it "under control of the Synod at all times." They also indicated that they wanted to appoint a "District Advisory Committee" for the University.

The whirlwind continued. On June 26, 1925, the organizing committee, which had adopted the name "The Lutheran University Association," traveled to Valparaiso and swiftly negotiated a purchase price of $176,500 for the property. They also confirmed the promise of the Valparaiso Chamber of Commerce that the cancellation of $331,000 in outstanding locally held debts had been secured. In addition, some Valparaiso businessmen pledged to the Lutheran delegation that they would raise $50,000 for the University. The next morning, Charles Scheimann, along with Pastors Baur and Schutes, met with VU President Evans. They agreed to conclude the deal and to begin the fall term without further ado, postponing discussion of potentially troublesome issues until they could meet with the existing faculty.

Fort Wayne was declared the headquarters of the LUA, and attorney Martin Luecke began the legal work under two important instructions.

First, the leaders had decided that an unusual dual structure would be the best defense against possible liabilities arising from the messy Valparaiso legal situation: A holding company would own the property against which there were still unsettled claims, and an operating company would run the University's operations. Thus on July 15, articles of incorporation of The Lutheran University Association, a nonprofit holding company, were filed in Indianapolis and Porter County, and on July 27, a separate Valparaiso University Association was notarized in Fort Wayne and Valparaiso as authorized to operate the institution.

The relationship between the new university and the NLEA constituted a second potential difficulty. Although the NLEA had promptly loaned $16,500 to the ALL organizers and had helped give them a certain legitimacy within the Missouri Synod, that organization's leaders appeared cagey about providing further support without exercising significant control. Therefore, the LUA leaders omitted all references to the NLEA in their incorporating documents. Many members of that organization did join the new movement, however, and looked on VU as the fulfillment of their goals.

On July 22, the LUA met in Valparaiso and created a board of directors, authorizing it to borrow the necessary money from a Fort Wayne bank to purchase the University. The first chairman of the board was Herman Duemling, the president of the ALL and part of the core group of Indiana and Michigan leaders who would remain instrumental throughout the early decades of Valparaiso University. The Fort Wayne laymen boldly put their own names and reputations on the line by personally signing for the six-figure loan. After a meeting with representatives of the Brown family, the board took a 30-day option on the property to allow time to insure that the tangled affairs of the institution were in some kind of order before the purchase agreement would be officially signed.

The next morning, at a specially called convocation, the campus celebration began. President Evans conferred honorary doctorates on the local leaders who had worked so hard for this outcome, including George Schutes. The Valparaiso University choir sang the "Hallelujah Chorus" and Pastor Schutes read from the Book of Genesis. Byron Holst related the story of the purchase and announced to the assembly the LUA's intention to make Valparaiso University into a major national institution of higher education: "We have many small schools, parochial and public, and small colleges which will serve as feeders to this great university." He assured the faculty that there would be "no serious changes" in the

University and that their organization expected every faculty member to stay on the job.

Holst's remarks were published in the local press and given wide circulation elsewhere. In some quarters, they were received with hostility, especially by Missouri Synod opponents of the purchase who noted the "unionistic" flavor of the ceremony and especially the Lutherans' public assurances that nothing would be changed. They were not amused.

At the moment when the final agreement was signed in Martin Luecke's Fort Wayne office on August 11, 1925, the bells rang out in Valparaiso, setting off a city and campus-wide celebration that lasted until a 2 A.M. rainstorm doused it.

THE STORM BREAKS

That was not the only cold shower to dampen the new university owners' exuberance. John Baur and Francis Lankenau immediately arranged to meet with the board of directors of the whole Missouri Synod to get their support for the broad financial campaign they planned to launch. The atmosphere was frigid. The Synod's president, Dr. Frederick Pfotenhauer, could not imagine endorsing a university of dubious reputation with no Lutheran faculty. It would not be a true Lutheran university, he declared, unless all of its faculty were Lutheran, like the rest of Synod's institutions. Nevertheless, recognizing the good intentions of the loyal Lutherans of Fort Wayne, and imagining that the NLEA had sufficient funds to start the venture, the board wished the effort God's blessing.

Despite the wet blanket from the Synod, O. H. Pannkoke agreed on August 24 to join Baur in directing the major VU kickoff campaign. Experienced and daring, the two men were prepared to design and launch an aggressive campaign, though the Synod's people already were spending heavily on the new seminary, new church building and remodeling, and other programs. On August 25, a letter from Pannkoke and Baur invited key clergy and laity to assemble in Fort Wayne for an important meeting regarding the new Lutheran university. At last, the letter said, Lutherans could have their own national university like so many other denominations.

On September 2, 1925, 30 leaders who accepted the invitation gathered in Fort Wayne for a carefully planned all-day meeting. LUA leaders spoke on the pressing need for a university to serve youth and the church, on Valparaiso University as a bargain and opportunity, and on the plan they had designed to raise the necessary funds. Pannkoke then spelled out a complex promotional and fund-raising plan supported with "educational" publications. The goal was to raise $883,000, of which $500,000 was to be for endowment.

The next day a letter went out throughout the Synod announcing that a Fort Wayne meeting of influential leaders in the church had authorized a major campaign on behalf of the new Lutheran Valparaiso University. It indicated times and places for clergy-laity leadership meetings at strategic midwestern locations during the next three weeks. "We are face to face with one of the most important undertakings in the history of our Synod if not of the whole Lutheran Church in America," the letter declared. Under the signatures of the 60 backers were the following two postscripts:

> P.S. The Central District has endorsed this movement and promised support. Also the Board of Directors of Synod has wished us God's blessing in this undertaking.
>
> P.S. Already a number of pledges of five thousand dollars are made.

President Pfotenhauer was upset. Pastors began writing, asking why he endorsed this unprecedented effort, as the Valparaiso literature seemed to suggest. But he had not endorsed it, Pfotenhauer wrote to Theodore Graebner. Valparaiso was misleading in its use of the board's "blessing." Graebner also was upset. To Duemling, he recalled his critique of the idea of a university a few years earlier. A college? Yes, you could develop a college for a million dollars. But a real university would require a minimum of $10 million. Instead of doing it right, the Valparaiso movement had purchased nothing but a ramshackle bunch of buildings and an institution of dubious background. The church had no business building universities. Such reactions shut many doors. The powerful clergy of the Western District, which included St. Louis, closed ranks around a refusal to participate in the Valparaiso drive. Pannkoke later recalled this as a "bitter struggle."

But there was no slowing the Valparaiso movement. If many official circles were cool or hostile, other voices within Missouri responded enthusiastically. Almost all pastors and leading laity in Michigan were supportive. From the executive committee of the Walther League board came a resolution that stated, "We express our joy because of the progressive movement that has been set on foot, and … we wish the Association the Lord's blessing for the consummation of this worthy project." Lengthy and favorable articles appeared in the *Walther League Messenger* and *The*

American Lutheran. However, all the official publications of the Synod were silent about Valparaiso and the campaign on its behalf.

Telegrams announcing major gifts and pledged totals went back and forth between headquarters and regional chairmen as the campaign approached the targeted date for its congregational phase. A few key congregations started the ball rolling. St. Paul's in Fort Wayne, led by prominent layman Henry Wehrenberg's pledge of $25,000, committed to a total of $75,000. St. Paul's of Hammond, Indiana, pledged $25,000. Finally, on November 29, 1925, the general congregational drive was launched. After the reports of its efforts came back to the Fort Wayne headquarters, Pannkoke was able to announce that $645,000 of the $883,000 goal already had been given or pledged.

A Campus in Transition

As classes began in the fall of 1925, there were only a few traces of the new ownership at the University. From time to time, Lutherans involved in the takeover would appear to speak on campus and reassure faculty and students, particularly with respect to the teaching of science. The Scopes Trial was still much in the minds of thoughtful people, and the tall, imposing Dr. Duemling spoke reassuringly of the University's commitment to the sciences. The new board chairman spoke with credibility as a well-known physician and the son of a science professor with a doctorate from a German university.

Others, especially John Baur, would come through occasionally to report on the progress of the fund-raising campaign: meetings all over the midwestern states, major advance gifts arriving, thousands of campaign workers organized as teams to visit Lutheran households. In nearby Chicago, Baur noted, a "mass demonstration" of 6,000 Lutherans had gathered at the Armory on November 29 to kick off a house-to-house visitation campaign on behalf of the new Lutheran university.

Despite such encouragement, among the veteran faculty members a sense of relief competed with the apprehension many felt at the coming of a new order. Despite the chaos they had lived through, the Lutherans were largely an unknown quantity. Gradually, more signs of the Lutheran presence began to appear at VU. A conference of Lutheran ministers held a meeting on what they proudly said was "their" campus. The Walther League contributed a conspicuous glass-enclosed bulletin board. Soon, trucks began hauling off the old bricks from the burnt-out Old Main College Building, erasing the campus's biggest eyesore.

John Baur's visits became more frequent, and he began signaling that the University would indeed have to change. Despite the desire to maintain continuity with the old Valparaiso University, he knew that the academic atmosphere had deteriorated badly. The tone of student life especially displeased him. *The Torch*, in particular, strongly reflected the party school atmosphere of the Roaring Twenties, and Baur did not like the roar. He spoke to several faculty members about appointing an adviser for the paper, but they simply shrugged their shoulders.

With the active part of the fund-raising campaign over, Baur decided it was time to make the Lutheran ownership effective. He pressured Evans to resign the presidency, and Baur himself became acting president at the beginning of the winter term in January. To the students, Baur minced no words:

> The University will be first of all a workshop where we are engaged in the pursuit of learning what fits us properly for later life. There will be pleasures, but the dominant thought will be: we are here to work and secure the best training that can be had. It is with this end in view that the Lutheran Educational Association [sic] wishes the University conducted.

Students apparently got the message that a new regime was in charge. *The Torch* at once announced that the policy of the paper had been altered to acknowledge the new control of the University by establishing a new "platform":

- Foster scholastic achievements.
- Manifest an interest in the students' welfare.
- Encourage an enrollment of 4,000 worthy students.
- Promote Brown and Gold athletics.

Despite this quick response, Baur determined to get a faculty adviser for *The Torch* as soon as possible.

Meanwhile, the board had turned to the important task of naming its first president. The short list contained some of the most prominent Lutheran clergy in the country: H. B. Hemmeter of Rochester, New York, a member of an accomplished family of strong Valparaiso supporters; Francis Lankenau, the forceful leader from Napoleon, Ohio; and Walter A. Maier, the rising preaching star of the Missouri Synod.

The board surprised everyone by appointing a senior Lutheran scholar, 62-year-old Dr. William H. T. Dau, professor at Concordia Seminary. If Dau could be persuaded to come, wrote Pannkoke, his reputation was worth a separate endowment. Born in Germany but educated in the Synod's schools, Dau had been a parish pastor; president of a small English District College at Conover, North Carolina; editor; and since 1905, the "English theologian" at Concordia Seminary. Dau was a productive scholar, a student of the Reformation, and a commentator on current church life through his editorial work on *The Theological Quarterly*. Dau had a reputation as a broad-minded churchman as well.

Dau had been following developments at Valparaiso with interest, and when the offer came, he was favorably inclined. He wrote to Pannkoke to get a true picture of the financial health of the institution. Eager to get him, Pannkoke overstated the resources, including a hypothetical $1,000,000 of "living endowment" based on projected annual $50,000 gifts from church members.

But the seminary faculty, believing there could be no more important role than teaching and editing there, refused to release Dau to go to Valparaiso. Dau argued in response that leading a university would better prepare laity to help the clergy, a limited but widespread "theology of the laity" at the time. But he met continued resistance. To his son-in-law Paul Miller, Dau wrote complaining about the seminary faculty's attitude: "Like a horse with blinders on they see nothing else. ... No vision! No horizon! And something that borders on idolizing Concordia Seminary! It is a pitiful spectacle." He added his irritation about the legalistic streak within the Synod by saying that his son-in-law, a teacher in Springfield, Illinois, was being hounded by his pastor for conducting an orchestra in a theater and because his wife was attending college rather than having children. Overcoming the objections from those at the seminary, Dau finally accepted the VU presidency by interpreting it as a divine call that he could not refuse. From Minnesota, Pannkoke wrote Baur, exulting over their coup. Shortly before Dau accepted on February 12, Dean Fritz broke the official silence of *The Lutheran Witness* by including the purchase of Valparaiso University in a summary of notable events in the Synod's history during the first quarter of the twentieth century.

Dau did not move to Valparaiso with his invalid wife until the following summer, but he already was active in VU affairs. In response to a request for a motto for the University, he immediately proposed Psalm 36:9, "In Thy Light We See Light." He also asked a well-known St. Louis designer to create a new official VU seal.

Soon Dau joined other VU leaders in an even more crucial task: the search for Lutheran faculty. They hoped to attract the best academics they could find, but in practice, they knew they would have to start with young Missouri Synod people with more potential than accomplishments. Together, Dau and Baur traveled to Scarsdale, New York, where a bright young scholar named Walter Bauer, with a master's in history from Cornell, was serving as a pastor until he could resume work on a doctorate. They also recruited Frederick Heimlich of Purdue University, an active layman in the Synod who had a Ph.D. in botany; young Alfred H. Meyer, who had a master's degree in geology; and Walther Miller, who had a master's degree in German. In addition to these five, they hired eight other Lutherans. These 13 would comprise nearly a third of the faculty in the fall. Conrad Moll, the son of a Fort Wayne Lutheran pastor, was named athletic director and coach.

Dau moved to Valparaiso early in the summer of 1926, determined "to make the intellectual and spiritual force of our school felt by pen and work in the academic world." In May, John Baur had unveiled sketches of new Tudor Gothic buildings for the campus that had been prepared by an Indianapolis architectural firm. The sketches depicted a new administration building, a library, a law school, and even a student union—the latest trend in accommodating the lively, socially minded student bodies on U.S. campuses. Excitement over VU's future was mounting.

For Dau, though, the next three years did not prove to be the great opportunity he had envisioned. Instead, they were largely an agony. The former seminary professor was completely unprepared for the multiple demands that descended on even a small university's president. That first summer of 1926 brought a taste of what was to come. More than 6,000 letters flooded in from prospective students or their parents. Lutheran students wanted information about programs, and Lutheran parents sought financial help or jobs for their sons or daughters so they might attend VU. Vendors were pushing for sales and favors. Some clergy already were criticizing the University for having a theater department or simply for being "non-Lutheran." A stream of visitors crowded in on Dau's schedule, wanting to see "their" university. There also were public relations trips to make and pulpits to occupy each Sunday on behalf of the University.

Furthermore, the situation with John Baur was almost guaranteed to create tension. While Baur was continuing to supervise the massive cleanup and remodeling job on the campus, he often crossed paths with the new president. Always action-oriented and impatient with any signs of what he considered to be dithering, Baur had no doubt that he was ultimately responsible to the board to get the University off to a successful start. It quickly became apparent that the scholarly Dau had no talent for administration but that he was conscious of the status of the presidency and desired the proper deference. Inevitably, these two strong personalities clashed. Thus, Dau quickly discovered that this university presidency, at least, was not an academic haven, but a pressure cooker. At the end of the summer, a few weeks before the fall term even began, Dau sent Baur a note stating that he already was worn out and was going to the Ozarks for some rest.

Despite these warning signs, Baur was working hard, with Pannkoke's encouragement, to make sure the inauguration of President Dau would be a "big event." Thus, on a hot and sultry Sunday, October 3, 1926, three chartered trains and several thousand automobiles brought an estimated crowd of 10,000 Lutherans to Valparaiso. Only a fraction could squeeze into the auditorium. For two-and-a-half hours, there was music by the new 100-voice Bach Choir of Chicago, a solo by the gifted daughter of Henry Baker Brown, Ruth Axe Brown, and much speechmaking.

Thunderous applause greeted the keynote speech on "The Aim of Our University Enterprise" by O. C. Kreinheder of Detroit, a member of the VU board and president of the English District. Kreinheder declared that Valparaiso would aid the church by "furnishing an educated laity," and he referred to "this historic hour, the inauguration of the first President of the only Lutheran University in America."

The crowd listened respectfully, if uncomprehendingly, to another speech delivered in Latin by Dr. Franz Pieper, the president of Concordia Seminary, St. Louis, and the leading theologian of the Missouri Synod. His speech was titled "On the Friendship which Should Be Cultivated between *Scientia* and the Christian Religion." It asserted that the present strife between science and religion could end when each respected its proper boundaries.

Then, after Dr. Duemling charged him with the responsibilities of office, the new President Dau turned to the audience to speak. His inaugural had an irenic, evangelical quality. He appealed to the meaning of Christian faith for students, namely, rejoicing in the goodness of the universe, natural and cultural. They should not fear its reverent exploration nor the results of science, Dau said, because of the sure knowledge of God's love in Christ. He gently criticized Darwin for pushing God away from life's center through his theory. Finally, he underscored the significance of the motto that he had chosen for Valparaiso University:

> The inspired truth of God's Book shall make plain and straight whatever is perplexing to man in any study, because it keeps him close to Him who said, "I am the Light of the world; he that followeth me shall not walk in darkness, but shall have the light of life."

The inauguration was widely and favorably covered. Noting that it marked the end of VU's 50 years under "the old regime," *The Porter County Vidette* called it "one of the greatest events in the history of the school." The festivities would, it said, "be entered in detail in the archives of Valparaiso's ancient hall of learning."

FACING REALITIES

Despite the inspiring spirit of the inauguration, VU's new leaders faced difficult problems. A few days after the crowds departed, Dau submitted his first report to the board. As he had previously told the deans, his goals were: (1) to develop the institution according to the "highest current educational standards"; (2) to secure accreditation with the North Central Association; and (3) to establish the Christian influence of the Lutheran Church. He was worried about the slender resources presently available, concluding, in what qualified as a considerable understatement, that "it will be some time, even after accreditation has been secured, before Valparaiso University will turn out many Ph.D.'s."

John Baur also was learning fast about university realities. Seeing the campus close up had made him realize more clearly that large-scale resources would be needed. Baur wrote to board member Harry Eberline of Detroit on October 1 that

> the more I think of this Valparaiso project, the more I am convinced that if we are really to succeed we must get away even from talking just about one million. If we talk about anything we ought to talk in terms of ten or twenty-five million, because ultimately we cannot succeed in building a high-class institution and appeal to big men unless we think and speak and act in the biggest possible terms. This, of course, would sound almost insane to some people!

Board members such as Eberline also discovered how quickly their responsibilities could expand. When Duemling suddenly and shockingly died early in 1927, Eberline succeeded him as the second VU board president.

Hopes for longer-term financial improvement had to give way to immediate pressures. Baur had calculated that it would take an enrollment of 800 to 1,000 students to balance the budget. Summer rumors optimistically suggested that as many as 1,200 students might enroll in the fall. But only 600 students showed up, far fewer than expected. Some of the decline was probably caused by former students who did not welcome the new administration and would not come to a church-related school. In addition, Catholic students were being systematically warned away from VU because of the Klan episode, though nothing had come of it. But it was also apparent that lay Lutheran parents would only send their children to a Lutheran college if it were accredited.

Thus, immediate accreditation was essential for VU's future. But it would be difficult to attain, especially because a substantial endowment was necessary. The enrollment shortfall and the extensive physical remodeling were eating up the funds originally designated for the endowment. Upgrading the university's academic quality would also be difficult. There was not a single genuine Ph.D. on the carryover faculty. Dau referred to the severing of 20 faculty members that year as a "painful and agonizing" experience. Lopping off the high school and preparatory divisions was another step taken with an eye toward meeting the accrediting standards of the North Central Association. The new administration also decided to move to a semester system.

After some wrangling with the faculty, acting academic dean Frederick Heimlich consolidated the existing eight departments into three schools—liberal arts, pharmacy, and law. To the board, Dau reported that the soul of the University would always be its School of the Liberal Arts: "There is in modern life a distinct danger of exaggerated specialization which imperils general education and culture and produces professional experts in one small study or research who are woeful ignoramuses in most other studies." He wanted graduates of broad culture and wide learning.

Inevitably, student life also came under scrutiny. Dau's earliest confrontation with students came less than three weeks after his inauguration when he denounced the fraternities and sororities as undemocratic "secret societies." The Missouri Synod opposed lodges as "false religions." To Dau, the Greek system seemed to be collegiate versions of lodges. He would not ban them, he said, but he insisted that the University would not recognize them until they eliminated all secret oaths and rituals. Although they comprised only 11 percent of the student body, the Greeks had become prominent on the campus. A battle ensued, and first the sororities, then the fraternities, grudgingly complied with the rules prohibiting secrecy, though not without strain and alienation. At times the confrontation took on a sinister tone, as when a shadowy Klan-like club hinted at violence if the old order were disturbed.

The battle with the Greeks was enormously complicated by Dau's discovery that, contrary to Missouri Synod policy, the local Lutheran church itself had many lodge members, the result of a previous pastor's practice. So his target now included the local congregation for its laxity. Pastor Schutes found himself in a fight with the president of the University, who refused to join the local congregation.

Dau despaired of dealing with the dancing and theater-going that were well established as part of the normal fare of the VU student body. The Lutheran students who began arriving in substantial numbers in the next few years also happily joined in these activities, though presumably at least some of them had been warned against such activity by their pastors. Reporting to the board on these lamentable developments, Dau said he was at his wits' end. Dancing, he complained, was virtually compulsory in the high schools, and he concluded plaintively: "It is becoming increasingly difficult to lead a chaste and decent life in this rotting world."

Dau was equally disappointed in what he hoped would be the salutary influence of the Lutheran-sponsored chapel. He instituted chapel as a devotional worship service held four times a week, but attendance was poor. The Lutheran students, Dau complained, seemed "overfed and indifferent," acting with regard to religion as if "they know it all." Yet when a board committee and the new dean of students talked about making morning worship compulsory—the normal practice at many church colleges—Dau reacted strongly. "Nothing that looks like religious coercion can be tolerated at a Lutheran university!" he declared.

By May, the optimism of the previous October was gone, and Dau had to address several publicly demoralizing rumors: that only Lutheran students would be admitted, that VU would become a prep school for pastors, that chapel would become compulsory, and that the music and pharmacy programs would be closed. None of these rumors was true, Dau said, and people should wait to see the proof of their falsehood. But he suggested that "antagonistic elements" within the University were behind these rumors.

Whatever the realities, Dau's tone suggested that he was reacting poorly to the pressures of the job. Toward the end of the academic year, it had become clear to many that Dau could not function as president. Ralph Richman, chairman of the board's Committee on Instruction, complained to Baur that they could not get Dau to act on faculty appointments. Dau himself was increasingly frustrated and exhausted. He requested a leave of absence for the summer, and the board agreed. Professor Albert Germann of the chemistry department was named acting president for the summer. At the end of the summer, Dau reported himself to be in deep depression, and the board, therefore, insisted that he extend his leave for a full year. Germann decided to return to industry, so John Baur again became acting president for the year 1927–28.

Despite this distressing turn of events for the fledgling Lutheran administration, its leaders were determined to pursue their goals of enhancing the academic standing of their new enterprise. For two years, the demands of the accreditation process dominated university life. A board consultant, Dr. Floyd Reeves of the University of Kentucky, thought the University had made the right initial moves and could be ready for a North Central visit by the spring of 1929. That became the goal.

The board worked hard. The Committee on Instruction—consisting of Ralph Richman of Cincinnati, Fred Wehrenberg of Fort Wayne, and the Rev. O. C. Kreinheder of Detroit—pressed the hunt for qualified Lutheran faculty. By the deadline, they had rounded up more than the required number of faculty with earned doctorates, enough so nearly every department was headed by a Ph.D. Two of the most notable new members of the faculty, Walter Thrun in chemistry and Frank Elliott in biology, were among their prize recruits. Thrun and Elliott, along with the earlier biology find, Frederick Heimlich, immediately set what became enduring high standards for Valparaiso University in the sciences.

Frederick Kroencke, newly appointed acting dean of the faculty after Heimlich's untimely death in 1928, was in charge of the academic drive for accreditation. A scholarly pastor with a doctorate from the University of Cincinnati, Kroencke quickly became a dominant figure on the faculty, known for his personal interest in his colleagues, as well as for his intellectual acumen. Students remembered Kroencke's lively classes as well. Reminisced one alumnus:

> He could quote chapter and verse from Aristotle, but he could also tell you who starred in the latest one-star movie and who pitched in what ball game. And the score. Doc Kroencke looked a little like Groucho Marx. He wore a high stiff collar and had a mustache. … I don't think Doc ever went to bed. No matter what the lateness of the hour, when we walked past his house, we could see him reading by the light of a living room floor lamp.

The consultant, Reeves, had pointed out that the law school was academically the weakest unit in the University, a casualty of the recent desperate years. There had been no money for faculty or the library. Already the Lutheran administration had moved the school from the old yellow wooden building on Greenwich Street to the Domestic Science Building (later renamed Arts-Law and eventually DeMotte Hall). With advice from a consultant and money from the Walther League, the law library was expanded to meet American Bar Association and American Association of Law Schools standards. A new dean, John Morland, was appointed to replace Milo Bowman. The school was reorganized and new courses added so when it observed its 50th anniversary in the spring of 1929, it did so freshly approved by the ABA, the equivalent of accreditation.

There also were quick efforts to improve at least somewhat the other professional programs. The College of Pharmacy, which President Dau had condemned as a mere trade school, was upgraded sufficiently to win the approval of its professional organization. Engineering and business were made departments and tucked into a newly streamlined College of Arts and Sciences. All the professional programs made a strong commitment to general education, which was expressed in several broad introductory courses.

As this rapid turnaround was achieved in the academic realm, the board turned its attention to the depleted endowment. Accreditation, and the future of the Lutheran university, depended on securing sufficient endowment immediately. Karl Henrichs from Fort Wayne joined the University staff and began his legendary career as a fund-raiser for the institution. The pressure to garner dollars was severe. Baur slept on a cot on the third floor of the administration building, his every waking moment given to finding funds. Despite his condition, President Dau also pitched in effectively. He spent much of his yearlong leave traveling across the country as far as California, speaking on behalf of the University and making friends among pastors and potential donors. When he resumed his on-campus duties as president in the fall of 1928, Dau continued to do his part in promoting the campaign.

Members of the board also worked tirelessly. Unpaid pledges from the 1925 campaign were followed up, as were similar promises from the Valparaiso Chamber of Commerce. Frantic appeals to friends of VU around the country brought the total to more than $300,000 by the deadline. To this was added what the North Central Association considered a permissible "theoretical endowment," which represented the annual gifts the University could reasonably expect to receive from its supporters. Taken together, the sum was enough. To be sure, as the accreditors noted, some of the endowment seemed shaky. One-third of it came from Lutherland Corporation bonds given by Henry Dahlen, a member of the board. A dynamic New York businessman and developer of a resort for Lutherans in the Pocono Mountains, Dahlen had placed these bonds in the endowment without formal condition but with an unwritten understanding that if his business experienced some future emergency, the University might have to replace the bonds with other funds. This was a real string, as the Depression was to prove, but in 1929, the bonds helped achieve the endowment goal.

On March 13, 1929, word reached Valparaiso that the North Central Association had granted full accreditation, touching off enthusiastic celebrations on campus and in town. Themes of university-community pride and accomplishment sounded forth at a celebratory dinner at Altruria Hall. The *Vidette* printed the letters of congratulation that came in from universities across the nation, beginning with the University of Chicago. The commitment of the LUA founders had paid off. In a few short years, the Lutherans had brought a venerable but stricken university back to academic respectability. The treasurer of the board, the genial Fort Wayne candy manufacturer W. C. Dickmeyer, promised that "the Lutheran people will not be satisfied with anything less than the building of Valparaiso University to a place where it will be acknowledged as one of the dozen distinctive educational foundations of the nation."

The board was looking to move toward that greater future. In the North Central Association self-study, John Baur projected an enrollment of 1,000 students in the near future. They were committed to building a new gymnasium. There was talk of a new endowment drive, and of constructing a new library.

The 1928–29 academic year also had turned out to be a positive one for the University, including President Dau. In his first speech in the fall, he expressed his joy at returning to the helm, contrasting the University's situation with its beginnings two years earlier. One reason for his happiness was the presence of two deans on whom he could rely. Dean of Students Henry Kumnick, a friendly pastor from Montana who also had a law degree, managed student affairs in addition to leading the chapel and teaching religion. Highly popular with students, Kumnick soon became a genuine campus character. At the same time, Kroencke had become Dau's strong right arm in the academic sphere.

The focus on the accreditation had been a good tonic for Dau, and its achievement ended the year on a high note. Throughout that celebratory evening in Altruria Hall, he was gracious and jovial to everyone. Nevertheless, he already had made the decision to resign. From his point of view, the president's office was still a place of constant interruptions and far too many decisions. Furthermore, Dau still found himself coming into frequent conflict with Baur. Dau and others wisely recognized that it was time for a change.

6

Holding On in Hard Times

Great Expectations

The high hopes generated by accreditation and an enrollment jump of 200 freshman students in the fall of 1929 assumed the continuation of postwar prosperity. Even after the Wall Street crash in October, many thought that the rebound to "normalcy" would be rapid. Instead came the harrowing years of the Great Depression, in which widespread poverty and social anguish left their mark on many institutions. Valparaiso University was no exception. The grand aspirations of VU's Lutheran founders languished. Yet the small university held on, serving its students as best it could while struggling to survive.

In 1929, still feeling the glow of accreditation and national prosperity, the VU board appointed an executive committee to set the agenda for the University and plan the next steps. The immediate goals were to replace the old gymnasium (which had burned in 1927) and create an endowment equal to their dreams. After a false start with a fund-raising firm, the board again approached Otto Pannkoke, who was between campaigns at other colleges. The board also attempted to approach the numerous alumni of the old school for help. This effort proved to be a fruitless disappointment. The break with the past created by the Lutheran takeover was too great, and with a few notable exceptions such as Lowell Thomas, support from graduates of "the old VU" was not forthcoming.

After digesting this bad news at the October 1929 board meeting, John Misch of Detroit proposed a brand-new campaign. He pledged $5,000 if other board members would match it. Henry Neils of Minneapolis pledged the same amount and added another $5,000 from friends. Misch matched the second offer. One by one, other board members—Nolde, Eberline, Boeger, Rohrman, and Hackstedde—made similar pledges. The two clergy members, Baur and Kreinheder, also chipped in, and the resulting handsome total of $80,000 became the first step in the new campaign.

Pannkoke next proposed a massive effort to raise the kind of endowment needed for a bright future. The board agreed, and set its sights at raising $2.25 million over five years. Using the tactic that had worked so effectively in 1925, Pannkoke invited leading clergy and laity to a remarkable November promotional weekend at Valparaiso to hear about "the greatest achievement in the history of Lutheran higher education." This was an exaggerated claim, of course. Besides the Missouri-owned Concordias, the other Lutheran bodies of various ethnic backgrounds had by the 1920s established about two dozen schools across the country, some of them fine liberal arts colleges. Yet it was quite true that there was nothing on the Lutheran scene quite like Valparaiso. VU was already the fifth largest Lutheran educational institution in the country, its academic offerings were the most diverse, and its founders had visions of creating a national Lutheran university with a variety of programs. The enrollment had risen sharply on the news of accreditation. Projections were for a student body of at least 1,250. But first, the VU leaders declared, the enterprise needed undergirding. It was time for that distinctly Christian move, "going the second mile." So went the speeches and, afterward, the campaign literature.

Shortly thereafter, a large mailing went out, written in Pannkoke's forceful style. It declared a five-year program to raise $225,000 for a gymnasium adequate for 1,500 students and an endowment fund of more than $2 million, which would include scholarships for "deserving and honor students." This was an enormous sum for the time, the equivalent of about $25 million in year 2000 dollars. Appealing to Missouri Synod pride, and evoking competition with other Lutheran synods, Pannkoke wrote that the other Lutheran bodies were convinced "that the most important place in maintaining the vigor of their Church lies in strong, high standing colleges." He pointed out their high levels of financial support.

As the publicity and appeals went out, complaints streamed in to the Synod's board of directors. At a hurriedly called meeting between representatives of the synodical board, including President Pfotenhauer, and Valparaiso University's board, numerous complaints were aired: unauthorized fund-raising, exaggerated claims of achievement, questionable Lutheran character, and draining money from the Synod. The meeting ended in an agreement to disagree on a number of points, together with the assurance from the synodical leadership that it would not oppose the move openly because it already was too far advanced. More constructively, both sides indicated they would consider setting up an "advisory committee" as a permanent channel of communication. Yet the cool atmosphere and lack of synodical support were palpable.

Besides fund-raising, complicated by church difficulties, the board had to select a replacement for Dau. After outlining its criteria for the presidency, it developed a short list that included two academics—Walter Bauer from the University's own faculty and Walter A. Maier, a fresh Harvard Ph.D. with a growing national reputation—and two prominent pastors—Paul Miller of Fort Wayne and Paul Lindemann of St. Paul, Minnesota. The nominating committee had nearly settled on the popular and energetic Maier when sentiment suddenly developed for the committee's own chairman, O. C. Kreinheder. Kreinheder was selected by the whole board and named the second president of VU in April 1930.

Kreinheder met few of the board's original criteria, especially the academic ones. The pastor of the large Christ Lutheran Church in Detroit, he had been president of the English District from 1918 until 1928 and was one of the earliest and most enthusiastic members of the LUA. His whole career had been in the ministry, first in East St. Louis, then in St. Paul and Detroit. But Kreinheder impressed the board with his quick practical intelligence, direct approach to problems, and keen-eyed, businesslike style. He consulted freely and easily, spoke plain midwestern English with no German accent (unlike Dau), and could build bridges to the church at a time when that seemed important to VU.

The inaugural activities were held on a warm fall afternoon, October 24, 1930, before a crowd of 1,500 in the auditorium. In his inaugural address, Kreinheder stated his simple, succinct vision of Valparaiso's mission:

> To offer college-going young men and women, especially those from our own household of faith, an opportunity for acquiring a higher education, whether it be for its cultural value, or as a preparation for a vocation in life, in a Christian environment and under positive Christian influences.

The week-long inauguration festivities defied the background of the growing Depression. So did that year's enrollment increase to 563 (62 percent Lutheran) and the knowledge that supporters had thus far pledged more than $862,000 to the VU campaign, of which $112,000 was in cash.

CONFRONTING HARD TIMES

Kreinheder was manifestly not an academic person. But he understood the centrality of academics to the University's life and future. He personally searched for the best faculty talent available and made plans to strengthen existing fields and even to launch new ones. But as the severity and duration of the national economic collapse became evident, it became harder to follow through on these goals.

The board already had mandated the creation of a new College of Engineering. It was launched with much excitement at a celebratory dinner in March 1931, which included a telegram of congratulations from President—and former engineer—Herbert Hoover. Dean Howard Moody and a student body of 101 students took their places in the University in the fall of 1931. The ambitious college offered six programs: civil, mechanical, electrical, chemical, industrial, and commercial engineering. That same fall the law school celebrated its final approval by the American Association of Law Schools. In addition, the law faculty was substantially strengthened by the addition of Marshall Jox, a graduate of the University of Chicago, who would become a notable academic leader in the wider Valparaiso University.

To bolster the humanities, Kreinheder recruited Walter G. Friedrich, a Johns Hopkins Ph.D. then teaching at the University of Pittsburgh, to head the English department. The English department also gained Herbert Umbach, a Concordia Seminary graduate with a Cornell doctorate who was a scholar of John Donne's poetry. Umbach and Friedrich, along with Walter Bauer in history and Walther Miller in foreign languages, each served the University for more than four decades, providing the core of VU's humanities faculty for many years.

The more talented young faculty tried to develop an earnest intellectual atmosphere on the campus, even amid the severe hardships of the Depression. Faculty meetings from those years reveal a strong concern for raising the academic quality of the institution. At the end of routine business, faculty members such as Richard Bauer, Alfred Meyer, and Walter Thrun would present papers on such matters as the exciting reforms going on at Robert Hutchins's University of Chicago, methods of improving teaching, or ways to enhance the University's academic reputation through research. Informal groups such as the Friday Faculty Forum met for further discussion of substantive matters.

The hard times of the 1930s bonded the small VU faculty and their families together, creating a strong sense of shared hardship and community. Salary cuts were common, as at many colleges. During one year, money was so scarce at Valparaiso that one 10 percent cut was followed by another, followed by a 25 percent cut of the remainder. Several times the University's budget was "balanced" only with a note indicating the thousands of dollars owed the faculty. Somehow they survived without the experience of the most painful poverty that the unemployed felt. Many faculty members took in student boarders to help make ends meet.

The Depression invigorated the social sciences in American academic life, and at Valparaiso, three young faculty members especially represented this ferment. With a fervent, single-minded energy, Alfred H. Meyer recruited student disciples who came to believe that cultural geography held the secret to understanding contemporary affairs. The two Cornell-educated history professors, Ernest Schwiebert and Walter Bauer, competed with Meyer for student interest. While different in their approaches, both presented history as a lively subject pertinent to current world events.

Like most of the country in 1933, people at VU hoped that the newly inaugurated President Franklin Roosevelt might do something, anything, to alleviate the Depression. Soon after Roosevelt's "Hundred Days," the faculty formed a Washington Committee under the leadership of Schwiebert to, as a *Torch* reporter put it, "help formulate policies." Just what policies this group intended to formulate was not clear, but the faculty did debate and sign a letter to Roosevelt, authored by the committee, praising the President for his initiatives. About the same time, the University also offered Community Forums that analyzed the crisis.

As a renewal of warfare in Europe began to appear more likely, Schwiebert also formed an International Relations Club that conducted discussions and invited various speakers to the campus. Chicago-based representatives of the governments of Japan, Germany, Poland, and China appeared for presentations presided over by Professor Albert Wehling, a young, debonair, liberal lawyer who recently had been appointed to the faculty.

A LUTHERAN PHILOSOPHY OF HIGHER EDUCATION?

While stimulating intellectual life and debating current affairs was important to many faculty on the campus, most Lutheran parents of the time looked to a Lutheran university as a place where their sons and daughters could get a good education in a religion-friendly setting. The appointment of vibrant young faculty, both Lutheran and non-Lutheran, enhanced that goal. For the ghetto-minded among the clergy, however, there could not be a Lutheran university without a completely Lutheran faculty and student body, as in the colleges and seminaries the Missouri Synod had created for educating teachers and pastors.

For the Valparaiso movement, this was neither possible nor desirable. In his final report to the board in 1929, President Dau had written that Lutheran identity was not a matter of quantity, but of quality. The key, Dau said, would be the gathering of exemplary Lutheran faculty and students. He also warned that the University should beware of attracting faculty or students who were nominally Lutheran but of dubious character. From the beginning of the Lutheran ownership, VU attracted and kept talented non-Lutheran faculty. Among the notable faculty from other backgrounds were Professor Hazel Guillamant (French) and Professor Edmund Chaffee (music). In the 1930s, approximately 60 percent of the faculty were Lutheran.

If an all-Lutheran faculty was not the way to be a Lutheran university, what was? Many of the strong religious models then available in the American environment were not helpful to Lutherans facing this issue. The Bible college movement, with its fundamentalist support and narrow style, had little appeal for Lutherans, and the general focus of evangelicals on immediate religious experience clashed with the mediations that comprised the Lutheran tradition: sacraments, education, liturgy, sermonic exposition of Scripture, and various expressions of doctrine, music, and visual piety. A coherent creedal structure underlay all these practices, assuring stability, coherence, and the possibility of a relevant argument with a changing world.

Yet the issue of how to translate the Lutheran outlook into the world of higher education was by no means clear. One first step seemed to be the direct teaching of religion. Already at its meeting in April 1926, the LUA had passed a resolution stating that

> Whereas the LUA has purchased the Valparaiso University for the purpose of converting it into a school of higher education to meet the exacting Lutheran educational ideal, therefore be it resolved that a chair of religion or of Christianity or of the Bible be established and endowed.

Although enough money did not become available for that chair, plans for a Department of Religion unfolded. The new department, created in

1929, was first called "Religion and Philosophy" and staffed by Kroencke and Kumnick. Its stated purpose was to "prepare the student for general lay leadership, or for such positions as institutional secretary." Initially, religion courses were optional electives. In 1930, a single-course religion requirement was instituted, then raised to two courses the following year. But the projected major disappeared amid the general belt-tightening.

Besides formal curricula, many of the VU faculty paid close attention to religious matters in all sorts of ways, and they helped stir similar concerns in students. Deeply interested in the affairs of the church, they regularly commented on religious and educational issues and spoke at conferences of pastors and teachers on matters of current concern. At the summer VU pastors' institutes that became a standard feature of campus life throughout the 1930s, faculty applied their expertise to topics of interest to the clergy. If practice indicates belief, then it was the general campus culture, and the strong sense of vocation among faculty and administration, more than any specific kind of academic work, that indicated the Lutherans' view of how to develop VU as a Lutheran institution.

In the 1920s and 1930s, the most visible intellectual issue for many religiously traditional church colleges was evolution. The course on evolution disappeared from the catalog when the Lutherans remodeled the University, and President Dau checked the books used on the campus for signs of this controversial theory. He reported that there was no "objectionable" textbook in use except for one in geology. But he believed that the "skill and piety" of the professor would adequately deal with whatever issues arose in this regard.

Little did Dau know that the instructor, Alfred H. Meyer, had long been in heartrending agony over this issue. As an undergraduate geology major at the University of Illinois, Meyer had aspired to an academic career in this field. Because his religious faith clashed with evolution, he decided to enter some practical branch of the discipline, such as oil geology. But as he was finishing his master's degree, Meyer plunged into a severe intellectual crisis. He even considered destroying his thesis because he had come to believe that the mere use of a term such as "biological development" was sinful.

Meyer wrote of his crisis of conscience to Missouri Synod theologian Theodore Graebner, whom he knew had written on such questions: "I want to get as far away from heretical ideas as I can and endeavor to be true to 100% Missouri Lutheranism. ... If I could but only recall my past mistakes." Graebner, a battle-hardened journalistic warrior on this issue, stated his view clearly in a letter to a Chicago pastor:

> Your young man must keep his geology and his Genesis in two compartments with a water-tight bulkhead between. He must not deny evident facts which are disclosed by the earth's layers and he must not give up his faith in the Bible because he cannot harmonize historical geology with the record in Genesis. It may be said that such contradictions imply an either or but experience proves that we get along with others of the same nature right in the field of science and they don't trouble us. Nothing can be more contradictory than the theory which makes light composed of waves and the other theory which deals in quanta, or small particles. Light cannot be both yet IT IS.

Graebner's approach was not entirely satisfactory. Meyer really wanted a "unitary view," a way of reconciling the claims of both theology and geology and creating some "religio-scientific synthesis." But he worked with the "double truth" approach and regularly used it to rebuke fellow Lutherans who did not take scientific claims seriously enough. Meyer's more personal solution to his crisis was to switch to geography, doing his doctorate in that field at the University of Michigan and proceeding to a distinguished, nationally recognized career at Valparaiso.

Something like this double-truth approach became paradigmatic for many VU faculty members. Trained at the best American universities in secular methodologies, the social scientists did not seek to discover the "hand of God" in major events. The humanities faculty did not, in the main, turn literature into edifying exercises. The scientists did not shape their inquiries toward religious outcomes. The Lutheran faculty at VU thus established a tradition of secularity congenial to Lutheranism, which became simultaneously a strength and a problem.

Such a tradition was a strength because it let the various cultural domains of the world be themselves, open to investigation by the best academic minds, requiring rigor and intellectual excellence. This seemed consistent with some versions of the Lutheran belief that in the everyday world God works through ordinary processes and institutions. It was a problem because the assumptions and worldviews behind various academic methodologies rarely were discussed and brought into a creative relationship with the larger Christian story.

Furthermore, except for its commitment to historic liberal education with its holistic implications, there was little evidence that the early Valparaiso faculty worried much about developing any specifically

Christian philosophy of education. This relative lack of attention to the assumptions of their enterprise stands in striking contrast to the approach of the other historic religious traditions that also were making strides into higher education during this period.

Within U.S. Catholicism, leading educators in the 1920s and 1930s emphasized the distinctive nature and purpose of Catholic education. Integrated by the renewed Thomistic philosophy that ordered every branch of knowledge, leading Catholic academics promoted Catholic art and literature, new social and lay initiatives, and the fledgling liturgical movement. These developments reached deeply into the souls and lives of thoughtful Catholics, and there was eager talk of building a Catholic culture. Among the Reformed, too, various sorts of "neo-Calvinism" created strong foundations for a "Christian worldview" that both justified and pervaded collegiate education at places such as Calvin College and reached out into other areas of life.

These concerns were heightened by the move of the major research universities, and even many of the mainstream Protestant liberal arts colleges, away from any serious connections with historic Christianity. The vast majority of elite private and state institutions, though sometimes still displaying in their official rhetoric some of the language of liberal Protestantism, were rapidly moving away even from such thin institutional gestures during the 1930s. The publication of Harvard's influential report on general education (known as the "Red Book") in 1945 signaled the ascendancy of a plainly secular liberal program for collegiate culture in much of the American academic domain.

Resisting such trends, conservative evangelical Protestants created more than 70 Bible schools in the period 1918–45, along with many small colleges that preserved old-time approaches to education, especially in the realm of behavior. These institutions often struggled financially, and with a few notable exceptions, such as Wheaton College in Illinois, had little intellectual vitality.

Lutherans, still for the most part linked to their immigrant origins and outlooks, had their own strong traditions and practices of education, but they were slow to articulate what they might mean in the modern American context or to develop any theoretical account of what they did. As a step in that direction, the Board for Higher Education of the Norwegian Lutheran Church asked Otto Pannkoke to lead scholars and presidents of that body's colleges in two substantial summer workshops, which were held at the University of Chicago in 1933 and at the University of Minnesota in 1935. The result was the first major attempt to enunciate a Lutheran approach to higher education on the American scene, including the outline of a proposed Christian approach to general education. Rejecting the regnant pragmatic view of education as training for success in society, the Lutheran academics focused on "integration" as a key term for their approach. The relationship of the student to God through Christ integrated one's personality into a dynamic being, living by faith, equipped with an integrated worldview that would enable the individual to be critical of a secularized world while understanding that that this world is "the theater of the Living God."

The two resulting monographs produced by the Norwegian Church's commission became the basis for discussion among a number of Lutheran colleges beyond that body. It also led eventually to the establishment of the Association of Lutheran College Faculties, which held periodic gatherings that addressed these broad concerns. Valparaiso, unfortunately, did not enter these discussions until the late 1940s.

SEEKING SUPPORT: ENTER THE WOMEN

One of Valparaiso's strengths from the beginning was its willingness to engage with wider American society. In the 1930s, many Missouri Synod leaders still pleaded for separatism among their people, warning against even friendship with "outsiders." But assimilation to American society was a powerful force. "Be ye separate!"—a favorite biblical admonition in synodical circles—was simply not working. In the 1930s, hard times and some recognition that newer approaches were needed led to some areas of cooperation between VU and the Synod.

One opportunity for working with other laity and church leaders came through attempts to help fund the *Lutheran Hour*, a lay-sponsored radio program that began broadcasting in October 1930. VU cooperated with the Lutheran Laymen's League in a campaign to keep the program on the air, winning many friends in the process. But the Depression badly hampered fund-raising, and the *Lutheran Hour* was forced off the air for three-and-a-half years.

VU's own fund-raising campaign soon fell into equal disarray. Initiating a major fund drive in November 1929 had proved to be a case of bad timing, to put it mildly. Big donors suffering financial reverses could not pay off their pledges, and gifts from ordinary Lutheran friends of VU virtually dried up. The major campaign launched with such ambition and confidence was also costly to run, and in the Depression climate, receipts did not begin to justify such outlays. Virtually all the money collected for the gymnasium and endowment was soon exhausted in paying existing debts and campaign costs. The campaign's failure became evident, and Kreinheder had to announce that balancing the annual budget was the top priority.

As the University tried to mend fences with the leadership of the Synod, President Pfotenhauer for the first time set foot on the campus in fall 1931 for a meeting of the LUA. Thereafter, a "Christian Education Sunday" was proclaimed by the Synod for November, which became the annual "Valparaiso Sunday" that permitted the University to appeal to cooperating congregations through an annual collection.

As it became evident that simple LUA memberships and giving from church members could not support a university, Pannkoke sought other forms of support. The University was well-connected to the Lutheran Laymen's League and the Walther League, but unfortunately the LLL declined into little more than a national dartball league until it recovered programmatic inspiration in the renewed *Lutheran Hour* at mid-decade. The Walther League provided a vigorous natural support group for Valparaiso, and its publication frequently featured the University, but it was more helpful in providing students than funds. VU did create a National Advisory Board of about 70 prominent men, but the board never developed a clear sense of purpose, and fund-raising alone was not enough to sustain the group.

The most innovative constituency the University developed in the 1930s was women. While U.S. women had won suffrage in 1920, Missouri Synod Lutheran women were still banned from voting in their own congregations. Nevertheless, the growing autonomy of women in American life inspired Missouri Synod women, too, to seek greater means to support the church and exercise their own abilities. Unlike their Protestant and Catholic counterparts, Missouri Synod women did not have large or national evangelical causes to which they could devote themselves. Congregationally sanctioned "ladies' aids" provided some space for women to act independently, and in urban areas, women's auxiliaries developed in connection with charitable institutions; but these groups operated under many restrictions. Thus, there was an enormous reservoir of female talent and energy seeking ways to be used.

In the late 1920s, a number of bold women in St. Louis and elsewhere designed a National League for Women as a parallel organization to the Lutheran Laymen's League. At the last minute, however, when the group's first national organizational gathering was about to be held in the fall of 1930, authorities in the Missouri Synod effectively quashed it by claiming that the Synod was getting so over-organized that pastors could no longer keep up with the proliferation without harming their ministries.

Several months later, in April 1931, Mrs. Adelaide Kreinheder and Mrs. Hannah Eberline invited 25 prominent Lutheran women to meet jointly with the Valparaiso University board and the newly organized National Advisory Board. Determined to form a "National Women's Committee," this group elected as their president Mrs. E. W. Schultz of Sheboygan, Wisconsin, an outspoken leader in the failed attempt to organize Missouri Synod women. Lily Fedder of Hammond, Indiana, was chosen secretary.

By the fall of 1931, this National Women's Committee had 86 members and was sponsoring Valparaiso University benefit events, hosting parties for prospective students, and drumming up general support. Members in Fort Wayne, Detroit, and Appleton, Wisconsin, formed the first three local chapters of the organization. By the end of the decade, there were more than 40 chapters.

Toward the end of 1931, representatives from the Valparaiso-centered group approached women in St. Louis, proposing that they start a chapter to support the University. "This was the spark that rekindled the flames of enthusiasm among the women," wrote Ruth Fritz Meyer in her history of the Lutheran Women's Missionary League. The women of St. Louis approached the Pastoral Conference of St. Louis, seeking approval to organize their own local organization with VU as one of its projects. Caught off guard and expressing surprise that Valparaiso could "go national," the pastors approved the request. The Lutheran Women's League, as the group called themselves, then maneuvered around the authorities by accepting members from beyond St. Louis, thus becoming a separate national organization. Eventually taking the name Lutheran Women's Missionary League, this, together with several other groups, became the major association of Missouri Synod women. Despite this organizational divergence, Valparaiso continued to occupy a special place in the activities of the St. Louis women's organization, which helped make the city a stronghold of VU support.

Meanwhile, the original Valparaiso National Women's Committee continued its own activities in support of the University. In 1932, the committee developed its first fund-raising project to raise the $5,000 needed for the physical education and home economics departments, plus a smaller project for Altruria Hall. In 1933, the committee changed its name to the Women's Auxiliary of the Lutheran University Association. In 1937, the name was changed again to the Valparaiso University Guild. This energetic group soon touched the campus in numerous ways, from planting evergreens to giving the library the *Variorum Edition* of Shakespeare. Most important, perhaps, the Guild created a national constituency that identified VU as the place where bright young Lutherans, especially women, could find an education.

The University *Bulletin* always featured the various activities of this group under the cut of the "The Pioneer Woman" statue, beloved of American feminists, at Ponca City, Oklahoma. Many Lutherans remembered their mothers knitting and sewing for the cause of Valpo, stimulated by Guild appeals that reached to the congregational ladies' aid societies. No other Lutheran educational institution had anything like the Guild. University-related projects fired its imagination and dedication, as did a sense of autonomy.

In the depths of the Depression and amid accumulating deficits, the University celebrated its 10th anniversary as a Lutheran institution on commencement weekend in June 1935. Despite the scarcity of funds, Karl Henrichs persuaded a number of VU friends to purchase adjacent parcels of land at rock-bottom prices, filling out the campus area south of the auditorium. Students pulled out the bricks and put in dirt, grass, and shrubbery, creating what they called University Park.

In the weekend ceremonies, the new Walther League executive secretary, O. P. Kretzmann, addressed the seniors at a banquet before they were received into the year-old Alumni Association, which was headed by Leonard Schramm (1931). A 10-ton granite rock from a local farm had been hauled onto the campus, and it was unveiled and dedicated as "Founders Rock." The bronze plaque affixed to it said: "To the Glory of God and in recognition of the faith and vision of the men and women who organized The Lutheran University Association in 1925 and fostered Christian Higher Education at Valparaiso University." President Kreinheder composed a hymn text for the anniversary set to a familiar tune and also, according to the program, a new school song, "Hail to the Brown and Gold."

Four to five thousand people gathered on Sunday afternoon in University Park near Founders Rock for commencement ceremonies. Honorary degrees were awarded to LUA secretary Paul Miller and organist Edward Rechlin. Dr. Walter A. Maier rose to give the commencement address when, as one alumnus remembered, "there came a frog-strangling, gully-washing downpour and the commencement exercises were over. We grabbed a diploma out of the box on the stage and headed for the Arts-Law building where we sorted them out."

DEPRESSION DEVELOPMENTS

Despite such bright moments, VU's financial situation was becoming increasingly dire. The Dahlen bonds, which had been crucial for accreditation, now became a point of dispute when his New York business interests deteriorated. Partly as a result of this conflict, John Baur decided to resign. At the same time, Otto Pannkoke, Baur's close friend and another central figure in the founding of VU, threatened to sue the University in a dispute over fees he felt he was owed. These disputes eventually were resolved amicably, but not without taking a human toll.

Amid the hard times, something of a rapprochement between VU and the Synod began. In the triennial synodical convention in the summer of 1935, the Synod passed a resolution of support for "our university." The University began to make more direct assertions of its importance to the church and to make direct appeals to congregations. The promotional material sent to pastors was blunt: We laymen have given you your education and have built a magnificent seminary. It is time you vigorously support the University as a layman's cause.

Despite the attempt to develop closer ties, or perhaps because of it, jousting continued between Valparaiso's board and the synodical authorities during the 1930s. The focal and symbolic issue for the church was dancing, on which no compromise seemed possible. "Dancing is a sin per se," declared members of a synodical committee led by the new president John W. Behnken. Today, the passions and energy that went into the dancing issue are difficult to understand. When modern popular dances first swept the nation in the teens and 1920s, conservative religious figures from many backgrounds took the lead in declaring them an assault on inherited morality. But through the years, young people clearly took up dancing, and in the Lutheran Church, many pastors, after initial opposition, simply stopped preaching against it. Although some progressive pastors flirted with sponsoring dances in church halls, official Missouri Synod publications continued to denounce dancing. At VU, officials checked with a dozen urban Missouri Synod pastors, and 11 of 12 had no objections to the University's practice. Even President Emeritus Dau changed his views by finding support in Luther for traditional German dancing, after his own conversations with students testified to the innocence of their pleasure in the pastime.

The University's practice had been not to sponsor dances officially on campus, but to chaperone them elsewhere. After increasing pressure from the Synod, and from some students' pastors, the policy changed. The board reluctantly agreed to ban dancing, but first it pleaded for time in which to "educate" students. This foot-dragging ended in 1938 when Kreinheder officially announced the ban at the end of the school year, doubtless hoping that the prospect of a new gymnasium in the immediate future would offset the groans of dismay from the dwindling student body.

Because most students had learned to dance in high school, they managed to find ways to continue to do so even after the ban. Alumni and other friends would sponsor dances for VU students at off-campus locations, allowing the administration to wash its hands of public responsibility, a mild form of hypocrisy not unfamiliar to colleges. Each fraternity and sorority also sponsored a formal dance each semester, to which others were invited. Except during Lent, there was a continuing round of enjoyable dances at VU, which for many students constituted an important part of their social lives.

Besides dancing, other fondly remembered pleasures of the time were the rituals surrounding "Student Bridge." The custom of kissing on the bridge at midnight while a train (hopefully a long one) rumbled through underneath was one of those traditions passed from student generation to generation.

Drinking alcohol was also part of the student culture inherited by the new Lutheran student body, though Prohibition had been part of the U.S. Constitution since 1919. Most German Lutheran students came from a culture where drinking was accepted. The official administrative line was that, of course, the law must be obeyed, though they, like most Lutherans, opposed it. Students at Valparaiso soon discovered the farms that brewed beer and the local speakeasies as well. Some fraternities even made their own bathtub gin.

The issues surrounding Prohibition were not without their complications, as one dramatic incident reveals. In the fall of 1931, students in Lembke Hall noticed that two somewhat older students in the dorm had become extremely popular. They owned one of the two cars on campus that year and had plenty of money to spend as well. They frequently invited other students to take them around to the speakeasies in Valparaiso and its environs to the point that by homecoming a few students had become suspicious.

The pair did not return after Christmas vacation. Then, on January 7, 1932, readers of the *Chicago Herald* opened their papers to read headlines about federal raids on illegal liquor establishments in Valparaiso, Indiana! The story claimed that the University had collaborated with federal agents posing as students, who had induced real VU students to map out all the illegal establishments in the vicinity.

President Kreinheder indignantly denied the reports of such a collaboration, though he also bragged that the agents had told him that far fewer students at Valparaiso drank illegal liquor than at the "large educational establishments" around the country. The local newspapers learned that the federal agents had indeed enrolled for a few classes, one of which was Dean Kumnick's religion class. Was this episode actually the dean's own personal effort at student control, unbeknownst to others? The answer cannot be determined from the record. In any case, the raids had little effect. To no one's surprise, within 24 hours the speakeasies were back in business.

YOUNG LUTHERANS AND THE COLLEGE CULTURE

Dancing, kissing, and drinking probably would have gone on under any circumstances, but the ways in which they were carried on at Valparaiso were a result of the particular forms of its collegiate culture. Although the young Lutherans who predominated at VU by the early 1930s were by and large pious Missouri Synod members who generally accepted their church's doctrines and outlook, their life at Valpo (as they called their school) was different from what most had known in their home congregations and communities. It was of great importance to the student experience at VU that the Lutherans had taken over a secular college with a preexisting student "culture" and patterns of behavior. While some modifications were made by the Lutheran administration, the Lutheran students at VU picked up and carried on many traditions of campus life that had developed earlier, while evolving some of their own.

Freshmen who entered VU in the late 1920s and early 1930s were immediately initiated into an inherited culture by older students. *The Torch* in 1934, for example, greeted new students with messages such as these:

> There are certain rules which you are to obey until homecoming. … Obedience to these rules will be a valuable lesson in cooperation, which must be learned on our campus. If you won't learn it at any

other school, it will have to be the School of Hard Knocks. It is to be for the first time your own choice. The Sophomore Enforcement Committee.

One initiation ritual carried over from the old VU was the "Pajama Parade Night." All freshmen were paraded down Lincolnway in their pajamas and herded into the local movie theater for "command performances" of cheers and recitations. A "paddling orgy" was one person's description of what often occurred. Unhappy with the hazing associated with the event, Dean Kumnick banned Pajama Parade Night in 1935, declaring that the pajama parade was not part of the tradition of the new VU.

Even after the ban on physical hazing, freshmen were supposed to follow numerous "rules." For freshman men, these were:

1. Wear the green beanie at all times and "button" when requested by upperclassmen.
2. Wear large red earrings.
3. Keep off Student Bridge.
4. No dating.
5. Carry matches and toothpicks.
6. Carry a rag, and be prepared to dust upperclassmen's shoes.
7. Wear no letters, numerals, rings, pins, or high school insignia.

For freshman women, there were similar rules:

1. On command, give name, home residence, and reason for attending Valparaiso.
2. No laughing in the presence of upperclassmen.
3. Carry bottles with water and a nipple attached.
4. Wear green armbands at all times.
5. Learn the Victory March and make up one verse of original lyrics.
6. Be in bed five minutes after all dormitory meetings.
7. Carry pillows and suitcases and dress back-to-front one day of the week.

The wearing of the beanie and armband, accompanied by demeaning commands from sophomores, continued until homecoming. Then, before the eyes of upperclass students and alumni, the freshmen battled the sophomores in a kind of free-for-all during halftime of the football game for the "right" to end hazing. Alumnus Walt Buescher remembered his days as a freshman in 1931 on a rain-soaked field:

> We frosh honed in on four of the most obnoxious sophomores. In calf-deep mud we knocked them down and stood them up. We stuffed mud in their mouths and defrocked them. Four mud-covered naked sophomores walked off the field that day. We frosh claimed victory and no sophomore challenged the claim. Our green caps went into the waste basket.

Homecoming, which had evolved from the traditional Brown Day observed in the old college, was a major event for VU students. On Thursday evening, an enormous bonfire stack was built and "defended" all night by the freshman men against upperclass attempts to light it. Usually, the freshmen were successful. At dawn, the freshman women of Altruria would bring their weary classmates a victory breakfast.

Homecoming Friday was "Hobo Day." The hobo motif also dated from before the Lutheran arrival and remained a homecoming fixture for more than 40 years. During the first week of October, the Student Council would announce with great pomp a requirement that all men must stop shaving until homecoming, with various penalties against the "lawless," including date boycotts by the women. On mid-morning of homecoming Friday, a German band (as it came to be called under the Lutherans) of raucous musicians would lead a swelling parade from classroom to classroom, ending the classes. The gathering crowd, eventually consisting of the whole student body, would proceed downtown to the theater for a pep rally and various contests, including the hobo king and queen, the man with the best legs, etc. That night another pep rally and the lighting of the bonfire took place as a warm-up for the next day's game.

Over the decades, the Saturday morning homecoming parade became increasingly prominent. Various organizations created elaborate floats, and the Greeks competitively decorated their houses. One of the most remarkable and best remembered house decoration was erected by the Phi Psis many years later. It was a 15-foot high plywood female nude seen from the rear. The homecoming theme that year was "Hooray for Our Side!"

ATHLETICS AND COLLEGE LIFE IN THE 1930S

Another element of student-life continuity with the old VU was the strong interest in intercollegiate athletics. Men's football, basketball, and baseball were the dominant sports, though tennis and other "minor" sports also continued. Intramurals were also strong, though the burning of the gym in 1927 meant that the outdoor sports necessarily became the most prominent. The University used Valparaiso High School's Boucher Gym for its indoor program.

Involvement in intercollegiate athletics was strictly a male affair, as women's intercollegiate athletics had disappeared. In the fall of 1926, *The Torch* had announced a meeting for women interested in continuing intercollegiate basketball, but nothing developed. The stifling of competitive women's athletics was in part a result of national developments. In 1923, a powerful group of female educators had announced their opposition to all intercollegiate competition for women. This precipitated a national decline in women's intercollegiate sports that was not reversed until Title IX legislation in 1972. In 1929, Valparaiso established a unit of the Women's Athletic Association, which promoted women's intramurals. But lacking a gym for more than 10 years, indoor activities were restricted. VU women did, however, play soccer and field hockey and participate in horseback riding, archery, and other outdoor sports.

In the first few years of the Lutheran administration, VU's intercollegiate teams faltered. In 1929, however, the University joined the Indiana Collegiate Conference, assuring good rivalries with a set of like-minded colleges. That same year, VU hired Jacob "Jake" Melius Christiansen, who served as athletic director and coach from 1929 to 1941. Son of a famous St. Olaf College music director and brother of another, Christiansen was the one nonmusician in this talented family, but he was equally brilliant in his own sphere. "Jake," or "Christy," coached all the sports at VU and taught the health courses for men. His basketball teams had a number of good seasons, winning the conference championships in 1932–33 and in 1937–38.

Football, though, was the glory sport during the 1930s. Christy's first season was a winless disaster, including an early 90–0 loss to John Carroll College. When those numbers were phoned back to Valparaiso, people thought it was a temperature report. Then Christy began recruiting heavily in the Calumet region, and soon names such as Kowalski, Christowski, and Gauthier stood out among the Schultzes, Luedtkes, Belzingloewens, and Berghausens at VU. The greatest football years were 1931–33 when the team compiled a 22–3 record, including 15 shutouts. The 1932 team went undefeated. Although VU offered no athletic scholarships, Christiansen was endlessly inventive in finding ways for his players to afford to attend the University. He spent his summers rounding up jobs in town for his athletes. They also washed dishes and served tables in Altruria's Hole, and some held down weekend steel mill jobs as well.

Christiansen's innovative strategies compensated for uneven talent. There were always some genuinely skilled athletes on the team, but most succeeded through hard work or intelligence. The team used deceptive shifts, and when playing defense, anything might happen. "Here comes that crazy-defense Christiansen," one alum remembers Butler coach Tony Hinkle, dean of Indiana coaches, calling out. Some believe Christiansen invented the linebacker blitz. Alums also remembered the coach's influence on everybody's life. He worked closely with his athletes, loaned them money, took them into his home, and became like a dad to them.

At first, VU teams had no nickname. Writers called them the "Brown and Gold," the "Flying Dutchmen," or the "Fighting Lutherans." In 1930, a *Vidette* sportswriter applied the label "Uhlans" in derision, but when a contest to name the team was held the next year, "Uhlans" won. The striking if mysterious name caught on in papers around the Midwest. *The Torch* explained that the Uhlans were "famous Prussian lancers (whose) dashing uniforms of blue with gold trimmings, silver helmets, magnificent horses and bannered lances were an inspiring sight. With reckless tactics and furious charges they struck terror into the hearts of their opponents." The yearbook soon changed its name from the *Record* to the *Uhlan*, and a campus hangout also adopted the name.

Despite the misgivings of President Dau and some other VU supporters, fraternities and sororities survived and even thrived with the increasingly Lutheran student body. Some of their practices were modified, and the VU Greek organizations remained "local," giving them a strong identification with the campus and keeping costs comparatively low.

Loyalty to Greek organizations was a hallmark of the era, though it did not seem to be destructive of the close bonding of the members of each class that occurred during the freshman year. There were a rather large number of fraternities and sororities for a small school, and over time, the percentage of students "going Greek" increased. Both fraternities and sororities had their own houses, though not all members lived in them.

Pledging fraternities and sororities took place each spring. Each male pledge had to acquire and carry a paddle with the names of the brothers inscribed on it. Some hazing was an accepted part of the initiation. "Hell week" and "hell night" concluded pledging. Sometimes the pledges were dropped off blindfolded at night at remote spots and forced to find their way back to campus. Female pledges might be taken to the cemeteries at night for various scary experiences or forced to scrub the courthouse steps with toothbrushes.

Some male students resented this hazing, especially when it gave license to sadism. But most VU fraternity men, and nearly all women, later looked back fondly on their Greek experience. Generally, upperclass students set a serious tone for fraternities and sororities in these years. In the fraternities, mature law students were generally in charge of the houses, and the groups vied for recognition as model organizations to which the administration might look for counsel on student life. Despite the generally successful efforts to maintain decorum, parties occasionally got out of hand.

VU students were joiners, and despite the pinched economic circumstances of the time, campus social life was highly active. *The Torch* reported one year that there were 40 organizations among a student body of 400 students, including intercollegiate debating teams. Among the most popular organizations were the many musical groups. Lutherans thought of themselves as the "singing church" with a famous musical heritage, and both instrumental and vocal ensembles flourished from the 1920s on. The touring VU choir quickly became the most popular and prestigious musical group on the campus. In 1931, the Valparaiso choir performed a Christmas concert for the University. It struck such a favorable chord with everyone that one of the most powerful and beloved Valpo traditions was born.

Early on, Karl Henrichs reminded the VU board of the tremendous impact that the St. Olaf Choir had made on the American public. As part of the fund-raising campaign, the 50-voice VU choir, under Director Frederick Schweppe, set out on its first tour in May 1930, visiting Detroit, Cleveland, Indianapolis, and Chicago. These tours became an annual highlight of the year for the choristers, who constituted about one-eighth of the student body. Schweppe took a two-year leave of absence in the mid-1930s, but the tradition resumed under Director Richard Schoenbohm in 1937. In 1939, the choir traveled for the first time by train instead of bus on a 2,500-mile tour that took them to New York, Baltimore, and Washington, D.C.

Students continued to publish both *The Torch* and the yearbook. Under Lutheran administration, *The Torch* was published with the "advice" of a faculty member, and the difference was notable. The old *Torch* that had offended John Baur truly reflected the spirit and activities of a party school of the 1920s, with full attention given to sports and an extremely active social life. Parties, dances, sexual innuendoes, and the social liberation of women observed from a dominant male point of view—often mocking women's new persona—occupied whatever space was not given to athletics. *The Torch* of the Lutheran era took on a more serious quality, exhorting students to attend cultural events and improve academics while still giving a great deal of attention to athletics. It began to sound "establishmentarian," reporting on the problems and progress of the University, faculty activities, the visits of church dignitaries, and similar matters. This sort of journalism was largely absent from the pre-Lutheran paper, which had blithely ignored VU's crises and narrow escapes from oblivion.

When the Lutherans arrived, the yearbook actually dropped out of sight for two years. There was a mysterious reference to "the turmoil of change," and plainly there were issues of control and tone. The yearbook had been a prime promoter of VU as a "party school." Soon a more sober version, with faculty advisers, reappeared.

The old Student Council also disappeared with the Lutheran takeover. When Dean Kumnick arrived, he did create a limited form of self-government in the two residences, Altruria and Lembke. Students soon appealed for a student government, and in 1929, the board authorized a Student Association. By 1930, they had a constitution and a Student Council, but at first its functions were so limited that quorums were hard to maintain. Students gradually pressed for more power over their own lives through an enhanced student government.

Although there were forums and discussions on public and international affairs, often sponsored by the faculty, politics and political organizations were largely absent at VU. There was, for example, no echo at VU of the massive "Peace Strike" of 1936, when more than 500,000 American students expressed opposition to future wars.

There was no discussion of issues involving race, either, and there were no black students. In 1925, the Reverend Andrew Schulze, a pioneering Lutheran pastor among African-Americans in St. Louis, wrote President Dau inquiring about the admission of black students. Dau at first responded affirmatively. He had immediately removed from the catalog the long-standing statement that "colored students" should not apply because there were no accommodations for them. Then he took it all back when he discovered conditions in the town of Valparaiso to be "inhospitable" to the move. Kreinheder responded in the same way in 1937 when similar inquiries were made. This rationale, or rationalization, sustained the gap between VU's religious profession and its all-white character.

Despite their active organizational and social lives, most VU students were far from affluent. As the Depression deepened, students had to bargain hard to attend college. Money became scarce at home, and most students had to work their way through college with little or no help from parents. Students worked in the dining areas, as school janitors, and in the library. Money did not exchange hands in these arrangements. Rather, students usually received in-kind subsidy in the form of room and board and sometimes in the form of tuition remission.

In 1936, Kreinheder announced that every single student application to VU had included a request for some sort of financial aid. But little actual direct aid was available for Valparaiso students. Eight endowed scholarships were established by the VU campaign at the beginning of the decade, but with the failed fund-raising, no more followed. Later the Aid Association for Lutherans, a fraternal insurance company, began a program of scholarship aid by establishing 10 scholarships. The National Youth Administration, an agency of Roosevelt's New Deal, provided some student subsidies. Although the dollar numbers were not large, these programs helped many students to attend college at VU, as they did elsewhere.

Residential life was highly structured but generally pleasant. Female students lived in Altruria Hall, while male students lived in Lembke Hall for their freshman year and moved into fraternity houses or other boardinghouses for their final three years. Altruria was the main social center on campus, and many alumni could remember its telephone number—268—even 60 years later. It housed the relatively small number of young women—never exceeding a third of the student population in the 1930s—and the University dining hall as well. Jay and Verdie Garrison (class of 1912 and 1915), a genial and much-loved couple who had managed VU dining operations since 1917, raised the quality of meals well above the usual level of college fare. Wednesday evening dinners were always special events. Men wore jackets and ties, and women wore hose and perfume. There were tablecloths, candles, and flowers.

Female students had stringent rules requiring them to be in their rooms by 8 P.M. on school nights, 11 p.m. on weekends. With permission, they could stay out until 9 P.M. on Wednesdays to go to the movies at one of the two theaters in downtown Valparaiso or to attend evening church services during Lent.

The Lutherans naturally brought new religious patterns to VU. A daily devotional worship service replaced the semi-secular "exercises" and visiting speakers that constituted "chapel" in the pre-Lutheran institution. But the Lutheran administration was increasingly embarrassed by the poor chapel attendance of the Lutheran students. Ignoring President Emeritus Dau's warnings about coercion, the board in 1934 decreed mandatory chapel attendance. The result was that chapel became a duty—a didactic experience rather than a worshipful one. But it also became a pleasant social event, as people were able to chat with one another after the services.

The faculty also were periodically admonished by the president or dean to attend chapel, which they did more or less frequently because their mail was distributed in boxes inside the chapel-auditorium building. Faculty members also occasionally led chapel services. Certain faculty members were remembered for their unusual homilies, such as Professor Thrun's annual discourse on the text "You are the salt of the earth," which included a demonstration of the chemical properties of salt.

Churchgoing on Sundays, and on Wednesday evenings during Lent, meant convoys of students walking downtown to Immanuel Lutheran Church, followed perhaps by a romantic roundabout stroll back to campus. Although weekly Sunday worship was not mandatory, attendance records show that a high percentage of the Lutheran student population did attend. Because relations with Immanuel Lutheran Church were strained by the unresolved lodge issue, which prompted Pastor Schutes to make periodic snide remarks about the University from the pulpit, students sometimes agitated for their own on-campus services instead. But when a new pastor replaced Schutes at Immanuel in the late 1930s, relations between the University and the parish improved.

When the Lutherans came, the YMCA and YWCA, as well as the Menorah Society, disappeared. The Catholic Society lingered for a time, but the number of Catholic students was too small to sustain it. A new student Lutheran Society was formed and warmly greeted by President Dau. Within a short period of time, a VU Walther League chapter replaced that organization. Through the league, students could continue the patterns of Bible study, fellowship, and service projects they had enjoyed at home.

During its first 15 years under Lutheran administration, Valparaiso University was a small, homogeneous community of young men and women who were friendly with one another and their professors. They were to some extent still Lutheran outsiders in American society. The University was a halfway house in this respect, providing security and a temporary haven from the anxieties of change while introducing students to the wider ideas and cultural outlooks most of them would encounter in their adult lives.

END OF A DECADE

By the late 1930s, many of the high hopes of 10 years before seemed far away indeed. The problems of funding were acute. Administration, faculty, and students alike struggled to make ends meet. The dream of building a great Lutheran university had become the reality of a small college of less than 500 students with few resources and little recognition. The daring and confidence of the founders had become the caution and anxiety of caretakers who saw other college ventures failing around them.

The death of Dean Frederick Kroencke in 1936, at the age of 62, was another blow. Simultaneously scholarly and pastoral, a sympathetic friend of faculty and students in times of distress, he had embodied and articulated the ideal of a Lutheran university as no one else could. His replacement as academic dean was Walter Friedrich, a Johns Hopkins Ph.D. from a well-known Lutheran family who knew the Missouri Synod well. Friedrich established himself quickly as a leader with a brusque style that could strike fear in the hearts of students and junior faculty.

Dean Friedrich's first tough task was to preside over a necessary reorganization of the University, preparatory to North Central reaccreditation. VU's enrollment, which had varied between the low 600s and the mid 400s, was again sliding downward. Difficult decisions had to be made. The venerable pharmacy program was eliminated. The fledgling College of Engineering, which had been launched with such enthusiasm in 1931, was reluctantly cut back to a basic two-year program that could be completed only by transfer to Purdue University.

In the face of the mounting difficulties, Kreinheder had one idea up his sleeve: He proposed to the Synod that pre-seminary students in the synodical junior college system come to Valparaiso University to finish their work in the liberal arts before attending Concordia Seminary in St. Louis. The Synod took no action on this suggestion, but it continued to study the situation, with the Valparaiso proposal simply one of several options. With Kreinheder's proposal becoming unlikely, talk began of moving VU to another location. These conversations again put the gymnasium project on hold.

Then slight improvements in the economy toward the end of the decade began to stop the bleeding as VU received several unexpected gifts in the $10,000 to $20,000 range. With nearly $100,000 already in the gymnasium fund, two-thirds of it in cash, the go-ahead to build was finally given in fall 1938. Building the new gymnasium was a tonic for the Depression-weary campus. Board chairman W. C. Dickmeyer turned the first shovelful of dirt on a fine October afternoon, and others followed suit while students sang VU songs. In an exuberant moment, President Kreinheder suggested that everyone join in singing "Happy Days Are Here Again." With that, the entire student body turned and marched downtown, holding up traffic in one of the first such demonstrations of collegiate spirit in the dying decade.

Authorizing the gym was Kreinheder's final significant act as president. Exhausted by bone-wearying service to the University and debilitated by his diabetes, in May 1938, he submitted his resignation to the board, who appointed Dean Friedrich, a layman, as acting president. Friedrich presided over the dedication of the new gymnasium on October 8, 1939. More than 2,500 friends and alumni gathered for the event, which included bestowing honorary degrees on former presidents Dau and Kreinheder and on Ludwig Fuerbringer, president of Concordia Seminary, St. Louis. Later that fall, the first basketball game of the season completed the dedication events. The opponent was George Keogan's Notre Dame squad, which defeated the Uhlans 63–26.

Meanwhile, the board decided to ponder more carefully the future of the University as it searched for the next president. Acting President Friedrich presented a study paper to the board at its October meeting in which he stressed the importance of liberal and general education and underscored the point that Valparaiso, while cooperating with the Missouri Synod, should remain outside the synodical education system. To build "slowly and soundly" toward these goals was his advice, envisioning "a great university rather than a large one."

Candidates for the presidency included the Rev. Alfred Rehwinkel, the progressive president of St. John's College, Winfield, Kansas; the Rev. O. P. Kretzmann, executive director of the Walther League; and Dr. Walter A. Maier, one of the most prominent figures in the Missouri Synod. There was strong sentiment also for Friedrich.

The board finally selected Walter Maier, whose dual career as seminary professor and *Lutheran Hour* speaker had made him a radio celebrity known far beyond the Lutheran Church. Maier was interested, but when he learned that he could not combine the presidency with his radio work, he declined. The board then turned to its second choice, O. P. Kretzmann.

PART III

Recreating the University (1940–70)

7

A Clear, Strong Vision

"O. P."

O. P. Kretzmann hesitated a long time before responding to the call to Valparaiso's presidency. Finally, on June 8, 1940, he sent a telegram to Chairman W. C. Dickmeyer:

> With a profound and prayerful sense of the challenge of our Lutheran university I shall … accept the call extended by the university authority. Deeply conscious of the courage and vision which has motivated the men and women who have carried our Lutheran university in their hearts and hands I pledge my full devotion to the ideals for which the University has stood for more than a decade. The passing years have emphasized the greatness of their courage and the depth of their vision. More than ever before the world of 1940 needs academic communities which will be lighthouses in our dark and anxious time. I pledge my administration to the American ideals of intellectual freedom and the Lutheran principles of spiritual obedience. It is my hope that our Lutheran university may increasingly become a meeting place of free courageous Christian minds who will approach the problems of the modern world in the fearless spirit of a church whose intellectual and spiritual traditions are long and glorious.

For 30 years, Otto Paul Kretzmann, known to everyone throughout his life as "O. P.," dominated Valparaiso University. He literally recreated the institution through the force of his personality and a cluster of ideas that he continually expounded in beguiling speeches to the University and its expanding constituencies. In his early life and career, Kretzmann had gathered many of the refreshing currents flowing in the Missouri Synod, and he channeled those movements into his work as president of Valparaiso University. More a churchman than an academician, he nevertheless drew a cadre of talented young scholars to VU, giving his vision a distinct institutional form. The fact that those ideas often ran contrary to the spirit of the times, and that he could marshal pitifully few resources to implement them, does not diminish his accomplishments.

Although born in Stamford, Connecticut, in 1901, O. P., along with his five brothers and two sisters, grew up "on the sidewalks of New York." Their father, Karl Kretzmann, was a scholarly, somewhat reserved, Lutheran pastor. To distinguish himself from nondescript Protestant ministers, he wore a clerical collar. On that account, New York cops regularly referred to him as "the Father with children." Karl Kretzmann's wife, Thekla Hueschen, was the daughter of a Lutheran pastor from Perry County, Missouri, the original Missouri Synod settlement. Where her husband was reserved, Thekla was outgoing and warm, a charming woman without airs who influenced her children through her quiet example and active encouragement.

All six of the boys—Otto, Martin, Adelbert, Edwin, Justus and Norman—became Lutheran pastors, though Edwin later pursued a diplomatic career. The two girls, Thekla and Anita, probably would have entered the ministry as well had the Lutheran Church permitted it. At the Kretzmann home, Christmas was always an especially memorable festival. The four older boys formed a quartet and sang Latin, German, and English carols in the Christmas services, for which they received a few coins from parishioners. The small change would add up, and they would then race to the neighborhood store to bargain for Christmas presents for their parents.

Living in the great metropolis of New York taught the Kretzmann children early on how to live in a multiethnic world. O. P. later remembered that world:

> Our house was surrounded by immigrants from Eastern Europe, the Balkans, and the lands about the Mediterranean Sea … . Our code of ethics was practical, though limited … . No telling a guy's mother anything when she tried to quiz you about Giusseppi Mattiani, or Moe Birnbaum, or Patrick O'Reilly. No making fun of a guy's religion unless he was a Catholic. Then an occasional jeer about incense and vestments was permitted.

O. P. always loved New York City. Later in life, he would return whenever possible to its teeming streets and waterfronts, its theaters and museums, its monuments and skyscrapers. He also loved the city's cathedrals where one could enter and for a moment imagine oneself living again in the age of Christendom. Growing up in New York made Kretzmann a truly urban and urbane person. The combination of gracefulness and wit, piety and worldliness that allowed him to be at home in every corner of the social or cultural world owed much to his cosmopolitan youth.

At the Concordia-Bronxville preparatory school, O. P. was a school leader who sang in the glee club and excelled in all sports: baseball, basketball, football, tennis. From there, he attended Concordia Seminary in St. Louis. The tall, lanky lefthander played semipro baseball to meet his expenses and tried out for the St. Louis Cardinals' organization, which offered him a contract. When his father protested against a baseball career, however, O. P. turned down the offer.

At the seminary, Kretzmann's close friends called him "John," and the nickname stuck with him throughout his life. There are two accounts of its origins. One has it based on the name of the Cardinals' star first baseman of the time, John Frank Fournier. The other is that a professor named him after the author of the fourth Gospel because he detected a similar mystical bent in the young student.

The seminary was not a particularly good experience for Kretzmann. Discipline was poor, scholarship was rare, and many of the good students quit in discouragement over these conditions or because of the "irrelevance" of their theology professors. O. P. was remembered by his classmates as a "brain," a bright student around whom the whole class would gather before tests.

O. P. spent most Christmas holidays in New York, sharing in his family's rich observance. But while at the seminary, he visited his mother's home in Perry County. His Grandfather Hueschen was pastor of a German-speaking congregation there that maintained the old custom of holding three straight days of Christmas services. As a lowly seminarian, O. P. preached on the third day to a relaxed congregation. He later recalled the event:

> If anyone is still living who sat through those efforts his longevity must be partially due to the rest and sleep he enjoyed while I struggled with Christmas and its meaning in that setting. The stove to the left of the high pulpit was a glowing pink, the heat rose straight up to the pulpit, and the deacons, comfortably stuffed with goose and sausage, rested snugly behind the stove. Only one had to stay awake to throw in an occasional shovel of coal. It was a warm, homey and somnolent occasion.

Recognizing Kretzmann's talents, the St. Louis faculty asked him to stay one more year after commencement for graduate work. Then, in a highly unusual move, the synodical authorities sent him in 1924 directly to the Synod's other Concordia Seminary at Springfield, Illinois, where he taught for 10 years.

Kretzmann's teaching assignment at Springfield was officially called "Bible and English," but in the pre-seminary division, he actually taught everything, including physics, algebra, geometry, and Latin—managing to stay three or four days ahead of the students. O. P. loved being with his students. Although custom dictated a social distance between faculty and students, he not only sat with them in church, but every afternoon, when the last class was over, he would be the first to join them on the athletic field for whatever sport the season permitted. He coached the baseball team that defeated many a good Illinois collegiate squad. There were also 7:30 A.M. sessions with students who met together to study Greek. Often he traveled to St. Louis to visit his many friends at the seminary. The word would spread that "John is coming!" and a crowd would gather for long sessions of talk, both playful and serious.

During the summers, O. P. pursued new opportunities and interests. One was academic. He enrolled in summer sessions at Columbia, Harvard, Johns Hopkins, and the University of Chicago to study English literature. He also worked at a Walther League camp in central Illinois, where admiring campers published his inspirational speeches as *The Road Back to God.* In April 1931, O. P. declined President Kreinheder's offer to teach English at Valparaiso because he had just received a year's fellowship at Johns Hopkins University to pursue his doctorate. But his academic plans were set aside when, in 1934, he entered upon a new and highly visible career as executive secretary of the Walther League.

KRETZMANN AND NEW MOVEMENTS IN LUTHERANISM

Throwing himself fully into his new role on the Missouri Synod's national stage, Kretzmann proclaimed his own version of a Rooseveltian "New Deal" for the Walther League. He backed this slogan with a set of programs and a travel schedule that put him on the road about 60,000 miles a year, speaking at rallies, conventions, and special events.

Kretzmann's remarkable speaking style had been developed through his own personal struggle to grasp the meaning and relevance of the central mystery of the Christian faith, which he came to see as God's "stepping into the stream of life" through the mingling of the divine with the human in the story of Jesus Christ. Although baffling to human reason, he came to believe that this mystery gave meaning to all human life, especially when it was embraced with childlike wonder and awe and celebrated through the arts, sacred music, and poetry. Kretzmann's preaching from this perspective came to be a kind of religious poetry, designed to evoke that same sense of mystery and wonder in his hearers, as he wove together the events and persons of ordinary life with the great events of the age, all against the background of the "Eternal," whose Word could be heard by those who had ears to hear.

While many speakers might raise their voices to make an important point, O. P. gradually would lower his tone as he approached his central message. Eventually, with his audience leaning forward and straining to catch every word, he would begin to speak of the mystery of the incarnation and the faith needed to apprehend it. Ordinary prose melted away, and the language became rich with imagery that seemed to touch many listeners deeply and personally. When Kretzmann spoke, even to an audience of a thousand, people could hear a pin drop. On less sanctified occasions, the same vivid style was punctuated by stories with funny, well-timed punch lines.

In the 1930s, the Walther League became a source of renewal for the Lutheran Church, both in the general way in which a younger generation renews and recreates any living tradition and in the specific impulses that O. P. Kretzmann imparted to the league. He divided the organization's work into two departments, Christian knowledge and Christian service. Among Lutherans, the formula "knowledge and service" was employed by energetic young leaders such as Kretzmann as a contemporary expression of the classical Lutheran slogan "faith active in love." Within Missouri Synod circles, it tried to infuse new elements of dynamism and personal growth into the traditional concern for "sound doctrine." Young Walther Leaguers and others formed by this revitalized and outward-looking Lutheran piety cultivated an unusual quality of alert Christian activism and service, and Kretzmann later drew many of them to Valparaiso University.

As his Walther League leadership demonstrated, Kretzmann was one of a relatively small number of fresh voices determined to bring the Missouri Synod out of its fortress mentality and into engagement with wider American society and with like-minded Christians. Most of these voices already were connected with movements such as the Associated Lutheran Charities, the youthful liturgical movement, the new journal named *The Cresset*, and the circle around the Rev. Paul Lindemann and *The*

American Lutheran. Kretzmann was involved in and shaped by all these movements.

The Great Depression of the 1930s formed the social backdrop that gave new urgency to these voices. In the face of diminished opportunities in the church and society at large, the new movements held out hope that the church could positively engage the world. The ALC movement took on new vitality in the 1930s as its leaders proposed ideas for reshaping church life and theology in light of the social crisis. The term "social gospel" was generally used pejoratively by Missouri Synod pastors, but within the ALC, the concept of the social meaning of the Gospel was endorsed when linked clearly to faithful "Gospel preaching" as an inescapable implication of the Gospel of salvation. Lindemann, for example, minced no words: The fact of Christ's concern for the lonely and needy "settles at least for us the question as to whether or not we have a social gospel."

O. P. Kretzmann became prominent in the ALC soon after he became the Walther League executive secretary in 1934. As a member of the board of the Wheat Ridge Sanitorium in Colorado, a Walther League agency that treated tuberculosis victims, Kretzmann had organized a Committee on Social Service. Speaking regularly at the ALC's annual conventions, his concern for reforming the social order became more specific:

> Where today is the capacity for moral anger and moral indignation over such things as our sweatshops here in Chicago, or, to be more specific, the Memorial Day Massacre outside of Chicago in 1937? Where is the moral anger over the treatment of the Jew in Germany? Over the share-cropper in Arkansas? Over the itinerant fruit-picker in California? There is sin there and it is about time somebody calls it sin.

Many of the programs that Kretzmann later developed at Valparaiso, such as the Social Work Institute and the Social Ethics Seminar, were rooted in the perspective he and other socially minded Lutheran pastors, such as Virtus Gloe and Henry Wind, had developed in the 1930s of the church, its youth, and genuine education all mutually engaged with needs of the world.

New patterns of thought and action also could be found in the tiny but growing liturgical movement represented by the Society of St. James and its journal *Pro Ecclesia Lutherana*. Many in the Missouri Synod were wary of such "Romanizing" tendencies, though the practice of the sacraments and liturgy traditionally distinguished Lutherans from many other

Protestants. The emphasis on the frequent celebration of the Lord's Supper, and of the real presence of Christ in the Sacrament, also seemed to critics to downgrade the preaching of the Word of God. But for a growing number of people, this movement recovered a fuller sense of the life of the historic Christian and Lutheran Church—its church year, its music and art, its appeal to the total person, its renewal of the laity, and its offering of a distinctive alternative to the revivalist traditions of evangelical American Protestantism. O. P. Kretzmann was deeply sympathetic to the movement. He was among the first Lutheran clergy in the Midwest to wear a clerical collar in public. His brother A. R. Kretzmann became a nationally renowned expert in the liturgical arts and architecture. Their fascination with ecclesiastical haberdashery and similar aspects of the movement was something of a joke in the family and among friends. But the piety, discipline, and love of worship, personal and communal, that the movement emphasized were serious matters for them. O. P. increasingly saw worship and meditation as central to the life of the church. Practices such as using candles for worship and prayer became a Kretzmann trademark.

In developing the realm of Christian knowledge to parallel the service activities in the Walther League, Kretzmann approached Theodore Graebner. Together, they founded, under league auspices, *The Cresset: A Review of Literature, the Arts, and Public Affairs* in 1937. In its first issue, Kretzmann set forth the purpose of the new journal:

> One of the major tragedies of the Church during the first third of the twentieth century has been the insidious departmentalizing of the individual Christian life and personality. ... *The Cresset* will devote itself to the orientation of the Christian life in relation to the world of human thought and aspiration.

When he became Valparaiso University president, Kretzmann retained the editorship of *The Cresset*. In 1952, the league officially transferred the journal to the University, where it became a vehicle of the University's intellectual work and an influence in the life of the church.

Many of the more thoughtful voices of Lutheranism were also finding their way into the pages of *The American Lutheran*, edited by Paul Lindemann in St. Paul, Minnesota, and published in New York. Along with Kretzmann, Lindemann was a forceful voice for reform in the Missouri Synod. By 1938, change was in the air in the church body. That year, the Missouri Synod convention declared that historical differences with another synod, the American Lutheran Church, were nearly resolved and that church fellowship (a close form of association) might be contemplated. The Synod also was debating the controversial and politically charged questions about its educational system—considering closing some institutions, altering pre-seminary education, or opening some of the colleges to the laity.

But in December 1938, Lindemann died. A figure admired as much outside the Missouri Synod as within, his funeral service was a notable event in the Twin Cities, packed with luminaries from all the Lutheran churches, as well as a grieving congregation. O. P. Kretzmann's funeral sermon was a dramatic and powerful oration that remained vivid in some listeners' memories 60 years later.

After Lindemann's death, a new editorial board for *The American Lutheran* came into being. O. P. Kretzmann was one of its leading members. For five years, he and several others had been meeting with "Lindy" on a regular basis, planning a major series of articles on the future of the church. The articles, which began appearing in the spring of 1939, indicate the perspective Lindemann, Kretzmann, and others had been developing on matters of the church and education. Kretzmann began by conducting a rather breathtaking survey of the state of American culture, criticizing its machine-dominated mass culture as a near-pagan purveyor of materialism and hedonism. Then he examined the positive signs of intellectual renewal in European and American Christianity, observing that modernism of various kinds were in decline and that fundamentalism and Roman Catholicism were now trying to shape the culture.

Lutheranism, Kretzmann argued, had become fully assimilated into American life, but it needed to distinguish what was central and unchanging in its message from the customs and traditions that could and should change. In the area of higher education, Lutherans needed to reduce the number of colleges for the education of the clergy and perhaps transform some of them into colleges for laity: "Cling to the principle that a few schools with high standards and hand-picked faculties and students, in accordance with the objectives of Lutheran education, are far better than a multitude of country club colleges seeking a country club enrollment." Kretzmann also asserted that a centrally located Lutheran university, eventually devoted to research, was also necessary.

It is striking that when this article appeared in March 1940, Valparaiso University was not mentioned, either as an existing "lay college" or as a candidate to become the desired Lutheran university. Kretzmann was doubtless reflecting some of the thinking of O. H. Pannkoke, who also was writing about higher education for the laity in *The American Lutheran.* Pannkoke advocated that Lutheran colleges focus on a Lutheran elite, becoming like Ivy League schools in the sense that they would educate a highly trained few for general cultural leadership.

In his article, Pannkoke did specifically discuss Valparaiso and included a set of bold ideas for enhancing its academic standing. Pannkoke asserted that he always had thought that Valparaiso, Indiana, was merely a temporary location for a leading Lutheran university and that the present VU should be relocated to River Forest, Illinois. Then Concordia Teachers College could become the College of Education of a new Lutheran university in Chicago, with all the urban advantages. Pannkoke's proposal was strongly supported by the Rev. O. A. Geiseman, the pastor of Grace Lutheran Church, River Forest, Illinois, a member of the editorial board of *The American Lutheran*, and also a member of Valparaiso University's board. Whether anyone on the VU board believed Kretzmann shared any of these sentiments when it offered him the presidency in the spring of 1940, the board's members must have known that they were not getting a shrinking violet.

"THE DESTINY OF A CHRISTIAN UNIVERSITY"

President Kretzmann's inauguration took place on Homecoming Sunday at the beginning of October. Two thousand people crammed into the new gymnasium, and representatives of 33 colleges and universities marched in robed procession. The new president's address, titled "The Destiny of a Christian University in the Modern World," was a rhetorical *tour de force* that changed attitudes and mind-sets and began the transformation of the struggling, impoverished school, at the time enrolling only 382 students, into a serious and unusual educational enterprise. It became, in effect, the intellectual charter of the modern Valparaiso University.

Beginning with the world war that already was on everyone's mind, Kretzmann conceded that it was a time when many felt the most important statements were being made by bombs and planes and guns: "We have come to the winter of the modern world, and there are few signs of spring." Nevertheless, the twofold task of the university, "the search for Truth and the transmission of Truth," must continue, even under these circumstances.

Kretzmann noted that because many Christians had reacted negatively to the threats of modernity, church-related schools often said no to modern realities and appealed to their constituencies in negative terms.

Here, they promise, your sons and daughters will be protected from the outside world. Kretzmann made it clear that this was not his vision of a Christian university. Valparaiso would be no escape from reality. It would offer everything a secular university could offer—and more. In his words: "Others may try to make men scientific; we must do that—and make them wise. Others may give men knowledge; we must give them that—and understanding. Others may try to make men useful; we must do that—and we must make them noble." There were really two battles going on in the world, Kretzmann contended. One featured guns and bombs. The other was the battle for minds and souls occurring in the quiet collegiate classrooms, libraries, and laboratories, battles over the great questions of God, church, the state, and humanity itself. "It is," he declared, "our destiny to throw ourselves into this battle."

By engaging such questions, the new president proclaimed, this small university and its graduates could have an impact on the church, the nation, and the world. Was this a practical goal? Although his address did include a seven-point plan for the development of the University, Kretzmann confessed to being suspicious of the word "practical." He said:

> If it means that we must always think in terms of compromise, in terms of financial support, in terms of our immediate material needs, then the word should be eliminated from our thinking. ... To be practical only in this sense of the word means that we shall go down in defeat. There is only one way of being permanently practical. Let the university set an ideal, a vision, a dream, if you please, for itself—and I am confident that there are still enough men and women in visible Christendom who will see the glory of the dream ... and help to make it a reality.

Turning to the students, Kretzmann emphasized their central role in the life of the University. He spoke of his "total distaste for authority predicated on vertical relations" and "his deep and consistent belief in the discipline of liberty." His peroration appealed directly to the young people's own yearnings:

> I shall join you in your impatience with all blind traditionalism; in your opposition to all sham and pretense. ... If you will leave this campus prepared to become thoughtful and intelligent citizens of a free and democratic America; sympathetic and understanding healers of a torn and broken society; great and courageous leaders of the Body of Christ in the world—then there is no power on earth that can stop Valparaiso University in the attainment of its destiny.

The speech brought down the house. The audience came to its feet and kept up a sustained applause that echoed across VU in the days and months afterward. John Strietelmeier, one of the students present for the dramatic occasion, remembered that "overnight the entire atmosphere of the campus changed."

Although the new president offered a new vision, he had no real blueprint for how to realize it. Little in his background had prepared Kretzmann for college administration. But he did have some key guiding ideas, and he was a brilliant opportunist who knew how to take advantage of situations as they developed. Many of his early statements and actions were designed to inspire confidence and drive out the defeatist attitudes that had taken up residence on College Hill.

Kretzmann's own personal style almost immediately helped alter the campus mood. The University's shrunken enrollment was contained within a small campus, effectively a couple of blocks, except for the new gymnasium and athletic fields a few blocks away. On any given day between classes, the entire student body might be seen milling about this campus, especially in fall and spring. Soon a new feature appeared on the landscape: the tall young president with a clerical collar and unruly red hair. Many students later recalled the familiar sight of students clustered around "O. P.," eagerly chatting with him.

Not far from the campus was the new president's house, which soon became something like a student union. Whenever the bachelor president was at home, students were welcome, and conversation and music were the fare. At special times, especially at Christmas, students who wandered into the house would find themselves silently listening to Bach in darkened rooms lit only with candles. During the Christmas season, too, the women of Altruria would sponsor a formal reception for the president. Lining up on the balconies overlooking the atrium, they would hold candles and sing carols. In 1942, O. P. married Flora Rosenthal, a music teacher and VU alum, but the couple's hospitality to students did not change. The birth of each of the three Kretzmann boys—John, Mark, and Stephen—became campus events.

Soon *The Torch* could report that a VU president was not simply speaking in Missouri Synod churches, but was appearing in venues such as Butler University, Northwestern University, and CBS's nationally broadcast *Church of the Air*. "This is the end of VU's isolation from the rest of the world in which we are living," wrote the proud *Torch*. Under editor John Strietelmeier, the paper expressed a willingness to trust the president in his efforts to create a revitalized social program, even with the ban on dancing. It also argued that Kretzmann's proposals for enhancing daily chapel by giving it a more devotional character should be given a chance.

NEW DIRECTIONS

Despite the immediate impact of Kretzmann's personal presence, few people had much sense of where he wanted Valparaiso to go. The "seven-point plan" he had included in his inaugural was the best clue to his thinking about directions. Briefly summarized, Kretzmann offered the following plans:

1. Interpreting the mission and message of the University to the church.
2. Building a faculty of great teachers to influence the student body.
3. Creating a system of faculty counseling to promote students' growth.
4. Extending the academic work to "metropolitan centers."
5. Developing plans for a "School of Higher Studies."
6. Supporting faculty research, especially in church-related areas.
7. Increasing enrollment.

These points reflected Kretzmann's intention to get Valparaiso and its people back to thinking in expansive terms rather than in the shrunken dimensions of the 1930s. He wanted to take tangible steps that would end the survival mentality and revive half-dead dreams of a great future for VU.

In the spring of 1941, Kretzmann proposed a five-year plan that elaborated on the seven points of his inaugural address. The centerpiece was to be a major financial effort to raise $1,025,000 for the construction of new buildings and the reduction of the debt. For these things to happen, he said, it was essential to expand the student body, improve the quality of life on the campus, and make Valparaiso University more publicly visible.

To reverse the declining enrollment, Kretzmann persuaded Fred Rechlin, a young, charming New Yorker and son of the famous Lutheran organist Edward Rechlin, to take over recruitment. Rechlin played a significant role in shaping the VU student body by also attracting a good number of non-Lutherans who appreciated the broadly Christian and tolerant viewpoint that Valparaiso came to represent. By the fall of 1941, the second year of Kretzmann's presidency, the enrollment of 480 students included more than 200 new freshmen.

Kretzmann worked in various ways to improve the quality of student life on the campus. He appointed the dynamic theater professor Vera Hahn as director of Altruria Hall. Betty Kelley Schwan remembered her frequent admonition to the young women: “We must elevate our tone.” The headmaster of Lembke Hall was Professor Albert Wehling, the most eligible bachelor on campus and a cultivated bon vivant. He regularly would invite numerous promising students into the headmaster’s apartment, where he taught them to appreciate good music from his huge collection of records. Students Alfred Looman, John Strietelmeier, Ray Scherer, William Schlender, and Ed Kurtz were among those who learned from Wehling not only the arts of listening and conversation, but also how to make and appreciate the dry martini.

To further enliven VU’s social life, Kretzmann appointed Sophia Heidbrink as director of social activities in January 1941. A former social director of the YWCA in Quincy, Illinois, “So” had become well known in the Walther League through her work in its summer camps. As VU dean of women and, later, as Kretzmann’s adviser and secretary, Heidbrink imparted to everything she did a gracious touch and a sense of distinction that became one of the hallmarks of the Kretzmann administration. Thousands of alumni remembered her personal warmth and concern.

Sophia Heidbrink, along with Walter Friedrich and business manager Albert Scribner, an alumnus of the old VU, formed the loyal inner administrative circle that Kretzmann needed. As dean of the faculty, Friedrich was the one person who could play devil’s advocate with O. P. or tell him the truth even when he didn’t want to hear it. Scribner (“Scrib”) was a shrewd and competent manager who developed a genuine affection for the new president and fully shared the dreams of a new kind of university. He usually could figure out ways to pay for Kretzmann’s ideas, even when the cupboard seemed bare. All three advisers came to know the president’s moodiness, especially those times of frustration or anger when, as someone said, “he made Vesuvius look like a slow mud-slide.” Not many saw this explosive side of Kretzmann, but a slowly rising red flush from his collar upward was a warning sign for those who knew.

The task of making the University better known was tackled by two students, Don Bohl and John Strietelmeier, who put together a low-budget film on the University titled “Building for Tomorrow.” Later in the year, student Ed Kurtz was able to persuade Lowell Thomas, Valparaiso’s most famous alumnus and a major celebrity, to dub in the narrative that Strietelmeier had written. Bohl took the film and script to New York, where Thomas intoned the script. The film was released in the summer of 1942, and Strietelmeier and former Student Council president Al Looman took it to Lutheran churches throughout the Midwest. Such promotion, combined with the talents of Rechlin and Kretzmann's broad popularity, drew another strong class to the University in the fall 1942 at a time when college enrollments generally were falling because of the war.

Plans for fund-raising and building were complicated by fundamental issues regarding VU's future that were up in the air. One of Kretzmann's strategic points had been to expand to "metropolitan centers," and the idea of establishing a branch in Chicago, or even of moving the entire University to Chicago or River Forest, remained alive. When the Walther League decided to build its own headquarters in Chicago, Valparaiso's leaders proposed that together the two groups buy enough real estate to form a "Lutheran Educational Center." Kretzmann gave this top priority, and the board came up with funds to buy its share of the land, a choice piece of real estate across from the distinguished, independent Newberry Library.

This was the kind of dramatic gesture Kretzmann loved, suggesting great things ahead. But apart from continuing vague ideas that VU and Concordia-River Forest might together develop a graduate center linked to the Newberry Library, nothing more happened, and the "Lutheran Educational Center" disappeared. The Walther League did build an impressive building on its part of the site. VU attempted to offer some extension courses in the Chicago Lutheran high schools, but the response was mediocre.

In the spring of 1941, the University board officially petitioned the Missouri Synod in convention to consider making Valparaiso University the "senior college" between the Concordia junior college system and the seminary, an idea that had first been broached by President Kreinheder. Kretzmann urged the board not to begin any capital projects until the Synod had responded to this trial balloon, perhaps another hint of a possible move. But the board then made it emphatically clear that its mind was settled as far as the location of the University was concerned: It would remain in Indiana. It did authorize the development of cooperative programs with Concordia-River Forest on the northside property, but these were never developed. For its part, the Synod chose not to act on the VU feeler.

As the second year of the Kretzmann administration began, many signs of a new era in the life of the University appeared. Rising enrollments (up 25 percent) added fresh energy to the campus. Daily chapel took on a new look with a new altar, candelabra, and a Matins choir that sang once each week in a liturgical service. Chapel addresses began to reflect Kretzmann's theme of the relevance of the Christian faith to both daily lives and events in the world. The president called for a "restlessness" among the students as they thought about the war and the coming mid-century mark. His talk about the "discipline of liberty" took dramatic form when he abolished the office of dean of students and replaced it with a Faculty-Student Council to manage student affairs.

Academically, too, Kretzmann moved to enliven the religious life of the campus. The religion department was separated from philosophy, and a new religion requirement of four two-credit courses was instituted. Ideally, one course would be taken each year of residence so religion was a constant subject of study and reflection as the student progressed through the University. Kretzmann himself taught a course on "Christianity and Modern Problems," taken by invitation only. It became for many students over the years a highly desirable academic prize. Students would gather in O. P.'s office for class and listen to Kretzmann range over all his favorite subjects and texts. Then they would write papers on broad topics of faith and culture; it was sometimes suspected that So Heidbrink graded them.

VU AND THE WAR

The background of Kretzmann's first year was, as he noted in his inaugural, the bombs and guns of a war in Europe that drew ever closer to home. For many at Valparaiso, the fall of France and the apparently imminent defeat of Britain created a dark and somber mood and a sense that all of Western civilization was undergoing a profound trial. When registration for the first peacetime draft began in fall 1940, *The Torch* headlined President Roosevelt's letter to college presidents urging students to remain in school as their "patriotic duty," suggesting that college students would be deferred. Even before Pearl Harbor, the first war casualty on campus was "Uhlan," the nickname for the yearbook and the athletic teams. There was much discussion regarding the propriety of the German term, including a formal debate in chapel. A subsequent student vote was inconclusive. But the board of publications decided in January 1941 to change the yearbook's name from *The Uhlan* to *The Beacon*, a change welcomed by President Kretzmann because the developing "light" motif in the University's nomenclature was symbolic "of Valparaiso's great purpose for existing—to give light to a darkened world." It took until January 1942, after Pearl Harbor, for the athletic teams to change their name to the "Crusaders," again approved by the president because it "connotes courage and devotion to ideals for which the University stands."

The Japanese attack on Pearl Harbor on December 7, 1941, shocked Valparaiso, as it did the nation. President Kretzmann remembered being in Fort Wayne, listening to a choir singing the "Hallelujah Chorus" when he first heard the news. At the first solemn wartime Christmas Vespers later that December, he told the students and faculty,

> Despite war and fear, or rather because of them, we have a clearer vision of our common task. ... We shall be tempted to look at the world and feel that nothing is silent and holy and calm and bright. That is a surface judgment. Beneath the roar of hate and fear, the Child still rules.

The faculty's committee on national defense met for the first time on December 18, 1941. Along with other war-related measures, the University eventually devised an accelerated program that would enable a student to earn a degree in two years and eight months by attending the University year-round. All holidays, except sacred ones, were canceled, and the spring 1942 semester was shortened. Many male students pondered the question of whether to leave school and join the military or to continue their studies under deferments and wait to see if they were drafted. "I am not sure just what is the right thing for a college man to do in a week like this one," wrote *Torch* editor Ray Scherer. Despite uncertainty about personal decisions, at least the collective direction was now clear: "There is the feeling that now we know what is to be done. There is relief from all that waiting and uncertainty. There is no more of that dread expectancy. Our course is clear. WE are in this thing for good."

Physical education became a special requirement with material drawn from the Army Physical Education Manual. It was energetically promoted by some students, dodged by others. The 13-day spring choir trip to the East Coast had to be dropped because of troop movements on the railroads. *Torch* editor Scherer sought to brighten the subsequent disappointment with a fictitious account of how the tour might have gone, describing travel by dog teams, riverboats, and trains full of milk cans.

Although patriotism was strong, some in the largely German-American VU community were sensitive about attempts to blame all of German culture for the war or to link their religion with Nazism. When W. M. McGovern's book *From Luther to Hitler* appeared in bookstores, Professor Schwiebert fired off an article in *The Cresset* entitled "From

Adam to Hitler?" Sweeping charges seemed particularly unwarranted to some because O. P. Kretzmann and *The Cresset* had been vigorous and outspoken Lutheran opponents of Hitler in the 1930s and had particularly protested Nazi anti-Semitism, as revealed in episodes such as the 1938 *Kristallnacht*.

The expected decline in enrollment did not occur in the fall of 1942. Female enrollment increased, and the men only gradually went off to war, many being deferred because of involvement in reservist programs designed to let them finish college before entering the service. "Education is Defense!" proclaimed *The Torch's* masthead. The University worked hard to enable students to graduate. When a low draft number brought senior Theodore Schwan a draft notice, Dean Friedrich immediately took the student to the courthouse and reminded the draft board that students were to be deferred until graduation.

A new column in the paper also began its weekly appearance: Valpo for Victory—News of Valumni in the Services. "As the drafting of man-power from the colleges throughout the country gains in momentum," the editor observed, "more and more of Valpo men will soon be peering down gun-sights instead of slide-rules, periscopes instead of microscopes." This reality hit home on September 10, 1942, when 1937 alumnus Eric Andres went down with the *U.S.S. Astoria* during the assault on Guadalcanal. In Valparaiso, Professor Kumnick, who knew Andres well, spoke at the memorial service, and the choir sang Bach's "Come, Sweet Death." Shortly thereafter, the hero was honored by the launching of a new ship, the *U.S.S. Andres.*

Soon deferments ran out and more and more students, mostly men but also some women, left to go to war. Eventually 500 VU students entered the service. As fraternity houses emptied one by one, the last members handed the keys to the president for safekeeping. Kretzmann wrote about one such farewell:

> I rose and we shook hands. I said a few things which sounded meaningless and trite. There really isn't much one can say in moments like that. He went out into the dark winter afternoon. Through the window I watched him go down the wind-swept street which he had walked in other days when his next class and the evening's basketball game were the most important things in life. Down an Indiana street on a winter afternoon towards Europe, Asia, Africa, and the islands of the South Seas.

WARTIME DEVELOPMENTS

As at most colleges, the wartime enrollment decline soon became severe. Most of the remaining students were women. The rising number of women had occurred partly by design as administrators recognized that female students were essential to the institution's survival. To the dismay of strict liberal arts partisans such as Friedrich, O. P. insisted on installing or enhancing more professionally oriented programs in education, home economics, and social work—the latter a particular favorite of the president because of his strong ties to the ALC and Wheat Ridge. In 1943, President Kretzmann also invited the Lutheran Deaconess Association, which trained young women for church-related service, to move its two-year educational program to VU. Six students came the first year and settled into a residence on Chicago Street. By 1946, the program required a Bachelor of Arts, and by 1950, 46 student deaconesses, organized as the Pi Delta Chi sorority, were studying at Valparaiso, a visible sign of VU's church relationships.

The faculty appealed to women to take courses in areas such as the hard sciences, where they were generally underenrolled, and many excellent students did just that. In fact, for the many women who did not believe that social life was the consuming purpose of college, the war years presented a great opportunity and challenge to develop their minds and talents to the fullest. Many VU women such as Carlene Heidbrink (later Professor Carlene Bartelt of the College of Nursing) accepted that challenge and later thought of themselves as precursors of the revival of the women's movement in the 1960s and 1970s.

Barbara Bernthal (later Gockel), a student leader who became the first woman VU Student Council president, left one of the most notable marks on the University: the Honor System. The faculty was extremely reluctant to go along with her proposal for a student-initiated and student-run Honor System, and some had to be warned not to ridicule the system publicly. But after a trial period, the faculty who came to believe in it devoted much time to making it effective and fair. The Honor System eventually came to be thought of as an expression of the Christian character of the University, though revisions were proposed nearly every decade. It was also a permanent monument to Barbara Bernthal's leadership.

The heavily female campus of the war years affected life in numerous ways. Because Altruria Hall could no longer house all the VU female students, they spilled into Lembke, private houses, and fraternity house "annexes" for the war's duration. *The Torch* regularly featured the opening of new houses, open house teas, and "bunking parties" between sororities. A women's choir was added to the singing groups, and plays and musicals were found that featured mostly female characters. Some were staged in the Altruria dining hall, known as "the Hole," before large audiences, including student-written revues such as one titled "The Russian Show" and set in the Red Goose Tavern in a place called "Valpoinske, Russia." (The Blue Goose Tavern, later called Jackson's, was a popular student hangout of the time.)

Student Bridge and its romantic activities remained, though "Sagerology" faded away. During the late 1930s, a new highway, U.S. 30, had cut off Sager's Lake from the campus. The lake became private property, no longer a cherished part of VU student life, except in remembered lore.

VU sports also changed under the pressures of wartime. For women, intramural athletics flourished as never before, and there were numerous teams in basketball, field hockey, and other sports. Women also benefited from increased attention to their athletic activities in *The Torch* and elsewhere. The near-absence of males naturally inhibited men's sports. The faculty canceled all men's sports except basketball for the duration of the war, but the basketball coach, Loren Ellis, persuaded enough men who were too tall for the military to attend Valparaiso to play basketball. For a few glory years, VU's "World's Tallest Team" played and defeated major college opponents such as DePaul, Holy Cross, and Long Island University.

The team that Ellis assembled had its first successes in the 1942–43 (17–5) and 1943–44 (17–8) seasons. Featuring giant Milton Schoon and the 6-foot 10-inch brothers Wally and Don Warnke, the team gained national attention in January 1944 when it defeated Coach Ray Meyer's top-ranked DePaul Blue Demons and their dominating center George Mikan, 65–57. The peak of VU's success came in the 1944–45 season, when the "World's Tallest Team," including its star All-American Bob Dille, defeated several nationally ranked teams. The highlight was a game in December with perennial powerhouse Long Island University. The game was played before 16,000 fans in New York's Madison Square Garden. Valpo came from behind to win in dramatic fashion, 64–59, prompting headlines across the country and in military papers such as *Stars and Stripes*. VU also defeated Hamline University and powerful Holy Cross in a game played in Boston Garden, finishing the season 21–3.

These national glory years ended after the war. But the widespread publicity in the national and G.I. press garnered by the basketball team's success made Valparaiso University more widely known and helped fuel its postwar enrollment.

The board and the administration spent a good deal of time during the war years planning for the postwar period. One central commitment for O. P. was that the University had to become a center of sacred music because music and Lutheranism had a long-standing special relationship to each other and Luther had described music as "God's gift to his sorrowing creatures" to banish their sadness.

St. Olaf College had developed a superb national reputation by renewing the tradition of sacred song in America. Many Lutheran colleges, including Valparaiso, had followed St. Olaf in creating touring choirs led by prominent choral directors. But there was an alternative Lutheran musical tradition to that of St. Olaf and the Christiansens, and O. P. was determined that Valparaiso represent it. Whereas the St. Olaf emphasis on choral music was natural for a fine liberal arts college, O. P. saw VU as pursuing a different range of emphases involving keyboard, orchestra, musicology, and liturgy. Ultimately, he hoped to create a School of Music on the campus.

In 1943, Kretzmann made his move to enhance music at VU. The first steps—firing several music instructors and removing Richard Schoenbohm, the popular choir director, from headship of the department—were painful and poorly handled. In Schoenbohm's place, Kretzmann appointed Dr. Theodore Hoelty-Nickel, an entrepreneurial German-born, Australian-educated church musician. Hoelty-Nickel brought an expansive vision of the renewal of Lutheran church music. In 1944, he created a Church Music Seminar and Workshop, which attracted not only the top musical figures in America, but after the war ended, it attracted leading European musicians as well.

At the same time, Kretzmann recruited as choral director M. Alfred Bichsel, a cosmopolitan French Swiss immigrant and bon vivant who was an ordained Lutheran pastor, a fine performer in voice and organ, and an expert on liturgy. Combining a repertoire of Gregorian works with Lutheran masterpieces, Bichsel's choirs established the high standard of excellence that came to define VU's choral tradition. Hoelty-Nickel had an uncanny ability to recognize and recruit faculty talent such as Bichsel. In short order, Hoelty-Nickel put together a remarkable group of musicians and musicologists at what was still a small college: the amazing William

Kroeger in piano, the internationally known Heinrich Fleischer from Germany in organ, the scholarly Newman Powell in musicology, the masterly John Golz in strings, and the promising Richard Wienhorst in composition. By the late 1940s, Valparaiso's music faculty could compare with some of the best undergraduate programs in the United States.

Another of Kretzmann's initiatives was to create the VU Social Ethics Seminar in the summer of 1944. Led by Professor Otto Piper of Princeton, it consisted of theologians and social scientists from Lutheran colleges and seminaries across the country who wrote papers and discussed issues of social concern and the Christian faith. The seminar bore fruit in courses and programs developed at Lutheran seminaries and colleges and in various publications.

The mid-1940s was proving to be a time of deep unrest in the Missouri Synod. Almost inevitably, Valparaiso was affected. The energetic action of those who believed that God's will was leading the church toward both Lutheran unity and wider Christian cooperation had called forth an active opposition. Starting in 1938, the opponents began pushing the synodical leadership into stalling the unity movement. By 1944, that stalling was visible. O. P. Kretzmann and others took the lead in shaping a public protest against a mentality that they regarded as legalistic and unevangelical. They called for a reorientation of the Synod back to its roots in "the gospel in word and deed," and forward to the "*Una Sancta*," the "one, holy, catholic, and apostolic church" of the Nicene Creed that the Synod served.

In September 1945, Chicago was the scene of a meeting of more than 40 prominent Missouri Synod leaders. Later called "the Forty-Four," this group of churchmen signed a pointed manifesto known simply as "A Statement." W. C. Dickmeyer, the chairman of the board of Valparaiso University, had raised the money that financed the effort. O. P. Kretzmann was the author of one of the "Ten Theses" that comprised the document, on the "*Una Sancta*."

Over objections from the synodical president, the Rev. John Behnken, "A Statement" was widely circulated within the Synod and quickly caused a sensation. Controversy continued to swirl around the document for years. Opponents demanded that its signers be sanctioned. A compromise was reached in 1947 when the signers agreed to withdraw it as a basis for discussion, but their ideas had been launched and the myth of synodical lockstep and mandated uniformity broken. Simultaneously, many leading laity in the Missouri Synod also became involved in a flurry of activities aimed at accelerating Lutheran unity, but synodical officialdom intervened to thwart them.

Valparaiso University was plainly implicated in the movement for Lutheran unity and a wider ecumenism. It became a place for many meetings of Lutheran leaders from all the church bodies, except Missouri Synod officials. In addition, O. P. Kretzmann led in the formation of a theological study group that met regularly at the DeKoven Foundation in Kenosha, Wisconsin, an Episcopalian retreat center. There leaders from all Lutheran groups, again minus top Missouri officials, met on an annual basis over many years to discuss issues and create intersynodical understanding through face-to-face meetings.

PLANNING A POSTWAR VU

Meanwhile, VU's leaders began to plan for the future after the war. Confident that the rise in women's enrollment presaged a general postwar increase, they decided that a women's residence would have to be built as soon as conditions allowed. In the spring of 1943, members of the board's committee on buildings and grounds stood with architect Edward Jansson near the gymnasium, trying to imagine a location for such a residence hall. "You should have that property," said Jansson, pointing to the open fields stretching eastward from the campus.

Thereupon, the three-man committee—Fred Wehrenberg, Paul Amling, and Robert Moellering—together with W. C. Dickmeyer, John Sauerman, and Paul Rupprecht, formed a temporary corporation and silently purchased the 92 acres in that tract at a total cost of approximately $43,000. Then they sold the land to the University for promissory notes, most of which they later returned as gifts. Two years later, the University rounded out the purchase by buying 15 additional acres along LaPorte Avenue. By this time, the cost had risen to $1,000 an acre. Jansson was asked to draw up a campus master plan with a cathedral-like chapel at its center on the highest point of the new land.

What kind of expansion should the University plan for, and what sort of campus should be envisioned to accommodate it? These were the difficult questions on the table. Planners variously projected building a campus for an eventual enrollment of 800, 1,000, or 1,200 students. Given the expected male-female ratio of 2 to 1, the enrollment of 400 women in 1944–45 suggested the highest figure.

But when World War II ended suddenly in August 1945, numbers swiftly outpaced all expectations. Seven hundred students arrived on campus that fall, and by spring 1946, enrollment had mushroomed to 1,126. The University desperately scrambled for housing. Appeals to the community to open boarding rooms in their houses helped a little. The University bought and refurbished ancient Stiles Hall. It also quickly signed contracts for building Guild and Memorial halls, two new women's residences planned for occupation in the fall of 1947. Ground for the well-designed new buildings, for which the University Guild was raising money, was broken at the Guild convention in the summer of 1946.

Even before those buildings were finished, it was apparent they would not be enough. Fourteen hundred students turned up in the fall of 1946, and 1,650 students arrived in the spring of 1947. Pandemonium seemed about to break loose in the crammed classrooms and dorms, and Kretzmann wrote to alumni that thousands were being turned away. That was not literally accurate, but it surely reflected the state of mind on the harried campus.

At this same time, the federal government was making surplus housing materials available to colleges if the recipient could provide an architect and a site. Scribner and his assistant, Robert Springsteen, traveled to Buchanan, Michigan, to acquire some of the available stock. Architect Jansson quickly drew up plans, and construction got under way. The lot across from Lembke Hall became "Greenwich Group," a set of one-story buildings with classrooms and a cafeteria. Further east, another vacant lot was filled with 16 mobile trailers—15 for occupants and one for toilets, showers, and laundry. The large parking lot west of Guild-Memorial held other hastily assembled and poorly heated dorms unpoetically named "A," "B," and "C." The construction superintendent lived in Stiles Hall throughout this frenetic building period, and Scribner, knowing his preferences, supplied him with a weekly bottle of the best whiskey, hoping it would speed construction.

By 1948, VU's enrollment had risen to 2,000 students, where it leveled off for a period of time before resuming its upward climb. In the span of only a few years, Valparaiso University had become the largest Lutheran institution of higher learning in the nation. This remarkable growth of more than 500 percent above the prewar level far exceeded the national average. Nationally, enrollment grew from 1,364,815 college students in 1939 to 2,444,900 in 1949. The number of GIs who returned to college was much higher than educational planners had predicted, and their example, plus the need for college graduates in science and technology, dramatically increased the percentage of American high school graduates who attended college compared to the prewar years. Subtly, the idea of a college education as a quasi-right insinuated itself into the public mind, and the postwar "academic revolution" was underway.

BUILDING AN "INTELLECTUAL ENDOWMENT"

After World War II, it soon became apparent to alert observers that American life would never be the same. The United States experienced a surprising economic boom that created an unprecedented new middle-class consumer society that featured suburban home life, a surge of patriotism, and a return to religion that reversed the losses of the 1920s and 1930s. It was a golden age for the churches: Everything suddenly seemed to be going their way.

The popular revival of religion, however, extended only unevenly into intellectual life and the universities. Harvard's influential 1945 self-study, *General Education in a Free Society*, acknowledged the historic role of "Judeo-Christian values" in Western civilization, but it said those values should now be transmitted in the context of the natural sciences and social sciences. As Christianity retreated into an increasingly marginal role at the elite research universities and liberal arts colleges, a few foundations and church organizations did provide some funding for the renewal of Christian higher education. Soon there were conferences and a journal, *The Christian Scholar*. Some of these efforts followed the line of inquiry suggested by Sir Walter Moberly in *The Crisis of the University* (1949), examining the presuppositions of the widespread scientific "cult of objectivity" and the implications of Christian thought for the individual disciplines of learning.

Lutherans still were not leaders in the national conversations on these matters, but they were beginning to develop their own voice. Building on the discussions led by Pannkoke in the 1930s, Lutheran academics addressed these issues through the National Lutheran Educational Conference and the Association of Lutheran College Faculties (organized separately in 1948). Speaking in 1947 to the Lutheran Theological Society at the DeKoven Center, O. P. Kretzmann argued that in the educational setting, the Lutheran themes of grace alone, faith alone, and Scripture alone could shape strong and courageous individuals who can be "radically critical of society, sensitively aware of its weaknesses and consciously prepared to assist in their elimination." In another address in January 1950, Kretzmann called on Lutherans to attend carefully to the relationship between worship and knowledge as a way of fusing the life of the spirit with the life of the mind at the highest level. He urged publications, seminars, symposia, and research projects to be made part of an agenda for cooperation among diverse Lutheran educational institutions.

Similarly, in *The Cresset*, Kretzmann set forth the goal of creating "a new unity of life and thought, of culture and religion, of faith and learning." He also wanted this to constitute the intellectual agenda of Valparaiso University. Although money was desperately needed for buildings and salaries, Kretzmann tenaciously sought to raise a different kind of capital as well. "We don't want to become just another Princeton," he often said. He gathered and cultivated people who would create an "intellectual endowment" off which the University could live in the future. The president's lofty rhetoric often lacked specificity, but he did generate new meanings and enthusiasm within a community of younger faculty, who sensed they were doing something fresh and important.

Faculty selection strongly determines the nature of any university. For such grand tasks as Kretzmann proposed, there were relatively few qualified men or women available and too little money to pay them. Nevertheless, he had a gift for luring interesting young people by looking far ahead and articulating his dream for the University. In the immediate postwar years, Kretzmann attracted a strong core of young faculty—Concordia Seminary graduates, returning veterans, VU alumni, some of them Lutheran and some not—who formed the University's character for many years.

Among those who already had arrived during World War II were stalwarts Vera Hahn and Thora Moulton and alumni William Bloom and Erwin Buls. Among the many graduates of Concordia Seminary who were acquiring advanced degrees in a variety of fields and who came to Valparaiso were: Jaroslav Pelikan, Ernest Koenker, Robert Bertram, Carl Krekeler, Victor Hoffman, Richard Scheimann, Ross Scherer, Luther Koepke, Martin Schaefer, and Erhardt Essig. There were VU graduates drawn back to serve their alma mater (after military service in the case of the men): John Strietelmeier, Richard Wienhorst, James Savage, Daniel Gahl, Rudolph Waldschmidt, Fred Kruger, Janet Sievers, Richard Koenig, Alfred Looman, and Robert Springsteen. Within a few years, other notable figures joined this faculty: Margaretta Tangerman, Louis Bartelt, Ruth Brown, Herman Hesse, Edgar Reinke, Byron Ferguson, Allen Tuttle, Theodore Schwan, Paul Phipps, Van Kussrow, and Lester Lange.

At Valparaiso, many of these faculty tried to develop and sustain a distinctive conversation, often led by O. P., around the themes articulated in

The Cresset and elsewhere. Meetings called for practical purposes often would end in discussion of issues only remotely related to the original agenda. In 1947, newly appointed academic dean Walter Bauer created an annual two-day faculty workshop designed to further discourse on matters of common interest.

One group of scholars assembled by Kretzmann was called the Palm Grove Group, named after a restaurant on the south side of Chicago where the group first met. It was an informal conclave that often included members of the VU faculty, along with guests or "associate members," such as Concordia Seminary Professors Arthur Carl Piepkorn, Richard Caemmerer, and Paul Bretscher; Robert Schnabel, a young philosopher then supervising Christian education in Indiana and Ohio; and provocative younger figures such as Martin Marty and Richard Luecke, whom O. P. was cultivating for the University. The participants regularly heard papers, often exploring the relationship between some academic discipline and the Christian faith.

No records of these meetings remain, but the conversations echoed in the pages of *The Cresset*, which regularly reflected faculty thinking. While O. P. remained editor of the journal, the actual editorial management was taken over by Jaroslav Pelikan in 1947. After Pelikan joined the Concordia Seminary faculty in 1949, the management was assumed by John Strietelmeier. Biologist Carl Krekeler wrote on science and religion, arguing that working with evolutionary theory does not require one to abandon faith in God the Creator and Redeemer. Martin Marty wrote on the arts and education. Pelikan called for a point-by-point response to neo-Thomism as a Lutheran contribution to the Christian presence in the culture. In his *From Luther to Kierkegaard*, Pelikan suggested the lines along which a philosophical effort informed by Lutheran insights might proceed. Ernest Koenker argued that the Christian existentialism of Kierkegaard, seen as a radical alternative to rationalistic modes of thought, demanded serious attention in philosophy, theology, and literature. John Strietelmeier called for Lutheran contributions to politics as the corollary of enjoying the benefits of the American political system, and he urged the same creative efforts in letters and the arts. He especially called the laity to go beyond catechization to develop a mature theology befitting their enlarged role in church and society.

These concerns, and others raised in *The Cresset* by VU faculty and their friends, set a tone that defined the spiritual and intellectual atmosphere at Valparaiso. Most VU faculty of the 1950s had too many responsibilities and too little support to pursue the kinds of scholarly careers to which they aspired. But in their teaching and in their exchanges with one another and like-minded people elsewhere, they made some progress toward suggesting what a Lutheran Christian institution of higher learning should be about.

STIRRING THE POT

For Kretzmann, a church-related university ought not to be simply an ivory tower. Its calling was to serve the church and society by sponsoring workshops and seminars and through generating and disseminating knowledge of use to others in many fields. For years, the University sponsored or cosponsored from six to 10 such gatherings a year, mostly in the summer, when O. P. would address and inspire the participants. Some were annual events, including the Church Music Seminar, the Social Ethics Seminar, the Liturgical Institute, and the Institute on Human Relations. Others were one-time or several-time meetings. Sample areas included a social work seminar that met quite frequently and other seminars on politics, radio, public relations, law, drama, the church and modern culture, and the church and rural life.

While some of these groups had a relatively limited impact, others created enduring relationships and made important contributions to their areas. The Church Music Seminar especially flourished and published its proceedings in a valuable "Musical Heritage" series. In 1949, the first Liturgical Institute was held under the auspices of the University, and it became an enduring feature of VU's life, drawing hundreds of people to its sessions each year. The VU faculty consistently included leading liturgical scholars and practitioners: M. Alfred Bichsel, Adolf Wismar, Van Kussrow, Ernest Koenker, Robert Schultz, Kenneth Korby, Hans Boehringer, Daniel Brockopp, and David Truemper. Liturgical Institute "graduates" regularly invigorated parishes with what they learned at VU.

Other significant institutes had large and mostly unforeseen consequences. Sometimes these directly affected the University itself. This was especially true of the institutes on human relations. Beginning in 1946, Andrew Schulze, a prophetic white pastor who had organized and led several "Negro" Lutheran congregations in the essentially segregated Missouri Synod, had held Lutheran race relations institutes in St. Louis and Chicago on an ad hoc basis. Kretzmann soon invited the small group supporting Schulze, many of them veterans of the ALC, to come to Valparaiso for the First Annual Institute on Human Relations in the summer of 1950. A second institute in the summer of 1951 attracted national press attention. By 1953, O. P. and others were suggesting that the ideas of the institute required a permanent organization to implement them. The participants, therefore, established the Lutheran Human Relations Association of America, with the future Illinois senator Paul Simon serving as one of its three directors. With O. P.'s prompting, the association hired Andrew Schulze as executive secretary in 1954, which included a half-time appointment in the VU religion department as well.

While the LHRAA was founded as a broad civil rights group with a particular mission to the Lutheran community, it also had a direct impact on Valparaiso University. In the late 1940s, a few black students with close ties to Lutheran parishes were the first African-Americans to attend VU as resident undergraduates. Hilbert L. Bradley commuted to the law school from nearby Lake County, becoming in 1950 the first African-American law graduate from VU. The creation of the LHRAA and its location on the VU campus provided support and encouragement for more African-American students. By the mid-1950s, each of the undergraduate classes had four or five black students. LouJeanne Bray (later Professor of Social Work LouJeanne Walton) was one of these students. She remembered their discomfort at the curious stares of people in the town of Valparaiso, as well as careless remarks by fellow students. Although the numbers of African-American students slowly grew, it was not until the early 1960s that many began publicly addressing the issues of prejudice and discrimination that were evident all around them, including at the University. Meanwhile, O. P. had recruited sociologist Jeff Johnson, an urbane Californian with a Concordia Seminary degree and a University of Southern California doctorate. For many years, Johnson was the only full-time black faculty member, until he was joined by Walton.

While the African-American presence on campus was small, the LHRAA and the faculty and staff who strongly supported it created an awareness of civil rights issues on the campus and beyond. The organization's presence at Valparaiso helped define the University and kept the nation's central social and moral problem on the agenda when much of the church and the public wanted to forget it. Members of the faculty from the law school and many other academic fields contributed formally or informally to the association's efforts. Because the LHRAA was early and active in the civil rights struggle, it maintained credible contacts at the highest levels of the movement. It regularly helped bring leading national and international civil rights leaders to the campus—a factor that became increasingly important in the 1960s and 1970s.

The LHRAA and other similar activities reflected O. P. Kretzmann's conception of what VU should be about as a university. Kretzmann lost no opportunity to remind his audiences that the founders had envisioned a university, not only a liberal arts college, related to the church and its mission. An excellent liberal arts core, he believed, should be surrounded by a small number of high-quality professional programs.

At the time, the law school was the most obvious basis for calling Valparaiso a university, and Kretzmann had insisted on keeping it afloat during the war years, even with only a handful of students. This commitment was rewarded immediately after the war when Valparaiso's law school was rejuvenated by the GI Bill. Enrollment boomed, reaching 158 students in the fall of 1949. In 1952, the faculty formally required that entrants not already in the Valparaiso 3/3 program (three years undergraduate and three years law) have the Bachelor of Arts degree. This higher requirement, combined with the lower enrollments of the early 1950s, created a plateau of about 75 to 90 students each year for the next decade.

In 1954, John Morland resigned his law school deanship of 26 years. He was succeeded by Knute Stalland, the assistant attorney general of Minnesota and a member of the influential Lutheran Preus family. Equally proud of his Lutheranism and the legal profession, Stalland firmly believed that the law school was Valparaiso's best chance to advance its Christian purposes in society. Under his leadership, the law school developed a fourfold self-description as a national, Christian, small, teaching institution. "National" meant it sought a nationwide student body and prepared students for the bar in all states. As a Christian school, it shared the life of the whole University, emphasized the nexus between law and Christianity in its required third-year jurisprudence course, offered personal care for students, and encouraged the Christian stewardship of the practicing attorney. Its small size fostered easy access to instructors, while the emphasis on teaching rather than faculty publication assured the student the best possible instruction. All these were ideals, of course, and represented aspiration more than achievement. But they did focus the school's policies and practices, which were carried out by outstanding faculty members added in the postwar expansion: James Savage, Louis Bartelt, Charles Gromley, and Jack Hiller. These gifted teachers played university-wide roles as well.

The most visible step to expand the University structure came with the reversal of an earlier decision: reestablishing a full College of Engineering.

After slumping badly in the 1930s, engineering was suddenly the hottest profession in the nation. Students attracted to Valparaiso University's pre-engineering program resented the fact that after two years they had to transfer to Purdue, receiving a fine degree but rupturing established relationships and leaving a milieu of which they had become fond.

The arguments against expansion at first seemed compelling. Upper-level engineering education was expensive, but a consultant believed that a carefully designed program in three engineering fields—civil, electrical, and mechanical—was feasible. Then, at the traditional spring engineering banquet in 1948, a student challenged the president to let the students build a new engineering lab for the new college through their own summer labor and fund-raising. The board backed the president's resolve to let them try.

The engineering students jumped enthusiastically into their major volunteer construction project. A year later, after a great deal of sweat and despite numerous obstacles, they completed the job. The building was dedicated and the College of Engineering reopened in the spring of 1949, soon after the arrival of its new dean, Herman Hesse, who came from the University of Virginia. The first class graduated in 1951.

The dramatic story of the student-built engineering building had all the ingredients of a movie. Indeed, it soon became one. In 1951, the Lutheran Laymen's League commissioned a professional film about the effort, titled "Venture of Faith." Professional actors arrived to play key roles, while various actual Valparaiso personalities added a touch of *cinema verite*. The film version varied from the actual story on some points, but it dealt with the essential realities the students had faced: raising funds, difficulty in getting the necessary building materials in the postwar era of government allocations, making agreements with 11 trade unions, and so on.

The movie was widely shown, establishing the saga of the building's construction firmly in VU's history and lore and contributing to a growing public image in some quarters that Valparaiso had an uncommon student body. Even before the film, something of that perception had taken hold even outside Lutheran circles. Various newspapers had commented on Valparaiso's student spirit when, in 1946, students pitched in to remove the bricks from College and Mound streets to complete the campus quadrangle. A similar student spirit animated Professor of Social Work Margaretta Tangerman's University Youth Council, which created a youth center that served several hundred local boys and girls. Soon students began agitating for a student union and began raising their own funds to build it.

STRUGGLE FOR QUALITY

The energy and spirit of VU's students and faculty were not yet, unfortunately, matched by academic quality or resources. When the College of Engineering applied to the Engineer's Council for Professional Development for accreditation in 1955, the disheartening word came back that accreditation had been denied. The inspectors had found much to praise, but several general university weaknesses were fatal. The uncertain financial structure and accumulating debt were intolerable. The VU physics department was described as an "academic slum," and its staffing was found to be woefully inadequate. Similarly, when a faculty committee led by Professor Tangerman applied for a Phi Beta Kappa chapter in 1955, it was turned down because of severe weaknesses in endowment, library, and admissions standards.

The College of Arts and Sciences, where most of the students flooding into VU were enrolled, was becoming aware that quantity was not quality. Initially, the overflowing student population was accommodated through larger classes in lower division courses and additional sections taught as overloads. As the flood of students rolled into upper division courses, new majors and departments were developed while administrators and faculty struggled to upgrade programs under severe constraints.

The long-planned religion major was inaugurated in 1946. Between 1946 and 1950, philosophy, history, sociology, government, and speech and theater were made separate departments. Foreign languages increased its Latin offerings and added Greek. In the same period, a new Bachelor of Science in education was added. Presiding over all this "controlled expansion" as chair of the curriculum committee was Professor Walter G. Friedrich, head of the English department. He stood for soundness and economy, not innovation—a style that left its stamp on the University curriculum.

A 1951 Lilly Endowment Report that generously praised VU's religious programs and activities such as *The Cresset* was much less complimentary regarding the academic strength of the University. It showed how the terribly low faculty salaries exerted a negative influence on academic quality by forcing many faculty to do extra work, to the detriment of their sustained scholarship. Of the 111 members of the faculty in 1951, only 19 had earned doctorates, putting it in the lowest 15 percent of comparable academic institutions in this respect.

As far as student quality was concerned, VU admitted students in the late 1940s who ranked anywhere in the upper two-thirds of their graduating classes. This undemanding standard, which was about the national average, soon began to change. The sons and daughters of relatively recent immigrants who had not themselves gone to college were aiming at higher academic goals and achieving them. By 1953, the quality of entering VU students had risen markedly, as measured by the number of valedictorians, the number of graduates in the upper 10 percent of their high school class, and so on. But the number of good students who were transferring elsewhere, sometimes in dissatisfaction with Valparaiso, was also rising—a less healthy indicator. Kretzmann wanted VU to continue to educate a cross section of the constituency, not only an elite group. He argued that "intellectual virtue is only part of what determines quality." But he also wanted Valparaiso to get and keep its share of top students. In 1953, he appointed a committee on the superior student to stem the loss of good students by making special provision for them. Their proposed programs, including major senior papers, comprehensive departmental examinations, and "proseminar" and "problems" courses for gifted students, came into place only slowly toward the end of the decade.

STRUGGLE FOR RESOURCES

"Ladies and gentlemen, we cannot afford to fail in this endeavor." Uncharacteristically, O. P.'s fist came down hard on the podium as he deliberately and slowly spoke those words to the faculty members and their spouses who gathered for the traditional faculty dinner in the dining hall of Altruria at the opening of the school year on a September evening in 1954.

He was referring to "Building for Christ," a $5 million campaign that the Missouri Synod had authorized to benefit Valparaiso University, the LDA, and several other church-related agencies. The campaign would be conducted from January through March of 1955. Failure would indeed be disastrous. But success would help the University reduce its debt and start building the new campus, particularly the rich symbol of a central chapel. It could be a turning point because $2.5 million was to come directly to the University. In year 2000 terms, that would be a $15 million gift.

The University had been struggling financially since the end of World War II. Despite its impressive expansion, many academic programs fell woefully short of the mark. It was plain that VU either had to solve its problem of inadequate funding or reduce its ambitions. A first financial appeal immediately after the war had badly fizzled, and VU's annual operating deficits were accumulating. The ever-ingenious board treasurer John Sauerman successfully appealed to Lutherans to buy "Valparaiso Notes." Several thousand did, thus financing the two new dormitories, Guild and Memorial halls, and refinancing the deficit. But such measures were stopgaps as long as the budgets for current operations were continuously spilling red ink.

At first Kretzmann bravely quoted Chancellor Robert Hutchins's remarks about how the University of Chicago had ridden to glory on accumulated deficits. A university is not a business, Hutchins had said. The purpose of a business is to make money, and universities are very different. But these assertions, however true, could not pay VU's bills or deal with the real problems of funding quality academic programs. A few board members tried vigorously to find new sources of revenue. The chairman of the board's finance committee and treasurer of International Harvester Corporation, Walter Gross, regularly admonished the board that its primary duty was to raise money, though many acted as if it were to spend it. Chairman Dickmeyer asserted that the Missouri Synod contained "great untouched wealth" and simply required greater education in the importance of Christian higher education.

Seeking help in its fund-raising, the administration had turned in 1948 to the St. Louis organization of Kelly-Zahrnt-Kelly, a Lutheran-Catholic firm that served several Lutheran agencies. KZK deployed one of its top agents, Herbert Knopp, to head the University Relations Department at VU. Knopp was a theologically alert churchman who tried to promote VU as a bulwark against threats to society with the theme "Center of Culture—Citadel of Faith." His "Patron Plan" eventually enlisted 20,000 small contributors, supplementing congregational collections and other individual solicitations. One of Knopp's more fruitful suggestions was that O. P. write *The Campus Commentary* for the clergy several times a year. Sharing news of the University, commenting on the life of the church, trotting out fictitious characters such as "Dean Sauerbraten," "Mrs. Schlukebier," and "Brother Theophilus" as figures in the church's life, this chatty newsletter defined VU for many supporters.

Knopp's endeavors did raise more money than any predecessor. Yet the deficits continued. Valparaiso University was hardly alone in its financial troubles. In 1950, *Time* magazine ran an article, titled "Crisis with

Colleges," that reported that all private universities were in serious financial trouble because of inflation and expansion. The president of Amherst College was quoted as saying that "frogs that cost seventy-two cents a dozen ten years ago now cost $2.25." It was clearly a time of crisis at Valparaiso as well. Serious tensions developed between Kretzmann and the fund-raiser Knopp. "We have no millionaires on this Board," complained Knopp, then immediately apologized for fear of having offended the members. The board responded with a resolution of confidence. But Knopp kept pressing for longer-term planning and thinking while the University wanted immediate results. Eventually, in 1955, KZK resigned the account.

Meanwhile, the Missouri Synod had lured the legendary John C. Baur out of retirement to run its huge $10 million campaign in 1953. In turn, Baur asked VU if he might borrow his friend Karl Henrichs, then in the position of athletic director, though still also responsible for wealthy donors. The University loaned Henrichs to the campaign for three months, together with other university-related volunteers. That fund drive was a huge success, raising $14 million before it was over. Baur declared that the Synod owed Valparaiso a debt of thanks. Like a number of other unofficial agencies with strong ties to the church, it had stood aside during the Synod's big drive and suffered setbacks as a result. Together, Baur and Henrichs pressed the Synod to return the favor.

Despite the cool relationships between the Synod and VU because of the church politics of the 1940s, President Behnken recognized the church's stake in this unique institution. Valparaiso's students came from more than a thousand Lutheran congregations from all across the United States. It was plainly the most influential lay educational force in the Synod's orbit. VU also was gaining recognition beyond Lutheran circles. In 1949, President Truman sent O. P. Kretzmann and several other religious leaders on a well-publicized trip to Japan to report on troop morale. In 1950, Indiana's Lutheran governor Henry Schricker cochaired VU's silver anniversary as a Lutheran school, adding to its visibility. So in October 1952, at Kretzmann's invitation, Behnken and the whole synodical board of directors came to Valparaiso for a campus visit, a Reformation Day address by Behnken, and a joint meeting of the boards of directors of the LCMS and Valparaiso University.

The meeting was one of mutual introduction. Behnken was impressed by the audience that (with O. P.'s prompting) had packed the chapel/auditorium. Students were standing in the aisles and even leaning over the balcony. The place could not hold the growing student body, explained O. P., as he displayed the new campus plan with its proposed large chapel. "We need that," he said. What the University also needed from the church's board was endorsement at the grassroots level. When people understood what VU was doing with the church's endorsement, Kretzmann contended, they would respond with funds enough for operations and for regular debt reduction.

The following year, VU awarded Behnken an honorary degree, conferred after a Reformation Day ceremony in which Behnken duly recounted the pope's latest errors and warned against the evils of evolution. Afterward, at another joint meeting of the VU and LCMS boards, new board chairman Paul Brandt presented a report that reviewed VU's financial condition and sharply posed the question: Does our church want this university? Among its other appeals, the report also strongly suggested that the Synod would be wise to counteract the academic influence of Catholicism, "which is presently gathering in so large a segment of the educated laymen of our nation." The report closed by painting a vivid picture of what VU might become: "The principal seat of Lutheran culture for the national continent, with junior colleges in the East, the West and the South. May God guide us unto wisdom and courage to do that which is pleasing to Him and helpful to all mankind."

Apparently, Behnken was impressed, and he asked how the Synod could help. The possibility of a fund drive either to build the chapel or reduce debt came up. Behnken promised to consult with other officials in the Synod and urged that VU supply more specifics. After further communications and clarifications, word came in April that LCMS officials had decided on a $5 million drive for five church-related agencies, including $2.5 million for Valparaiso University. Of that sum, $750,000 would be for a chapel and the rest for debt reduction and working capital. This was welcome news to a campus whose future was still very much to be determined.

8

A Turning Point

Between Realities and Hopes

The mid-1950s proved to be a turning point for Valparaiso University. While O. P. Kretzmann and his collaborators had succeeded in attracting students and reviving the school's sense of its distinctive mission and vision, VU was far from the kind of academic institution it aspired to be. Despite the often heroic exertions of many committed faculty and staff, the quality of most programs and majors was spotty at best. With the exceptions of the gymnasium, Kroencke Hall, the engineering laboratories, and the Guild and Memorial residences, the physical campus was still essentially the one built by Brown and Kinsey at the turn of the century. Many of the old buildings were the worse for wear. These problems, in turn, were clearly related to the need for capital funding. At the same time, VU student life was changing in response to the more affluent times and a much-expanded student body. VU's now-thoroughly assimilated Lutheran constituency was comfortably engaged with prosperous American life. At the end of the decade, a centennial celebration and dedication of the chapel signaled that a corner had been turned, and these celebrations offered hopes of better things ahead.

An infusion of funds from external sources that began in the mid-1950s was both an economic lifeline and a boost to morale. The successful synodical fund drive brought VU a badly needed $2.25 million. Shortly thereafter, in December 1955, the Ford Foundation announced that it was giving half a billion dollars to qualified private universities and hospitals. As part of this program, Valparaiso University received more than $500,000 for the endowment of salaries of faculty in the liberal arts. While VU missed out on a selective supplementary grant that greatly benefited neighboring Notre Dame, the recognition inherent in the Ford grant was a confidence-builder.

That same month, a deeply moved President Kretzmann announced to a special meeting of the board that VU had received a gift of $375,000 from Mrs. Margaret Moellering for a library in memory of her late husband and Lutheran university founder Henry—the largest individual donation to that date. At the same time, additional funds came from the Scovill family, the Lilly Endowment, and the Kellogg Foundation. Some substantial gifts, such as $375,000 in stock from Minna Scheele, were simply used to cover operating deficits, not for capital projects or endowment. Not for some time would the board and administration really understand the full dimensions of university fund-raising.

Kretzmann did talk about tapping the "third source" of funding (after tuition and the church), and he participated in a new joint effort of Indiana private colleges to raise money from corporations in the state. But the amounts gleaned from this effort were small, and there was no targeted effort to approach funding sources elsewhere. Nor was there any move to hire a fund-raising expert to replace Knopp. For several years, fund-raising was in the hands of a few people who simply continued the Patron Plan and Valparaiso Sunday. Individual donations were handled by Karl Henrichs, who kept in touch with many well-off families. Finally, Kretzmann appointed the Rev. Otto Toelke as vice president for development—a sign that VU still was looking principally to the church for support.

Despite financial uncertainties, there were enough dollars and high hopes to push ahead with plans for a new campus on the empty farmlands to the east. Campus planning was placed in the hands of Professor Jean Labatut of Princeton University, a distinguished architectural planner. Labatut was associated with Charles Stade, a leading church architect who regularly collaborated with A. R. Kretzmann, O. P.'s brother and a noted ecclesiastical art expert. While Labatut developed overall plans for the new campus, Stade was named architect for the new building, and A. R. Kretzmann became the church art consultant.

Suddenly, there was a rash of groundbreakings, each carried out with the sense of ritual for which the University already had become noted. During its commencement, the class of 1954 witnessed the first: the groundbreaking for the new Student Union that was the first building to rise on the East Campus. In January 1955, construction on the Dau-Kreinheder residential complex began, funded by a local bond issue. In October 1956, a crowd of faculty and students, led by Professor Bichsel's Chapel Choir, met near the site of the new chapel. With excavation already begun, and surrounded by the colors of a spectacular Indiana fall, they consecrated the plot of land to the worship of God and the service of God's people.

Just over a month later—November 27—President Kretzmann had gone to bed at 11:30 P.M. after starting work on his Christmas *Campus Commentary*. Shortly thereafter, the telephone rang and an excited voice said, "The auditorium is on fire!" Then the phone went dead. Kretzmann hurriedly dressed and dashed to the campus a few blocks away to find firefighters dragging hoses through the snow and pouring water into a burning classroom at the rear of the building. Soon, the whole structure was a blazing inferno. The chapel-auditorium was lost, and 20 feet to the north, hot cinders already were falling on the roof of the library.

It was 1:45 A.M. Hoses were turned on the library walls, and the decision was made to attempt to rescue the books. Within a few minutes, 500 students had formed lines to pass books out of the threatened building and into the Arts-Law Building, a hundred feet to the north. An hour later, the books were saved and the danger past. O. P. sadly recalled:

> Most of us stayed and watched until about 5:00 A.M., looking at the dying flames, each with his own thoughts of the proud history of the Chapel-Auditorium—the baccalaureate services and the commencement exercises during the war years, the plays and concerts, the anniversaries of faculty members, the occasional funerals, the chapel service on December 8, 1941, the annual Reformation convocation, the Christmas concerts and Christmas vespers—all the memories of the long years during which this building has been the living heart of a living institution. I must confess that when I finally turned away there were some tears in my eyes—not caused by smoke.

There were no injuries, and the University's vital records in the registrar's office were found safe in fireproof compartments. Special appeals from students and Missouri Synod President Behnken brought in more than $400,000 to the campus. The students proceeded to decorate the gymnasium so there could be a traditional "Valpo Christmas"—concert, Vespers, and all.

Despite difficulties such as the chapel fire and financial strains, the mid-1950s represented the beginning of a turnaround in the University's academic work. The failure of the College of Engineering to attain accreditation proved to be one strong catalyst for improvement. When the physics department was declared to be an "academic slum" by visiting accreditors, action was swift and brutal. Chairman Ansel Thomas, who for years had operated the department with a low budget and homemade equipment, was unceremoniously relieved of his duties. Nearly the entire physics and mathematics faculty resigned in protest over this autocratic action.

The administration immediately brought in two talented physicists, Armin Manning and Manuel Bretscher, both well connected with the Atomic Energy Commission and other professional agencies. Money soon poured into remodeling and equipping laboratories in the half-century-old Science Hall, which still shook at the passing of trains, ruining experiments and creating endless undergraduate lore. The chemistry department also was upgraded and successfully applied for membership in the American Chemical Society. By late 1957, the University could announce that the U.S. Atomic Energy Commission was loaning VU three tons of uranium and the necessary plutonium to create a subcritical nuclear reactor.

O. P. already had pressed on the board the urgency of a new science building. It was the era of Sputnik, and among the anxious American responses was the National Defense Education Act of 1958, which channeled huge amounts of money into science, foreign languages, and social science programs in an effort to "catch up" with the Soviets. Kretzmann declared that the sciences were "the most important departments in our university today, because of the nuclear age in which we are living." Soon, almost all the VU science faculty possessed doctorates from leading universities, and most were active in the Lutheran Church as well.

The dramatic improvement in the sciences at VU was accompanied by an equally strong upgrading of engineering. When another tough team of accreditors—the department heads from Yale, Maryland, and Swarthmore—arrived for an inspection visit in 1958, they found the program much enhanced and approved accreditation. With 430 students, the College of Engineering was larger than the entire student body had been when Kretzmann arrived. It also was attracting academically top students. To staff the burgeoning college, Dean Herman Hesse had drawn on some of the college's own alumni. For example, after Edgar Luecke and Merlyn Vocke graduated in 1955, they immediately found themselves traveling to Notre Dame for graduate study in the mornings, then returning to teach at Valpo in the afternoons. Such VU alumni, along with a core of fine professors recruited from elsewhere, made VU's engineering college, within a few years, comparable to the best undergraduate programs in the country.

THE ARTS AND SOCIAL SCIENCES

Equally striking was the growth of the arts. In 1952, Theodore Hoelty-Nickel had started the University Composers Exchange in Valparaiso. Through its annual meeting of composers and performers at major midwestern campuses, Valparaiso became identified with some of the finest contemporary music. Among the most original young composers was VU's own Richard Wienhorst, who gained an international reputation for works such as the "Missa Brevis," first performed at an international church music conference in Oslo, Norway. The tradition of outstanding VU organists was continued after 1958 by Philip Gehring. Active in the American Guild of Organists, which awarded him first prize for improvisation in 1970, Gehring was equally gifted in performance, leading worship, and teaching.

Professor Vera Hahn headed a lively Department of Speech and Drama that attracted not only prospective theater and speech teachers for the schools, but also creative students who found in the Valparaiso Players and their four or five annual dramatic productions the basis for a truly liberal education. Hahn attracted a loyal following of bright and talented students who admired her staunch advocacy of the highest ideals in the arts and her personal courage in the face of physical handicaps. She brought a sensitive humanism to her teaching and dramatic interpretation that established a strong VU theatrical tradition. Hahn's student and eventual colleague, Van C. Kussrow, extended her vision to explore the relation of drama to Christian liturgy and the arts, constantly pursuing the goal of "faithful excellence."

In 1958, the University created a genuine art department with the appointments of Ernest Schwidder and Richard Caemmerer Jr. Both were high-impact professors dedicated not only to technical instruction, but also to teaching students the importance of art in society and church. David Elder followed Schwidder in the department and created the great *Christus Rex* crucifix above the altar in the Chapel of the Resurrection, as well as the suffering Christ in the Gloria Christi Chapel. Caemmerer remained at VU for more than two decades, much in demand nationally for his liturgical work, especially in stained glass. On campus, he frequently took on the artist's role of disturber of the peace.

Professor Alfred H. Meyer continued to be the most nationally recognized scholar at VU in this period. His research on the natural and human ecology of the Kankakee Marsh and the Calumet Region established his national reputation, while his passionate teaching attracted many of the best students. Long before "ecology" and "environmentalism" became common terms, Meyer was discussing the realities they signified with a genuinely religious passion. The earth was the Lord's, he declared, but humans were despoiling it. For Meyer, the proper study of geography as the interrelation of things on the earth was an antidote to environmental disaster because the world and its people were terribly threatened.

In the social sciences, there were other forceful personalities who strongly affected students. Paul T. Heyne, a graduate of Concordia Seminary who held advanced degrees in economics and ethics, blended economic theory with a Christian humanism of rare sophistication. Professor of Government Victor Hoffman was a visible and controversial presence on campus. For *The Cresset*, he wrote a regular column called "Minority Report," and he reveled in the role of critic and gadfly. Trained as a Missouri Synod clergyman, Hoffman had done a dissertation at Indiana University on the classical theorist Max Weber and was strongly interested in the social consequences of faith, which he also explored by practicing Democratic politics and aiding those in need. Students remembered Hoffman bringing to the classroom some passage from his incessant current reading, quoting it with a familiar quizzical look on his face, cocking his head slightly to one side, scratching it, and asking, "Now what do *you* think about that?" Well versed in the new behavioral social sciences, and a believer in the tradition of "Christian realism" in politics, Hoffman saw power as something to be used for justice, while standing, as he often said, under the cross and under the forgiveness of sins.

Combining the "empirical" with the "normative" in this way was rare in the discipline, but it was the sort of thing O. P. regularly called for. However, the president was sometimes dismayed when the results turned out to be unsparing criticisms of the power structures on which the University, in part, depended. O. P. spent a lot of time dealing with the public relations fallout from faculty who, like Hoffman, took seriously the call for a prophetic, truth-seeking university. Together with his colleague Donald Mundinger, Hoffman worked especially hard to get top VU students into good graduate schools, with considerable success. Many of them went on to distinguished academic or diplomatic careers of their own.

No sampling of notable VU professors could omit historian Willis Boyd, who joined the faculty in 1954 and died in August 1993 while preparing for yet another semester. For 40 years, he enlivened the classroom for bright and mediocre students alike. The single Boyd lived for his students and was a strong intellectual and moral influence on many of them. His classes overflowed, often requiring extra sections that he eagerly accepted. Over the course of a semester, one of his goals was to take each student out for coffee or lunch, singly or in groups of three or four, and he often succeeded.

Teaching both Western civilization and Latin American history, Boyd often traveled with classes to Europe and Mexico, as well as to other parts of the globe. His foreign study tours never failed to produce tales of narrow escapes and student foibles, humorously recounted. Like a number of the leading faculty at the University, Boyd was not afraid to be critical of the administration. He regularly wrote irate letters to *The Torch*, complaining about administrative action on student or fraternity issues. Steeped in the traditions of the Enlightenment, Boyd promoted a humanism tinged with skepticism, though in later years, he became a regular at the VU chapel. Countless students owed him much, well beyond the money he so easily lent and the books he so freely gave away.

Professor John Strietelmeier's students were not only those in campus classrooms, but also the readers of *The Cresset*, a journal that grew in influence under his editorial leadership. Trained as a cultural geographer, he was also a lay theologian grounded in the Bible and the work of C. S. Lewis. He was often off campus giving speeches, attending conferences, or serving on committees. After O. P. Kretzmann, Strietelmeier was VU's principal theorist of Christian higher education and brought a layman's suspicion of clerical omniscience as he articulated the ideal of Valparaiso as a crucible of lay Christianity.

In 1951, Strietelmeier inaugurated a *Cresset* column, "Letter from Xanadu," purportedly written by G. G.,

> a dauntless ecclesiastical Babbitt. A sometimes shaky pillar of his congregation, the man from Xanadu was proud that he had retained his childhood religion without one whit of change, was ready to make any sacrifice for his church as long as it was not too great, and was open to all contemporary thought as long as it did not affect the status quo.

Readers met this pious Nebraskan—who later became president of the International Lutheran Implement Dealers of the United States and Canada (ILIDUSC)—together with his pastor, the Rev. Zeitgeist, just as their congregation had erected a gymnasium with a small prayer chapel attached to make it more Christian. For more than a decade, readers eagerly followed the adventures of G. G. and Rev. Zeitgeist in the column. They also found Strietelmeier's more sober editorial comments on current affairs among the best and most thoughtful opinion pieces in the Synod or, for that matter, in the nation.

INNOVATIONS IN THEOLOGY

At the urging of board member Dickmeyer, in 1954 Kretzmann began to invigorate the religion department by appointing a number of top young Concordia Seminary graduates in the process of completing their doctorates in the U.S. or Germany. Familiar with the more recent approaches to Lutheran theology developed in Europe, they gave the department a new visibility and dynamism. In 1958, the president appointed as head of the department Robert Bertram, a highly regarded theologian and philosopher who was also something of a visionary and reformer.

Bertram, aided by two creative German-trained theologians, Edward Schroeder and Robert Schultz, developed a curriculum that he believed would vitalize the religious character of the entire University. Taught by scholar-pastors who regarded their teaching as a form of ministry, the "New Testament Readings" curriculum was designed to integrate religious instruction with the liturgical church year. The package included raising the religion requirement to 12 hours (six two-credit courses), comparable to that at most good Lutheran colleges of the time. While some talented students majored in theology and went on to seminaries, divinity schools, or varieties of professional church work, the focus of VU's department was on developing a working theology for use by the laity.

The new program, and the department's general initiatives, attracted considerable favorable attention from outsiders, especially Roman Catholics. An article in the Catholic lay journal *Commonweal* by Jeremy Taylor of Notre Dame said that Valparaiso had instituted "an experiment in religious instruction of no small interest to all concerned with Christian education and the formation of Christian youth." Taylor noted that many students declared that, despite the heavy work load, the course was "meaningful and life-changing."

Catholic theologians at Notre Dame also took note of what was happening at Valparaiso and in Lutheran theology generally. Following up on conversations about liberal education that Dean Allen Tuttle and Ernest Koenker had held with Notre Dame leaders, the Valparaiso and Notre Dame theology departments began holding groundbreaking Catholic-Lutheran dialogues that continued twice a year for more than a decade. This was during the papacy of Pius XII, well before Vatican II. A synod in Rome had just repeated its sharp warnings for Catholics to be wary of

Protestants, and the Protestant attitude toward Catholics was doubly suspicious because of the new papal initiatives in Mariology. While there were some other ecumenical straws in the wind, the Valparaiso-Notre Dame dialogues were genuinely pathbreaking and helped to lay the basis for the deeper Lutheran-Catholic conversations after Vatican II.

The ideas being developed by VU's department were quite distinctive on the American scene, perhaps not surprising because the Missouri Synod and its people, while no longer outsiders in U.S. culture, still understood themselves to be different from other forms of American Protestantism, both mainstream and evangelical. The New Testament Readings courses reflected this difference by working out of scriptural stories, the liturgy, and reflections on the materials that frame and form the Christian community, rather than from many of the psychological or social concerns that preoccupied many contemporary religious thinkers of the time. The program revolved around themes such as "The Theology of the Cross versus the Theology of Glory," "Incarnational versus Gnostic Christianity," "Baptism and the Lord's Supper as Dying and Rising with Christ," and "Christian Life as Conformity with Christ." The figure of Christ, present in Word and Sacrament, was always the religious linchpin, distinguishing this theology from a good deal of American Protestant religious language.

Despite its religious creativity and favorable notice from outsiders, however, the New Testament Readings curriculum was soon enveloped in controversy on the VU campus. Some of this reflected competition for scarce financial and curricular resources, compounded because the rapidly growing department of high-impact clergy professors appeared to some to be developing a privileged position in a church-related school. Some internal critics found the emphasis on God's judgment too harsh. Others believed that the recurrent emphasis on judgment and grace, Law and Gospel, led to a neglect or distortion of the full range of Christian teaching.

Bertram ably defended the program against various criticisms, showing how these theological themes in effect threatened the prevailing religiosity so comfortably wedded to the affluence, conformity, and moralism of U.S. culture. O. P. called in his brother Martin ("Mickey") and other distinguished visitors to evaluate the curriculum, and they responded favorably. But in the end, the decision was made to establish a "two-track" program, with New Testament Readings as one option. At the same time, the theology department was relieved of responsibility for the chapel program as VU began to sponsor its own Sunday worship as well.

Recognizing the changes, Bertram left for Concordia Seminary on amicable terms. Although the particulars faded, something of the spirit and dynamism of the New Testament Readings program remained within VU's (now renamed) Department of Theology, which continued to aim at producing a theologically literate and engaged leadership for the church.

One particular religious program that tapped into the mostly quiet and "underground" spiritual and social idealism of some students in the 1950s was the Youth Leadership Training Program (YLTP), developed in 1956 and first directed by Coach Walter Reiner. Reiner was a skillful and successful football coach, but people who knew him recognized that behind his athletic persona was an intense man who could quote Kierkegaard on "risk," who possessed wide-ranging religious and social concerns, and who yearned to act on them. Established in cooperation with the Lutheran Laymen's League, the Walther League, and the Missouri Synod Board for Young People's Work, YLTP was a fresh idea at the time, linked to the theology of the laity that several churches were articulating and Lutherans were discovering—or rediscovering. It also reflected, in part, the churches' recognition of the power of the new "youth culture" that was emerging amid the affluence of postwar American society and of many pastors' inability to understand or relate to it.

Applicants for the program were screened carefully to draw exceptional young men and women who combined good scholarship with a strong religious and service orientation. In 1959, the *Walther League Messenger* featured Dean Kell as the type of Valparaiso student attracted to this program. A straight-A former premed student who had shifted into YLTP, Kell played football and ran track, led his fraternity to sponsor programs for underprivileged kids, served as president of the junior class, and was a freshman residence hall counselor. With their combination of theological and practical training, "YLTPers" such as Kell were in high demand with pastors and congregations. Several of the synodical schools soon followed in developing programs that trained young people to work with youth of the church.

Soon the impulse behind YLTP took a more active and socially conscious turn. In 1962, O. P. declared in chapel that "once more we are embarking on something unusual and exciting. Some pioneering needs to be done again." He announced the creation of an "Inner City Peace Corps," another Reiner brainchild that placed VU students in American inner-city locations for a year. These young people were to be "Christophers"—Christ-bearers—to those in need whom the affluent society had passed by. *The Torch* printed accounts of the ICPC students' activities in places such as Detroit and New York, and they received other media attention as well. Within a few more years, the operation expanded to an even more ambitious and far-flung international version, operated by the Synod, called the "Prince of Peace Volunteers." POPV sent students from Valparaiso and other colleges into church-related service programs around the world.

Student Life in the 1950s

While such programs appealed to some VU students' idealism, most followed more traditional paths. As the immediate postwar phenomena of older veterans and makeshift housing arrangements receded into memory, undergraduate student life returned to more familiar and stable patterns, and tenacious collegiate traditions again prevailed. Generalized freshman hazing was among them, until an accident in 1959 that sent several students to the hospital led to the banning of this form of "initiation." Most students of the 1950s accepted the University's parental role as part of their transition to independence, while still managing to find ways to assert their autonomy and to enjoy themselves in the process.

Greek life also revived and turned to revised versions of traditional patterns. In the years after the war, fraternity houses remained under the strict rule of seniors and law students. Fraternity men were proud of their houses, keeping the public rooms clean so at any time guests could be entertained with a sense that, however humble the structure, it was well presented. Within a decade or so, though, returning alumni had a hard time recognizing the old places. In the early 1950s, Valparaiso's fraternities joined national fraternities, bringing them closer to general collegiate norms. The influence of the new "youth culture," especially including increased drinking and ownership of automobiles by the more affluent students, led to more incidents of hazing and decreased attention to the "civilizing" function of fraternity house living. During the late 1950s and early 1960s, a more aggressively "rebellious" ethos developed, similar to what eventually would be featured in the film *Animal House*.

Throughout the 1950s, VU sororities still rented houses in the vicinity of campus. Most of them were firetraps, with ropes hanging from upper-floor windows for use in cases of emergency. Although they had their own residences, sororities maintained the same 9 P.M. curfew, with lights out at 10 P.M., that governed the dormitories, though students found ways to evade the rules. Some of the houses had housemothers, but most were under the charge of a senior student. Every house and residence hall had a "door-buzzer-girl," whose job it was to let in after-hours students with "late permits." Sorority Vespers held immediately after the curfew were common.

The condition of most of the houses was so poor that opportunities were sought to find alternative sorority housing. In 1961, the University took advantage of government funding to build Scheele Hall, which was designed with as much individuality as possible to house the eight sororities. When Scheele opened in 1961, alumna Dolores Ruosch joined VU as assistant dean of women and director of sorority affairs, carrying out her work with style and care for students.

The Greeks continued to sponsor much of the social life on campus in the 1950s. There were date parties between sororities and fraternities, with themes such as Swinging Safari, Catacomb Party, the Gangster Party, the Fireside Party, and the like. Many events were open to independents as well, so the fraternities and sororities actually organized much of the campus social life for all students, especially before the Union was built and began sponsoring campus-wide activities. One real advantage of Greek life for many students was that, by living in a house and hiring a cook to prepare meals, the cost of living could be reduced significantly.

For VU students of the 1950s, who were often the first in their families to attend college, the Greek organizations, despite their weaknesses, did teach skills and responsibilities. Internal organizational activities fostered leadership skills of cooperation, organization, and public speaking. Young men learned from their "big brothers" how to do laundry, shine shoes, clean rooms, and care for a house and lawn. For social events such as the spring formals, they learned how to dress properly and wear tuxedos. The college issue of *Esquire* taught them "what men are wearing on campus." Monday evening meetings still required jackets and ties. Greeks and others patronized the special forums on "dress and manners" sponsored by Union Director Helen Olson, in which women were taught such things as how to guide the flame of a man's lighter to the tip of her cigarette. They also learned that they were supposed to smoke only while seated and never while walking.

Spring weekend was largely a Greek event, featuring such things as bicycle races, rope pulls, and track events, followed by a festival ball with a big-name band and Songfest. The Greeks also reigned supreme during homecoming. Its traditions changed little from previous decades: the German band breaking up Friday classes, Hobo Day, the crowning and kissing of the queen by O. P., and the pep rally, the freshman bonfire made of logs and railroad ties laced with creosote, which sent black smoke a hundred feet into the air. Eventually the bonfires became so immense that they were seen as a threat to the new buildings, and the long-standing tradition was discontinued. During the infamous homecoming of 1955, someone—everyone suspected students from arch rival St. Joseph's College—set fire to the bonfire a night early, but the freshmen got local merchants to donate materials and cooperate in rebuilding the bonfire in time for the proper ceremonies.

Sports were an important part of VU student life in the 1950s. Although the success of the "World's Tallest Team" was not duplicated, it had encouraged the belief that Valparaiso could compete at high levels of intercollegiate athletics. The board adopted a policy to maintain at least one sport at a level of national recognition, consistent with the University's effort to be a national institution for Lutherans. That sport was basketball, which was the most affordable.

For nearly two decades, a new style of fast-break, jump-shooting basketball had been developing in the Midwest and especially in "Kentuckiana," the basketball-mad states of Kentucky and Indiana that took even their high school basketball tournaments with the seriousness of the World Series or the Super Bowl. The universities of Kentucky, Indiana, Purdue, and Notre Dame were the high-profile athletic powers of "Kentuckiana," but more than a dozen smaller universities and colleges in the two states played a similar style of basketball. Butler, Evansville, Louisville, and Valparaiso regularly challenged major national teams, and sometimes they beat them.

The Indiana Collegiate Conference (ICC) was the organizational vehicle of such colleges in Indiana. In 1950, Butler, Ball State, Indiana State, St. Joseph's, Evansville, and Valparaiso became charter members of the conference. DePauw was admitted in 1953. For 15 years, this alignment of seven schools remained intact. Its members competed in a wide range of sports, but it was in basketball that the conference achieved recognition on the national scene.

The rivalries of the ICC created what many later regarded as idyllic days of college sports at Valparaiso. The competitors were evenly matched, though Evansville was the perennial power in basketball as Valparaiso was in baseball. The schools were of similar size, and the majority were private. Healthy and enjoyable rivalries flourished in all sports. Fiercest for Valparaiso was the rivalry with St. Joseph's College. Because it was only an hour away by car, sizable student and faculty groups of fans could follow their team for games at the rival's campus. There was the potential for pranks at each game, and people would be on watch for several days before a St. Joe football game, guarding the victory bell against theft and keeping an eye on the field for possible shenanigans. The pranks went both ways. On one occasion, St. Joe students awoke to see all their stop signs transformed to read "ST.O.P."

Moreover, players were thoroughly representative of the student body and participated in other areas of campus life, often as leaders in student government and fraternity offices. Athletics shared the budgetary austerity of the whole VU campus. There was as yet no dominating professional basketball league to serve or imitate, and college sports were only beginning to be televised. Spectators enjoyed winning, but even more, they appreciated the high quality of "wholesome" collegiate sports, no matter the outcome. Students cheered and avidly followed the teams, crowding the facilities, all the more so because the players were so much a part of their common college life at Valpo. That was a point regularly stressed by Athletic Director Richard Koenig in his reports to the president: "As you know one of the key principles of our philosophy is that student-athletes should be truly representative of the school they represent." He went on to cite VU athletes' achievements and recognitions on Awards Day, at the Honors Convocation, and in various student organizations. Coaches relied on good contacts with high schools, pastors, and key alumni to recruit the kind of players that fit with Valpo's approach.

Basketball started the decade with a resoundingly successful 1950 season, led by All-American honorable mention Bob Metcalf. Coach Ken Suesens took the reins in 1951 and coached for most of the 1950s. Although the basketball team never won an ICC championship during the 1950s and 1960s, it was often near the top. VU basketball did upset Evansville's top-ranked small-college team, 73–71, in 1959. Earlier, in 1956, VU played in the Orange Bowl tournament, defeating Miami but losing to Stanford and LaSalle. At home that year, Valparaiso lost only to Purdue, Evansville, and San Jose State.

Paul Meadows, a member of the "World's Tallest Team" in the 1940s, returned to VU as coach in 1958. In 1962, Valparaiso hosted the Great Lakes regional NCAA tourney, won it, and moved to the national NCAA college division eight-team tourney in Evansville. In 1964, Gene Bartow became head coach, and VU basketball reached a new high point of interest and excitement. In the first home game that year, the team set a new scoring record by beating Western Ontario 132–53. The following season, Valparaiso was ranked fifth in its small-college category and won the first round of the NCAA Midwest tournament.

In 1966–67, VU's team finished second in the ICC with a 21–8 record and progressed in NCAA postseason play from the regional tourney at Terre Haute to the national quarterfinals at Evansville. The next year, VU's star Dick Jones set a new career scoring record of 1,520 points. That season also featured a game against the University of Houston, the nation's top-ranked major college team, and its star Elvin "Big E" Hayes. Houston slaughtered Valparaiso 158–81. During the next two years, basketball continued its winning ways, dominated by the great play of Bruce Lindner, who set records in nearly all scoring categories by the time he graduated in 1970. In 1968–69, VU again placed second in the ICC and hosted the Great Lakes regional, where it lost in the second round.

It was the end of an era when Bartow left VU in 1970, moving on to a career as one of the top college coaches at Memphis State, Illinois, UCLA, and Alabama-Birmingham. By that time, the college basketball world was changing dramatically and moving beyond the nostalgic era of the 1950s and the ICC.

While football, baseball, and other sports could not match the enthusiasm for basketball on a Hoosier campus, they were competitive and had their followings. In football, a group of beefy veterans who had played football in the armed services brought Valparaiso a pair of undefeated seasons in 1950 and 1951 and a bid to the Cigar Bowl in Tampa, Florida, on New Year's Day in 1951 against undefeated LaCrosse State Teachers College in Wisconsin. With 12,000 fans cheering the two teams, Valparaiso lost 47–14.

VU's two-year winning streak brought with it domination of the ICC. The team featured Joe Pahr, little All-American in 1951; all-conference player Arol Amling; and such future members of the VU staff as Don Findling, future coach Bill Koch, and in 1952, future athletic director William Steinbrecher. Guard Fred "Fuzzy" Thurston later became a star with the Green Bay Packers. There was also a "Lutheran Bowl," played during the season at Cleveland, then at Fort Wayne, with strong Wittenberg University as the opponent. Three hundred students took a special train to Fort Wayne for that contest.

One reason for VU's football success in the 1950s was the appointment of Walt Reiner to the coaching staff in 1949. Emory Bauer, the quarterback on Christiansen's undefeated 1932 team, was head coach, but as

Bauer's assistant, Reiner brought a special discipline and intelligence to the game, reflected in his long hours spent studying opponents' game films. In 1957, Reiner was named co-coach. The next years in football were especially exciting, with many outstanding players named to all-ICC teams. In 1963, quarterback Dave Lass was second in the nation in passing with 1,883 yards, and he led VU to a five-way tie for the ICC championship.

"Complete and total domination" are the words for the VU baseball team's record in the 1950s and early 1960s. By 1970, VU had won 14 ICC championships and was a regular in NCAA postseason play. In 1963, Coach Emory Bauer was named NCAA Baseball Coach of the Year. VU seemed to produce especially outstanding pitchers, such as Randy Goede, Richard Beumer, Douglas Seltz, Robert Lohse, Tim Juran, and Jon Robisch.

College baseball had little attraction as a spectator sport, but VU players nevertheless gave themselves wholeheartedly to the game. They were dedicated athletes and survived on absolutely minimal budgets. While football players ate steak after a game, baseball players ate hamburgers. Gloves, shoes, and other equipment were normally supplied by the players themselves. None of the budgets for any of the sports, of course, was ever adequate. Coach Bauer remembered that in the 1940s he and his wife did the football laundry on Sunday afternoons. On the road, two 200-plus pound football players commonly had to bunk in a single bed.

Valparaiso also fielded competitive track teams. The three Schroeder brothers, Don, Ted, and Art, consistently led VU teams to cross-country victories, with Ted winning the ICC championship twice. In the 1960s, Steve Cook was a little All-American hurdler. Rhodes Scholar Richard Nehring continued the cross-country tradition. ICC track championships or near-championships were frequent during those years.

Men still dominated the postwar sporting world, and at Valparaiso, as around the nation, the old arguments against women's participation in major intercollegiate sports were still heard. The strength of women's intramurals and their participation in physical education classes, however, belied the attitude that women were somehow unsuited for highly competitive sports. Women's athletics included softball, volleyball, basketball, badminton, bowling, gymnastics, track, golf, tennis, swimming, and field hockey. In golf, VU's Patty Shook Boice became the national collegiate women's champion. A modest form of intercollegiate women's sports did exist under the auspices of the Women's Athletic Association, which sponsored "play days"—occasional all-day (usually Saturday) meetings of schools in a variety of sports. Teams were differentiated by "pinnies" (pinafores worn over blouses) rather than uniforms.

Richard Koenig was named athletic director in 1957. At that time, enrollment was rising and student demand for athletic facilities far outstripped the capacity of the old gymnasium. Another former VU athlete, Koenig was an ardent advocate of intramurals for all students, as well as intercollegiate activities for the talented. In memos, announcements, and public appearances, Koenig pushed the idea of "a sound mind in a sound body" as an essential goal for college life and after, and he worked to expand athletic opportunities for everyone on campus. As part of their centennial gift in 1959, the alumni donated Alumni Park, a tract of land across U.S. 30, to the University for future athletic purposes. By 1962, a second gym, a swimming pool, additional workout space, and other improvements were added. In 1965, the University acquired the large "Eastgate" property across old Highway 49, which was developed for baseball, track, soccer, and intramural use.

As a former multisport athlete and continuing fan, O. P. thoroughly enjoyed following VU sports. When he was in town, he could be seen sitting in his balcony corner seat at basketball games or on the players' bench for football contests, conspicuous in his clerical collar. When he could, he attended other sports contests as well. O. P. was enthusiastic about winning and would openly express his disappointment—"Well, they played like monkeys tonight, didn't they?"—when the teams lost.

Besides athletic events, O. P. was an especially visible part of VU student life during annual homecoming rituals. He always wanted homecoming to go well, so he tried to prepare students and put them on good behavior. On Homecoming Sunday, the chapel would be jammed. For many alumni, hearing O. P. again would be the high point of the weekend, and he rarely failed to deliver a stirring sermon. In 1959, the centennial year, a special Service of Remembrance was held. A member of each class since 1883 placed a wreath on the altar steps in memory of classmates who had died in service of the United States.

Even as the University grew, O. P.'s memorable speaking was one of the things that held it together. His speeches and writing were marked by grace, wit, and a penchant for large ideas that typically clustered around memorable phrases and images. "The university under the cross" suggested that VU was responsible to an authority other than the institutional church or denomination. "The postmodern age" suggested the evident implosion of the secularist and scientific Enlightenment as the ultimate ground of truth and an emerging new configuration of cultural forces. "Convergence" hinted at the coming together of the Christian faith and selected cultural themes toward a new cohabitation of "Athens and Jerusalem," Kretzmann's regular shorthand phrase (borrowed from the church father Tertullian) for the best in human thought and the biblical revelation, respectively.

Besides his public addresses to VU's numerous constituencies, O. P. made a special point of speaking directly and personally to students, and his papers reveal the care that he devoted to these public utterances. He constantly reiterated and elaborated on his favorite themes, drawing his young listeners into a sense of a common enterprise. He spoke at Student Council installations before the student body, at Honor Council meetings, at fraternities and sororities, and at student organization banquets. He always addressed students at the opening and closing convocations of each semester. In 1955, for instance, students gathered for the final chapel service of the school year heard these words:

> In this student body and faculty we have a growing number of outstanding men and women who have joined us in our quest for the leaders of tomorrow—men and women of critical spirit, dispassionate mind, and the cool reflection that must precede final commitment.
>
> Everyone, especially seniors, agrees that there is a perennial miracle, a timeless magic about college: the memory of changing seasons across campus and ivied walls, the lingering words of close friendships throughout the years, the first clear shock of truth, football on long afternoons, Christmas in chapel, a long talk with an instructor to whom years have given wisdom. All these make college a great and remembered thing, something which I am sure you will never quite forget.
>
> And yet beyond all these—let us say it again this morning—there is something else infinitely greater, and finally determining of the greatness of any college or university. It must be a place where hope has not died, where the prison house of the modern world is not yet closed, where the door is open to yesterday and tomorrow, where no battle is quite yet lost; finally, where God moves, in quietness and in strength, to take our hopes and our dreams, for ourselves and for the world, and begins to build them into reality. I hope this has happened also this semester. A blessed and happy summer!

There were times when Kretzmann scolded the students. Sometimes he would refer to manifestations of pride, jealousy, and dishonor on campus; sometimes he talked of cheating, failure to attend chapel, sexual immorality, drunkenness, and abuses of freedom. "You may break the law, but the law will break you!" he could thunder. But John Feaster, a student and later a faculty member, recalled above all O. P.'s pervasive high spirits and sense of humor: " 'On this solemn and auspicious occasion' was his routine opener on occasions that were not even superficially either of these things. We knew it was coming. It always did. But we were charmed nonetheless and knew that things were not quite so bad as we thought after all."

TOO AMERICAN?

As the 1950s drew to a close, Valparaiso University was very Lutheran, very American, supported by a more national and increasingly affluent church body that was showing many signs of success and was very far from its struggling immigrant beginnings. The Americanization of the Missouri Synod and its people was well advanced when World War II broke out, and the war served to strengthen many Missourians' attachment to the United States.

The patriotism kindled by the war flared again as the Cold War followed, and this increased patriotism linked itself closely to the postwar revival of religion. In the early 1950s, VU Professor Ernest Koenker noted the rising phenomenon of "civil religion" in a *Cresset* article titled "The Threat of American Shintoism," pointing to the danger signals in this kind of blurring of religion and nationalism. A few years later, Martin Marty contributed a piece on what he called "The Emergent Religion of American Democracy." When Congress moved in 1954 to insert the phrase "under God" into the Pledge of Allegiance and to make "In God We Trust" the official national motto, *The Cresset* vigorously denounced it. It was significant that thoughtful voices of the Missouri Synod, which for so long had stood outside the mainstream of American life, were able to bring a critical perspective on what scholar William Lee Miller called the uncritical linking of "religion and Americanism, God and country, cross and flag."

But there was no doubt that most Lutherans were now at home in the United States and loved their nation. While some people in VU circles retained a bit of the immigrant outsiders' more critical perspective on some features of American life, others reflected the former outsiders' enthusiasm at finally being "inside." Within the board, there were those who talked of how VU could help the United States return from its recent "moral decline" and corruption to a more virtuous condition. For some, the University was seen as contributing to this end, and some financial appeals certainly were based on a patriotic and anticommunist pitch.

Amid the 1950s' atmosphere of upward mobility and patriotism, at least some of the tensions that had often dominated relations between VU and the Missouri Synod hierarchy seemed to diminish. Some in the Synod, who recognized the significant role that Valparaiso played in moving Lutheran laity into wider areas of American society, looked more positively on the institution. At a joint meeting of the University and synodical boards in 1956, LCMS president John Behnken declared, "The progress of Valparaiso University and Synod are intimately related," and Secretary Martin Kretzmann chimed in, "Valparaiso is part of Synod!" Behnken then proposed, following a custom in the Synod, that everyone present rise and sing. Normally the song would be "Now Thank We All Our God" or the common doxology, "Praise God, from Whom All Blessings Flow." But in this case, Behnken proposed that those assembled sing "God Save Our Native Land."

Bonding with U.S. culture and trying to find a place in it took many forms during the late 1950s among Missouri Lutherans and others. One way was to embrace American popular culture and to identify with representatives who had "made it" into visible positions within that world. The Lutheran press was fond of featuring star Lutheran athletes in collegiate and professional sports, as well as Lutheran movie stars and beauty queens. Valparaiso often figured into these stories. The 1956 Miss America was Sharon Kay Ritchie, the grandniece of VU patron Emma Ritchie. Three VU coeds also became prominent as contestants in the Miss America Pageant: Miss Indiana 1958 (Gloria Rupprecht), Miss Wisconsin 1960 (Mary Alice Fox, who became the first runner-up that year), and Miss Indiana 1960 (Barbara Kummer).

Martin Marty later recalled watching the 1960 pageant on TV, in which each young lady was required to do a "cultural piece." Mary Alice Fox was introduced as a student from Valparaiso University, and her piece was delightfully clear and attractive. She spoke with the faintly German accent of Sheboygan citizens in the 1950s. Self-congratulatory Lutherans in the national audience were anticipating further satisfaction when she was asked, "What do you think could do most to promote world peace and understanding?" In front of approximately 30 million people, Fox said, "The most important thing that's going on is Pope John XXIII's call for an ecumenical council to unite Christians." As Marty related it, his phone started ringing off the hook with people calling to ask what a Roman Catholic girl was doing at Valparaiso University! Marty's point, when he recounted this story to the Association of Lutheran College Faculties, was that in the coming decade many of the old lines separating social groups and communities would be breaking down as the conditions of American pluralism asserted themselves.

VU's movement into the American mainstream, as well as its slow but steady academic improvement, was stimulated by and partially responsible for the surge in highly competent students who came through the University in the late 1950s. Especially after Sputnik in 1957, and even more so with the election of John Kennedy and his emphasis on "the best and the brightest," the word "excellence" came into vogue on American campuses, including religious colleges. In these years, Valparaiso students began a long streak of winning prestigious nationally competitive fellowships. In 1963, Valpo seniors copped six Woodrow Wilsons, nearly matching much larger Notre Dame and Indiana. Rockefellers, Danforths, NDEA Fellowships, and even a Rhodes Scholarship in the mid-1960s were signs that VU students could compete with the nation's best.

Moreover, many of these eventual fellowship winners and other top students were increasingly prominent in a variety of leadership positions on the VU campus. Alan Graebner and James Nuechterlein, for instance, were both *Torch* editors of great distinction. *The Torch* regularly carried sophisticated commentary by such students that was hardly the typical fare of college journalism. For example, by way of criticizing the social passivity of VU's pre-seminary students, political science major David Leege wrote:

> The category of the holy, i.e., religious value, consists not only of the understanding of the nature of being, but also of the practical determinants of action or morality. Religion, therefore, gives meaning to life, to social, economic, and political phenomena. Clergymen are faced with the momentous task of applying the Gospel to a society existentially distorted by evil. Whether in the pulpit or in the vestry, they must make judgements on the morality of everyday affairs.

This period also brought several new student media into existence. In 1958, under the leadership of Jack Lawson, the *Lighter* was founded as the VU student literary and humor magazine. "You are putting your head in the lion's mouth," wrote O. P. in a letter of congratulations. Lawson similarly took the lead in launching the campus radio station, WVUR.

The emphasis on academic excellence proved to be a benefit to women at Valparaiso. After the war, coeds largely had reverted to a less visible role on campus, with many of them envisioning a future of domesticity according to the widespread ideal of the 1950s. Others still cherished the memories and stories of the wartime experience, when women ran VU's campus and contemplated going against the grain by fully developing their talents and pursuing careers. Even those women who did earnestly prepare for careers were dismayed to enter a world of work in which women were paid far less than men for doing the same job. Just as some women were inspired by accounts of female achievement, others were discouraged by witnessing the many barriers to success.

As the attention to academic achievement and "meritocracy" increased in the classrooms, however, the overt emphasis on gender differences lessened. In 1956, Kathy Sandborg was one of four VU engineering students to graduate "with high distinction" as she achieved the highest-ever grade point average in engineering. When Professor Margaretta Tangerman established a chapter of Alpha Lambda Delta, the women's honorary society, in 1955, guest speaker Dean Miriam Sheldon of the University of Illinois urged VU's female students to "acknowledge their gift of a keen mind, keep their minds clear and open, dare to show flair and see the world a little differently, and use their minds in the service of others."

Toward the end of the decade, a few VU women were in the vanguard of that rather small group of students who were reading Beat poetry and forming pockets of nonconformity, quietly questioning the then-prevalent U.S. culture and searching for a more authentic life. Such independent-minded women, usually gathered around such activities as the University Players or student publications, especially chafed under the sororities' domination of social and cultural life. Irked by the protected life of the female social organizations, Julie Becker petitioned O. P. to be allowed to live off campus. O. P. was not about to alter the rules until he noticed that Julie was the granddaughter of the Rev. F. J. Lankenau, one of the University's founders and an early visionary leader. "Lankenau!" O. P. exclaimed. "Why, he died in my arms!" He instantly granted Becker permission. Others followed her lead, and this first group of young nonconforming women moved off campus.

CENTENNIAL YEAR

Already in the 1940s, O. P. had begun calling attention to the importance of VU's upcoming centennial celebration in 1959. A committee headed by Walter Friedrich planned a series of religious and academic occasions linked to three major dedications: a residence hall (Wehrenberg), the library, and the chapel. The committee arranged for the publication of *Valparaiso's First Century*, a history of the University by John Strietelmeier. It also renamed all the buildings on the West Campus after major figures from the pre-Lutheran university: Kinsey, Bogarte, Baldwin, Heimlich, Heritage, and DeMotte.

The year was started and closed with religious services. President Kretzmann opened it in January by appearing on NBC-TV's *Frontiers of Faith*, speaking on the theme of Luther's dying words, "We are all beggars before God." The centennial observance concluded in December with a Service of Dedication for the second century, followed by dedication of the new Henry F. Moellering Library. In between were many events and ceremonies. Major religious services during the year included a Te Deum Service, at which Professor Wienhorst's setting received its premier performance; the Service of Remembrance at homecoming; and a special Reformation Day service.

In a more academic vein, the University brought speakers of international reputation to the chapel for a series of convocations. Among the notables were Clement Attlee, former prime minister of Great Britain; Roscoe Pound, Dean Emeritus of the Harvard Law School; H. Richard Niebuhr, Sterling Professor of Christian Ethics at Yale University; Bishop Hanns Lilje, former president of the Lutheran World Federation and a fierce opponent of Hitler; and Robert Maynard Hutchins, former president and chancellor of the University of Chicago. Perhaps the most notable memory for those present at the centennial convocations was the remarkable Dean Pound. Unable to read his manuscript because of the glare from the still-clear chancel windows, the 90-year-old Pound delivered the final 45 minutes of the lecture from memory, without hesitation.

The centennial year contained many events VU and its friends would long remember, but there were other events it would have preferred to forget. There was an unusual series of unpleasant incidents on campus. Just before graduation in June 1959, a senior committed suicide. After a homecoming party in October, there was a fatal automobile accident. Also that fall, a group of freshmen leaving the gym spotted some sophomores waiting to haze them. In the pushing and shoving that followed, eight female students were trampled and hospitalized. O. P. was furious: "There will be no more of this sort of thing. Shall we get it clear? I think the campus should grow up. We can't justify this before the academic world, much less before God." Hazing was banned, and other traditions suddenly were canceled.

By late October, fraternity drinking had gotten out of hand, and the academic record of members was in decline. O. P. called a summit of fraternity leaders and declared an end to drinking in their houses. A week later, two students stole an airplane at 3 A.M., hit a power line, which interrupted electricity for many homes, and crash landed in a corner of the airport. Besides this, a member of the U.S. Senate rackets committee claimed, in televised public hearings, that "the mob" had an operation "on the VU campus." The University quickly pointed out that the establishment in question was a private building near the campus and had nothing to do with VU. But in the new age of TV, facts had trouble catching up with allegations.

As *Lighter* editor, Dick Lee wrote in the Christmas issue:

> Incidents similar to these, I'm told, are nothing new to the campus—but the sheer concentration of them in the year past has been a bit overwhelming. And not a little saddening and depressing. Who would have imagined that Valpo had so much dirty linen. ... Perhaps as the University is repeatedly called to defend and purge itself, it will eventually approach closer fulfillment of its defined ideals.

The high point of the centennial year was the chapel dedication. No single building had been as controversial as this one. The idea of constructing at VU a "cathedral embodying the highest art for the glory of God," in W. C. Dickmeyer's phrase, had seemed attractive in the abstract. But when funds were tight and other needs more desperate, many began to look more skeptically at planting such a building in the middle of Indiana farmland. When the plans were presented to synodical authorities, Behnken worried about "high churchism" and feared that too many superior features would make students complain when they returned to their ordinary churches. The original budget was to be $750,000 derived from the Building for Christ campaign. With other funds gathered by the Guild and special memorial gifts, that should do it, said the Kretzmann brothers. But board member Robert Moellering said that there was "no way" to keep within those limits—and he was right. The final cost was a little more than $1.6 million, a figure that included most, but not all, of the special memorials.

Some faculty members and certainly many parents who had to pay the growing tuition bills found this to be an extravagant expense. Detractors thought its size a monument to the Kretzmanns' egos. Its domination over the campus suggested a past age of Christendom and made it a target for antiauthoritarian impulses. But for O. P., the chapel symbolized the centrality of the living Christ in the University and the life of learning. "If this place departs from its purposes, the chapel should be an accusing embarrassment," he said often. In his sermon of dedication, A. R. Kretzmann described the chapel as "a way station for a vast pilgrimage of young people for years to come."

As the liturgical consultant for architect Stade, A. R. Kretzmann had been influential in patterning the chapel after one of the first churches in Christendom, the fourth-century Church of the Incarnation in Bethlehem, which was built over the place where, tradition held, Jesus was born (thus the name Gloria Christi for the lower chapel, corresponding to the traditional birth site). Whatever its historic resonance and symbolism, the chapel also was especially important as a place where the entire student body could gather under one roof, preserving a sense of community as the University, now with an enrollment of 2,600, continued to grow. (The chapel was designed to seat three thousand.)

Within the group planning the details of the building, there had been considerable controversy over various features. Musicians Hoelty-Nickel, Bichsel, and Fleischer battled for a superior organ worthy of "Lutheran culture," able to set the highest standards for the Lutheran church in the United States. The board supported their arguments, the Reddel family added the necessary funding, and a great Schlicker organ was designed with the balcony reinforced for future expansion.

The evening before the dedicatory services, the Guild dedicated Gloria Christi Chapel in a long, solemn service of Holy Communion, with 700 people communing in the small space. The events of the next day can be seen through the eyes of sophomore Gail McGrew (later Professor Eifrig of the English department), who wrote the following letter to her family:

> Dear folks—
>
> I am still so up in the air about yesterday that I can hardly sit still. How can I ever tell you about it. I just can't—but I must try. Well. The processions were in two parts—faculty from the Union; choir and officiating clergy, President, crucifers, mace, and torch bearers from the library.
>
> *Sketches*

> Dig this with the crucifers wearing those white belted albs like Episcopal acolytes, the torchbearers wearing white gowns covered by red and gold capes, the acolytes the same, the flag bearers in black robes, the choir in white and black (freshly laundered) and the clergy in black robes, white surplices and red and gold stoles, except for OP who wore a new gorgeous huge black cape with red and gold tassels and do-dads *and* a big gold U. seal on a chain around his neck. Plus the usually resplendent (and large) faculty. Oh too much. First our procession went around the building singing "Veni Creator Spiritus" and then into the building at the Gloria Christi Chapel up and into the nave and down the aisle out to the front where the ceremony of opening door was done and the choir sang "I was glad when they said unto me" then into the building again to the congregational singing of the chorale we finished—the whole procession. Then up to the Chancel and from here I haven't too much idea what happened as I couldn't hear a thing except when the liturgist faced the altar. But even to see was one thing. I'll try to describe the Chancel.
>
> *Sketch*
>
> The people—there were hundreds outside standing, the narthex was full, the balcony, the Gloria Christi Chapel, the steps down to the Gloria Christi Chapel, the steps to the balcony, the aisles—there wasn't breathing space. I don't know how many people but I should guess around 4,500. Well after the recessional we all recessed outside to the campanile and carillon and these were dedicated—and the largest bell struck three times, then the complete scale (every bell) three times, then the large one seven times more and that was the end.

The letter also describes E. Power Biggs's evening dedicatory concert for the Reddel organ, with 1,000 people unable to get into the building.

The new chapel had a powerful impact on student life. It challenged pastors and faculty to the highest forms of public address and preaching. It challenged musicians to sing and play well, designers to create banners and bulletins expressing the best the visual arts could offer, theater students to experiment with reconnecting drama and the church. It was a place for student weddings, memorial services, crisis convocations, great festival services, and for the famous to speak and sing—though the acoustical quality from the beginning depended on variables of weather, humidity, type of voice, care in speaking, and the type of music being sung or played. Some students found the cathedral-like character of the services too distant from their accustomed way of worshiping, but many others welcomed it, as it was intended, as a "way station on their pilgrimage" and perhaps as a link to the great cathedral culture of Christianity.

In any case, the Valparaiso University chapel became one of the notable places of worship in North America, and Stade, the architect, won a prestigious award for the design. When the distinguished guests for the Centennial Convocation examined the place, they recognized its grandeur. The most iconoclastic comment came from Robert Maynard Hutchins: "It looks like intellectual rock and roll." A few years later, theologian Paul Tillich, also renowned for his art criticism, looked up at the giant piers that form and uphold the chancel and said that the VU chapel was to him a symbol of "courage," Tillich's favorite synonym for faith in the modern world.

A "VALPO CHRISTMAS"

The long-standing emphasis on Christmas at VU took on new richness in the chapel, and celebrating the "Feast of the Incarnation" became the most beloved of Valpo traditions. A Valpo Christmas was a special time. Decorated houses and residence halls, Christmas parties, collections and events for underprivileged people at various venues, group caroling, the concert, and finally, the night before the last classes prior to everyone heading home for Christmas: the Christmas Vespers. If you wanted a seat, you had to come very early.

Decorations, common singing of favorite hymns, beautiful special music by various choral groups, candlelight, and always O. P.'s Christmas address—these were the ingredients of Christmas Vespers. O. P. was at his best in these addresses. Already in October, he had begun playing selections from his large Christmas record collection to get in the mood for the writing he would do for various seasonal publications. In 1959, in the newly dedicated and beautifully decorated chapel, he spoke on the theme "Point and Counterpoint." He said in part:

> I imagine you may be wondering why a theme reminiscent of a book by a modern agnostic should become the subject of our Christmas meditation—point and counterpoint. It has a musical derivation, two or more melodies running side by side, a composite melody which gives beauty and power by the recognition of its several elements. Taken alone any one of them is incomplete, may even be poor and thin, but taken together there is meaning and beauty in their rise and fall, even in momentary dissonance which is reduced into final harmony, and the joined melodies fall sweet and sure on the listening ear.

My theme, you see, is simple. Point. Counterpoint. Christmas has done that for life, and history. Introduced another melody into life, great and eternal, without which the discord of history and the broken music of our own lives cannot be understood, nor perhaps even endured. You cannot hear all of life unless and until you hear beyond the roar and confusion, the little clatter of our hurrying lives, the counterpoint which alone can give them sense and harmony. The new melody which began when the earth was at quiet midnight and the world in unquiet sleep—the Almighty Word leaped down from heaven. There was the voice of an angel: "Unto you is born ..." And then, after an interval of silence to enable the audience to reach a stable, the real theme of the melody, the new song, the eternal counterpoint to the crying of men—the cry of a Child, the whimper of a Baby, the voice of a Mother. Now the music of life is really complete. Point and counterpoint, man and God become man, a new song. Want to hear a few measures of that song this pre-Christmas night? "Come unto Me." "I am with you alway." "Because he was obedient." This is the new choral melody, the counterpoint. There is nothing more important than the power of this basic truth about life and history.

Some years ago Mr. Auden, one of England's most brilliant poets, suddenly published a work which was quite unexpected. Slowly and quietly, he had come to the manger, as so many modern minds have come, through a valley of disillusionment and despair. It is called "For the Time Being—a Christmas Oratorio." He cites the narrator, a proud Roman, living as men today live, in a world of headlines, a world half secular and half real, hearing only the surface noises of life. The Roman speaks. It has a strangely modern ring. ...

And at that very moment, Mary was lulling an infant to sleep in a manger and the shepherds heard her song in the gracious night and the hands of a Child were beginning to tug at the foundations of Empire and the melody of Christmas was beginning to sound over the discord of time. Oh, I know, seemingly the nations would stumble on, but beyond them all was the power of lowliness, of faith, of love, of hope, dominating and controlling in the end. The living power of the living God, lying helpless and supreme in a manger. The final melody belongs to God on Christmas night.

And now very personally. The Church wisely makes Advent a penitential season. Why? Because so many things in our lives cannot harmonize with the melody, the song of Christmas. They strike the wrong note. And so, before we can really come to the Manger to sing our little carols and bring our little gifts, there must be a sweeping of the heart, a cleansing of the spirit—"Except ye become as little children"—wonder, faith, and love. Where shall we start? Our pride? Looks bad, sounds bad, beside the incredible humility of the manger. Our selfishness? That child gave up the choir of heaven, the gates and the City, for the love of us. Our fears and anxieties? Angel: "Fear not!" He came to take them into his hands. No, if there is to be no discord and no disharmony in our Christmas we must come to the manger very light and very clean, past our sins and our hates, our sentimentality and sophistication—to come at long last to the place where all journeys end, with a child lying in a Manger. Certainly that must be my Christmas wish for you: quiet, so that you can hear what only faith can hear, God and man now singing together, and their song the ultimate eternal melody of life. I wish you much joy, for there is nothing greater than that.

9

THE 1960s

EXPANSION AND CHANGE

A NEW DECADE BEGINS

On the twentieth anniversary of his arrival in 1940 at a struggling Lutheran university of 380 students, President Kretzmann reflected on his inaugural address: "None of the phrases I used twenty years ago have lost their charm or their verity; they have merely returned hauntingly, to ask me to give them life and meaning." He insistently restated the centrality of Christ's atonement and public worship for the Christian university. Then he added: "Personally, I too have come to the quiet afternoon of my journey and the shadows now lie longer to the east."

O. P.'s reference to his advancing years was pertinent. Although he appeared to be in relatively good health as he turned 60 years old, the following years were not kind. Loving good food and drink, he put on too much weight. This aggravated an old football knee injury, and he soon had to be assisted up the chancel steps in the chapel. O. P.'s doctor incautiously treated him with a new cortisone medication whose side effects were not well known. They soon appeared in two forms: an onslaught of cataracts that severely limited his once extensive reading, as well as mood swings and bouts of depression. Thus, Kretzmann faced the difficult 1960s with increasing health handicaps. The daily functioning of the president's office increasingly depended on Sophia Heidbrink, her secretary, Dorothy Herscher, and Alfred Looman, who became the president's official assistant and unofficial right-hand man on campus and elsewhere.

In the 1960–61 academic year, there was a sense of change in the air on the campus, as in the nation, where youthful John Kennedy was elected and inaugurated as president of the United States. A fall conference on law and theology brought leading scholars in the Lutheran community to campus, including law school alumnus Richard Duesenberg, then on the faculty of the New York University School of Law, and two future VU presidents: Dean Albert Huegli of Concordia-River Forest and Professor Robert Schnabel of Concordia Senior College-Fort Wayne.

The philosophy department sponsored a series of interdepartmental lectures that established its strong intellectual leadership on the campus throughout the 1960s. Professor Van Kussrow led a panel on "Alienation as a Tragic Theme for Modern Man." Dr. Hans Rosenhaupt, director of the Woodrow Wilson National Fellowship Foundation, spoke to an Honors Convocation on "The Intellectual and the Affluent Society," denouncing the intellectual who merely talked and did not act. "What he thinks must lead to action, and in action he will tie himself to his fellow man," Rosenhaupt said. In April, Bishop Reeves of South Africa, a powerful critic of apartheid, addressed the issue of racial justice. In retrospect, these topics directly anticipated the developing issues of the coming decade.

Of great interest to everyone in the fall of 1961 was the appointment of Dr. Albert Huegli, whom O. P. described as "probably the top academic man in The Lutheran Church—Missouri Synod," to the new post of vice president for academic affairs. Huegli was familiar with VU through his family's long associations with the University. His father, a Detroit physician, had been active in progressive church causes, including the Valparaiso movement, and his brother Wilfred (Bob) had been a premed student at VU. A Concordia Seminary graduate, Huegli earned a Ph.D. at Northwestern University and became the academic dean at Concordia-River Forest. He was an expert on church-state relationships and eventually edited a well-regarded book on the subject, *Church and State under God*. Huegli successfully had practiced politics himself by winning election to the council of Oak Park, Illinois, and he was a regular consultant-examiner for the North Central Association. Within the Missouri Synod context, these were impressive credentials. Huegli enjoyed a deep personal respect throughout the Synod and served on numerous important synodical committees.

This cautious man with a scholarly demeanor and a quiet smile came to the campus at a time of faculty restlessness. That fall of 1961, fully a fifth of the faculty, including many of its leaders, formed a chapter of the American Association of University Professors (AAUP), the national organization that championed faculty rights and academic freedom. Huegli was an associate member. At the fall 1962 meeting of the board, he presented the sad state of VU faculty salaries, using the national AAUP tables that ranked salaries according to quintiles in each faculty rank. Valparaiso's salaries were so noncompetitive, he reported, that only two of the 24 appointments made in 1961 had their doctorates in hand.

Huegli had other assignments to address as well. He was in charge of synthesizing the new Ten-Year Plan and of gaining North Central approval for the new graduate program that the faculty had unenthusiastically approved. He also undertook the reorganization of the academic administration by forming a Deans Council that met regularly to discuss an agenda of short- and long-range concerns. Accustomed to personal involvement in every aspect of the University's administration, President Kretzmann sat in on the council and wrote a long commentary on the minutes when he missed a meeting. Kretzmann also concluded that because all important VU committees met in his office, the same should be the case with this council. Soon he literally took over the council, adding Vice Presidents Scribner and Toelke and renaming it the Administrative Council. Actually, this arrangement worked well and functioned during the rest of the Kretzmann presidency. But it was clear that O. P. Kretzmann would not easily delegate authority to anyone.

Despite difficulties, the general atmosphere at VU was expansive. Throughout the 1960s, the noise and sights of construction were part of campus life, as students shuttled between two campuses in fair weather and foul. The continuing growth in enrollment, the unsatisfactory condition of the older student housing (especially the firetrap sorority and fraternity houses), and the availability of federal funding for student housing made residences the first priority in developing the new campus. By 1966, five large residence halls had sprung up on LaPorte Avenue, the northern boundary of the East Campus. At the east end was Wehrenberg Hall (1959) and at the opposite end Scheele Hall (1961). Between them came Brandt (1962), Lankenau (1964), and Alumni (1966).

Designed by Stade to house the sororities, Scheele was named in honor of Minna Scheele, the widow of an Avon Products founder and a generous benefactor. Lankenau Hall was named in tribute to the great preacher and VU founder from Napoleon, Ohio. Brandt Hall recognized alumnus Paul Brandt, chairman of the board and tireless worker for VU and the Lutheran Church. Throughout this huge building program, Physical Plant Director William Domke and Business Manager Robert Springsteen worked day and night to assure both quality and economy in construction and interiors.

The five new LaPorte Avenue residences were quickly occupied, allowing the demolition of the temporary postwar housing and the transformation of Lembke Hall into a faculty office building. The faculty, already troubled by low salaries and remoteness from decision making, was no longer tolerant of crowded classrooms that trembled when trains passed or boilers went into action, that were invaded by bees or wasps, and whose knocking and hissing radiators competed with class discussion in the winter. The class schedule that began at 7:30 A.M. and included Saturday morning classes added to faculty and student woes.

Most successful private colleges, relying on large numbers of prosperous alumni, concentrated on enlarging endowments to attract talented faculty with good salaries and conditions. With only a small, young Lutheran alumni cohort, Valparaiso faced the daunting task of creating an endowment from scratch while building a new campus. Residences were largely self-financing, but where would the money be found for the numerous other needs?

Pressures from the law school's accreditors led the board to approve a new $500,000 law building for the campus. But a synodical fund-raising drive for "the only Lutheran law school in America," fully endorsed by synodical leaders, failed to raise even half that amount. The Synod was losing some of its famed cohesion, and no more funding for capital projects would come from that source, though the annual congregational efforts continued to aid the operating budget.

Part of the answer was found in private gifts, the results of seeds planted long before. The 1960s turned out to be the Rev. Karl Henrichs's triumphant decade in fund-raising. Years on the road in inexpensive hotels; thoughtful notes written in German; meals for visitors cooked by his wife, Luetta; visits with older Lutheran families now sharing in the economic boom—all these efforts came to fruition in a series of major donations. The first came from Judge Adolph Wesemann, a prominent attorney and supporter of Lutheran causes, whose trust eventually brought more than $3 million to VU, with part of it funding law school scholarships and a new law building.

Another source was the Neils family, prosperous Lutherans from Montana. The 13 children of Mary and Julius Neils, led by daughter Anna, raised $1 million as a memorial to their parents. Stade designed a beautiful building, and with federal money augmenting the donation, the main unit of the Neils Science Center, housing the biology and chemistry departments, was occupied in April 1967. A physics wing was added six years later.

In 1965, Henrichs announced a bequest of more than $1 million from the estate of Californian William Gellersen, an officer of Libby, McNeil, Libby, whose VU connections dated to the Depression. Stung by complaints about the breakdown of communications on campus, O. P. invited everyone to submit suggestions for the best use of the Gellersen bequest. Given available federal funding, a proposal emerged to construct two separate buildings, one for engineering-mathematics and another for foreign languages. The former was named for the donor and the latter for Richard and Oma Meier, the progressive board treasurer and his wife, both supporters of the humanities. The two buildings were dedicated together in 1968.

Besides these major structures, several smaller projects also went forward in the early 1960s: a bookstore addition to the Union, a gymnasium expansion, the remodeled education building (the former Immanuel Lutheran School), the Henry Loke Home Economics Center, and a Guild-funded admissions center, which was renamed Heidbrink Hall in the 1980s to honor the late Sophia Heidbrink. Groundbreakings, cornerstone-layings, and dedications for all these buildings were moments of fanfare, liturgical ritual and music, and celebration of the progress and purposes of the University. None surpassed the dedication of Wesemann Hall in the spring of 1964. The major addresses were given in the chapel by Supreme Court Chief Justice Earl Warren and Secretary of State Dean Rusk; LCMS President Oliver Harms preached at the dedicatory service.

THE LHRAA AND CIVIL RIGHTS

Besides growth in programs and buildings, VU was also opening more to the wider society. It was especially remarkable that throughout the 1950s and 1960s Valparaiso University hosted a civil rights organization that addressed the nation's central social problem of racial justice. The University proudly identified itself with the Lutheran Human Relations Association of America located on its campus and often sent out news releases about LHRAA activities on its own letterhead. "You did more for Valparaiso University than Valparaiso ever did for you," said O. P. Kretzmann in a moment of reflection.

In 1959, clergyman Karl Lutze came from Tulsa, Oklahoma, to serve as associate director of LHRAA and part-time theology professor. Karl and his wife, Esther, soon demonstrated their special gifts to the university community. Deeply sympathetic to anyone in need, Karl and Esther found plenty of such people in the VU student body and beyond. Their residence near campus became a home away from home for many students, a sanctuary for the troubled and confused, and a headquarters for the bold in spirit who wanted to change the world for the better.

Largely through the efforts of people such as the Lutzes and LHRAA director Andrew Schulze, the University became engaged in the huge social problems associated with race and poverty. Although the number of actively involved people was small, they had an impact far beyond their numbers. Schulze helped organize a student Human Relations Club, which sponsored discussions, movies, and visiting speakers. In 1960, a VU news release announced LHRAA's advice to Lutherans that civil rights organizations such as the NAACP, the Urban League, the Southern Regional Council, and others, as well as actions such as "knee-ins," deserved support from Christians.

In the fall of 1962, Schulze joined Martin Luther King Jr. in an Albany, Georgia, campaign that had been under way for some time. The demonstrations were designed to support black voting and school registration. Schulze and about 75 other demonstrators from Chicago, New York, and New Jersey picketed the Albany courthouse and, when they refused sheriffs' orders to disperse, were arrested and thrown into a filthy jail for six days and nights. Kretzmann sent bail money and wrote a long telegram of public protest to President Kennedy. The avalanche of critical mail that landed on Kretzmann's desk as a result included a letter from board member Paul Rupprecht, urging O. P. to dock Schulze's pay for committing an illegal act when he should have been teaching. This perspective accorded with a prevalent Lutheran view that tended to abhor street politics and insist on the self-correcting processes of democratic politics to right social wrongs. Unfortunately, this ordinarily sound approach does not contemplate a situation such as that in the South, where the democratic electoral process was systematically blocked for blacks.

This was never more clear than in the spring of 1963. Martin Luther King's demonstrations in Birmingham, Alabama, and the harsh overreaction of Eugene "Bull" Connor with his dogs and fire hoses, aroused a new national civil rights constituency. The subsequent jailing of King, his widely read "Letter from a Birmingham Jail," and the rise of more militant voices such as that of Malcolm X convinced many people that the promotion of civil rights was the only just solution to the crisis. Until then, President Kennedy had disappointed the civil rights movement. But a new

Kennedy appeared in a passionate speech on June 11, 1963, in which he elevated the civil rights issue to the level of a national moral crisis. That night, a white sniper assassinated NAACP leader Medgar Evers in Jackson, Mississippi. Building further national support for civil rights, Kennedy summoned 90 American religious leaders, including O. P. Kretzmann and Andrew Schulze, to a White House conference on the moral dimensions of the issue.

These events had a significant effect on Valparaiso's campus. On September 15, just as students were gathering for the fall semester, six people, including four young Sunday school girls, were killed in the infamous bombing of the Sixteenth Avenue Baptist Church in Birmingham. Two weeks later, a special memorial service was scheduled in the chapel. Student Senate president Fred Bernthal concluded a searching piece in *The Torch*: "When you attend chapel Thursday, do not let the sorrow over six untimely deaths remove from your minds the repulsive specter of the cancer which caused those deaths." Kretzmann personally invited the Valparaiso Town Council and many civic leaders to attend, together with the children of Immanuel Lutheran School. The main speaker was the Rev. Joseph Ellwanger, pastor of St. Paul's Lutheran Church in Birmingham, who had participated in the funeral for the Birmingham children. Ellwanger was president of the Alabama Council on Human Relations and a member of the board of directors of LHRAA.

Later that month, Karl Lutze discussed with the VU Human Relations Club the mounting peaceful demonstrations of the summer. He gave a firsthand report on the March on Washington where he and hundreds of thousands heard King deliver his "I Have a Dream" speech. "People are being willing to stand up and be counted," he said. "This is something we haven't seen too much of in the past few years." To the students who wanted to "do something," Lutze's injunction was to "keep informed … do not miss some of the most important days in the history of the world."

One of those days came soon. O. P. Kretzmann described it in his *Campus Commentary*:

> It was exactly 1:25 P.M. CST on Friday, November 22, when the news hit campus: "President Kennedy is dead." Professors closed their books, and students filed dazedly out of classrooms. … Within twenty minutes, the University Chapel was crowded with three thousand students and instructors. Some sat quietly, staring at the cross above the pulpit. Others knelt on the cold floor. The only sound was an occasional sob. The organ began to play, and I read the only words

that could matter at that moment: "I am the Resurrection and the Life." ... We sang a few hymns and resolved to have a memorial service four hours later. Soundlessly the students left the Chapel.

A CHANGING UNIVERSITY AND CHURCH

While such dramatic national events created an increasing sense of social awareness and imminent historic change, VU also attended to its internal concerns. Puzzled by signs of faculty discontent, Kretzmann proposed creating a committee on faculty welfare. Nine highly regarded faculty leaders served, with Louis Bartelt as chairman and John Strietelmeier as secretary. In the first meeting, they recommended changing the name and enlarging their responsibilities. "Welfare" had overtones of paternalism, so the committee proposed to substitute "concerns." The president approved, and the Faculty Concerns Committee came into being.

Soon after, a case arose involving Professor Ernest Moses, who protested a terminal contract on the grounds that he had *de facto* been awarded tenure. He appealed to the national AAUP, and though O. P. sputtered and fumed over outside interference, the University eventually reached a financial settlement with Moses. It clearly was necessary to develop clear definitions and procedures for tenure. Kretzmann appointed a faculty committee, chaired by law school professor Marshall Jox, who produced a careful document that ultimately was passed by the faculty and approved by the board in 1964. A further statement on academic freedom and responsibility was passed by the faculty in May 1966, then approved by the board.

The Faculty Concerns Committee also inaugurated far-reaching changes in academic governance. First, it proposed a system of departmental chairmanships to replace the "headships" that had produced near-feudal conditions in some departments. More important was the proposal for a streamlined, working University Senate of 32 members, in which faculty and administration would share authority in debating and adopting legislation. As various versions of the proposal were circulated and discussed, differences developed along generational lines. Many senior faculty looked with suspicion on the "young Turk" faculty who wanted a voice. These older voices felt the veteran faculty had built the University and that younger faculty should wait their turn to have influence. On February 21, 1966, the faculty gathered in Heritage Hall for a long, tense meeting. When Professor Friedrich came forward with a cluster of amendments, the "young Turks" scrutinized them carefully for signs of sabotage. After a series of close votes, in which some amendments passed and others failed, both the department chair proposal and the University Senate were adopted essentially intact. A quiet revolution had occurred. Afterward the younger and older faculty who had tenaciously fought each other settled in somewhere, probably Walter Friedrich's living room, for a reconciling drink.

Similar senates were established across the nation as a new generation of faculty leadership came of age. Although these changes at VU were painful for Kretzmann, they came none too soon. Within a year, students would be pressing for membership on senate committees, as well as other changes on the campus. By that time, the faculty had assumed a share of leadership responsibilities within a viable governance system that could address the more volatile issues emerging on the horizon.

Within the church, too, politics heated up during the 1960s. In 1961, conservative dissidents against the increasingly "moderate" synodical leadership mounted a major "State of the Church" conference in Milwaukee. One of their prime targets was Valparaiso University. Some VU leaders were worried by the long list of complaints: the teaching of evolution, the dialogues with Notre Dame, "liturgical excess," and a variety of theological positions taken by members of the theology department that seemed to depart from conventional Missouri themes.

In a speech to the board, W. C. Dickmeyer saw opportunity rather than threat in these developments. The Missouri Synod was in the process of splintering, he declared, and this was the time for Valparaiso to take a leadership role. It should begin by publishing a statement of the University's general position, and individuals should tone down approaches that might suggest freelancing to the contrary. Such a document was widely distributed. The Ten-Year Plan had emphasized that one of Valparaiso University's goals was to give intellectual leadership to its major constituency. Many of Kretzmann's policies and statements, backed by other leaders such as Dickmeyer, were designed to give VU a key role in remaking the Missouri Synod into a church body worthy of its "high destiny" as a progressive, confessional voice in American Lutheranism and American Christianity.

The next several years seemed to move toward that promise. In 1962, the Reverend Oliver Harms, a strong friend of Valparaiso, was elected president of the Synod. Within a few years, members of the VU faculty—such as Robert Bertram, Edward Schroeder, Richard Baepler, Paul G.

Bretscher, and John Strietelmeier—were appointed to important synodical committees. In 1963, Concordia Seminary bestowed an honorary doctorate on Strietelmeier. There were suggestions that the Synod might subsidize VU for educating church professionals—deaconesses, youth leaders, parochial school teachers, social workers—but these plans were wisely discarded with the realization that control inevitably would follow subsidy, which would be inimical to the University.

In a conservative denomination trying to distinguish itself from "fundamentalism," the evolution question persisted. Within the Missouri Synod, a variety of opinions were held. The orginally antievolutionist Theodore Graebner had been persuaded by a number of outstanding German and American Lutheran theologians that Christianity and evolution were compatible, while others in the Missouri Synod took up banners of resistance. At Valparaiso, biology professors Carl Krekeler and William Bloom regularly dealt with the issue in their classrooms and writing. Along with both theology and science colleagues—Robert Bertram, Ernest Koenker, John Strietelmeier, Theodore Schwan, and Robert Hanson—Krekeler and Bloom formulated the view that both evolution and creation were valid answers to the question of the origins of life's diversity. Evolution is a valid answer in terms of scientific evidence and logic, natural cause and effect. The answer in religious language is creation: "Thou hast formed me in my mother's womb" (Psalm 139). New understandings of Genesis, these VU faculty believed, fit these conclusions.

This was the "double perspective" taught in Valparaiso theology and science classrooms. When an irate pastor wrote to O. P. stating that his congregation would no longer support Valparaiso, Kretzmann asked Krekeler how he should reply. Before answering, Krekeler made some inquiries into how much the congregation had contributed in the past, then suggested that O. P. tell his critic that he would deduct the average amount of the congregation's previous years' contributions—zero—from Krekeler's salary.

Replying to such critics was a long-standing practice at VU. When Dr. John Klotz, a science professor at Concordia-River Forest, published *Genes, Genesis, and Evolution*, VU scientists reacted negatively. Krekeler reviewed Klotz's book in the January 1956 *Cresset* and called parts of it "reprehensible." He said that "to promote writings of this sort with the implication that it provides a correct interpretation ... can do immeasurable harm by binding consciences of those struggling in this area." Krekeler did another scorching review of a 1959 book, *Darwin, Evolution, and Creation*, edited by Paul Zimmermann, then president of Concordia Teachers College, Seward, Nebraska. He accused the authors of presenting false alternatives for young students who are struggling with the relationship of science to their Christian faith. Subsequent meetings of Krekeler and others with synodical and seminary leaders—which included towering scientific figures such as Francis Schmitt of MIT, a loyal LCMS member—suggested strongly that the Missouri Synod had opened itself to new understandings of Genesis and the modes of divine creation.

In 1963, D. Van Nostrand published Krekeler and Bloom's text on introductory biology, which included a chapter on faith and science—unusual in such textbooks but insisted on by the authors. The text was ridiculed in the tabloid *Lutheran News* and stirred angry letters to Missouri Synod president Harms. At O. P.'s request, Krekeler wrote a lengthy and widely circulated statement asserting that, while biologists at Valparaiso taught evolution as a "working hypothesis," there "was no doubt whatsoever that Scripture teaches that God was and is Creator." Scripture simply did not reveal the method of creation. In 1965, the protagonists in this debate met face-to-face at a conference in Valparaiso. Neither side budged. Throughout the various controversies, O. P. vigorously defended Krekeler and Bloom, whether at pastoral conferences or in his *Campus Commentary*.

ACADEMICS AND FINANCES

VU's Ten-Year Plan for the 1960s charted ambitious proposals for academic expansion. It committed the University to create a School of Graduate Studies and a College of Business Administration. In March 1960, the faculty approved a proposal developed by the meticulous Alfred H. Meyer for a Master of Arts in Liberal Studies (MALS) program. Kretzmann appointed his wise friend John Conrad Seegers, the recently retired president of Muhlenberg College, to be director of the new program when it was inaugurated in 1963. Under Seegers's successor Howard Peters, the program was expanded to include a Master of Arts in Teaching (MAT). It enjoyed considerable success, especially with teachers from Northwest Indiana, helping to develop a new regional constituency for the University.

While the graduate program was not research-oriented, a 1959 self-study prior to the Ten-Year Plan had made clear that VU needed to promote more faculty research. That same year, leading faculty research scholars Krekeler and Les Zoss of engineering proposed the creation of a committee on creative work and research to support such work. Although the campus-funded research money for summer grants and a university research professorship was modest, it served over the years, under chairpersons such as Walter Rast and James Startt, to encourage VU faculty in many fields to maintain active research programs.

Neither the music nor education departments was transformed into a new professional school distinct from the College of Arts and Sciences, as some had hoped. But they each attained professional accreditation for their programs with the National Association of Schools of Music and the National Council for the Accreditation of Teacher Education. The highly respected Paul Lange and Gerald Speckhard, leaders in the growing Lutheran high school movement, brought a host of new contacts and interests into the VU orbit, though the department frequently faltered because of internal quarreling. The Bachelor of Music in church music, established in 1963, while not the School of Music that O. P. had dreamed of, reinforced Valparaiso's strong commitment to that field.

Kretzmann launched the College of Business Administration with the appointment of economist Harold Gram as dean designate in 1963. The next year, four existing arts and sciences departments—economics, finance, management, and accounting—were reconfigured to form the new college. A legendary professor of accounting, Janet Sievers, anchored the new faculty, but there were insufficient faculty with doctorates to apply immediately for professional accreditation. That goal, thought to be imminently attainable, would actually take 30 years.

The Ten-Year Plan also proposed programs for gifted students. In 1961, the Directed Studies Program began under Ernest Koenker's direction, following a several years' trial period of honors work among senior students. Modeled on Yale's program of the same name, it worked with about 40 invited students each year. The students took enriched sections of Western civilization, philosophy, theology, and English. Two remodeled classrooms above the Faculty Club and some common extracurricular activities created a small, low-key program. President Kretzmann, however, had a more ambitious scheme in mind for "Christ College," a special college within the University that would more directly embody VU's academic vision. It would take many years for such a college to take shape.

The Achilles' heel of the University continued to be its structure of financial support. It needed more money for operating expenses, especially faculty salaries, but its tuition-driven annual budgets were consistently in the red and were bailed out only by one-time bequests or by counting on continually rising future enrollments. The University needed money for building a whole new campus, but it had to rely on irregular and inconsistent donor gifts or government opportunities that might or might not fit needs. It also became evident to some board members that VU needed a substantial endowment, the traditional source for funding beyond tuition. Congregational donations remained fairly steady at around $200,000 per year, but these donations could not be expected to grow. Overall, external income was static, and the gradually rising tuition did not match rising costs.

In the January 1963 board meeting, the accounting firm of Peat, Marwick, and Mitchell examined the University's finances and identified its weaknesses: failure to secure major gifts from corporations and from major individual donors. Vice President Toelke, who was keenly aware of the subtle ways in which his hardworking staff had to be a kind of scapegoat for VU's main weakness, resigned in some discouragement. Once more, the University had no plan to move forward, so a member of the board, Fred Reddel of Michigan, became interim vice president of development.

In May 1964, at a retreat-like board meeting in the Poconos, John Conrad Seegers presented the results of a comprehensive six-month study of the University he had undertaken. Seegers raised many questions about the expansionary mode in which VU operated, particularly about allowing the enrollment to grow to 4,000 students, as the Ten-Year Plan recommended. In general, he urged consolidation and improvement of what VU was doing, rather than further expansion. O. P., as usual, had other ideas; he was going to get some things done before he retired. Seegers also pointed out Valparaiso's financial weakness: It should have an endowment of about $1 million for every 115 students, which came to $31 million—an unthinkable sum. Somehow, for the present, the church would have to come through, though Seegers worried about VU coming under church control. Whatever else might happen, Seegers insisted, the president of the University would have to become actively involved in fund-raising. The American university presidency was simply evolving in that direction.

Also present at this meeting was Frank Sparks, the retired president of Wabash College and another of O. P.'s friends. Sparks proposed reorganizing the Department of Development to include new directors for corporations and foundations, as well as a new volunteer structure. Sparks stated his own willingness to serve in implementing his proposal, and the board agreed. Unfortunately, Sparks died before he could undertake this assignment. So nothing was done. Perhaps the spate of extraordinary gifts coming in at this time from Gellersen, Neils, and Wesemann, as well as significant new gifts from northwest Indiana citizens Fred Smoke and Floyd Seib, lulled the board into complacency. Vice President Reddel did present to the board a grand fund-raising plan, a new five-year $21 million drive that included $10 million for endowment. But the truth was that no one at VU really knew how to plan or implement such an ambitious campaign, and administrators could only propose to study how other universities managed successful fund-raising programs.

Meanwhile, the Lilly Endowment recommended that VU engage Dr. Ralph Cooper Hutchinson, a consultant noted for his studies of how to achieve efficiencies in colleges. Hutchinson did a business-oriented report on Valparaiso that appealed to some board members but not at all to the administration. To end the annual deficits, Hutchinson contended that the University's operating expenses should be financed by tuition and fees and a much-enhanced endowment, with annual fund-raising going for capital projects or similar purposes. To achieve this, Hutchinson proposed eliminating a large number of "mediocre" faculty and relying on large classes taught by a few well-paid lecturers. These classes would be supported by expanded student "independent study" through technological devices such as the computer and television.

For more than a year, the Hutchinson report loomed in the background as the administration stalled and kept it from faculty eyes. Vice President Huegli and Dean Allen Tuttle prepared a confidential study, trying to show that these ideas were not suitable for Valparaiso. The need for further argument was ended, however, when Parsons College in Iowa—a thriving institution for whom Hutchinson had become a major architect—was roundly criticized by the North Central Association for implementing some of these very ideas. Within a few years, the Parsons bubble burst, and the college passed into the hands of the Maharishi Mahesh Yogi as Maharishi International University.

In January 1968, Kretzmann announced the appointment of alumnus Max Nagel to develop deferred giving. Then in the spring of 1968, Edward Hekman, a business executive with a strong church commitment, was appointed vice president for development. Hekman hired the Robert Johnson Corporation to advise on modernizing VU's fund-raising. Their report in the fall of 1968 contained plans that, when implemented over time, would begin to put Valparaiso's fund-raising on a modern basis.

"THE 1960S" REALLY BEGIN

Meanwhile, the mood of the country was turning increasingly sour, and the outlook on campuses was turning sour along with it. The early 1960s had brought a sense of high energy and, for many, a belief that America was moving forward to address national problems and mobilize its youth for education and social service. By 1965, that optimism was rapidly undermined by the expansion of the Vietnam War and the numerous troubles and even violence afflicting the nation's cities. In the late 1960s and 1970s, many cultural beliefs and social practices underwent criticism and upheaval, and some things would never be the same.

There are several interpretations of those profound changes, many of them still controversial. One recent interpreter, historian James Patterson, describes the "rights-conscious spirit of the era" as the heart of this period. By 1965, the Supreme Court already had upheld blacks' rights under the Bill of Rights and the Fourteenth Amendment; banned prayers in public schools to protect the rights of minority religious adherents; defined the rights of criminal suspects; and protected the use of contraceptives as part of a right to privacy. Similarly, much of the Great Society legislation could be seen as furthering the drive for the rights of the poor and elderly, ethnic groups, women, newcomers, and so on. Higher education, like all social institutions, clearly was impacted on many levels by this "rights revolution."

The young people who came of age during the 1960s, and came to colleges and universities in vastly increased numbers, had grown up in a time of great American power abroad and unparalleled wealth at home. Some, at first only a few, committed themselves to change what they saw as a society afflicted with social and racial injustice, empty materialism, and violence. But by the late 1960s, the idealism of the Peace Corps, the civil rights movement, and the early Students for a Democratic Society, with its call for "participatory democracy" and a "new humanism" in the 1962 Port Huron Statement, had largely disappeared. Street politics, domestic violence, racial backlash, political murders, mounting Vietnam War casualties, drugs and psychedelic pop culture—all of these created intense disillusionment with government and with society in general. These developments and attitudes washed onto the campuses, where they inevitably changed college and university life.

The way they changed higher education was not uniform, however. Much depended on the context, history, and culture of each institution and its constituency. Wealthy and elite institutions did not change in the same way as those that served a more middle-class student body. Large state institutions in the Midwest reacted quite differently to "the 1960s" than small evangelical colleges in the South. Catholic and Lutheran colleges provided a different context for social change than secular private institutions.

Valparaiso University had a distinctive geographic and social context. The town in which it had grown up had a largely conservative Republican political tradition. At the same time, it was a part of the Calumet Region of northwest Indiana, with its economic and ethnic variety. Valparaiso also was being integrated into the greater metropolitan area of "Chicagoland." There was regular traffic between Valparaiso University and Chicago, and that dynamic city was a powerful and growing influence on VU throughout this time.

The administration and faculty were by and large political "moderates," ranging from liberal Democrats to moderate and conservative Republicans. Only a small number, often clustered around the various Reiner-connected groups and, later in the 1960s, the law school, were actively involved in social causes. *The Cresset*, while regarded by many conservative constituents as tending toward the left, was, in fact, a centrist voice that promoted civil rights but editorially supported the Vietnam War for a long time. Professional faculties in the sciences, engineering, and business were traditionally conservative throughout the nation, and these made up a large and growing proportion of the VU faculty as well. On the whole, institutional loyalty to VU and its mission, only slightly diminished from earlier decades, was still much stronger than the loyalty to particular disciplines or national political alignments that prevailed at many larger universities.

The VU student body remained 75 to 80 percent Lutheran throughout the 1960s before it began to drop toward 50 percent in the next decade. But the non-Lutheran students who came to VU in significant numbers were also often from similarly strong religious backgrounds. The number of Catholic students in particular began to rise significantly. In 1969, Catholic students petitioned on behalf of 150 coreligionists for space to celebrate Mass on campus. While Catholic students might be more interested in social justice concerns, they were otherwise generally conservative and tended to support the Vietnam War until its late stages. VU undergraduates from all religious backgrounds still tended to be first-generation college students who intended to prepare for vocations, and they often experienced enormous psychological tensions when their idealism led them, against parental advice, to subordinate studies to involvement in greater social causes.

There were, however, other distinctive factors that encouraged a degree of social awareness and involvement among VU students. A substantial number of students were idealistic and service-oriented, as demonstrated by programs such as the Inner City Peace Corps and deaconess training. The student body was liberally sprinkled with the sons and daughters of Lutheran pastors. Often such "PKs" (Preacher's Kids) who had attended Lutheran parochial schools were among the active student leaders. Some of these sons and daughters of the parsonage became prominent rebels against what they saw as moral and social complacency as well.

At Valparaiso, as at most other colleges, student political awareness and activism began to pick up in the early 1960s. In 1960, the VU Student Council became the Student Senate, suggesting a loftier collegiate conception of student government. Especially after John F. Kennedy's exciting election, more VU students saw politics as an interesting and noble way to affect the world, beginning with their own university. This became a time when some of the best students were regularly involved in VU campus politics: William Karpenko, Fred Bernthal, Frank Gray, David Hessler, Theodore Buhlmann, Joyce Pelz, Mark Hellman, Mark Schwehn, Michael Turner, Peter Lutze, and Rick Barton. Student politics imitated national and local politics. Leaders identified various interest groups and possible trade-offs, deals and ideals clashed, and charismatic personalities competed with efficient organization. There were parades, debates, political rallies, and even the most popular rock bands were hired to promote candidates. Almost the whole student body joined in the process. If voting participation fell below two-thirds of the student body, it was regarded as a great disappointment. While there was much hoopla, serious issues of academic and student life also came to be part of the campus political process.

In the 1960s, *The Torch* took up the role of raising such issues, especially those that affected the university community. Top students vied to become writers and editors for the twice-weekly publication. Many went on to highly successful academic or journalistic careers, though some fell prey to the falling grades and "burnout" that were the occupational hazard of student leaders. *Torch* and *Lighter* editors—such as Theodore Steege, Sharon Haug, Pat Sullivan, Mel Piehl, Janet Karsten, and Kathy Wille—and writers—such as David Nord, Ronald Roschke, Sandra Govan, Gary Weinhold, John Hill, and many others—challenged the University to live up to its principles, in more or less critical tones. Kretzmann and others sometimes saw this as adversarial and periodically complained that *The Torch* (which was distributed off campus) was costing the University "something like $100,000 a year" in lost donations. But in the end, Kretzmann always acknowledged the value of the student publications' independence and appreciated it when they engaged in well-thought-out critique and analysis. When he once called a *Torch* editor in to complain about the lost donations, the editor replied, "But President Kretzmann, who always tells us that it's essential for people in a Christian university to pursue the truth and let the chips fall where they may?" There was a pause, then O. P.'s voice rumbled, "Well, the next time you write an editorial advocating longer library hours, I want you to think hard about that $100,000."

At first, only a small but vocal minority on campus questioned national policies on matters such as race and foreign affairs. Their numbers increased with the escalation of the Vietnam War, but until May 1970, they never included a majority of students. At VU, any turn toward activism was complicated by the absence of any Lutheran tradition of "street politics" and the strong tradition of "vocation," which was understood to mean that students should be students and not activists in "outside" affairs. Within the University, this teaching seemed to imply that authorized instruments of expression, such as the publications and the Student Senate, were the proper channels of action.

The swirling winds of the 1960s at Valparaiso University brought more collaborative governance, increased student autonomy, curricular change, and a more accommodating environment for black students. It also resulted in some loss of trust among members of the once-close university community as political disagreements and controversial values and behavior created fracture and division. How participants and observers evaluated these changes depended on many variables. For some faculty, there was a welcome rise in student engagement, while others saw a lowering of both academic standards and cherished values. For some students, there was a sense of living in a heightened way with moments of intense bonding and moments of fierce rage. For other serious students, the rapid pace of change threatened their studies. For some fraternity men, it created an urge for angry retaliation against "the radicals" who were spoiling the joys of "college life" with politics. For many women, it represented a gradual liberation from the double standard that had governed earlier generations' lives, as well as the opening of new opportunities and life paths.

For some devout Lutherans, there was a diminishing of the "special" religious character of Valparaiso University. If the changes of the time were difficult to understand and evaluate, then and now, they were impossible to ignore.

ACTIVIST STIRRINGS

As in the nation at large, the year 1964–65 marked a redirection of life at Valparaiso University and signaled the end of the seemingly innocent idealism of the early 1960s. Kennedy's assassination had led to Johnson's landslide election and the subsequent Great Society and civil rights legislation, which heightened the "rights revolution." At VU, *The Torch* opened its pages to national news and began reporting regularly on the rising national student movement. Affiliations with groups such as the National Student Association (NSA) and the United States Student Press Association (USSPA) contributed to a new sense of being part of major national developments on campuses similar to Valparaiso. These affiliations also provided information, ideas, and strategies to the relatively small but increasingly influential groups of interested students. Events such as the Free Speech movement at the University of California at Berkeley and the growing civil rights activism of groups such as the Student Nonviolent Coordinating Committee (SNCC) in the South fueled the belief that it was the right and duty of young people on college campuses to speak out and shape public affairs.

At Valparaiso, this outlook encouraged *The Torch* to take a more adversarial position toward the University administration. Early in fall 1964, Harold Scheub, a young English professor with strong commitments to civil rights, diagnosed what he saw as the root of all VU's ills in a chapel talk: "Paternalism!" *The Torch* puffed this address and began expanding on the theme in its editorials: Students were treated as less than adults; women, even those over 21 years old, were "protected" by curfews; VU students accepted spoon-feeding by weak professors; the fraternities fostered a "playboy" mentality. This indictment was apparently confirmed a few weeks later by O. P.'s highly uncharacteristic act of banning production of an Arthur Kopit play, "Oh Dad, Poor Dad." Apparently, Vice President Huegli had learned that the play contained "offensive lines," and he somehow persuaded O. P. to ban it. Kretzmann had never censored any campus publication or production before, and it was ill timing that he chose this year to take such a step for the first and last time. In any case, one paramount issue of the 1960s—freedom—was dramatically launched.

The ban became a constant reference point throughout the year. "Blatant censorship!" cried *The Torch*. Reaction to the ban also led to the formation in February 1965 of SCOPE (Student Committee On Positive Expression), which became the vehicle for organizing further debates and activities. Even before SCOPE's formation, some "student rebels" at VU had launched attacks on "college men" (to use historian Helen Horowitz's terms). The Greek organizations seemed to represent student allies of "the establishment," and throughout the 1960s, students promoting change—often themselves disaffected fraternity and sorority members—engaged in a running battle with the social organizations. For example, *The Torch* blasted fraternities for failing to contribute to funding Mississippi "Freedom Schools" and for refusing to help raise money to bring Dr. Martin Luther King Jr. to campus. Eventually, such criticism by *The Torch* and other student groups led the fraternities to contribute, meanwhile defending themselves by citing their many good works.

A similar critique was leveled by *Torch* writer Pat Sullivan against the Associated Women Students (AWS) for its preoccupation with such things as Miss America and the "Best Dressed Girl" contests. Noting that many VU women increasingly protested the annual fee for membership in AWS, Sullivan wrote that the group should begin focusing on real women's issues:

> There is much discontent among women students over the fact that even junior and senior women may not live in apartments, nor may they visit members of the opposite sex who do. AWS could foster open discussion on this controversial subject and perhaps take a stand on the matter.

Another *Torch* writer, Sherry Haug, did a lengthy review of Betty Friedan's pathbreaking book, *The Feminine Mystique*, and urged VU women to think deeply about their identities.

Although the Vietnam War was still a remote and relatively small affair in the fall of 1964, *The Torch* did a sophisticated analysis of the conflict, accusing governmental authorities of deceptive practices in giving U.S. citizens flawed information. *The Torch* called for an end to the war. To counter such increasingly "liberal" views being expressed in student publications and organizations, a campus Conservative Club was organized and eventually evolved into a chapter of Young Americans for Freedom. Meanwhile, SCOPE was actively engaged on many fronts in promoting its views. It sponsored forums on such issues as the extent and nature of student freedom, student power to protest, censorship for economic reasons, and the meaning of a university.

While many issues were trivial by later standards, the discussions and protests did affect campus life. After *The Torch* severely criticized the chapel for its domination by clergy and its lack of involvement by lay students, the student chapel committee announced new student-shaped and student-led services. Similarly, when a student hangout, "The Hole," was shut down by the administration, a student wrote in *The Torch* that "the real issue is that a certain amount of P.D.A. is going on in the Hole." Shortly thereafter, a headline read: "Administration, SCOPE, Cooperate to Re-Open Hole Coffee Shop Again." This kind of response would be one pattern of bringing about change at Valparaiso.

As students tackled issues such as academic freedom, some also searched for avenues by which they could help and free others. At VU, the emphasis on "freedom" frequently took the form of asking how Christians ought to engage themselves in the wider world. Walter Reiner, on a leave of absence to run the Prince of Peace Volunteers, returned to recruit VU students and said: "We're all after the same thing: how can we be better channels of God's love to people? We want to work with some people for change without dangling a carrot in front of their faces." In March 1965, SCOPE organized 30 students to picket the Valparaiso post office, mourning the assassination in Alabama of civil rights activist the Rev. James Reeb.

Civil rights concerns quickened on the VU campus throughout 1965. The Rev. Joseph Ellwanger took time off from his activities in Selma to address the campus. Ellwanger was greeted warmly by O. P. as the Alabama civil rights leader urged students to help blacks obtain their legitimate rights. In response, students gathered for a nighttime prayer vigil in Gloria Christi Chapel on behalf of the Selma protestors. In March 1965, 33 VU students joined four faculty members in the memorable march from Selma to Montgomery. VU students could read firsthand accounts in *The Torch* by David Sheriff and Timothy Warfield. Late at night on the climactic March 25, as the marchers arrived in Montgomery, the sounds of "We Shall Overcome" rang out from the Brandt campanile at VU, played by an anonymous person who had gained access to the keyboard.

Fifty VU students proceeded to organize a "Friends of SNCC" chapter, which was recognized by the Student Senate. Its executive committee of five immediately criticized Kretzmann for moving too slowly in dealing with racial issues at Valparaiso. Black students also leveled charges of discrimination against the University, including the use of photographs in the admissions process, presumably for racial identification. White female students were asked if they would object to a black roommate. The University responded by ending the practice. Black students also accused the fraternities of including discriminatory clauses in their constitutions and bylaws. The fraternities were forced to explain their actual procedures, and several organizations joined in applying pressure at the national level to alter restrictive clauses.

RACISM AND THE VIETNAM WAR

The sense of heightened moral and social responsibility took many forms in the mid-1960s. The growing critique of the fraternities reached a new level in 1966 when Student Senate president Mark Schwehn, himself a fraternity member, published a lengthy *Torch* article asserting that fraternities were anti-intellectual, sponsored detrimental programs (particularly hazing), and were guilty of discriminatory policies toward minorities. He then proposed that fraternities should withdraw from their national organizations, sign an antidiscrimination pledge, abolish all blackball systems, and change their relation to governance on campus. Finally, the University should meet the crisis of substandard fraternity housing by building a group of small houses that would become dormitories if the fraternities did not show the desired improvements. If that should be the case, Schwehn said, the fraternities should be abolished. Amazingly, the article was signed by the presidents of all the VU fraternities, though a close reading of the text showed that they were agreeing only to discuss this proposal.

"I can't believe it!" was the typical student response to this manifesto. While no fraternity finally accepted the proposal, all of them started talking about change and took some steps to reform "rush." Kretzmann took these discussions seriously enough to report to the board that a disposition of the fraternity housing problem, then under urgent consideration, should wait until deliberations were further along.

The 1960s were, everywhere, years of heady talk. O. P. Kretzmann readily joined in, seizing every opportunity to contribute to public debates and demonstrate how Christian intellectuals might approach current issues. To the delight of the campus rebels, he regularly denounced "Joe College." He also called for a dialogue between what he called the "modern and postmodern mind"—a debate between no-faith and faith, between selfishness and service. And he reminded his audiences that the context for all such discussions at Valparaiso should be "Christian hope."

But Kretzmann soon learned that civil rights issues, in which he had been a genuine leader in relation to American society at large, took on a very different shape when applied to the university community itself. More VU students were involved directly in racial concerns. In the spring of 1966, another group of students traveled to Birmingham to work on voter registration. Professor Karl Lutze then created a regular course on "The Church and Race Relations" in cooperation with black Miles College in Birmingham. In this course, students read relevant texts, visited each other's campus, and met with local community organizations. A visiting Miles professor also taught a course at VU on "Black Humanities."

But for the 40 to 50 African-American students on VU's campus, such activities were increasingly unsatisfactory. Newly assertive, and increasingly sympathetic with the "black power" movement appearing to challenge more mainstream civil rights efforts, they began presenting a new set of issues. Increasingly, they turned their attention to racism on the VU campus itself.

In the fall of 1966, a group of black Lutheran Walther Leaguers visiting campus were met with racial insults from unknown persons. O. P. was incensed and called a university convocation that nearly filled the chapel. He denounced the racial slurs, ordered an investigation of the incident, and proceeded to rehearse VU's record of commitment to civil rights. That was not enough for black students and a number of whites, who were also irked by Kretzmann's criticism of black power spokesman Stokely Carmichael as "dangerous." They demanded more action and developed a catalog of racist features of the campus, beginning with the fraternities. *The Torch* also criticized the president's disposition to talk and not act. So strong was the feeling in response that the vice presidents and deans issued a statement of support for Kretzmann and his policies.

Tensions mounted. Accusations and counteraccusations regarding race swept other issues aside. John Hill, a black *Torch* writer, wrote about sentiments of "Nigger, go home if you don't like it here." He declared the "white problem" at VU much more acute than any supposed "black problem," and he endorsed the new and ominous-sounding "black power." But Hill balanced his catalog of problems with signs of hope. For example, the freshman women of Alumni and Kreinheder Halls were circulating a statement declaring that they would like to have an integrated sorority on campus. The University Senate addressed racial issues in a special session, and the Human Relations Committee apologized to the Walther League guests from Milwaukee and made numerous recommendations.

Race was not the only issue causing sharper debates at VU. As the Vietnam War escalated from 1965 to 1967, antiwar sentiments on U.S. campuses grew as well. Some of this protest was clearly linked to the threat of being drafted, while others saw the war as fundamentally unjust or shared the sentiment of "win or get out." For most people on VU's relatively conservative campus, these perspectives were long subordinated to patriotic support for the President and the war. On a more sophisticated level, represented at Valparaiso by *The Cresset*, Vietnam was justified as another manifestation of the collective security and containment policy that had worked in Europe and could be expected to work again in East Asia, given enough patience and determination.

But from 1965 onward, small antiwar activist groups appeared on the VU campus and skirmished with pro-war students. When the Selective Service asked universities to rank students academically so only those with lower rankings would be drafted, a moral crisis ensued. One group of students wanted the University to refuse cooperation with such life-and-death decisions, but a larger group wanted the chance to avoid the draft through good academic performance. VU resolved the matter by reporting the broad class standing of students in each college only if the student requested that the information be sent to his local board. In a campus referendum, students voted 523 to 248 in favor of this policy over the proposed alternative of noncompliance with Selective Service. Professor Richard Lee undertook the task of counseling students on the technicalities of the draft, including conscientious objection for nontheists. He also unpacked for many the forgotten Christian (and Lutheran) doctrine concerning just and unjust wars.

Self-Determination and Academic Renewal

While much of the spirit of the 1960s was determined by the great national controversies over racial justice and the Vietnam War, there was also a great deal of attention on university campuses to issues that affected primarily academic and student life. Just as many young people questioned the practices and wisdom of their elders in regard to public policies, they also challenged long-standing habits on campus and demanded a larger say in their own lives and education.

At VU, students steadily pressed for a greater degree of self-determination and participation in policy matters, such as required class attendance and residential rules. The latter issue was especially focused on women's dormitories, which still maintained curfews and tight regulation of activities and hours. Only gradually were these relaxed. In 1966, an appeals board was set up in the women's residences to review the dean of women's decisions in disciplinary cases. When Student Senate president Schwehn persuaded the faculty in the spring of 1967 to overturn an action of the University Senate and put two voting student members on each of the University's four major policy committees, student participation in academic policy suddenly increased in a marked way.

The deeper fact, however, was that throughout the nation many students and faculty alike were being led by the times to ask fundamental questions about the methods and purposes of education. At Valparaiso University, a group of student leaders focused on the questions of improving the academic quality of the institution. It was easy for detractors to see this concern as a smoke screen for student self-indulgence—a suspicion confirmed for some by the appearance on campuses, including VU, of the mores, dress, and music associated with the counterculture that had come on the scene after the 1967 "Summer of Love" in San Francisco's Haight-Ashbury district.

In truth, however, student critics of VU academics had plenty of ripe targets. The goals of academic improvement still lagged behind the physical expansion of the campus, a fact acknowledged by the University's own leaders. The 1960 self-study had criticized the intellectual tone of the College of Arts and Sciences and the fraternity/sorority domination of student social life. A growing number of faculty and students began agitating for change. A philosophy department lecture series on "The Idea of the University" in 1962 had begun with Professor Boyd's speech to a capacity crowd in the Union's West Hall. *Torch* reviewer Robert Ayres wrote: "If we accept the contention that transmission, creativity, and criticism are the historical constants in the life of a university, how do we measure up? The answer, lurking behind the lecture's facade like a ghostly gadfly, is: not exceedingly well."

Ayres noted that the fast growth of Valparaiso, overtaxing its resources, seemed motivated by a desire to educate any Lutheran, and he asked, "Are we doing enough to insure that the campus will not be submerged in a vast pool of mediocrity?" The graduate program raised similar questions, as did the state of faculty research. While there was a core of excellent faculty, poor financial underpinnings had led to the appointment of weak professors, and there was apparently no zeal to implement the periodic calls to "cut out the deadwood."

Students' complaints about such ills were more often than not conveyed in ambiguous terms, such as the popular demand for "relevance"—one of O. P.'s favorite terms too. Students created an instrument of faculty evaluation, *The Candle*, that aimed to improve teaching by declaring that "it is better to light one candle than to curse the darkness." But the most brilliant student innovation at VU was the idea of the Week of Challenge. Student leaders Mark Schwehn, Barbara Lewis, Mike Turner, Eileen Ash, Fred Oster, David Simpson, David Nord, and others proposed in 1965 to pool certain funds available for Lyceum and similar purposes into a high-impact set of public presentations. They won O. P.'s support and received more funding from him. He also encouraged faculty to alter class work so students could attend the wide range of events scheduled for a single week in the spring of 1966.

Major figures such as poet and critic Mark Van Doren, historian Henry Steele Commager, poet John Ciardi, the Berkshire String Quartet, and the Joe Daly Jazz Trio spoke and performed. The common theme was "Man Entangled." The student and faculty response was remarkable as thousands turned out in venues from the chapel to the Union to Kroencke Theater to hear impressive speakers demonstrate what a great lecture could mean. They gave substance to the call for "relevance" by presenting issues that pertained to contemporary student questions and issues while reaching beyond them to create new questions. For a number of years, this stimulating Week of Challenge was a source of intellectual awakening on the campus and must be judged as one of the most outstanding products of the 1960s at VU. In the spring of 1967, the VU board of directors commended the students for their initiatives and the high quality of the week's events.

O. P.'s Final Flurry

The year 1965 marked the 40th anniversary of the Lutheran purchase and the 25th anniversary of Kretzmann's presidency. There was talk of succession, but O. P. showed no signs of stepping down. To observe the anniversary, prominent guests, such as Tom Mboya of Kenya, addressed the theme "Toward the Year 2000." At a faculty banquet honoring O. P.'s anniversary, Walter Friedrich used a line from a William Butler Yeats poem—"How can we know the dancer from the dance?"—to unfold what he saw as the "mystery" of this "embattled but unbowed" paternalistic figure by enumerating a dozen major achievements. Each of these achievements had been controversial and autocratically imposed on Valparaiso

University, but when taken together, they constituted much of what made VU a distinctive institution.

The "dance" was not quite over. At the October board meeting, O. P. took note of the storm clouds hovering over the nation's campuses. In many ways, Kretzmann declared, he wanted to join the student rebels: "The younger generation—now better trained than ever before—will no longer tolerate the vast, unfamiliar impersonality of many of our larger colleges and universities." Education must be personal if it is to be meaningful at all, he said, and suggested that VU should be broken down into a set of smaller colleges and units. But if some students raised valid concerns, he asserted, others were not really motivated by social awareness, acting out, instead, their own psychological distress in public. For these emotionally disturbed students—this is how Kretzmann interpreted some of the student unrest—expensive counseling would be necessary. The Week of Challenge showed the need to focus on American society, which was the generator of "postmodern culture." In this growing crisis of meaning, academic experimentation was essential. The newly proposed Christ College, Kretzmann insisted, should be a school not only for students with "high I.Q.'s," but for those with "high Q.Q's"—"Quest Quotients"—who thus could take the lead in genuine experimentation to address contemporary educational needs.

A true university, furthermore, would surround the teaching and learning community with a number of "research institutes," led by a powerful Institute on Church and Society. These activities would bring the best academic thinking to the church in the world, while keeping scholars, teachers, and students engaged with the deepest moral and social needs of society. We are engaged, Kretzmann concluded, in a race between "education under the cross" and a spiritual and social disaster.

So there began one final explosion of activities that O. P. wanted to launch before he retired. As he intended, a College of Nursing, Christ College, and overseas study programs in Europe were begun in the final two years of his presidency. He also spoke of initiating study programs in Japan and Africa, of constructing a major fine arts building, and of developing a VU medical school.

For several years, Kretzmann had been talking about Christ College as a new, vital unit of the University. At various times, he had defined it by describing urgent contemporary moral and religious challenges, the explosion of knowledge, the need for educational experimentation, and the laudable desire of many of the best students to influence society. He imagined that Christ College would meet these challenges in an exemplary way by integrating knowledge, involving students in public affairs, promoting genuine learning by discarding such conventional devices as credit-hours and grades, and in general challenging fine students to perform at their highest level. A planning committee tried to sketch out the design for such a college under the four themes of "honors, experimentation, involvement, and integration." Professor Richard Baepler, who had followed Bertram as head of the Department of Theology, accepted the appointment to be the first dean of Christ College, which began its life in the fall of 1966.

Christ College was established entirely by fiat, without consultation with the faculty. At first, to get it under way, the first two years of the earlier Directed Studies Program were simply rebaptized, its budget enhanced, and the planning committee given a fairly free hand with which to experiment. Initially, most Christ College professors were borrowed from other departments. But the plan from the beginning was for the college to have some full-time faculty of its own so as not to be entirely dependent on departments of the College of Arts and Sciences. Two young instructors, Richard Lee and Strachan Donnelley, were soon appointed to devote their efforts to the college. Together with Dean Baepler, they attempted to create an original academic unit during one of the most challenging periods in the history of U.S. higher education.

As an honors college aimed at highly gifted and motivated students, Christ College was to feature the humanities, with special emphasis on the relationship of theology to the liberal arts. But the college also was conceived to be a source of constant academic innovation and stimulation for the whole university. As a consequence, it offered courses in areas such as Russian literature, "Black Humanities," and the first East Asian Studies courses on VU's campus. Other innovations were pedagogical, undertaken with the idea of breaking down rigid disciplinary boundaries by connecting and integrating areas of knowledge. So law faculty taught undergraduates. Team teaching by faculty from different disciplines was frequent. The arts were brought into the classroom and the cocurriculum. All faculty were encouraged to reach beyond their standard approaches and materials to address common questions.

In the 1960s, the ideas of experimentation or involvement often took on connotations of experiential learning. Such was the case in Christ College also as it developed an Urban Studies Program as well as active engagement with the arts. Led initially by Walter Reiner, this program became residential in Chicago and evolved into the Urban Studies

Program of the Associated Colleges of the Midwest. VU remained affiliated with the ACM and regularly sent students to Chicago, but the program eventually was disconnected from Christ College.

Of the dozens of experimental colleges that appeared in the 1960s, few survived for even a decade or two. That Christ College not only survived, but contributed to Valparaiso's character is partly the result of its visible and attractive building, the gift of Ewald and Joan Mueller of Ridgewood, New Jersey. They were longtime admirers of O. P. Kretzmann who shared his daring vision and had long worked on behalf of VU and other Lutheran church-related causes.

In contrast to the long planning curve for Christ College, VU's College of Nursing appeared rather suddenly on the scene. In some ways, the earlier neglect of nursing at Valparaiso was odd because Lutheranism had a strong tradition in nursing. Theodore Fliedner, a 19th-century German Lutheran pastor, had established a world-famous hospital and deaconess nursing program at Kaiserswerth, Germany. Kaiserswerth-trained nurses had come to Pittsburgh, Milwaukee, and other cities to staff Lutheran hospitals and nursing schools. After World War II, VU provided liberal arts courses for nursing programs at the Lutheran hospitals in Fort Wayne, Cleveland, and St. Louis. Finally, in the 1960s, the decision was made to establish a program on the campus. Porter Memorial Hospital, at the edge of campus, was ready to cooperate fully.

Consultant Ida Strieter, a well-known Lutheran faculty member at Case Western Reserve University, suggested that VU hire Dorothy Paulsen, one of her students completing a doctoral program at Yale at the time. Paulsen (later Dorothy Paulsen Smith) arrived in the fall of 1967 with the assignment to plan the curriculum and recruit the first class for the next fall. With start-up funds from the Guild, the first class of 55 students began classes in the fall of 1968. Paulsen also applied for federal funding that, along with a gift from board member A. W. J. LeBien, enabled the construction of LeBien Hall to house the nursing college. It was dedicated in 1971.

O. P. Kretzmann made several trips to Europe during the 1960s with the intention of developing relationships with some European universities and establishing a VU presence abroad. The first probes occurred when Professors Richard Scheimann and Van Kussrow visited Coventry Cathedral in Britain, whose imaginative program of international centers featuring reconciliation, renewal, and involvement in the social environment suggested a possible model for VU's developing chapel ministry.

Therefore, in 1963 the chapel adopted a form of ministry with a dean and a "collegiate chapter" with canons responsible for various areas of service. Kussrow saw even greater possibilities in the Coventry connection, and by 1966, 10 students interested in drama were in residence at Coventry with Kussrow conducting their highly successful experimental year abroad. VU became formally linked with Coventry as a member of its international "Cross of Nails" network, which featured Christian witness and projects of reconciliation.

Shortly thereafter, Friedrich was dispatched to establish two study centers, one in Britain and another in Germany. The tiny Lutheran Church in England had its own House of Studies at Cambridge University, and VU was able to develop this connection. In Germany, a well-connected German acquaintance of Friedrich assisted in creating a VU center at the *Paedagogische Hochschule* (Teachers College) at Reutlingen, only a few miles from the ancient university town of Tuebingen.

The first contingents of carefully selected students were sent to these study centers in the spring semester of 1968. At Cambridge, Dean Donald Mundinger directed the program, as did veteran Professor Walter Bauer in Reutlingen. They set the pattern of appointing local instructors to teach other subjects and developing a cocurriculum that included travel and engagement with the local culture. The whole effort proved to be a stunning success. Involvement in these overseas studies programs became a valued privilege for students and faculty directors and an enrichment for the University.

Some critics called such programs "frills." But O. P. continued to talk about the importance of creating similar VU study centers in Japan and Africa. After he sent Professor Tuttle to Japan to investigate, Tuttle came back discouraging a separate center. He suggested establishing cooperative programs with established institutions instead, a plan later implemented. As for Africa, Kretzmann was not able to realize this goal during his presidency, but eventually a program in Namibia was established in cooperation with Augsburg College. The idea of a VU medical center also failed to materialize, but it had not just been idle chatter. There was, for a time, serious interest in developing a Valparaiso medical school in cooperation with the noted Lutheran General Hospital in Park Ridge, Illinois, but the hoped-for funding failed. Similarly, VU was, for a time, part of a consortium of Lutheran colleges planning to open a medical school in the Milwaukee area, but an anticipated major funding bequest was instead directed into public medicine.

In January 1967, O. P. secretly appointed a committee on the state of the university that consisted of leading faculty members and chaired by Professor Friedrich. Its real purpose was to advise O. P. on whether he should retire. His knees were wobbly. His cataracts were bad, though he was planning to undergo surgery for those in the summer. "Are you sure you would be able to retire, O. P.?" Friedrich asked. "I don't know," the president replied.

The committee, however, concluded that it was indeed time for him to retire—as Kretzmann himself perhaps realized. In a number of ways, he had become dysfunctional. Professor Leon J. Tolle, a business professor interested in management styles, was privately circulating among faculty and student leaders a paper subtitled, "A Case Study in the Collapse of Charismatic Leadership." He detailed O. P.'s lack of serious planning, his undermining of vice presidents and deans, his overexpansion, and the mediocrity of a number of departments that had no resources for good faculty or curricular depth. General education had not changed for decades, Tolle asserted, and these deep-seated problems would not be cured by adding new programs.

When Kretzmann accepted the committee's recommendation and announced his retirement plans to the board and the faculty, the committee on the state of the university was turned into a faculty advisory committee for choosing the next president. Some assumed that Kretzmann would be less visible. Not only was O. P. not a lame-duck president, however, but his final kaleidoscopic year turned out to be a personal triumph.

It was a year bracketed by the 1967 "Summer of Love" in San Francisco and the summer of 1968, perhaps the most violent season in American history in a century. Numerous political confrontations, punctuated by violent riots, formed the backdrop for the academic year. The Vietnam War escalated, reaching a peak in the February 1968 Tet offensive. To many sober observers, American society was more divided than at any time since the Civil War. Social disorder on a large scale seemed possible.

With growing national political turmoil, several academic events on VU's campus helped maintain a sense of normal activity. A church music seminar brought Dutch and German choirs to observe the 450th Anniversary of the Reformation, as well as a conference on Christian humanism that pondered the relevance of that sixteenth-century movement to modern academic life. On All Saints' Day, VU conferred an honorary doctorate on Father Theodore Hesburgh, president of the

University of Notre Dame. Hesburgh delivered a major address appreciating the positive influence of the Reformation on Vatican II. For Hesburgh, the invitation to Valparaiso was a personally moving sign of reconciliation between Catholics and Lutherans:

> Not long ago, this would have been unthinkable. Like most Catholics, my personal view of Martin Luther was shrouded in myths. ... The first Reformation, unfortunately, separated us. Let us hope and pray that this present reformation will unite us as we face together the great modern challenges of Christianity.

The performing arts were highlighted by the return from Coventry of 10 theater students, the "Coval Players," who presented dramatic fare of high quality and relevance, much of it developed by the group's members.

But politics was never far from view. Toward the end of October, the largest demonstration to date against the Vietnam War took place in Valparaiso as students and faculty members marched from campus to downtown Valparaiso. As the marchers passed "Herb's Club," the right-wing proprietor, Herb Ross, called out, "Make way for the Benedict Arnolds of VU!" At least one egg splattered the marchers.

Meanwhile, O. P. was publicly talking of creating a new "International Studies Program," including a center in Japan, of the imminence of nursing education, and of a possible medical school. "The Sun Never Sets" was the heading of a *Torch* editorial in which editor Mel Piehl echoed the sentiments of many faculty when he pointed out that the University had only barely begun a graduate program and a new College of Business Administration and was now facing a dizzying set of new proposals and ideas. How thinly could VU spread its limited resources without addressing the need for consolidation and quality improvement?

In October, *The Torch* had editorialized in favor of legalizing, though not of using, marijuana. O. P. was greatly upset because of the widespread distribution of the newspaper off campus. *The Torch* also regularly editorialized against *in loco parentis*, saying its time was past and it was not possible at a university of Valparaiso's size. *The Torch* suggested exploring the idea of community as a way to develop better approaches to shaping and governing the university's common life.

Larger numbers of students were becoming involved in discussions about academic and social issues at VU. As part of his campaign the previous spring, Student Senate president Peter Lutze had promised an "All Campus Congress" in which students, including the majority who did not identify with some of the more "liberal" proposals under discussion in the Student Senate, could express their views in preparation for senate action.

Appearing before the first session of the congress, O. P. put on a bravura performance. He assailed the failure of the University to become truly distinctive. VU had, he declared, been drawn into too many national movements without a Christian basis. "We have become a 'me too' school," he said. VU students were right to be concerned about public issues, but they should not simply imitate their secular counterparts. Much of the activism he saw was "a cheap, pale copy of all sorts of schools that are not of our kind." He would advocate careful study of the relationship of Christian faith to Vietnam rather than march on Washington. He personally opposed the war, but students at this university should be asking and answering different questions than those in Berkeley or Ann Arbor. He had begun studying the black power movement with appreciation, he said, but he had to turn away from the hate some of its representatives generated. He shared a suspicion of *in loco parentis*, but in some ways, he believed a caring university could not help being a parent, citing cases where the University intervened with civil authorities on behalf of students or stood with them in medical or personal crises. While he still maintained that *The Torch* was costing the University "$100,000 a year" because of its "bad judgment," Kretzmann apologized for some of his "extreme" statements about the newspaper. Most of the gathered students roundly cheered the president. Others thought he had contradicted himself. But no one could deny his personal authority or the way he could hold an audience. Marveling at the performance, *The Torch* reporter concluded, "The magic that is 'O. P.' is still there."

The question of how to be authentically Christian in turbulent times was one that students did consider. In his farewell editorial in January 1968, Piehl wrote,

> While the oft-repeated admonition to make VU "distinctive" was frequently a veiled defense of parochialism and quietism, the fundamental assumption that this university has something unique and exciting to contribute to our society cannot entirely be dismissed as shallow administrative platitudes designed to forestall student activism. ... Beneath heavy layers of mediocrity and indifference, Valparaiso University does still evoke excitement, affection, and even love in some of those who are associated with it.

Dramatic national events continued to affect VU throughout 1968. The murder in April of Martin Luther King Jr. again brought the entire student body to the chapel for services and a vigil. O. P. made it clear that the whole country and the campus shared the guilt of that hateful act. But VU's black students boycotted the services. Inconsolably and conspicuously, they held their own prayer meeting outside the Union.

As national events turned toward the 1968 presidential election, the campus became caught up in the remarkable campaigns of the Democratic contenders, Senators Eugene McCarthy and Robert Kennedy. With the Indiana primary in May as a crucial test, both McCarthy and Kennedy came to Valparaiso. McCarthy, widely identified with the cause of "getting us out of Vietnam," drew 1,000 people to the Moellering Library parking lot for a speech. Student Sue Brandon was a member of the National Committee for McCarthy, and she and others organized about 100 students to canvass Porter County on his behalf.

As Kennedy prepared to bring his campaign to both the white and black areas of northwest Indiana, where he was extremely popular, friends of VU, including alumnus Mayor Richard Hatcher of Gary and Senator Vance Hartke, urged him to visit the University. Student Ernest Berndt arranged Kennedy's appearance on Monday, April 29. Five thousand people packed the gymnasium. Kennedy clearly awakened the idealism of the VU audience, but in some ways, it was Kretzmann, who was to introduce Kennedy, who stole the show. As O. P. was introduced by a student organizer, unexpectedly, the audience stood and roared as the familiar figure, towering over everyone in his black suit and collar, unsteadily rose to speak. "I'm glad I don't have to run against *you*," quipped Kennedy to the delight of the crowd. Afterward, Kennedy was besieged by people reaching to touch him, amazing even veteran politicians by the powerful emotions he seemed to arouse. Kennedy's subsequent assassination the week before VU's commencement added to the many sorrows of 1968.

The search for a new president to follow, if not replace, O. P. Kretzmann had gone on quietly throughout the academic year. In May, one of the candidates, Professor Norman Graebner, the widely respected Edward H. Stettinius Professor of History at the University of Virginia, visited the campus to meet with administrators, faculty, and students. To many, Graebner seemed an exciting choice, a fitting successor to O. P. He would continue the trajectory of developing a first-class Christian university. After his campus visit, Graebner accepted the board's offer. The first wave of public announcements went out. Then the publicity had to be halted. Graebner had had second thoughts about abandoning his scholarly career, and he decided that he should decline.

10

THROUGH THE FIRE

A TIME OF CRISIS

As students returned to Valparaiso University in the fall of 1968, the sense of distress and disillusionment throughout the United States was palpable. Just past was the violence of the August Democratic National Convention, when 12,000 police, backed by thousands of national guardsmen and military reserves, had bloodied a large group of protesters. Despite the beginnings of negotiations, the Vietnam War was still raging fiercely, creating soaring death tolls in Asia and more bitter divisiveness at home between doves and hawks, both of whom despised government policy. On many campuses, protest was endemic, and strikes and violent confrontations occurred at more than 120 colleges in 1968–69, including at Columbia and Harvard universities.

Compared to many such places, Valparaiso University still seemed relatively peaceful, though certainly not isolated from turmoil. Issues of race, drugs, sexuality, and the environment were topics of concern, and Vietnam and the draft affected nearly everyone. Issues internal to the University were in many respects even more compelling in the next few years, issues deeply colored by the contemporary "generation gap" between young people and their elders, especially anyone in authority. VU was undergoing its own transition from the long presidency of O. P. Kretzmann, and it experienced a period of self-examination and internal stress that tested its goodwill and fundamental values.

The deepest test of those values occurred during the culminating spasm of national violence in May 1970 in response to Cambodia and Kent State. The burning of the VU administration building, Kinsey Hall, seemed to mock the efforts by nearly everyone at Valparaiso to address profound national and local problems with civility. While "the burning of Kinsey Hall" later came, for many, to symbolize the anger and divisions of an unhappy time, the real story of these transitional years probably was VU's ability to come through that fiery furnace with its essential identity and convictions intact.

Efforts by board members and students failed to get Norman Graebner to reconsider his decision to decline the appointment as president, so Valparaiso University became one of more than 300 colleges and universities without a president. The board turned to Albert Huegli and asked him to be acting president. Huegli loyally agreed to serve. He appointed Donald Mundinger to the position of vice president for academic affairs and Alfred Looman to the new post of dean of student services.

Acting President Huegli immediately encountered the urgent issues facing the campus. He approved a set of recommendations, produced by black students working over the summer, to improve the racial climate. A house-center, dubbed "The Ghetto" by black students, came into being. New courses on black history and humanities were offered, as was a Black Arts Festival. Professor Jeff Johnson was named black student adviser, and along with others, he met with the mayor of the city to discuss points of friction, especially with landlords and the police. The new Black Caucus successfully fought for a special seat on the Student Senate. When a delegation of Black Panthers later came to the campus to explain black power, courtesy of VU's Chicago connections, they found a small VU black community growing in self-confidence.

Vietnam and the draft continued to concern the campus. About 20 VU students had participated in demonstrations at the Democratic convention, and *The Torch* was filled with their vivid accounts. In late September, about 100 VU students carrying a Valpo banner joined thousands in a Chicago march protesting the summer debacle. Many students also noted that 25 students did not return to VU's law school that fall. They had been drafted because Selective Service Director General Lewis Hershey had decreed that graduate students, except dental and medical students, were no longer exempt.

Amid such sobering realities, students generally worked for constructive change. A group of activist freshmen formed their own caucus, led by David Samber, with the slogan, "Jahweh, Light Our Fire!" The fraternities brought prominent antiwar Vietnam journalist David Halberstam to campus to lecture. One hundred and fifty students signed up for a new "Free University," like those on many other campuses, which offered noncredit courses taught by faculty volunteers on such subjects as "The Vietnam War" and "The Current College Generation." It was considered a success, though many students could not keep up with their regular courses and the noncredit ones at the same time.

In the aftermath of the All-Student Congress, O. P. agreed to appoint a summer task force of eight students, led by alumnus Mark Schwehn, now a graduate student at Stanford University, to do a thorough study of the University and make recommendations. In November 1968, the task force unveiled its heavily documented report. It was a formidable document, with recommendations so far-reaching in the academic realm that its prospects for enactment were slim. It proposed the "4–1–4" academic plan, a core curriculum administered by Christ College, two integrative upper-division seminars, and—inspired by the Week of Challenge—lecture courses by top professors accompanied by discussion sections. Professional college faculty raised eyebrows at once over the ideas, including the generous use of pass/fail grading for the core courses.

The report's analysis of student life identified many issues that immediately became part of the agenda for campus discussion and continued to be prominent for many years. Its language bore witness to the fact that the sexual revolution was touching Valparaiso University. Throughout the nation, the old consensus that colleges should care about such matters was breaking down, and at VU there was no longer agreement about how the University should treat its students' nonacademic lives. In this climate of rapid change, the pressure for liberalization of hours, and eventually for inter-visitation privileges, was interpreted by some as a quest for the University's tacit endorsement of premarital sexual intercourse, though most proponents did not see it that way. In any case, the context of such issues, particularly for females, was plainly changing. *The Torch* noted that more women were now living off campus and that plans were well under way to eliminate curfews for women over age 21 or with senior standing. Coed dorms were fast becoming a hot issue.

Sexuality in general became a major topic for campus discussion. Writers in *The Torch* argued that sexual morality was a matter of personal choice. The incipient women's movement provoked discussion on the availability of contraceptives and abortion procedures. Toward the end of the academic year, *The Torch* printed two huge double-page displays of information: one on the various kinds of drugs available to college students, the other on the various kinds of contraceptives available. These were not advocacy articles, but they startled the administration and faculty and offended sensibilities, including those of some students.

In December 1968, the board offered Huegli the presidency and he accepted it. A month earlier he had turned down an offer to be provost at Kent State University in Ohio. The VU presidency was not exactly a Christmas present for him—he had contracted debilitating pneumonia and his mother died during the same month. President Huegli did not have a strong constituency among faculty and students, and the prospect of following O. P. Kretzmann, still a presence on campus with the honorific title of chancellor, would have discouraged a lesser person. *The Torch* expressed disappointment with Huegli's appointment, but it said, in effect, let's put O. P. in the past and get on with it. But some student leaders remained unforgiving and viewed Huegli with suspicion.

THE CHALLENGES OF COMMUNITY

As thoughtful men and women pondered the future of VU at a time when many fine universities were being torn apart, there was strong sentiment for finding ways to avoid the kind of polarization that pitted students and faculty against each other. Among some, the idea of a joint Student-Faculty Senate gained ground. Students strongly favored it; faculty were decidedly mixed. A perceptive *Torch* reporter saw the basic issue at stake in the emerging discussion as the nature of the university itself. Is the university primarily a "chastity belt," a community, or an organization? she asked.

It was plain that even if Valparaiso University could not preserve "chastity," it would not abandon its moral concerns. It wanted to be a "community" but an educational as well as a moral one. Nor did it want to be merely a functional organization, providing educational services much as a supermarket provides food: Find out what students want and give it to them. In the next three decades, such a consumer-driven understanding of what a university is would increasingly come to the fore, as colleges competed for students. But in 1969, few at Valparaiso saw it that way. But though it chose "community" as its defining self-image, VU soon learned in 1968–70 that this was no easy choice, either at the level of definition or of actualization.

The idea of a university community was soon tested. President Huegli proposed the "Design for the Seventies," an 18-month comprehensive study of the University and its needs to be carried out by a number of task forces, a study that would culminate in a fund drive. Then the president created a fourth vice-presidency that the board had authorized some years earlier, the vice president for student affairs.

Following precedent, Huegli simply offered the position to his hand-picked candidate, Dr. Walter Rubke, president of Concordia College-Austin. Huegli earlier had indicated that students would be consulted in the appointment, but he was so sure that Rubke was the right person for this difficult task that he offered him the position without telling the students that he had done so. A group of students were then quietly invited to meet with the appointee but were not won over. They doubted the suitability of a Texas Lutheran clergyman for such a task and regarded Rubke's Christian discourse as so much ideological weaponry to be used against the students' current drive for rights and self-determination.

The president would not back down. Nor would the students. When editor David Schroeder published the facts of the affair in *The Torch*, a storm of protest arose. Aroused leaders from nearly every student organization on campus rallied to form a "Student Coalition." The language at the coalition's meetings was often angry, but the document sent to the president on March 11 combined reason with resolve:

> In the wake of recent developments on campus the Student Coalition feels that there is an acute need for greater student participation in the affairs of Valparaiso University. There are a number of areas of student life where students feel that the present university policy does not meet their needs. Students are ready to take responsibility for their own affairs in living in this community. We expect a response to these proposals by 10 A.M. Friday March 14.

Six "requests" (not "demands") followed. The first request was rescinding the appointment of Rubke and the nomination of a candidate by a student-faculty committee. The other five were matters of student life policy already under active discussion. On March 14, Huegli, advised by trusted counselors, sent the student body a well-crafted two-page letter: "Let me say that the wide-ranging interests of the students expressed through the Coalition and others in so many aspects of our campus life is impressive." Recognizing the slowness of normal procedures, he stated his readiness to call off classes for two days to hold an "All-Campus Conference" that would hold hearings and take action.

Then, Huegli took up each of the requests. Regarding the first, he asserted the right of a president to choose vice presidents whom he trusted and with whom he could work. There was to be no compromise on this, but Huegli said that in the future he would appoint student affairs officers with more student involvement. On each of the other five requests, he commented positively. In a special meeting of the University Senate on

Sunday afternoon, March 16, the president announced that the All-Campus Conference would be held the next two days.

On March 17–18, 1969, more than 1,200 students and faculty jammed the floor of the VU gymnasium. The group met continuously from 9 A.M. until 10 P.M., engaging in sometimes-heated debate. The form of the conference consisted of a series of committee hearings. Three committees met on a stage in front of the vast, noisy assembly and invited comment on propositions dealing with a proposed combined senate, rules for living units, control of the Union, and so on. The whole assembly cast an advisory ballot on each proposal before the committee took its final public vote. Another outstanding Week of Challenge had just concluded, and students were keyed up to participate in such intense debates.

When a consensus was reached that a new form of governance should be drafted that could address the issues raised, a "Committee of Five and Five," representing students and faculty in equal proportion, met night and day—sometimes in faculty homes, sometimes at local restaurants—to produce the broad terms of agreement on a new University Senate. Behind the scenes, leaders such as Vice President Mundinger and Professors Strietelmeier and Friedrich worked hard to convince the president of the viability of the new developments.

On March 19, the existing University (Faculty) Senate approved in principle the formation of the new body, which was to have a two-to-one faculty-student ratio in its senate and a one-to-one ratio in its committees. The faculty retained exclusive jurisdiction over such matters as promotion and tenure, academic graduation requirements, professional school requirements, and similar traditional faculty prerogatives, except for general education, which came under "community" (joint student-faculty) jurisdiction. The faculty as a whole also reserved the ultimate right to rescind University Senate legislation.

The deliberations had many moments of drama. Most memorable was a Faculty Senate meeting, held in the chapel to accommodate the enormous crowd, dealing with issues especially dear to students, such as a student court and living unit autonomy. When the proposals in question were not immediately adopted but instead referred back to the Committee of Five and Five for further refinement, more than 1,000 students rose and marched out of the building!

On April 16, the senate approved the new "Instrument for the Internal Governance of Valparaiso University" by a vote of 20 to 2. Approval by a student referendum and faculty vote followed, and the new constitution and governance system went into effect. At a time when many colleges and universities were being torn apart by hostile and even violent confrontation, the creation of the new University Senate through such a dramatic but essentially civil process was a triumph—and proved that the will for community at VU was strong. Although no one who had put the governance system together at the time could be confident that it would work, the new University Senate proved to be a durable and, for most members of the University, legitimate governing institution for the academic community. It was a framework that would soon be tested.

On Wednesday, September 10, 1969, the inauguration of President Albert G. Huegli took place in the splendid setting of the University Memorial Chapel. Signs of continuity were abundant. Veteran faculty leader Walter G. Friedrich presided as master of ceremonies, board chairman Paul Brandt conducted the installation, and Chancellor O. P. Kretzmann bestowed the Presidential Medallion on his successor. Student Senate president Ronald Roschke referred to the present unsettled state of university life in the nation and to the events of the previous spring at Valparaiso, which "differ(ed) from some other campus confrontations in that students here were met with dialogue rather than threats of retribution." Professor Carl Krekeler, vice chairman of the new University Senate, praised the president's flexible response to the legitimate claims of the students in the spring. Also present and speaking were the Rev. Oliver Harms, who had just been narrowly defeated for reelection as president of The Lutheran Church—Missouri Synod, and the man who had defeated him, Synod president Jacob A. O. Preus.

Huegli's inaugural address was titled "The Present Imperative." He invoked the "pioneering spirit" that he said was part of the tradition of this particular university since its nineteenth-century beginnings. Avoiding "defender of the faith" language that might defer to the resurgent right in the Missouri Synod, he declared that a modern university would have to find a balance between scholarship and action, combining academic integrity with passionate concern for questions of moral and social significance. He emphasized the nature of the University as a community and the importance of developing a Christian lifestyle, though he was short on suggestions on what this might mean. Huegli welcomed VU students to their new role in university governance and demanded of the faculty good teaching done with personal warmth and concern, along with increased attention to research. To achieve all this amid rapidly changing conditions required above all faith—"the present imperative."

Huegli had reason for optimism. Despite the controversy over Rubke's appointment, Student Senate president Ronald Roschke had worked well with him in preparing the new Student Handbook that summer. Student leaders such as Roschke and *Torch* editor David Schroeder were able Christ College students who operated within the framework of their own generation's outlook and concerns but also within the University's traditions that had been enunciated by the president. A few weeks after the inauguration, on October 5, the chapel was officially named the "Chapel of the Resurrection" with Chancellor Kretzmann preaching. The name was especially appropriate because "resurrection" was a meaningful, multilayered Christian doctrine that seemed to have particular resonance during the apocalyptic turmoil of the times.

LAW AND POLITICS

Part of that turmoil was the growing clash between institutions and the demand for individual rights. The legislation of the "rights revolution" launched a litigious phase in American life that would, over the next decades, see law school enrollments more than double. For many students, changing society apparently meant going to law school, and Valparaiso's law school was one especially interested in civil rights. "Law is where the action is!" one student declared. The VU School of Law soon faced a phenomenon like none other in its history, with more than 800 applicants vying for 100 places in its first-year class.

During Louis Bartelt's five-year deanship, VU law students began working for the courts, assisting attorneys and judges, particularly as President Lyndon Johnson's war on poverty provided increased incentives for studying the various kinds of "poverty law" affecting the disadvantaged. On the intellectual side, a small group of bright, highly motivated, and immensely energetic students founded *The Valparaiso University Law Review*. For several years, students such as Frank Gray, Frederick Thomforde, and Norman Buls had worked to get the publication under way, and the first issue came out in 1966 under the editorship of Michael Swygert, with Bruce Berner, later a member of the faculty, serving as a member of the first editorial board. On June 5, 1966, the law school conferred the new Juris Doctor (J.D.) degree on 12 law students as the school phased out the old "3–3" program and tightened standards.

Legal education was turning to clinical education as a way of providing students the kind of practical experience once associated with the old apprenticeship system, though now within an academic context. The Ford

Foundation granted the school $30,000 to create a clinic and program in conjunction with Gary's Legal Aid Society. Selected students worked in law offices and social agencies, handling cases on behalf of welfare recipients, low-income tenants and consumers, and indigent mental patients. Commented Professor Seymour Moskowitz, a Harvard law graduate: "The obligation of the bench and the bar is to provide equal justice under law to all persons in our society, rich or poor. The law school, training the lawyers and judges of tomorrow, is the logical starting point in meeting that obligation." The appointment to the faculty of religiously and ethically serious young scholars such as Moskowitz was part of the surge of vitality that redefined the VU law school. Within three years, its enrollment jumped from 155 to 349 students, exceeding the capacity of the new building.

Professor Alfred W. Meyer, a VU alumnus who had joined the law faculty early in the decade, followed Bartelt to the deanship in the summer of 1969. A new assistant dean, alumnus Michael Swygert, brought incredible vitality to the recruitment and retention of students and to promoting the school's involvement in the affairs of the day.

The law school was particularly visible on October 15, 1969, the day of the national moratorium on campuses called to focus on issues raised by the Vietnam War. President Huegli declined to dismiss classes, but in a sympathetic manner, he made it clear that no student should be penalized for being absent from class. He also expressed his own distress over the war and its conduct. Right next to the president's statement in *The Torch* was another statement signed by Dean Meyer of the law school, former Dean Bartelt, and other law faculty, urging colleagues throughout the University "to join us in leaving our classes on October 15, 1969—taking into account our students' wishes—so that each member of the University community" might participate in the planned moratorium events.

The centerpiece of the moratorium was the march of many students and faculty downtown from the chapel to the courthouse for memorial services, which included a reading aloud of the names of the Porter County war dead and a wreath properly placed. It was a solemn and orderly ceremony, full of emotion for participants and witnesses. Major speakers for the day included the prominent Mennonite scholar and pacifist John Howard Yoder of Goshen College and the Rev. Hazaiah Williams, a leading civil rights and antiwar activist from Oakland, California. During the moratorium, the chapel held round-the-clock prayer vigils.

Among undergraduate students, the issues of campus life were often as important as the war or more so. The Instrument for Internal Governance had made it plain that the ordering of university living units was the exclusive domain of the Student Senate, working through mechanisms that it was to set up and subject only to the authority of the president. But in the process of implementing residential regulations, students stressed the term "exclusive jurisdiction," while administrators had their eyes on the final presidential authority.

When the first batch of liberalizing legislation came through from Student Senate, all residences devised new rules acceptable to the administration, except Altruria and Lembke, which legislated 24-hour visitation privileges. A debate ensued between the president and the affected students. Huegli invoked the notion that the "tone and character" of the University set the parameters for the residence rules. *The Torch* thought the administration was worried about sex, while the students claimed to be concerned with developing responsibility. The president admitted that he was worried about appearances and their effect on parents sending their sons and daughters to Valparaiso. He preferred not to discuss sex, but he did talk about "opportunities for selfishness." In the end, Huegli referred the matter to the University Senate's Committee on Community Life. Here the matter was discussed at great length, and the attempt to define "tone and character" led to the formation of a "Blue Ribbon Committee" that was to produce a definitive document on the matter.

The document was not forthcoming until the end of the semester, so the University Senate confirmed whatever new university rules it could that were consistent with the president's thoughts about the University's tone and character. The phrase was used countless times as a code for something the members regarded as important but were unable to define to everyone's satisfaction.

As the semester went on with the issue of intervisitation unresolved, the students of Altruria announced in *The Torch*:

> A coffee house for Old Campus, named the Tone and Character, will open Monday, March 1, in the basement of Altruria Hall. The nature of Tone and Character has not yet been defined, but dorm president Carrie Schueler has assured us that a special blue ribbon committee to define the goals and parameters of the Coffee House will be appointed.

Such wit perhaps reflected a general weariness with the consideration of weighty issues. The student Week of Challenge committee that spring chose the theme "Comic Relief" for the event and brought the usual cast of prominent speakers—but this time the list included people known for their sense of humor. To many on campus, the theme was a stroke of genius.

There were a number of students who did not find comic relief in the year's events. They thought the great gains of the previous year were being frittered away. Others hammered away at the still-pending academic matters. A group of freshmen and sophomores sponsored a conference with some notable off-campus speakers to dicuss further academic reform at VU. That soon became a hot topic for the new University Senate as well.

SPRING 1970

It was not local agitation, but explosive national events that brought a new upsurge of student activism to campuses across the country, including VU. Friends and alumni were shocked to learn through the media on Ascension Day, May 7, 1970, that during the week of the greatest turmoil on U.S. campuses in the history of the nation, Valparaiso University also had lost a major building, Kinsey Hall, through arson.

When Richard Nixon took office in 1969, Americans waited for him to unveil the "secret plan" that he had said would end the war. Instead, the President escalated the bombing, including secret bombing of Cambodia, while cutting back America's contribution to the ground war by slowly withdrawing U.S. soldiers. In the fall of 1969, draft calls were cut and Congress approved the lottery system. The antiwar movement spread beyond campuses to include a vocal minority of veterans, as well as people who were not opposed to the war on moral grounds, but who wanted simply to cut the nation's losses. Nixon's pointed refusal to respond to the massive protests on National Moratorium Day (October 15) and Mobilization Day (November 15) heightened political conflict over the war.

When Nixon ordered U.S. and Vietnamese troops to invade Cambodia to clean out Viet Cong sanctuaries on April 29, 1970, he seemed to be expanding the war that he had been elected to end. The campus response came quickly in waves of protest. Students firebombed ROTC buildings at Maryland, Michigan State, Washington, Wisconsin, and Yale universities. At Kent State University, the ROTC building was firebombed, and students smashed store windows and threw bottles at police cars. Ohio Governor James Rhodes sent the National Guard to keep order. On May 4, some of the gathered protesters threw rocks at the

National Guardsmen. Sixty feet away, several guardsmen opened fire, killing four students and wounding nine. Two of the victims were women who were simply walking to class.

News of the killings inflamed campuses nationwide. A few days later, Mississippi policemen killed two black students at Jackson State College and wounded 11. Before May was over, 350 campuses experienced student strikes, demonstrations involved some 4,350,000 students, and 30 ROTC buildings were burned or bombed. The National Guard was called out on 21 campuses, and more than 75 campuses had to be closed for the remainder of the academic year.

At Valparaiso University, the expansion of the war to Cambodia did not draw immediate protest, but the killing of fellow students galvanized VU students into clamoring to join the nationwide college strike called by the National Student Association. Eight hundred VU students gathered on campus to request that the University shut down. Huegli assured them that any student who did not attend class for reasons of conscience would be respected and that they should respect the rights of students who wished to attend class. The University would remain open, Huegli said, because of the nature of a university as a place for the free exchange of ideas.

An unofficial strike began the next Tuesday morning, May 5, when approximately 2,000 VU students and faculty participated in a march, bearing a coffin in memory of those who died at Kent State. They marched from the chapel to the Porter County courthouse and back. The long, quiet processional, with marshals directing traffic, resembled the solemn liturgical and academic processions in the University chapel.

Early that evening, some 30 faculty met to "discuss possible actions to relieve campus tensions," but no clear plan resulted. Then a group of students and faculty meeting in *The Torch* office decided to bury the coffin that had been carried in the mass procession in a ceremonial fashion, after holding a memorial service. A large number of participants processed from the chapel to a burial site on the campus grounds for the ceremony. Originally, the students' plan had been to bury the coffin across Highway 30, near the local National Guard Armory. Dean of Men Carl Galow later remembered, "All I could do was hope that they didn't come because the National Guard had been activated. They were in combat gear. They had masks and live ammunition, and the guy in charge was of that intensely patriotic mindset." Had cool heads not persuaded the students to conduct the burial on campus that day, Valparaiso might well have become another Kent State.

On Wednesday, May 6, the strike was clearly waning. Student activists picketed some classes and invaded at least one, trying to promote the strike. A sound car circulated on campus, stating that two more Kent State students had died. Many students believed this report, though the information was false. That evening student leaders organized a rally on the east side of the Union. About 500 students showed up. A non-VU student who claimed to be from Kent State spoke, with little effect. The news that President Huegli would address the crowd brought out more students. The president said the University recognized and sympathized with the concern of the students for the tragic events of the preceding days, but it also owed an obligation to those students who believed that their proper course of action lay in continued class attendance. He called off classes for Friday as a day of mourning. (Afternoon classes traditionally would have been called off for Spring Weekend.)

Students responded harshly. The official university report says, "A few students subjected him to unmitigated baiting thinly disguised as an attempt at dialogue. ... The baiting episode apparently was calculated to accomplish two objectives—to embarrass the president and to incite students to further action." Others disagreed with this characterization. Student Rick Barton, one of the speakers, insisted that he was not disrespectful. His was "a cry from the darkness" for Valparaiso students to join with other students around the country. He only wanted the president to listen, he asserted.

A smaller group of about 200 students, dissatisfied with the president's statement, gathered at the Union to talk about further steps. Eight of their leaders left the meeting to call on the president at home, where he was meeting with a number of administrators and faculty members. Their meeting proved unsatisfactory, especially for the students, because Huegli was frequently called from the meeting for phone conferences.

During this extended meeting, someone phoned in the information that students were marching on Kinsey Hall. The students at President Huegli's house left at once for Kinsey. A group of antistrikers also were reportedly getting ready to "guard" Kinsey Hall from the marchers, and Vice President Mundinger and Professor Strietelmeier hurried to head them off. The chanting pro-strike marchers circled Kinsey Hall several times, then sat down in front of it. These students planned to occupy the administration building the next morning when it opened in hopes of persuading the administration to make a formal statement.

About 1 A.M., the group of student leaders resumed their discussions with the president, joined later by all the deans. At 2:30 A.M., everyone went to Kinsey to tell the protesters that "many members of the faculty and administration were in sympathy with their views of the war and supported their objectives." Conversation continued for an hour and a half. The students then asked the faculty and administrators to retire so they might plan by themselves. A number of them entered the nearby Faculty Club for coffee. Soon thereafter, at 4:15 A.M., a fire was discovered inside Kinsey Hall, and pandemonium broke loose. Firefighters responded at once and, together with the remaining students, battled the fire. Students also formed a chain to remove records and music department papers, saving many but not all of them. By 6:30 A.M., the fire was extinguished, but the building had been destroyed. Authorities quickly determined that the fire was arson, and word went out on press wires that "the administration building at Valparaiso University has been burned down."

While some shocked students and faculty gathered in the Great Hall of the Union that morning at 9 A.M., more than 1,200 others attended the Ascension Day chapel service. Missouri Synod president Jacob Preus, who was visiting VU, spoke evangelically to the traumatized campus. The faculty met in the chapel later that morning, hearing the president's report on the events of the week and passing a resolution urging "no recriminations." They also called for a faculty committee to investigate and evaluate the events surrounding the fire.

The atmosphere on the campus remained tense. The flurry of subsequent events in the next few days included the circulation of a request for amnesty for any culprits who might be caught, information centers trying to "get out the truth," and several "liberation" classes held by a number of faculty members on subjects relevant to the crisis. On Friday morning, May 8, there were four services of reconciliation, numerous meetings by various groups and caucuses, public statements, and more ad hoc "liberation classes." Students created a "Kinsey Fund." Senior class money went into it, as did receipts from a Saturday night concert by the rock group Late Edition, who also donated part of their fee. Local churches offered to loan pianos to the music department. Students from Concordia-River Forest and Concordia-Seward sent their sympathies and offered to loan instruments.

But the issue of official response to the events was still a source of serious conflict. On Sunday evening, May 10, the University Senate convened in a tense special session. A proposal by which students who had missed classes could make them up without penalty passed quickly. But intense debate focused on a proposal for optional conclusion of the final three weeks of the semester, which would allow students to take a Satisfactory/ Unsatisfactory grade in all courses but one. The single graded course would be a special group independent study project with a faculty sponsor.

Administrative and faculty leaders clashed over this idea. Strietelmeier, who had advised the president against the strike, now spoke on behalf of this proposal. A Christian university had four responsibilities in the current crisis, he said: (1) to maintain the social fabric which is a gift from God, even if that fabric must be changed; (2) to sanctify reason, which must be preserved; (3) to challenge disruptive passions with constructive action; (4) to be about its primary business—the ministry of reconciliation. Powerful and articulate faculty members and administrators spoke against the plan. But Strietelmeier concluded the discussion with an eloquent plea for a realization of the depths of the passions stirring within the nation and the University. The proposal passed 24–11.

More than 300 students proceeded in collaboration with faculty to hammer out the independent study projects envisioned by the resolution. Some of these projects, filed in the University archives, provide a unique and valuable historical record of the issues and passions of this extraordinary spring. Besides the undergraduate efforts, the entire third year of VU law students left their classes to engage in three weeks of community-oriented discussions and research, an action unique among American law schools.

The investigation of the arson proved successful. Three students were identified as the culprits. A deal was cut by which they were separated from the University, their identities were withheld, and no legal proceedings were undertaken. They were not among the student leaders or those who had participated in the nonviolent march, but they had come from a fringe group who admitted they were on drugs that evening.

The loudest reaction of the polarized nation to the national calamity of Kent State and its aftermath ran strongly against the students. There were public murmurings that "a few more should have been shot." At Valparaiso, too, the mail ran against the students and against the University for permitting a "student minority" to "prevail." The Indiana Supreme Court demanded that Valparaiso's law school show cause why its graduates who did not properly finish their courses should be allowed to sit for the Indiana bar exams. (Nineteen law students previously had signed up to take the bar.) Dean Alfred Meyer and University attorney James Chester appeared before the court to plead their case. One member of the five-man court was absent, and the remaining four justices split evenly. The fifth justice finally voted to allow the students to sit for the examination. "You men better pass that exam," sighed the dean. The results came back weeks later—all 19 passed on their first attempt, a rare achievement.

Question: "What happened at Valpo in the 1960s?" Answer: "The students burned the administration building down!" As the years passed, variations on this exchange became increasingly frequent among people who came to know VU but were not present for the events. It was true that Kinsey Hall was burned by some students. But such a summary probably does an injustice to the complexities of history and especially to the many VU people—students, faculty, staff, and administrators—who worked so hard to follow their convictions while maintaining the traditions of the University amid the powerful emotions and divisive political crosscurrents of a tragic time. They, too, should be remembered, along with the fire through which they passed.

PART IV

Negotiating with Modernity (1970–2000)

11

The 1970s

CONFRONTING CONTEMPORARY CHALLENGES

The Challenge of Modernity

For more than 300 years, the word "modern" has suggested the increasing mastery of the world for the benefit of human life by people who claim to think for themselves without reliance on tradition or revelation. Since the nineteenth century, the new secular university has become a primary symbol and generator of this kind of modernity. With relentless rationality, it contributed to the specialization and segmenting of society, as well as to stunning advances in agriculture, medicine, and other technical realms. But the rational processes that seemed to work so well in the mastery of nature fell short in the realm of human affairs. By the time the twentieth century ended, the intellectual assumptions of modernity were under assault, though in many areas of society the "juggernaut" of high modernity rolled on.

As universities themselves became more complex, a new kind of modern managerial approach came to the fore, focusing more on immediate means and results than on any distinctive educational vision. The faculty professionalization that had begun at the turn of the twentieth century became even stronger under the influence of grant and research money and through the domination of colleges by faculties trained in the research universities. This meant that institutions with distinctive intellectual traditions had a more difficult time recruiting faculties who could sustain and develop these traditions and not simply reproduce the dominant models.

National economic pressures also made it more difficult to uphold distinct academic perspectives or even to maintain the old liberal arts tradition—the principal secular alternative to the research university model in U.S. higher education. As the U.S. economy sputtered and stalled in the

1970s, career preparation seemed uppermost in the minds of many students. The traditional liberal arts, which aimed to teach students to "see the world steady and to see it whole," became for many students a requirements to be met, a means to certification and a career. Higher education became a middle-class entitlement, not a privilege, and a functional service, not a source of personal growth or wisdom. Increasingly, students and their families shopped for a college as a customer shops for an automobile. Competing for their favor, many college administrators adjusted to their new consumers, organizing to serve their varied needs and desires. Such accommodation verged on being an abdication of the college's traditional role of transmitting a valued culture and transforming lives. Furthermore, as students increasingly asserted their legal rights as young adults, the older nurturing role of "alma mater" yielded to management by a class of professional student officers. The ideal of the university as a corporate body of teachers and learners engaged in a shared enterprise gradually gave way.

Religion inevitably changed under the pressures of the times. In the 1970s, a dramatic revival of post-fundamentalist evangelicalism surprised prophets of religion's demise. Some evangelical colleges prospered by beginning to engage modern culture intelligently from an orthodox Christian base rather than simply building barriers against modernity, as had their fundamentalist forebears. Roman Catholic universities attempted to balance their inherited tradition with the new openness decreed by Vatican II. But not all churches safely negotiated the passage into the intellectual and cultural dimensions of the modern world. Several church bodies experienced schism, including The Lutheran Church—Missouri Synod and, later, the Southern Baptist Convention.

As often happens in times of profound change, young people bore a special burden. Many traditional church youth organizations, including the Missouri Synod Lutherans' venerable Walther League, succumbed. Among mainstream Protestants, the once vital Christian Student Movement simply disappeared amid the turmoil of the 1960s. The broad "formation" of young people into patterns of faith and life—which in the United States had been maintained by a loose partnership of communities, religious institutions, families, and the culture at large—could no longer be assumed to happen automatically, if at all. Christian institutions, including universities, had a rich history of conducting moral education in uncongenial or even hostile environments. But amid the pressures of modernity, especially in the United States, much of that past lay half-buried and largely forgotten. Sustaining any kind of moral education would present an especially profound challenge to the Christian university concerned with teaching contemporary students how to think and live as Christians.

FACING UP TO FINANCES

The front page of *The New York Times* of December 4, 1970, carried two items of interest to friends of Valparaiso University. The first showed a picture of President Nixon presenting Young American Medals to four American youths, one of whom was Debra Jean Sweet, a student at Valparaiso University who had left VU after her freshman year to work for the Walther League's successful Hike for Hunger program. These four students were being held up as models to refute the notion that "young Americans have lost faith in their country." But when Sweet received her medal, she told the President, "I can't believe in your sincerity until you get us out of Vietnam." Soon thereafter, the President abruptly left the room. To the media, Debra Sweet commented, "The leaders of the youth of America are resisting, and certainly aren't happy. I was prepared to accept the protocol, but I saw him using me as a symbol, and I refused to become that symbol."

The other item was more serious. Earl Cheit, a distinguished educator from Berkeley, California, had been commissioned by the Carnegie Commission to do a study of the economic situation in higher education. Its title caught its gloomy conclusions in a much-quoted phrase: "The New Depression in Higher Education." In the article, Cheit argued that the current financial crisis of the universities far outweighed student unrest as the most critical problem in academia. Costs were rising far faster than income, and red ink threatened to drown even some of the best-known universities in the nation. Endowments supporting private education had gone stagnant, and voluntary giving was going into a 10-year slump. After 1967, inflation began a steady and unaccustomed climb, reaching "double-digit" levels by the end of the 1970s.

If all these negative factors were impacting well-endowed institutions, they were even more dangerous for less wealthy universities such as VU. Valparaiso University's fund-raising remained stagnant, and in the late 1960s budgets were balanced only by some kind of annual windfall. The real crunch arrived, however, when the board decided not to raise tuition for the 1969–70 budget despite rising inflation. Huegli announced in the July meeting prior to his inaugural that the coming year's budget would have a major deficit of between $600,000 and $800,000. Some of this could be overcome with windfall income, but loan notes would have to be sold to friends to avoid a cash flow problem.

At the same time, a consulting firm submitted the results of an intensive survey, including in-depth, eye-opening interviews with 60 key members of the University's constituencies. Few of these people thought the University had any financial problems. They generally believed that the Kretzmann-Scribner-Henrichs triumvirate "knew where the money was." Valparaiso University was thought of by them as a place of high quality, but they described this largely in terms of the dedication, devotion, and loyalty of the faculty, students, and alumni—not in terms of scholarship. Some thought *The Cresset* to be snobbish and ideologically wrongheaded, and many condemned *The Torch* for its criticism of the administration and faculty, despite its admittedly professional writing and editing. Those who knew O. P.'s *Campus Commentary* regarded it as "about right" for a university publication. They saw Valparaiso alumni as active leaders in the church, and for the most part, they were strongly admiring of President Kretzmann. But there was some sense among them that during O. P.'s final years the University had been drifting and that senior administrators seemed unable to articulate the case for Valparaiso University in any depth.

The consultants praised the people of the development office but not their programs. There was no systematic "prospect research." Fundraising had proliferated into 15 different annual appeals. An essential volunteer structure was missing. The consultants proposed a total reorganization and a new strategy, employing modern concepts of annual giving campaigns and club memberships as the preparation for major capital campaigns. Despite its clear identification of problems, the report was optimistic about the future of Valparaiso University, which it said should "assume the mantle of prophetic leadership in Lutheran higher education in America" as a "collegiate university," focusing primarily on undergraduate work. The University would need to raise $50 million over the coming decade to achieve this, but they thought this was entirely possible. The consultants praised Acting President Huegli for introducing updated methods of administration and opening up avenues of communication within the university.

Huegli recommended to the board in December 1968 that the consultants' report should be the basis for his "Design for the Seventies," which envisioned two major capital campaigns during the coming decade.

Vice President Hekman immediately invigorated the President's Club, inaugurated a university-civic campaign, and began conducting research into corporations and foundations that might support VU. When Hekman later resigned, the president appointed Athletic Director Richard P. Koenig as vice president for public and alumni affairs. Koenig had no fund-raising experience, but the president gambled on his hardworking promotional ability, his loyalty to his alma mater, and his tenacity. "He's like a bulldog," said one of his close colleagues. Together, Huegli and Koenig developed the new approach to fund-raising for the University.

The immediate problem, however, was how to deal with the approximately $700,000 debt resulting from the failure to hike tuition in 1969–70. Business vice president Harold Gram proposed a sharp 21 percent tuition hike. By raising tuition at such rates, however, VU found itself coming sharply up against the limits of its traditional constituents' ability to pay. Vice President Rubke observed, "We are pricing ourselves out of our market." There was growing evidence to support this concern. Enrollment dropped. The percentage of Lutherans in the student body also declined as tuition levels rose, a problem aggravated by turmoil in the Missouri Synod and the nonportability of the new state scholarships. At Valparaiso it was also apparent that "occupational relevance" was replacing political and social relevance. The College of Arts and Sciences declined by 900 students over the decade of the 1970s, altering the tone of the University. Professional programs flourished, partially offsetting these losses.

If rising tuition was the first step in creating a new financial underpinning, the second was increased attention to constituencies and an appeal to them for support. Valparaiso's Alumni Association was young in average age and had never been seriously cultivated as a source of support. Only about 15 percent contributed to their alma mater. The first senior class five-year pledge in 1970 was a step toward changing that.

Unfortunately, Valparaiso's most natural constituency, the Missouri Synod, was at that very moment tearing itself apart. Although its new president, Jacob Preus, always supported Valparaiso University, many of his allies did not. The bonds tying together the Synod and the University were deeply personal and could survive political change, at least for a while. But it was also clear to VU's leaders that the University had to ponder other constituencies for added support.

One new constituency appeared rather suddenly and unexpectedly in substantial numbers without much direct cultivation. "Do you realize," Huegli asked the faculty in the fall of 1974, "that we have 400 Roman

Catholic students?" Valparaiso was becoming attractive to families in greater "Chicagoland" and other nearby metropolitan areas as an institution of quality that attempted to uphold traditional academic and spiritual values. Catholics were especially prominent among this constituency and became a more visible part of VU's changing student body.

In June of 1973, Koenig advised Huegli that a "staff-directed, volunteer oriented" plan for a quick capital drive was taking shape. The Lilly Endowment had announced a million-dollar endowment grant available to qualified private colleges, if it were matched within three years by the recipient institution. VU succeeded in doing so. A year later, an increasingly confident President Huegli addressed a special meeting of the faculty. Enrollment was recovering, the deficit had been wiped out, and the University could strengthen itself internally through a campaign called "Forward to the Eighties," which would be chaired by Indiana governor Otis Bowen and 1911 alumnus Lowell Thomas. The goal of this comprehensive drive was to raise $28.15 million by 1980 to cover current expenses, add $10 million to the endowment, provide for extensive remodeling of the campus, and undertake several major building projects. The endowment also should provide for faculty salary increases, Huegli declared.

This was good news for the faculty, and none too soon. Restive in part over its low salaries, the faculty had a year earlier passed two resolutions. The first was that salary increases should be at least equal to the rise in the cost of living. The other was that the administration should prepare a five-year plan to bring faculty salaries to the 40th percentile of colleges in Valparaiso's appropriate AAUP categories. At the board meeting that fall, John Strietelmeier, who had succeeded Donald Mundinger as vice president for academic affairs, said, "The inauguration of this drive marks for them [the faculty] the end of what some of our colleagues had considered a period of drift."

The Forward to the Eighties campaign created many occasions in cities across the country for friends and alumni of VU to gather and discuss the University's future. Vigorous campaign efforts drew many corporations and foundations to make first-time gifts to VU. At a special dinner in Chicago honoring Lowell Thomas, corporate and industrial leaders of that city came to hear the Valparaiso story and a speech by another illustrious alumnus, former NBC newscaster and media celebrity Ray Scherer, who by that time had become a vice president of RCA Corporation.

In 1977, Huegli announced that the first phase—more than half the amount—had been completed well ahead of schedule, and he launched the second phase. A modern system, with its flow of information and opportunities for giving, was finally in place. The impact was visible. The old student-built engineering laboratory was remodeled into the Arts-Music Building, and a modest structure for the music department was built next to it and named for the late W. C. Dickmeyer. In 1972, ground was broken for the Klingsick addition to Neils Science Center, which was partially funded by the Guild and the Schoknecht family. In 1975, the law school added a new wing funded by the Lutheran Spencer Werner Foundation. Two major gifts for the business college electrified the community. The Krannert Charitable Trust gave $1 million, and the Urschel family of Valparaiso gave $600,000 in memory of their father, William Urschel, a graduate of the old Valparaiso University and the founder of Urschel Laboratories.

So the 1970s, a decade that had opened in financial disaster, closed on a solid footing, more solid than anyone knew. Because Huegli's annual budgets were constructed on a conservative basis, the tuition increases actually began yielding annual surpluses, which were channeled to current reserve funds of various kinds. In 1970, the University had less than $100,000 in current reserves. By the end of the decade, Huegli's administration had paid back the initial $700,000 deficit and increased the current fund reserve to more than $2.1 million. In 1968, the total endowment was $1.7 million. A decade later, the endowment had grown to $15.7 million, of which $10 million had been added as new gifts during the 1970s. President Huegli, by relentlessly focusing on the endowment, had given the University its fiscal health.

INITIATIVES FOR LEARNING

In the spring of 1970, responding to the general campus clamor for academic improvement, the University Senate asked the president to undertake a major reform of general education. Huegli responded by appointing Deans Richard Baepler of Christ College and Louis Foster of the College of Arts and Sciences to lead the effort.

A large number of universities were abandoning general education requirements, or reducing them to a bare minimum, in response to student demand. Those that did so were in effect abdicating the essential educational task of providing a broad knowledge of the arts and sciences as the best possible preparation for the professions, for scientific learning or scholarly research, and for democratic citizenship. General education so conceived bears many fruits, including a critical idealism that leads to religious and ethical vision and informed social change. Furthermore, long experience has shown that all knowledge is connected and that insights in one field are often expanded or illuminated through interaction with other fields of knowledge.

But to remain vital, general education must be continually renewed through connection with both modern learning and classical traditions. At Valparaiso, the basic framework of general education had not been altered for three decades, though some components, such as theology, had undergone revisions. After a summer's labor, the two deans proposed a new, flexible framework for general education within which the faculty could further shape the curriculum.

Baepler and Foster personally favored the 4–1–4 curriculum that had been pioneered successfully by a number of top midwestern liberal arts colleges. It included a January term (the "1" of "4–1–4") that would invite genuine academic innovation. But anticipating faculty resistance, they designed a curriculum that could move toward the 4–1–4 or operate within the two-semester format, with the first semester ending before Christmas. Baepler and Foster also recommended more four-credit-hour courses to reduce the number of courses and preparations for both faculty and students. They proposed that more attention in basic courses be given to methods of inquiry and awareness of how knowledge was constructed so beginning students would understand the "how and why" of their studies, as well as the fruits of contemporary scholarship. In a proposal intended to elevate the intellectual level of the major, Baepler and Foster proposed that all seniors take a required comprehensive examination in their major field.

The proposals were hotly debated. The professional colleges (nursing excepted) led a successful fight against the 4–1–4. The proposed comprehensive major exam was defeated. The January term became an experimental miniterm in May. During the debates, it also turned out that some students thought theology requirements should be abandoned in favor of courses in urban reform, following the then-popular notion that because God was redemptively at work in the reform of society, engaging in social action and studying religion amounted to the same thing. Theology chairman Edward Schroeder made a strong case for keeping academic theology a key part of VU's general education. But he acknowledged that the now often half-empty chapel showed a considerable new secularist presence in the student body that would have to be addressed in the courses' content. In the end, the senate approved a solid three-course, nine-hour theology requirement. Besides English and theology, other strong general education courses were developed in life sciences, physical sciences and math, social sciences, and history. Foreign language requirements were retained for the Bachelor of Arts.

Despite the strengthening of general education, the trend toward professional and career programs in the 1970s was unmistakable. The core liberal arts departments steadily lost students, majors, and, eventually, faculty members. To compensate, the College of Arts and Sciences developed programs in journalism, speech therapy, and computer science, housed initially within existing departments.

Nevertheless, the liberal arts departments did not entirely lose momentum. The theology department was a pacesetter. Meeting on academic business every week, it faced the intellectual challenges of the time in both curriculum and research directions. It increased offerings in non-Christian religions, brought black instructors to teach on a part-time basis, invited noted Catholic scholars from Notre Dame to be visiting professors, secured the service of Rabbi Joseph Edelheit of Michigan City to teach courses on Judaism, and began a significant series of Christian-Jewish dialogues with leading Jewish thinkers. Walter Rast developed an international reputation in biblical archaeology, and Gottfried Krodel, holding a position in Reformation Studies in both history and theology, finished a highly regarded three-volume translation of Luther's letters with his critical commentary on their social and religious setting.

As North Central visitors noted, VU's science departments lagged in attracting outside funding for research, but they continued their strong tradition of demanding, student-centered instruction that prepared students well for graduate school. The initiative for introducing computers came from the mathematics department, seconded by physics. As early as 1959, Professor Diane Krebs had incorporated the university's first primitive computer into her course on "Numerical Analysis." In the early 1960s, Computing Director Norman Hughes used the early IBM 610 and 1610 for payroll applications and the like, but soon other math and engineering faculty began to experiment with academic uses and to introduce courses in FORTRAN and other computer languages into the curriculum.

A faculty committee first proposed the acquisition of a major computer precisely at the time the University discovered its huge deficit in 1969, so the request died. But as it became clear that VU was falling behind other institutions in this revolutionary technology, another faculty committee approached Vice President Strietelmeier in 1976 and put before him the case for a major computer acquisition. Strietelmeier, convinced that it was a top priority, began to lobby Huegli. Professor John Sorenson visited Dartmouth College, then the leader in time-shared computer uses in education, and returned with a long-term plan. Funds were put together from several sources, including a gift from the Guild, and in October 1976, the HP3000 arrived.

Sorenson directed the new Academic Computing Center in Gellersen Hall. The physics department joined the math and engineering faculty in developing computer applications, and as the 1970s ended, further expansion plans were under consideration. Given the cost of the equipment and the rapidity of change, the faculty committee adopted the wise policy of waiting for other universities to innovate, then acquiring well-proven technologies.

While students turned to rock music and other forms of popular culture in large numbers, the music department continued its tradition of teaching, study, and performance, primarily in the classical Western tradition. Jazz was added toward the end of the 1970s and flourished under Professor Jeff Brown. Early in the decade, Professor Larry Fleming took the VU choir on a European tour. Fleming was succeeded by Eldon Balko, who considerably extended and enlarged VU's choral and liturgical tradition, including, among other things, a choral society that attracted several hundred music enthusiasts from outside the University.

Christ College had the freedom to innovate, and it did. Its Freshman Program—"Problems of Inquiry I and II," a two-semester, 16-credit "nondisciplinary" course combining theology, humanities, and social sciences—was inspired by the core courses of the University of Chicago's New Collegiate Division. The entire Christ College faculty—including Richard Lee, William Olmsted, Warren Rubel, Donald Affeldt, and Dean Richard Baepler—together with leading faculty from outside the college, collaborated in the original creation of the Freshman Program. But it was Professor Sue Wienhorst—a theologian, philosopher, and literary critic—who provided the leadership and imparted a steely quality to the curriculum. Students read Plato, Aristotle, Thucydides, the Bible, Machiavelli, Hobbes, Shakespeare, Freud, modern social science, and fiction. It was a course in the classical liberal arts, but one containing an edge of "relevance" to contemporary society and attention to the nature of Christian commitment.

The experience of close reading of difficult works, along with ruthless criticism of weekly essays, proved so overwhelming for students that the faculty instinctively rallied to create supporting activities. Most prominent of these was the "theater-in-education project" led by Professor Van Kussrow, which eventually developed into student-composed musical theater productions. The first was titled "Peanuts, Popcorn, and the Peloponnesian War" and was staged in 1975. Professor Warren Rubel and others developed an equally strong tradition of incorporating the arts, especially visual arts, into some of Christ College's many interdisciplinary seminars.

The tremendous growth of the law school in the early 1970s was matched by the undergraduate professional schools later in the decade. At the new College of Nursing, large numbers of bright young women studied to be nurses, giving the newly accredited college a fine academic reputation. The science-based curriculum was difficult, and nursing students soon found themselves closing the library late at night along with engineering students, whose equally demanding programs left little time for social life. Lest they become total "grinds," however, the nursing and engineering students arranged periodic parties that showed they could put some of their late nights to purposes of enjoyment.

When engineering student Peter Schmalz won the national Tau Beta Pi scholarship award in 1972, he became the sixth VU engineering senior in consecutive years to do so, a record still unmatched in the nation. Under Dean Fred Kruger's leadership, laboratory work became a hallmark of the college, and the faculty began requiring of each student a major senior project that included public presentations. When Huegli appointed Kruger vice president for business affairs, his successor, Gilbert Lehmann, nurtured the established traditions of the college, with the help of a dedicated and talented faculty, at a time when the University cupboard was often too bare to finance much innovation.

The College of Business Administration was, in contrast, often a faculty war zone. Low faculty salaries led to the appointment of marginal faculty, four of whom kept up an almost unremitting battle with Dean Richard Laube. When Vice President Strietelmeier concurred in a recommendation to fire them, the University had its first major run-in with the newly vigorous regulatory agencies of the federal government. The dissidents appealed to the National Labor Relations Board, joined by two faculty from the social work department, one of whom was a woman who sued the University for sex discrimination.

Thus was VU rudely introduced to the intrusive regulatory atmosphere of the 1970s. It appeared that the earlier civil rights emphasis on equal rights and opportunity without regard to race and gender had rather suddenly become conscious group entitlements, vigorously enforced. Universities counted heads by gender and race, appointed compliance officers, and were swamped by expensive paperwork. The IRS threatened private schools with the loss of tax-exempt status and their students with the loss of federal loans if compliance with the rules could not be proved. The litigation in this particular case continued until the end of the decade, when the University finally won. Meanwhile, federal agencies had put VU on notice to appoint more women, especially to supervisory positions.

Other cases appeared as well, and VU sometimes found it expedient to settle them out of court, even when it believed no wrong had been done. In every case that was followed to the end, VU was exonerated of discrimination, though it was sometimes found to be procedurally sloppy. The faculty proposed better procedures for avoiding such entanglements, including an annual review of progress toward tenure and an annual visit to each department by the college dean to discuss the state of the department.

ARTS ON THE RISE

The 1970s saw the growing impact of the visual arts on campus. The VU art collection began with a gift of art from Percy Sloan, an art teacher in the Chicago public schools, who, while searching for a place to leave his collection of more than 380 paintings and its accompanying endowment of $150,000, found in O. P. Kretzmann an enthusiastic patron who promised to carry out Sloan's wish to operate the collection as "actively as is the college library" for the benefit of students and the community. Much of the collection consisted of paintings by Percy's father, Junius Sloan, a minor but respected member of the Hudson River School. It was clear that the donor's intent was that the collection expand along these somewhat conservative lines, concentrating on landscape painting, as exemplified in other works of the collection by Frederic E. Church, Robert Reid, and Frank Dudley.

By 1960, a committee appointed by the president to administer the endowment, chaired by Professor Albert Wehling, had acquired 13 additional paintings, including notable works by the two most distinguished Lutheran painters of the time, Charles Burchfield and Siegfried Reinhardt. Burchfield's own gift to the University, entitled "July," was plainly so far outside the Sloan Collection guidelines that it became the first work in what came to be called the "University Art Collection."

With the arrival of Professor Richard Brauer in 1962 to head the art department, a new era in collection development and in the Sloan Arts program began. Brauer mounted major exhibitions, brought guest speakers to campus, and made annual purchases of works of art. Under the expert guidance of Brauer and Wehling, additions to the collection included works by William Glackens, Georgia O'Keeffe, Kenneth Callahan, John Marin, Walt Kuhn, John Sloan, Childe Hassam, Moses Soyer, and Eastman Johnson.

Huegli personally enjoyed the arts and thought students were being deprived of their heritage through their attachment to inferior rock music and popular culture. He established and funded a Cultural Arts Committee, headed by Professor Arvid Sponberg, to broaden offerings and to encourage attendance at the rapidly expanding number of cultural events. Huegli also appointed Brauer as director of art galleries and collections. Two years later, the Sloan Committee became the "University Museum Council" and formally recognized the University Art Collection.

Soon afterward, Brauer engaged Milo Naeve, curator of American Art at the Art Institute of Chicago, to appraise the aesthetic value of the combined VU collections. In his report, Naeve wrote: "You have an amazing person in Richard Brauer. His keen judgment is exceptional, and the proof is in the paintings, drawings and prints selected with extremely limited funds. Through his efforts you have a collection of national significance, a treasure for the University." This kind of recognition stirred a greater enthusiasm on the campus. Under the extraordinary leadership of Brauer, assisted by enthusiastic faculty members such as Jack Hiller, the visual arts gathered momentum for future moves ahead.

SIGNS OF THE TIMES

While academic and institutional activities continued apace, the campus climate and the outlook of VU's students were altered considerably in the 1970s. Gwen Sayler, a deaconess student who had spent time away from VU on a required internship, was struck by the changes she saw upon her return to Valparaiso's campus in 1970. The most visible difference was in clothing styles. Before she left, a female student would not have gone to chapel, classrooms, or dining halls in anything other than a dress. Now it was all jeans and informality—even deliberate sloppiness. For some, the new style was a form of protest against the consumer society and the empty materialism of American culture. For others, it represented a new attitude toward the body and a celebration of sensuality. For most, it probably was sheer conformity, a fashion trend shrewdly promoted by the clothing industry and no different in principle from the earlier era of skirts and chino slacks. Still, informality was the new norm. Some faculty and students now addressed one another by their first names. *The Torch* described the four different settings of the Eucharist now available to students in the chapel in varying styles and levels of liturgical formality. Everything seemed up for grabs and often stayed there. When Sayler returned again in 1974 to teach for a year in the theology department, she was even more struck by the way that nothing at VU, and in the world, was beyond questioning on the campus. A deep dialogue between established values and various emerging alternatives was quietly, almost subliminally, under way.

By the early 1970s, however, much of this questioning of values, beliefs, and lifestyles no longer took overtly political form. Political protest no longer appealed to the more pragmatic students of the decade, though the counterculture's quest for new values had made its mark. Among students, as indeed among some faculty, the covenants underlying traditional community life had been strained and, for some, broken. Many components of "traditional" student life weakened or disappeared, at least temporarily. For a time, *The Torch* and the Week of Challenge fell into the hands of a few students deeply alienated from the University who tried to whip up protest and confrontation. But this phase did not last, as several such students fell victim to academic deficiencies or drugs. Before long, more representative student leaders and editors reappeared.

Observers called the students of the 1970s the "me generation." As ties with traditional values weakened or were threatened, many students turned inward or ardently sought personal fulfillment. Individual or family anxieties seemed to exact an increasing toll on VU students. When Rubke opened the Student Development Center, later called the Student Counseling Center, more than 800 students sought help in the first three semesters. Rubke worked hard to make the center effective, including creating a "drug loft" where counseling and discussion on drugs could go on in a setting of confidentiality. The chapel significantly increased its counseling services as well. Theology professor Thomas Droege set up faith-encounter groups for students and developed a substantial following for his scholarly work on the psychology of faith and faith development. Around the nation, a general therapeutic approach to life flourished.

Dormitories were now called "residence halls" to reflect the many new efforts to make them more attractive, including more lounges, room telephones, cultural programming, and arrangements to accommodate small groupings of students. In 1973, Rubke told the board that students seemed more willing to listen than they were three years before,

> and do not come with the expectation that they will be oppressed here and deprived of their rights. ... They have been given more freedom than their parents had while growing up, they express and accept behaviors considered improper a generation ago, and they need to learn Christian bases for decisions.

Substance abuse, sexuality, and cheating were the three perpetual areas of concern for campus student affairs officers. Drugs were a problem, and on at least one occasion, Rubke threatened to ban rock concerts if drugs and liquor got out of hand. Much of his attention was given to alcohol. "There has been a tradition of drinking at Valpo," he wrote to the board. "In our American culture it is a symbol of 'growing up.' "

Official university policy banned alcoholic beverages on campus. Rubke knew that this policy could not be enforced except in cases of flagrant public behavior or other visible violations. Fraternities were deemed to be technically off campus. Most fraternities held keggers from time to time for the student body. The events were popular, with attendance sometimes reaching as high as 800 students at a single event. But the practice of serving beer without a license—especially to minors—together with abuses such as drunkenness and vandalism, led to growing concern. After much pleading and cajoling with fraternity leaders, Rubke and his assistant dean, William Beilfuss, banned the keggers for the entire year 1973–74. The abuses decreased dramatically, but so did the campus social enjoyment, and it became clear that this was not a satisfactory solution. In the spring of 1974, the senior class petitioned to hold a kegger outside the Union during Senior Week. Rubke and Beilfuss declined, though the University Senate upheld the students. The matter was referred finally to the board of directors, which overruled the vice president and authorized the kegger. Over the summer, a special task force headed by Professor Albert Trost labored to produce new policy recommendations on the use of alcohol.

While the quest for personal fulfillment took various forms, another discernible trend was the increasing visibility of new subgroups on campus that were united by concerns for identity and rights. The Black Caucus had shown the way and continued its assertion of black students' special identity and needs. Professor William Neal, an African-American professor of social work, replaced Jeff Johnson as faculty adviser and worked closely with the students. A growing black law student population helped bolster the Black Caucus's numbers and confidence. In April 1974, a fraternity event involving students appearing in blackface angered members of the caucus and led to demonstrations and demands that the University increase efforts to combat racism on campus.

Another identity grouping was religious in character. Roman Catholics came in growing numbers to the University, said Mass in Lankenau's chapel, and finally secured a student pastor and a Newman center, Thunderhouse (named after Sts. James and John, the "Sons of Thunder"), adjacent to the campus. Catholic students felt at home on VU's campus and made full use of the new variety of styles that shaped Catholic worship and life after Vatican II. Within a few years, various evangelical Protestant groups also began to appear on campus. Intervarsity was the first, and others of various types followed. Later in the decade, "One in the Spirit" was created as an umbrella Christian organization and clearinghouse, bringing together leaders of the numerous religious groups on VU's campus, including, of course, the residential ministries that the chapel developed. In a secularizing context, religion still asserted its identity and claimed its rights.

The most numerous and visible of the new groupings on campus grew out of the women's movement. It proved to be the strongest crusade of the 1970s in most universities, as it was in the wider society. The first phases of the women's movement followed in the wake of the drive for civil rights and made demands for the elemental equity that women were denied. In higher education, women gained numerical parity with men before the 1970s were over. By the end of the decade, approximately 25 percent of students in U.S. legal and medical education were women.

At VU as elsewhere, many women still had to fight various obstacles to equal treatment. One coed wrote a furious letter in *The Torch* because once again the Week of Challenge had no female speakers. Another wrote against leering fraternity men whistling and yelling at female students as they walked down Mound Street from West Campus to East Campus. Meanwhile, rape counseling was made available and Dean of Women Dolores Ruosch provided information on self-defense. In April 1973, Rubke told the board, "All the editors for next year will be women." In 1975, Mary Fitz was elected Student Senate president, the first woman to hold the office in 30 years.

In 1972, VU law school alumnus Rosalie Levinson joined the faculty and immediately offered a course on "Sex and Discrimination." Levinson became the first of many female faculty in law who, in addition to their teaching and scholarship, served as role models for female law students before and after graduation. In other areas, the Department of Athletics was put on notice to establish comparability in women's sports. The student affairs office had to eliminate the concept of separate "women's hours." Sometimes the movement toward gender equity worked both ways. In the late 1960s, the VU women's honor society, Gown and Gavel, had become affiliated with the national female honor society Mortar Board. In 1975, a federal agency ruled that Mortar Board had to accept men into membership as well, and it did.

The agitation for coed dormitories at VU got nowhere for a number of years. Finally, however, the new ratios of men and women required the University to change one dormitory to an arrangement by which men and women occupied alternate floors. This version of "coed dorms" seemed to work well and to satisfy students. There was at VU no movement for men and women to live on the same floors.

In the larger society, the availability of the birth control pill in 1960 marked a new phase in women's history, as did the U.S. Supreme Court's legalization of abortion in 1973. In the ensuing public discussion of *Roe v. Wade*, *The Torch* took a pro-choice position, and on one occasion, it objected to a pro-life sermon preached in the chapel. The pro-life adherents in the student body and faculty, however, appeared to be a substantial majority. There was growing agitation for distribution of contraceptive devices by the Health Center, a proposal that was turned down without mincing words. It would, said university health officers, be condoning fornication. With glee, the *Torch* noted that Planned Parenthood had set up shop nearby and that university students comprised more than half of its clients. The Student Senate even voted to donate money to the organization, to the obvious embarrassment of the administration. Announcements and ads for pregnancy termination appeared regularly in *The Torch*.

THE SILENT REVOLUTION

As such controversies demonstrated, the deeper social and cultural context for addressing students' nonacademic lives had been permanently altered. In addition to the obvious changes, a silent revolution had been taking place on American campuses, at first almost imperceptibly, yet as the 1980s and 1990s were to show, clearly and irreversibly. Carl Galow sensed it when he resigned as dean of men in 1969 to study journalism. "*In loco parentis* is gone and I don't know what has taken its place," he said.

The older view had consisted of four elements: (a) The University had the power to make whatever rules and regulations for student living it thought necessary and (b) to enforce them through disciplinary action. This meant the University had (c) the duty to care for students and take responsibility for them and (d) was, therefore, exempt from the usual requirements of legal "due process" when acting in its caretaker role for young people.

Galow was right that the set of assumptions behind this historic practice, as well as the policies themselves, had disappeared. As major beneficiaries of the Rights Revolution, students in the traditional 18 to 22 age group gradually were seen by the law to be adults, and academic institutions were no longer viewed as fictive parents. This changed view was summarized by the U.S. Court of Appeals for the Third Circuit in 1979 when it said: "Whatever may have been its responsibility in an earlier era, the authoritarian role of today's college administration has been notably diluted in recent decades. Trustees, administrators, and faculties have been required to yield to the expanding rights and privileges of their students." The courts consistently have upheld the right of universities to make and enforce rules, so long as they follow the rules they themselves establish and do not violate students' constitutional rights to privacy and due process. But this consensus has left large areas of conflict.

In the long (and continuing) debate concerning residential rules of conduct, especially intervisitation rights, university authorities who wanted to maintain some degree of regulation of residential life sometimes acknowledged and sometimes denied that its limitations were based on opposition to premarital sex. Over time, this wavering made cynics out of students and made the university appear to be hypocritical because everyone knew that residence rules could not create or maintain student celibacy. The genuine difficulties in thinking about how to deal with the related issues of group living and sexuality were seldom explored from the standpoint of the Christian moral tradition. Even when students directly requested thoughtful talk about sexual matters, the university faltered. When the Catholic Newman Center, Thunderhouse, began holding discussion seminars on sex, the University promised to do the same, but it did not do so because, as a concerned Dean of Men Robert Schroer was quoted as saying, "There weren't enough resources."

After experiencing health problems, Walter Rubke left VU in 1975 to take a pastorate in California. Rubke's winsome and fair approach to student life had gained the support of many faculty and students, even amid the profound changes occurring in the larger society, the faculty, and the student body. The new vice president for student affairs, Daryll Hersemann, was a good modern manager who saw his main duty as delivering services to students through the Union, Health Services, the Placement Office, the Security Department, Counseling Services, and so on. This he did well. But while Rubke had seen his deepest task as promoting the moral education of students while dealing with their issues and problems, it was not clear that Hersemann felt under any such deep obligation. He maintained a smooth bureaucracy that gave the appearance of all things being in order most of the time. When concerned members of the faculty would pick up word through students that intervisitation rules were sometimes flagrantly breached or that racial issues were not being addressed, their questions or complaints often were lost in the bureaucratic maze.

Increasingly, it seemed that the functional and bureaucratic standards of modernity were eroding VU's strong sense of community. Student affairs officers were assigned to care for students outside the classroom while faculty tended professionally to the cultivation of their disciplines and related academic matters. At a place such as VU, there were many concerned professors who genuinely cared about their students, but inevitably faculty and students alike gradually tended to make their relationships more functional and less personal. Under the new governance system, faculty no longer gathered to receive reports from student affairs officers or register their own concerns, as in an earlier time when faculty felt some corporate responsibility toward student life. Despite talk about "educating the whole person," there were fewer and fewer people on campus who saw others' lives that way and perhaps fewer still who wanted to.

SPORTS IN THE 1970S

Even collegiate athletics experienced momentous change during this decade. The NCAA by now had become a cartel of politically powerful athletic departments. Embedded in the large organizations associated with the major universities, especially those that played big-time football, the NCAA was firmly in control of intercollegiate athletics, and it developed a remarkable bureaucratic power in its sphere.

For many years, men's intercollegiate athletics had been conducted within the framework of two divisions—for the larger and the smaller institutions. Valparaiso was in the second, called the college division. But the rules of participation were flexible so in basketball, for example, Valpo traditionally scheduled a number of university division teams, including Notre Dame, Air Force, Northwestern, Marquette, and Loyola, while playing smaller schools in other sports.

To take full advantage of the increasing radio and television receipts that the NCAA controlled through its broadcasting contracts, the large universities with big-time football programs promoted a restructuring into three rigidly defined divisions. The new Division I required that a member had to play all of its sports except football in that division and that 75 percent of a school's basketball team's schedule must be played against Division I opponents. The dramatic rise in revenue especially affected college basketball, which the media found tremendously attractive, especially when the expanded championship tournament (at first consisting of 48 teams, then 64) attracted millions of viewers and many new advertisers. Basketball was also the sport that gave even medium-size universities the chance to participate in the prestige and income of Division I status at relatively low cost. As the three-divisional structure came into operation during the second half of the 1970s, smaller universities had to choose whether to play at the Division II (fewer scholarships) or Division III (nonscholarship) levels, or to pursue Division I, dominated by much larger football-oriented institutions.

These developments posed a major question for Valparaiso University. Its budget for athletics was extremely low, and the genuinely amateur, student-centered approach of the ICC accorded well with its values. But the ICC was breaking up, forcing hard choices. Indiana State and Ball State, now large institutions, readily withdrew from the conference to seek their fortunes in the big time. Closer in size and character to Valparaiso, Butler and Evansville were also lured by Division I status and began meeting with a number of urban universities, such as Xavier, Detroit, and Loyola, that eventually would form the Midwestern Cities (later the Midwest Collegiate) Conference. Soon they, too, declared their intention to enter Division I. In this situation, what should Valparaiso do?

VU began holding meetings with the MCC schools, and in early 1976, the board of directors decided to enter Division I. There was only rudimentary administrative consultation with the Intercollegiate Athletic Committee of the University Senate, such that the committee did not even have a chance to consult with its parent body. Athletic Director Norman Amundsen and most of his staff opposed the move, knowing that Valparaiso was not yet prepared for Division I and had vastly underestimated its cost. They were especially concerned with the negative consequences for all other sports besides basketball because they would now have to enter Division I contests that they had little chance of winning. The faculty were unhappy with the apparent shift of values. The campus consensus regarding athletics that had existed for decades had dissolved.

On top of these concerns came the movement for equality in women's athletics. The passage of Title IX of the revised Civil Rights Act in 1972 sent shock waves throughout the collegiate athletic world because on its face, the legislation mandated complete gender parity in sports. In practice, slow government machinery and pressure from the NCAA, especially the big football schools, meant delays in enforcement. Meanwhile, the Association of Intercollegiate Athletics for Women (AIAW) came into existence with ideals and practices of classical amateurism: Winning was subordinated to the joy of playing well together, and highly informal structures prevailed. Like most colleges, Valparaiso joined the group. But the NCAA soon decided to take over women's athletics, and by sponsoring championships in women's sports, the NCAA eventually crowded the AIAW out of existence.

VU women's varsity athletic competition began in 1972 in intercollegiate field hockey, tennis, volleyball, basketball, and gymnastics. Professor Ruth Brown almost personally carved out a place for women on VU's sports scene. Brown became associate athletic director in late 1974, coaching both the basketball and field hockey teams, which, along with swimming, had been the only women's team sports for a number of years. Almost casually, a full-blown VU women's intercollegiate sports program appeared, scarcely noted even in *The Torch*. In 1974–75, the VU Parents Fund gave money to boost this new program. Contrary to the myths surrounding the subject for decades, if not centuries, women loved participating in sports and enjoyed intense competition. They learned to play in the dynamically expanding precollege girls' sports programs around the country.

For VU sports teams, the 1970s was a transitional time. The venerable ICC finally dissolved toward the end of the decade. There were outstanding players such as Gary Puetz in football, Joel Oberman in basketball, and Daniel Wilson and Joel Bretscher in swimming. Female standouts also appeared: Lee Ann Berning became state tennis champion and placed high in national tennis meets. Together with teammate Patty Giannis, Berning helped VU women dominate in state tennis for a number of years, winning both singles and doubles state championships.

The decade did not end on a positive note, however. Valpo's hopes to be included in the Midwestern Collegiate Conference were dashed. Blame was put on the size of VU's gym, the low population base of the area, and similar factors.

A CHRISTIAN UNIVERSITY IN A POST-CHRISTIAN AGE

Some bright *Lighter* editors of the mid-1970s saw that the deep changes occurring in U.S. culture required new understandings of Valparaiso's character as a Christian university. Marie Failinger (later a professor of law), Patrick Keifert (later a professor of theology) and Joan Lundgren Hunt (later among the first women ordained in a Lutheran church body) turned to two leading faculty members, John Strietelmeier and Richard Luecke, for essays to explore the question. The students asked whether, in light of the then-prevailing sentiment that secularization was itself a religiously proper outcome of cultural change—because God was assumed to be at work in that process—the idea of a "Christian university," seemingly derived from an earlier period of Western culture, had any contemporary viability or rationale?

In his response, Strietelmeier revealed some of his own gloomy assessment of the current situation. Supreme Court decisions, as he saw them, were going against church-related schools, and in the prevailing economic distress, the "educational depression" threatened the very existence of institutions such as Valparaiso. But the worst problem was the loss of any sense of tension between Christianity and society, which went for church-related schools as well. "We will survive by being different, not by being one of the boys," Strietelmeier said. "But of course survival is not the issue. We have taken upon us the name of Christ, and our first concern must be to bear that name with humility, power and integrity." He then identified five characteristics that he believed essential to "a Christian community gathered to pursue the academic vocation in a particular place."

In the succeeding issue of *The Lighter*, Richard Luecke affirmed each of Strietelmeier's five propositions but put his own glosses on each one, teasing out their implications. Conflating the two essays produces the following summary of how some reflective people at VU in the 1970s were attempting to preserve continuity in the University's mission while acknowledging the tectonic plate shifts that were occurring in the cultural landscape.

1. Christians at the University should continue to draw from the Word and the Lord's Supper—in chapel (whether or not campus life still

"revolves" around it) and elsewhere—for failure to do so constitutes a "failure of nerve." Luecke found that the old words and rites could suddenly produce new meanings in unsettling contemporary settings. Where college catalogs could talk about their students becoming "well-rounded" and "fitting in," the old language of Scripture and liturgy heard in fresh ways could produce "strangers and pilgrims."

2. Christian institutions should affirm servanthood but squeeze everything "servile" out of the Christian servant. The focus should not be on society's self-defined and felt needs. *Alma mater* dare not become a "whore," but it must try to uncover the real needs of the society and to develop the courage to meet them.
3. Christians in the University must care for one another in "apostolic" ways, not being indifferent in the spirit of "do your own thing" morality, but functioning as a Christian community through evangelical, not legalistic, means. Further, Christian memory requires looking backward to prophets and crosses, then outward again with a fresh intention, caring enough to ask no less of one another.
4. Christians should seek an institutional excellence not standardized by other academic institutions. Indeed, they must outdo their contemporaries but in original ways.
5. Christians ought to respect the meaning of vocation, with each member of the University following his or her calling. Full integrity of vocation, however, includes being called out of conventional definitions to reform old functions and help create new ones in ways that are not predetermined.

Some students, faculty, and staff continued to take this kind of reflection seriously and to try to incorporate a wider vision of the Christian university into their teaching, learning, and scholarship. During the Huegli years, John Strietelmeier in particular assumed the mantle of articulating the fundamental assumptions that shaped VU as a Christian university. Speaking to the faculty in various venues, Strietelmeier emphasized that to "redeem the time being" meant to "take seriously our calling to be role models to a generation which has been taught to despise both culture and the faith. ... It means, for those of us who can do so with a good conscience, participation in the life of the on-campus worshipping community." He also stated that though for Lutheran Christians the Ten Commandments and the Sermon on the Mount were not the heart of the Christian faith, the times urgently required both church and university to undertake their calling to moral education. He remembered, Strietelmeier said, the disappointment students had felt a few years before when they vainly pleaded for moral leadership from the faculty: "My own feeling is that it is against this refusal of their elders to speak and act with conviction and passion that the activist students of a few years ago revolted."

Speaking to engineering faculty and students on one occasion, Strietelmeier reminded them of the larger dimension of their Christian calling. He pointed out that "civilizing roads and bridges and pure water systems" was directly translatable into better schooling, better food, better administration, and more available medicine in developing lands where people often died young, "never having known what it is to have a full stomach or a day without pain."

While Strietelmeier was regularly applauded when he delivered such stirring calls to the faculty and others, the context in which such conversations occurred was changing. The difference was not so much in what was said, but in who was listening. Just as the student body was changing, so were the faculty, administration, and staff. By the late 1970s, the original core of religiously informed and committed people from both Lutheran and non-Lutheran traditions who had been drawn to VU in the 1940s and 1950s, often at the great sacrifice of opportunities elsewhere, was beginning to age. And quality junior faculty were harder to find. Language about the "moral obligations" of faculty, much less talk about the larger Christian dimensions of the academic calling, landed somewhat strangely on the ears of some newer faculty who had little experience of religious higher education and for whom the idea of Christianity as a cultural presence was quite foreign. With fewer factors in either the academic or general culture reinforcing their message, those who sought to maintain Valparaiso's mission had to work harder to rally their forces and reconceive their ideas and strategies for a new time.

Yet Valparaiso was able to attract and retain at least a core of excellent younger faculty from a variety of religious and academic backgrounds. Those appointed in the 1970s and early 1980s became faculty leaders in the next generation, including Donald Koetke (physics), Michael Kumpf (classics), Frederick Niedner (theology), Edward Uehling (English), Arvid Sponberg (English), Warren Kosman (chemistry), James Caristi (mathematics), John Feaster (English), Sandra Kowalski (nursing), Carole Pepa (nursing), Sarah DeMaris (German), Ann Reiser (education), Renu Juneja (English), Gail Eifrig (English), William Marion (mathematics), John Steffen (engineering), Gerald Seeley (engineering), Linda Ferguson (music), Larry Baas (political science), and others. While few of them had been immersed in the Missouri Synod system or tradition in the same way that earlier faculty had been, and they held a variety of religious commitments, they came over time to value what VU stood for and to carry on its mission in times that were not congenial to Christian higher education.

VALPARAISO AND THE SYNODICAL TURMOIL

Just when the University needed its nurturing church body the most in this perplexing age, the Missouri Synod tore itself apart. Although Valparaiso University had never been owned or operated by the church and had carefully guarded its institutional independence, the University was bone of its bone, flesh of its flesh. The names on the buildings, on innumerable plaques around the campus, and on student scholarships were a constant reminder that the University had been built primarily by the people of the LCMS. The personal ties that bound members of the Synod to VU students, faculty, and supporters were both numerous and thick.

During the 1950s and early 1960s, the Missouri Synod had appeared to many observers to be ready for a new and larger role in American culture. A generation of unusually talented theologians, well-educated clergy, and vigorous congregations, previously sheltered by immigrant ways from the erosions of modernity, seemed poised to step onto a larger stage and contribute their gifts to the invigoration of American Christianity. Young Missouri Synod scholars such as Martin Marty and Jaroslav Pelikan were highly regarded both inside and outside the Synod, and others were preparing to follow in their path.

A substantial party within the Synod, however, disagreed with the direction of change and what they understood to be the new teaching by the faculty of Concordia Seminary, St. Louis. Later, that faculty admitted to not having kept in touch with the concerns of many pastors and congregations and to a touch of arrogance about their own avant-garde role as well. Building on the discontent first manifested in the "State of the Church" conference in 1961, conservative activists began mobilizing at the grassroots level to reverse the Synod's direction. A coarse but widely distributed tabloid, first called *Lutheran News*, then *Christian News*, exploited these anxieties and gradually gained a wider audience. Its articles and editorials pilloried institutions and individuals, undermining the thoughtful deliberations of the church body. Some simply viewed the publication as filled with half-truths and cheap shots. But even many who did not share its extremism began to feel that something "dangerous" was going on in the Synod.

At first, the dissenters could not destroy the broad support within the church for engaging the contemporary world. At the Detroit convention in 1965, the Synod joined the new Lutheran Council, USA, and approved the Mission Affirmations, a set of principles on how the church in mission should approach the contemporary world, and adopted a "Statement on Woman Suffrage in the Church." These moves were supported by wide margins, but they further galvanized the opposition, strengthened by the reaction to the social upheavals of the 1960s, into a more effective activism. The movement to change Missouri's direction culminated in the 1969 convention at Denver, where highly organized and effective tactics led to Jacob A. O. Preus's narrow defeat of incumbent President Oliver Harms on the third ballot.

Thus Preus, who had come to the Missouri Synod from a smaller Norwegian Lutheran church body, attained the office of president of the Synod through a series of events that climaxed a decade of militant political activity within the church body. While Preus moved to assert his control over Concordia Seminary and the church bureaucracy, he did not include Valparaiso University among his targets. In all his dealings with VU, Preus warmly acknowledged the connections between university and church, though he knew that many at Valparaiso saw him as a stranger in their midst.

Although Preus expressed his personal support of Valparaiso University, Huegli and his advisers were alarmed at the tactics of his allies. They sensed VU's vulnerability to the same kind of politics that they had witnessed in the Synod and moved to insulate it. Technically, under the older bylaws, anyone who contributed to Valparaiso University became a "member" of The Lutheran University Association and was eligible to vote for the members of the board of directors. It would not have been difficult for an organized and zealous group to have taken over the university in a relatively short time. To forestall this, the LUA was restructured so the board became a self-perpetuating entity, electing its own membership. No one questioned whether this move might come at a cost, that of diminishing the church-relatedness of the University.

In 1969, the same year that Preus became synodical president, John Tietjen, an ecumenical spokesman who was little known in the midwestern heartland of the Missouri Synod, became president of Concordia Seminary, St. Louis. For the next several years, Tietjen and Preus publicly faced each other down as the principal leaders of two opposing parties. Through the use of appointive powers, Preus steadily increased his influence over the Synod. The 1973 convention in New Orleans became, as advertised, the "confrontation convention" that revealed profound disagreements regarding the location of authority in the church, how to read the Bible in the modern world, and a host of other theological issues. The St. Louis faculty responded to the attacks on their positions with an impassioned plea to the synodical membership, declaring that "the Gospel is at stake."

Huegli met periodically with the Department of Theology to help guide it in understanding its important task within the University. The board decided that the University itself would not take positions in the confrontation, and this applied to the theology department as a collective entity as well. Many individuals did speak out in various ways. Under Professor Kenneth Korby's editorship, *The Cresset* presented searching analyses of the key issues. Professor Walter Keller, the new chairman of the department, collaborated closely with the president in monitoring both the complex theological issues and the intricate political maneuverings in the Synod.

By October 1973, the resisters to the new leadership, calling themselves "moderates," formed the Evangelical Lutherans in Mission (ELIM), a dissident organization. On January 20, 1974, Tietjen was suspended. A majority of the faculty declared themselves in solidarity with their president, and many students supported Tietjen as well. There was a moratorium on classes, as well as demonstrations and confrontations, and the national media descended on the campus. Because a number of Valparaiso alumni were involved, *The Torch* covered the events as well. Alumnus Rick Mueller became the editor of *Missouri in Perspective*, a "moderate" publication that provided a reliable account of what was happening. Valparaiso's administrators and faculty had many friends on the Concordia faculty and were deeply concerned. On February 5, 1974, many faculty and staff of Valparaiso University signed a letter to Concordia Seminary's board, protesting Tietjen's suspension.

On February 6, Huegli assembled the VU faculty in Neils Science Center. Keller rehearsed all the recent dramatic events in St. Louis, and Huegli provided his own analysis of the situation together with copies of a position paper he released that day called "The University and the Crisis in the Church." In this position, Huegli expressed sadness at the present distress of a sister institution. But he insisted that "the University as such is not partisan in matters of controversy, whether they be doctrinal or political, but it opens its doors to wide-ranging discussion in the search for solutions and for truth." While urging patience and forbearance, he pointedly added, "As individuals we have an obligation to speak out against all that would hinder academic honesty and spiritual growth in the schools of the Church." He then offered the services of the University for the reconciling of differences within the Synod.

But the time for mediation was past. In vain, a series of meetings initiated by various parties sought reconciliation. On February 19, 1974, a majority of the faculty and students at the seminary marched out and created Concordia Seminary-in-Exile, also known as Seminex. Faculty pay had been cut off and eviction from faculty housing was imminent. Tietjen came to Valparaiso, where he was given a standing ovation at an address in the chapel. By August 1974, the second assembly of ELIM sounded more like an incipient church body than a confessional movement within the Missouri Synod.

Many wanted the University to enter the fray. Emotions ran high at VU because friends were being treated unjustly at synodical schools and in the mission fields. Leaders of ELIM and Seminex appealed to Huegli to lead the University to join them in a common cause. They met late in 1974 to discuss this possibility, but in the end, Huegli declined to openly ally VU with ELIM. Of course, this was not a personal decision, though he fully joined in it. The board, some of whose members were deeply involved in ELIM, finally concluded that their essential duty was to preserve the University. This precluded taking an institutional stand on the church conflict. Huegli himself had disagreed with the walkout from the seminary. He believed that had the faculty remained in the institution, the church, including the constituents of Valparaiso University, eventually would have rallied to their support.

In his travels and correspondence, Huegli discovered that many alumni felt the same way. They were not supporters of Preus. Often they were the lay leaders of congregations that did not want to get caught up in what they understood to be a narrow theological quarrel or a political struggle or a combination of both. In any case, they had not been convinced that the issues, as they understood them, rose to the level of a great confessional conflict. There was a considerable distance, it appeared, between the seminary and the pulpit and between the pulpit and the pew.

About two years later, the strongest Seminex supporters officially broke with the Synod and formed a new body, the Association of

Evangelical Lutheran Churches (AELC). About 200,000 members eventually joined the new body, though a large majority of the "moderates" stayed on quietly and powerlessly within the LCMS. More than half of the AELC congregations were contributors to Valparaiso University, including many of the English District congregations that had been so important throughout VU's history. The schism, culminating over a decade of increasingly bitter conflict, split families and strained friendships throughout the once close-knit Missouri Synod. For many people, including a large number at Valparaiso University, these events were traumatic and heartbreaking, creating a deep sense of loss from which it was not easy to recover.

More practically, the synodical crisis added to VU's troubles in the 1970s. Forward to the Eighties was just getting under way, and its outcome was uncertain. Budgets were pinching. Lutheran enrollment was dropping, and the new, more diverse student body challenged deeply rooted outlooks and practices. Furthermore, the Missouri Synod split seriously depleted the academic pipeline that had long furnished Valparaiso with many of its best faculty. For some on campus, the earlier dreams of building a unique Lutheran institution seemed threatened, and many wondered what kind of a university would emerge from an increasingly attenuated relationship to a church body, or bodies, with which VU was no longer as well connected. For the first time, the prospect of becoming a vaguely Christian university, sliding down the "slippery slope" to becoming just another private U.S. college, began disturbing those who had worked hard to make Valparaiso a strong Lutheran representative of the United States' religiously pluralistic higher education.

At the Missouri Synod's convention in Anaheim in the summer of 1975, the last hopes for reconciliation disappeared. Preus declared that for two decades there had been two different theologies in the LCMS, one more than the church could bear. Those who could not agree with the theology as established by convention resolution, he said, should seek another church. In response to the failure of reconciliation attempts, Huegli wrote in his July 1975 board report that Valparaiso University must now seek new constituencies. In October, he wrote of rebuilding a whole support network but stressed the importance of avoiding confrontation while that task was under way. In the long run, the question of how to maintain Valparaiso's Lutheran and Christian character and relationships in an altered ecclesiastical environment would be one of the primary challenges facing the university.

A GOLDEN ANNIVERSARY

Throughout the 1970s, Huegli took steps to reaffirm the University's church connections. He established the Center for the Study of Campus Ministry, which sponsored many conferences for Lutheran student pastors as part of its program. Campus conferences for Lutheran pastors included "Congregation and Confession" on the 400th anniversary of the Lutheran Confessions. In 1977, the entire 60-member College of Presidents (regional judicatory heads) of the Missouri Synod conducted its five-day meeting on campus.

A special opportunity to address the difficult issues of church relations occurred during the fall semester of 1975 as the University paused to observe its golden anniversary as a Lutheran institution. There was a series of convocations, observances, and special events. The music and art departments had special golden anniversary performances. Richard Wienhorst composed a choral cantata, "Clap Your Hands," and a major symposium of on-campus and visiting scholars was held on the future of church-related higher education. James Albers wrote *From Centennial to Golden Anniversary*, a well-researched monograph on VU's turbulent history from 1959–75. Jaroslav Pelikan's Miller Lectures concluded the observance by showing how church doctrine had often changed precisely to preserve the central intention of Christian teaching.

Despite evident difficulties, the tone of the observance was bold. In his opening convocation address, Huegli said:

> Even if the church body with which we have been affiliated for half a century should be torn apart and new organizations emerge, we must remain true to our calling as a university. ... We must commit ourselves with whole heart to the high principles of Christian learning as they are embodied in the Lutheran tradition, reaching out in academic fellowship to all who wish to share these treasures with us.

At a later special convocation, Huegli presented three Lutheran Presidential Scholarships to be annually granted by the presidents of the three major Lutheran church bodies of the Lutheran Council to whomever they selected. On hand to receive them were Jacob Preus, his cousin David Preus, president of the American Lutheran Church, and Dr. George Harkness, general secretary of the Lutheran Council, representing the president of the Lutheran Church in America. In his remarks, Huegli said, "The church-related college or university is not merely an agency of the church but has a calling of its own to do the work of the people of God in the world." Therefore, "A Lutheran university must be assured of non-intervention by the church, lest the character of the university be warped and the minds of scholars made captive by misguided zeal."

In September of the golden anniversary year of 1975, O. P. Kretzmann died. "He was the keeper of the dream," wrote *The Torch* in a special issue devoted to him. As his body lay in state in the Chapel of the Resurrection, an honor guard of 92 male and female students stood at the coffin, two at a time for 30-minute intervals. Student sons of alumni were the pallbearers, and the coffin was carried elevated on their shoulders during the procession down the chapel aisle. Several thousand mourners, including Jacob Preus, heard President Huegli conclude his eloquent funeral oration with the words from Bunyan's *Pilgrim's Progress* that had been Kretzmann's lifelong personal motto: "And all the trumpets sounded for him on the other side." The long funeral procession wound through the campus before stopping at the gravesite in Graceland Cemetery, which was directly across from the chapel.

Despite the encouragement of the executive committee of the board to stay on as president beyond the official retirement age of 65, Huegli announced his retirement to the board on April 19, 1977, effective at the end of the next academic year. The board accepted his decision and began the search for the fifth Lutheran president.

In late winter of 1978, the final five nominees for president visited the campus for meetings and interviews. Later in spring, the board announced that Robert V. Schnabel, vice president for academic affairs at Wartburg College, had been selected as the new president. As the year drew to a close, President Huegli was given a send-off with a round of elaborate dinners. By the end of his presidency, Huegli had become a figure highly respected on campus and off for steering the University through the turbulent waters of the times. At its final meeting of the year, the faculty passed a resolution that represented its genuine sentiments, acknowledging the "excellence of Dr. Albert Huegli's accomplishments as administrator, educator, builder, financier, churchman, and gentleman."

12

THE 1980s

BOLD MOVES AND GROWING STATURE

PROMISE, PURPOSE, AND PLANNING

The new president, Robert V. Schnabel, had many ties with Valparaiso University. Born in Scarsdale, New York, he attended Concordia College-Bronxville, where he became acquainted with the liturgical movement through his teacher, M. Alfred Bichsel. Graduating from Bowdoin College with honors in music, Schnabel attended Concordia Seminary in St. Louis but never sought ordination. Schnabel completed a Ph.D. at Fordham in 1955 and served as professor of philosophy and academic dean at Concordia Senior College-Fort Wayne. O. P. Kretzmann had brought Schnabel into the Palm Grove group and unsuccessfully tried to recruit him for Valparaiso's philosophy faculty. In 1971, Schnabel became president of Concordia-Bronxville, but when synodical politics undermined the integrity of his presidency, he resigned in 1976 and accepted the position of vice president for academic affairs at Wartburg College in Iowa.

Schnabel was not the Valparaiso faculty's first choice for president, but the board saw him as well-suited for the task, especially at a critical time in the University's relationship with the Synod, where he had wide contacts and experience. Vice President Strietelmeier addressed the faculty's skepticism at the opening faculty meeting in August 1978:

> I have known our new president for thirty years. … I can substantiate what we have heard from our colleagues at Concordia Senior College, Concordia College-Bronxville, and Wartburg College about his integrity, his collegiality, his skill as an administrator, and his diligence. We have every reason to be confident that once again the Holy Spirit has given us the right person for the moment and that the auguries are right for bold moves along many fronts.

Strietelmeier's warm endorsement proved prophetic. Quickly this small, jaunty, energetic man won the hearts of his faculty colleagues, showing himself to be a straightforward person without pretensions who was not afraid to make bold moves to push Valparaiso ahead.

The new president's inaugural address was titled "Promise and Calling, Purpose and Commitment." The faculty and student body soon learned to expect such alliterative titles and paired expressions in Schnabel's complex but precise public speeches and writings. Schnabel had worked hard, he said, to grasp Valparaiso University's "genesis and genius, heritage and hopes, problems and progress, potentialities and prospects." He discerned five aspects of VU's calling. Central to its work was the proclamation and teaching of the Gospel, focused in an excellent Department of Theology that should operate "at the interface of scientific, humanistic and theological inquiry."

The second aspect of its calling, Schnabel declared, was the academic quest for truth through "critical and constructive reason and creative imagination." Freedom was common to the third and fourth aspects. The University should be a setting for free and responsible inquiry, and the freedom of the Gospel should prevent the Christian university from making a "god" of human knowledge and from falling prey to partisan or political special interests. Finally, the new president asserted that the calling of the University includes a commitment to serve humanity as a whole: "Along with a concern for academic learning there is a concern to create and sustain a community of care, a fellowship of persons who respect and love each other."

Reviewing the speech, *Torch* editor Jeff Smith pronounced it "adequate." In his generally friendly criticism, he asserted that the whole VU campus was too comfortable with itself. Smith was a talented writer who would spend two years taking on the fraternities, the professional colleges, and what he called the university's cult of "niceness," in a running critique based on the idea that a university should be a community of scholars locked in perpetual argument. His fellow *Torch* writer Dan Friedrich, looking at the broader scene, followed up by asserting that "the dull days of inactivity seem to hang forebodingly on the whole age. Carelessness, blind acceptance, and shallow critical thought are its symptoms."

In *The Lighter*, student Jon Siess took aim at what he saw as another issue facing VU by writing on unexamined issues of Lutheran identity. Noting Schnabel's heavy emphasis on "calling" in the inaugural, he observed that such a view seemed to presuppose a static status quo into which people simply fit to find their callings. He thought that the real question of identity was not "Who am I?" but "What will I become and what are the resources at hand for the future?" Such intelligent student questioning, while in the minority, effectively targeted campus complacency and met with both support and criticism from students and faculty.

There was little controversy about the student editors' critical judgment on the 1970s. Some of their outlook undoubtedly reflected the wider skepticism of younger people coming of age in an era of limits and disillusionment. Nationally, it had been a dismal decade, from the oil shock, through Watergate, the Three-Mile Island meltdown, and finally the American hostage episode in Tehran. The public mood was more pessimistic than at any time since the Great Depression. President Carter's pronouncement of a national "malaise" rang true to many, though it may have cost him his reelection.

The future of higher education did not seem bright either. Demographically, the number of 18-year-olds peaked in 1979, and the projection for the next decade was for a decline of 26 percent. The roaring inflation that continuously accelerated from 1973 to 1980 also had a negative impact on college faculties' inflation-adjusted income, injecting further pressures on presidents and boards to raise tuition. Moreover, President Ronald Reagan was no friend of higher education, and proposals to restrict severely federal aid began to come from the White House.

The actual developments of the 1980s, however, proved to be unexpected. After the sharp recession of 1981–82, the economy rebounded and began a sustained period of growth. With federal aid to education being scaled back, private universities turned more and more to the private sector, which responded with a philanthropic boom. Academic leaders also worked hard to save programs of student aid that made their colleges affordable. Throughout the 1980s, VU President Robert Schnabel spent many days and weeks in Washington, D.C. as a member of the board of directors and secretary of the National Association of Independent Colleges and Universities (NAICU). Through this "voice of independent higher education," he provided leadership in the eventually successful efforts to maintain federal support for college and university students. By 1986, the decline in federal assistance was finally halted. During this decade, the economic advantages of a college education also reappeared. Enrollments held steady, especially for those private colleges that emphasized quality—and raised tuition accordingly. Following the pattern, VU's tuition more than doubled during the 1980s, but the expected devastating loss of students did not follow. Enough wealth was being created to support the higher tuitions, and people proved willing to spend it on quality education.

Despite improved economic prospects, the 1980s brought other sharp challenges to institutions such as Valparaiso, challenges that went to the heart of an institution's identity and mission. The "negotiation with modernity" that an institution such as the Christian university necessarily engages in means many things. It is easy to say yes to technological aids, to modern medicine, and to many of the other advances that are universally cherished. But the "acids of modernity," as Walter Lippmann called them early in the century, also have been at work, corroding tradition, loosening the structures of even legitimate authority, and making human beings believe more and more that they can be creators, achievers, and completely free actors in shaping human life to their own ends, without the constraints of nature, history, or God. How to survive while maintaining a critical perspective on this widespread cultural assumption presented a growing concern. Valparaiso could no longer depend on the informal but rich structure of relationships with its historic church partner to furnish a steady stream of students who shared its religious assumptions. It had to devise ways of making fruitful contacts with good Lutheran students when fewer of them were swayed by family and church considerations in their college choices. At the same time, it had to convey its ecumenical Christian vision to students and faculty from other religious backgrounds as well. This was plainly leaning against the wind.

Soon after taking office, Schnabel appointed a blue-ribbon Council on University Priorities and Planning (CUPP), chaired by Richard Baepler. CUPP proposed recruiting a stronger student body and strengthening the internal academic life of the University. It made clear that money was required for more scholarships, endowed professorships, more attractive salaries, and several new buildings. After the board adopted a revised and condensed version of the CUPP Report in July 1980, Schnabel presented it to alumni and supporters under the title *A Decade of Decline or of Decision and Reaffirmations?* In his foreword, Schnabel summoned the University to see its goal as becoming a "national Lutheran University of high academic standing."

At the same time, a more theoretical paper entitled "Four Hallmarks of Valparaiso University" was circulated among faculty for discussion. It identified these defining features as Lutheran character, character as a university, scholarship, and residentiality. It declared that while Valparaiso sought a prominent Lutheran presence, it also required and cherished a diversity of viewpoints. A genuine Lutheran university, it said, should require of all its members a willingness to understand and relate to the Christian intellectual tradition, though some might withhold personal religious commitment.

While the critical secular spirit should be welcomed, "Four Hallmarks" said, it should also encounter critical Christian perspectives as well, lest academic secularity go unchallenged and eventually secularize even religious expression. Thus, even as they carried out highly practical planning processes, some VU faculty continued the internal dialogue concerning the nature of a Lutheran university, a discussion that had begun the moment the Lutherans acquired the school. How well such perspectives could be incorporated into institutional life remained to be seen.

STUDENTS OF THE 1980S

The campus found Schnabel and his wife, Ellen, a former Lutheran school teacher, to be warm and approachable people, equally at home with faculty or students. Each fall, hundreds of new students followed the tradition of tramping through the presidential home on campus in long lines to greet them. Some years Schnabel discovered as many as 50 or 60 sons and daughters of his own former students among the VU freshman class bringing greetings from home. Sons and daughters of VU alumni also appeared in growing numbers. Whether alumni children or not, Valparaiso was attracting more students with college-educated parents than at any previous time in its history.

Within a few years, most students were also the sons and daughters of Baby Boomers, acutely aware that the affluence of their parents might not be theirs. The world had changed, as had the assumptions their parents had brought to college in the 1960s. Consequently, they signed up in large numbers for professionally oriented courses that might fit them for competition to get into good graduate professional schools—the aspiration of a growing number. They streamed into undergraduate business programs, into the new computer science major, and into communications and media programs opened by the College of Arts and Sciences.

Helen Lefkowitz Horowitz, in her study of changing college generations, found college less a special time in the life of 1980s students than it had been in any previous era. In high school, they had prepared for college, and in college, they prepared for what followed; but the earlier assumption that college was a special, unique place and time of life was rapidly diminishing. Long before coming to college, they had faced the teen conflicts of drugs, alcohol, and sex with their peers, and often they had become in important respects independent of their parents. Yet, strangely, as a generation they did not want to stray far from home (fewer and fewer students traveled more than 300 miles to attend college), and high telephone bills suggested more dependence than they imagined.

When this generation went to college, they came loaded with their "stuff"—TVs, VCRs, computers, microwaves, stereos, hair dryers, and much more. Schools everywhere rewired their residences. College life was no longer an enclosed experience, but it blended into TV serials, phone calls, trips home, and visits to party and entertainment venues in northwest Indiana and beyond—places that at Valparaiso were now duly reviewed and rated by *The Torch*. Boundaries became indistinct and permeable—between home and campus, campus and community, Greek and independent, academics and employment. Fraternities and sororities, while gaining back numerically the strength they had lost in the 1960s and early 1970s, were no longer the primary source of status on campus. Organized college activities of all kinds drew fewer students. Students largely lived and moved in small groups of like-minded friends.

In the mid-1980s, *The Torch* ran its own analysis of "Students of the Eighties." The picture was clear. Valparaiso was similar to other colleges: Suburban conformity and too much attention to grades prevailed. The faculty agreed. Cramming for grades seemed far more important than trying to understand large issues, noted political science professor Albert Trost. It is a generation without a cause; there are no heroes, summed up Professors Arlin Meyer and Mark Schwehn. English department chairman Edward Uehling found, nevertheless, a strong value system underlying these quiet lives: "I find there's a pretty serious Christian commitment among them," he observed.

There were rebels against the conformity. One regular columnist for *The Torch*, Carole Nuechterlein, would have none of the vocationalism of her generation. Her personal rebellion was on behalf of the liberal arts. "There is a great deal of pressure on students today to major in something which will get them a job after they graduate," she declared. "You see, I am one of those increasingly rare liberal arts majors and I mean liberal arts … English. And history. And, hopefully interdisciplinary humanities. I've made my choice but there are fewer and fewer students today who care to share my choice."

There was among some other students a stirring of social and political concern from varying perspectives. *The Torch*, more professionally edited than ever, attempted to bring social and political issues of the larger world to the attention of the student body. Around mid-decade, the Student Senate renewed the Week of Challenge, though it was more modest in funding and attendance. An activist group called BIONIC attracted several hundred students to four days of lectures and discussion on world hunger, apartheid, and the threat of nuclear war.

In 1982, the faculty, though not unanimously, awarded conservative politician Edwin Meese, counselor to President Reagan and a Missouri Synod Lutheran, an honorary doctorate. A faculty minority signed a protest; alumni, many from the 1960s, wrote letters of protest to President Schnabel and to *The Torch*. At the commencement exercises, a visible minority of liberal arts students wore badges of protest while the graduating engineers rose as a group to give Meese an ovation.

TRAGEDY

Whenever death suddenly appears in a university community of young people with their futures before them, it is a disquieting, intrusive affair. In December of President Schnabel's second year, there was a violent death that resulted from a fight between two students at a fraternity house. It was one of the most tragic events ever to occur on the VU campus.

Around midnight on Friday, December 7, 1979, *Torch* reporter David Yamada received an urgent call at the newspaper's office and immediately headed to a location on Mound Street. He later wrote:

> By the time we arrived, the scene looked like something out of a television crime show. Six police cars flashed their whirling lights. Officers questioned possible witnesses. Small groups of people stood around with bewildered looks on their faces. Some people were crying. The people we talked with were understanding and cooperative. Yes, a young man had been stabbed, they said. Yes, he was taken to the hospital minutes ago. No, they didn't know the extent of the injuries.
>
> Then the tragic news came. "He's gone. ... Mike's gone."
>
> There was no doubt now. It was a real tragedy with real-life consequences. A male student had been stabbed to death and it was here at Valparaiso University.

> A friend of the victim was crying tears of anger and pain that come with the utter frustration of such a needless death. Others yelled and cursed—not like in a locker room, but when there's nothing else you can do. And some just stood silently in shock and disbelief.

Student Mike Spagoletti was dead. The alleged assailant, Todrei Sanders, an African-American student, had escaped, and a multistate manhunt started. The mayor of Valparaiso claimed that the incident was a damning indictment of the Mound Street fraternity culture and an administration that, in his eyes, had proven incapable of dealing with the problems there in the previous few years. Some fearful black students stayed overnight at Deaconess Hall.

On Sunday morning, theology professor Edgar Senne was the preacher in an unusually well attended chapel. He said to the worshipers, "If we are in any true sense a community and not simply a collection of strangers and little cliques, then this event belongs to all of us." Senne took up the theme of prejudice and animosity on campus: "In the chaos of that dark night, there were other cries too, cries of hatred and revenge, adding hate upon hate. In the face of such cries it is no wonder that groups of students huddled together in fear." He called the whole community to account for its failures to address the causes of such events. Finally, Senne reminded them of the season of Advent in which this terrible event took place and of "the light of the face of Jesus Christ who has come to save us." The next day, the Chapel of the Resurrection was again packed to hear President Schnabel describe the University's reaction as "dazed disbelief, sore distress, and outraged shock" as he summoned the members of the community to become God's "healing agents to one another."

Sanders was finally apprehended in Detroit, and his trial took place the following spring. The defense, including members of the VU law faculty, mounted a major effort on his behalf. There had been a long-standing feud between Spagoletti and Sanders. On the evening of the killing, Sanders had been harassed by four white people in a jeep. Later that night, he had gone to the fraternity house. Spagoletti, far bigger than Sanders, had been drinking. The two fought. Sanders drew the knife. Spagoletti died in a pool of blood.

On May 12, a jury found Todrei Sanders guilty of second degree murder. He was sentenced to 38 years. He finally was released in 1998 after his term was shortened for good behavior.

Unnatural death came to the campus again in 1982. In September, a promising but apparently troubled young woman in the freshman class wandered away from campus and was found dead in a field, an apparent suicide. The University gathered around the words of chapel dean Norman Nagel, who preached at the memorial service. The mother of Karen Rhiness later wrote in *The Torch* of her gratitude to the University family, and especially to Dean Dolores Ruosch, for their rallying around at a tragic time. Only a month later, Professor Donald Palm of the Department of Physical Education committed suicide. Many students and faculty knew and admired Palm. Therefore, the shock was widespread. "Why, God?" headlined Diana Montague's column in *The Torch*. She cited Palm's diary, which told how he had not been able to sleep for three years. Confronting yet another tragic loss, Schnabel admitted that "God ... understands things we do not. And I truly believe that. But the tears of pain and regret that I wasn't able to help a fellow human being in need still fight to surface sometimes."

LAW SCHOOL TROUBLES

The Valparaiso University School of Law was skilled in staging mock trials, but in the late 1970s and early 1980s it underwent a severe trial of its own. In Huegli's final year, 1977–78, the school's accrediting agency suddenly presented the president with a set of sweeping criticisms. Law dean Charles Ehren later remembered watching Huegli's face turn ashen as the list of alleged defects was cited, including low salaries, insufficient support staff, and an inadequate building. When the dimensions of the problem were presented to the board, the question of continuing the law school was seriously raised.

The board created a special task force under the direction of new member Harold Bernthal, a major corporation president with a reputation for quickly getting to the bottom of things. The newly arrived Schnabel asked Vice President Strietelmeier to address the issue, and much of Strietelmeier's final year was devoted to finding some way out of the dilemma. Despite its sharp criticisms, the American Bar Association accreditation team had found much to praise in the School of Law: its size, its spirit, its faculty, its tradition of unembarrassed engagement with questions of values. But the problems were huge, and addressing them would require a lot of money: a $600,000 annual increase in the budget, plus a sizable capital investment to supply additional classroom, library, and office space. One solution was to expand substantially the school's size from about 300 students to 500 students. This proposal raised questions about character, quality, and the difficulty of maintaining the faculty's traditional sense of common purpose and close association with students.

Ehren saw the task as one of modernizing the school while attempting to preserve its distinctive features, a unique heritage that had produced outstanding alumni. He recruited John Farago, a brilliant New Yorker, as assistant dean. His quick, creative, analytical skills provided an exact counterpoint to the dean's methodical, painfully thorough style. By April 1979, Strietelmeier could report to the board that both planning and implementation of a solution were well under way, though a final decision for or against the law school had not yet been made. A plan for additional faculty, salary improvements, library enhancement, and facilities was in place. But this plan required an immediate reallocation of about $390,000 from other parts of the University budget, the equivalent of a 4 percent salary increase for every employee of the University. This news was not received kindly by everyone on campus.

Amid these anxieties, the University celebrated the law school's centennial, which featured a lecture on the history of the school by Louis Bartelt, a symposium on natural law with Lutheran theologian Richard Neuhaus and Notre Dame theologian-lawyer Edward Gaffney, and a lecture by Haverford College president Robert Stevens on the history of American legal education. The centennial celebration could not conceal the continuing strains in the school. The possibility of increasing enrollment to 500 to produce needed revenue continued to generate tense discussions of the impact of scale on the quality and character of VU's legal education. Senior faculty worried that an influx of new faculty and a focus on publication would erode the distinctive quality and tone of a Valparaiso legal education. Assistant Dean Farago wrote about the importance of keeping the law school's connection to VU's Christian mission through its underlying educational philosophy and foundation:

> The School's emphasis on personal, student-centered education; its inquiry into the underlying values and philosophy of the legal system; its involvement in the community through its Legal Aid Clinic; and its firm resolve to support the education of members of underrepresented minority groups, these are the hallmarks of Christian concern at the University.

Law school spirits rose when instruction in the new LEXIS computer system was introduced in 1981 and when student teams began placing well in various national law school competitions. The most dramatic morale boost, though, came when Professor Bruce Berner and a dozen student researchers, along with others from DePaul University, participated in a pioneering Ralph Nader-like case being tried in Winamac, Indiana. The public, industry, and the legal community watched with fascination the case of the *State of Indiana v. Ford Motor Company*. Ford had been indicted for faulty design, manufacture, and sale of the Pinto in the deaths of three teenage girls in a rear end collision. Berner and a team of VU law students, cheered on by the entire law school, worked day and night over many weeks to help develop the prosecution's case with brilliant and innovative research, while the national media celebrated them as Davids taking on Goliath. In the end, Ford's huge team of lawyers found a defense which satisfied the judge. But Berner's team had raised safety issues in automobile manufacture, and VU legal education had received flattering recognition and a healthy distraction from its troubles.

STRENGTHENING ACADEMIC QUALITY

In the July 1979 meeting of the board, John Strietelmeier presented his last official report, accompanied by his successor as vice president for academic affairs, Richard Baepler. Strietelmeier declared that every feasible step was being taken to save the law school. He concluded his report on a doleful note, pointing out that VU faculty salaries had now sunk to the lowest quintile in the national professional tables. He warned that the strains this placed on VU professors "effectively forbid the full development of those powers which might lead on to greatness. These salary levels, if maintained, will first weaken and ultimately kill the University."

When the board prepared to move on to other business, the two academicians intervened by asking whether the board would clearly address this crucial matter. The result was a resolution that began: "WHEREAS the Board ranks its faculty as its most valuable asset. ..." The resolution cited the esteem in which the VU faculty were held, the importance of promoting scholarly excellence, and other considerations. The resolution concluded "that the Board of Directors commit itself fully to the raising of compensation levels of all ranks of the faculty and that this priority goal be second to none in its plan for the future." It was a critical moment. At last the board had clearly committed itself to addressing a persisting critical issue affecting VU's academic future.

Raising faculty salaries in the face of high inflation and probable enrollment decline was daunting. Nevertheless, the administration promised a reallocation of funds derived from increased operational efficiency. An increase in enrollment in 1979 permitted small but symbolically important salary bonuses. Taking heart from the board resolution, the Faculty Concerns Committee in December 1980 pressed two modest goals on the administration:

1. By 1983–84, the levels of compensation would equal or exceed that of a six-institution cluster of universities similar to Valparaiso, such as Pacific Lutheran, Drake, Capital, and others.
2. By 1985–86, Valparaiso would rank at least sixth-highest among Lutheran institutions.

Eventually, these two goals were achieved and new, higher ones set.

Administratively, Schnabel instituted a new policy of opening the whole budget for inspection by his vice presidents. This closer look revealed that the combined Wesemann bequest was much larger than first imagined, permitting the Spencer Werner Foundation gift that had funded the first extension of Wesemann Hall to be replaced by the Wesemann bequest. In turn, this released much of the half-million dollar Werner grant for law school scholarships, thus easing the severe strain on the law school budget. Then, in honor of his parents, Edgar Seegers completed the endowment of a chair in the law school, widely publicized as the first fully funded chair in VU's history. It was first occupied by Louis F. Bartelt and subsequently by Alfred W. Meyer and Bruce Berner. An annual lecture also was attached. While dollars remained tight, the law school had now been put on a path of fiscal stability and academic improvement.

While there was a new determination to enhance academic quality across the campus, the actual meaning of that term was often elusive. Conventional measures such as test scores, percentage of doctorates, and library holdings provided one measuring stick for judging progress and setting new, higher goals. Schnabel pointed out to the board that, even with improvements, the SAT profiles of the VU student body still lagged behind schools such as St. Olaf and Gettysburg among Lutheran colleges and behind Notre Dame and Rose-Hulman in Indiana. But the administration also used more subjective techniques, such as extensive exit interviews with graduating seniors, to evaluate the quality and effectiveness of a VU education.

To signal a focus on higher standards for the faculty, Vice President Baepler announced a two-year freeze on promotions to full professor. Following the law school's example, previously weak tenure and promotion criteria were strengthened to demand excellent teaching and recognized research, as well as a formal inaugural lecture by new full professors in the undergraduate colleges. Gary Greinke was appointed director of insitutional and faculty research to assist faculty in finding external grants. He worked with a revitalized Committee on Creative Work and Research to cultivate resources for faculty scholarship. Eligibility for sabbaticals was expanded even as they carried more strict performance requirements.

The new focus on postdoctoral scholarship provoked a valuable discussion of the nature of scholarship and its role in an undergraduate institution. Some at VU began to examine the strengths and limits of the kind of research promoted by the modern university and to consider alternative understandings of the life of the mind. In the mid-1980s, Professor Mark Schwehn authored a pair of articles in *The Cresset* that attracted some national attention by probing the nature and role of scholarship in relation to "the academic vocation," which he understood as inducting students and faculty alike into an intellectual tradition rather than only the making of new knowledge.

The new emphasis on scholarship was seen by most thoughtful faculty members as intimately linked with improved teaching, which remained the most prized quality for Valparaiso faculty members. A faculty committee headed by Professor Edgar Senne developed extensive proposals, including certain kinds of student evaluations, to be used to improve teaching. Uniform salary increments gave way to selective increases based on the particular contributions of faculty members as teachers, scholars, and contributors to the University and beyond. The emphasis on good teaching also gave rise to a permanent faculty committee on teaching effectiveness and to the eventual appointment of Professors Kenneth Klein, Joel Lehmann, and Kathleen Mullen as teaching consultants. Baepler also created a "venture fund," administered by the committee and his office, which granted modest sums for faculty reading groups or experimentation in the classroom. Summer workshops in support of professional development, often supported by Lilly Endowment grants, became regular fare.

A grant from the Aid Association for Lutherans supported a program of "faculty foyers," in which about a dozen groups of 10 to 15 faculty members met several times in faculty homes for reflection on the University and their work. Such reflection and motivation was crucial for VU because the new emphasis on high academic quality, including challenging scholarship, ran counter to the pattern produced by the powerful U.S. historical experience. Church-related colleges had come to be identified with poverty, complacency, and mediocrity, while secular or secularizing schools had rigor, wealth, and sophistication. Few church-related schools disconfirmed this view.

This strong belief that first-rate academics and church-relatedness competed in a "zero-sum game" also was present at Valparaiso University. Put simply, the question was framed in many minds as an either/or choice: "Shall we be Christian or shall we become really good?" Rarely was the matter stated that baldly, but such a dichotomy was often the underlying and subtle assumption at work among faculty members of all opinions. Leaders who tried to maintain religious commitment and support for institutional mission as criteria for hiring sometimes were met by uncomprehending stares and hints that taking such considerations into account might constitute illegal discrimination—which in fact it did not. The more sophisticated argued that high academic quality itself was, in the Lutheran view, a virtue for Christian institutions because the Creator, as Lutherans might put it, works through human competence, without regard to religious labels. This was a powerful argument. But when standing alone, it tended to ignore the broader question of how one creates a truly excellent institution that is clear in its mission and unembarrassed by its Christian character.

The new emphasis on research at VU raised another question. That was the well-known problem of the kind of faculty "professionalization" where attachment to the discipline and its culture trumps both attention to undergraduates and institutional concern. How to support and advance professional scholarship while maintaining Valparaiso's traditionally strong sense of commitment to the campus community and personal attention to students was a new issue.

The student movement toward vocationalism, which continued unabated through the 1980s, hit the College of Arts and Sciences hard. To some extent this diminution of the traditional liberal arts was countered by a strong tradition of general education more comprehensive than at most colleges. General liberal education was also one of the central purposes of the college, and it received new impetus in the 1980s from VU's participation as one of 14 universities in the foundation-funded Project GEM (General Education Models). Led by Christ College professor Marcus Riedel, who had garnered the grant, the VU GEM faculty committee in late 1979 proposed a completely new program in general education that strongly reflected Riedel's own University of Chicago philosophy background.

It quickly became clear that the faculty was not ready for such radical change, and the Educational Policy Committee turned it down. Under the leadership of Professor Judith Peters, a revised GEM proposal created a core freshman program to be followed by other courses more or less on the distribution model. It would conclude with a capstone "University Course" to be taken in the senior year. In the April 1980 VU board meeting, Indiana governor Otis Bowen, a member of both the VU and Lilly Endowment boards, announced that VU had received a $105,000 grant to implement the program.

The major innovation was the Freshman Seminar, an idea borrowed from the hugely successful program at Notre Dame. VU's Freshman Seminars also reflected the Christ College experience, whose dean, Arlin Meyer, played a major role in the course's design. Edward Uehling, one of the English department's experts on writing, directed the program in its early formation. Freshman Seminar proved to be a striking success, and VU's new general education program received national attention in a book written by Jerry Gaff, the director of Project GEM.

When nursing dean Dorothy Smith became interim dean of the College of Arts and Sciences, she reinforced the new emphasis on both quality and streamlining by reducing the faculty by more than 10 percent in one year. At the same time, she called the first meeting of the College of Arts and Sciences faculty and began the process of giving that faculty a more distinctive identity within the University. The new permanent dean of the college, psychologist Forrest Vance, set the tone of his office with an inaugural lecture on "vocation," displaying a learned theological perspective on contemporary conditions of work.

INTERNATIONALIZATION AND PROFESSIONAL DEVELOPMENT

Throughout the 1980s, the University increased its role in building international understanding through further internationalization of its programs. VU scholars in several fields brought commitment and expertise to the emphasis on internationalism. History professor and alumnus Keith Schoppa's scholarship on the history of Chinese civilization in books such as *Xiang Lake* and *Blood Road* achieved national acclaim. In theology, Theodore Ludwig authored an imaginative text on the history of religions, *Sacred Paths*. When Ludwig advocated a new and more sympathetic approach to non-Christian religions in *The Cresset*, he drew some lightning from the more conservative elements in the church. Although such study fit with VU's growing international emphasis, it also reflected the church's reorienting position toward non-Christian religions, a long and difficult task immensely helped by the Second Vatican Council's declaration *Nostra Aetate*. The campus Jewish-Christian dialogue begun in the 1970s was deepened through an annual conference in which leading scholars studied common roots and approaches to contemporary issues, as well as current differences.

The most impressive curricular expression of the growing international emphasis was the program in International Economic and Cultural Affairs, a highly successful interdisciplinary major created by the Department of Foreign Languages and Literatures and the Department of Economics. The University also promoted international education by enhancing and expanding its formal programs abroad, adding a residential program in Puebla, Mexico, and joining a Paris consortium run by Central College in Iowa. Schnabel oversaw major changes in Reutlingen as VU's host, the *Paedigogische Hochschule*, became the *Fachhochschule*, a specialized school for international business. While on a trip to Reutlingen, Schnabel also met with President Adolf Theis of the University of Tuebingen, confirming an exchange program facilitated by board member Richard Duesenberg and former Valpo law professor Erich Markel, director of the influential Max Kade Foundation. Professor Martin Schaefer, followed by Professor Hugh McGuigan, administered VU's growing international programs while also significantly expanding recruitment of international students.

Over time, the spirit of international studies spread into the professional colleges as well. Toward the end of the decade, VU established a study program in China that was later expanded to include other Lutheran colleges. Through a relationship with Hangzhou University, law and engineering professors became involved in faculty exchanges with that Chinese university. Eventually, cooperative arrangements also were established with Kansai Gaidai and Osaka International Universities in Japan. At the same time, an East Asian Studies Program consolidated VU's growing on-campus resources in the field and encouraged the introduction of Chinese and Japanese language instruction and several new appointments, including Zhimin Lin in the social sciences and Christ College professor Janet Lynn Kerr in Chinese religion.

The Interlink organization, a group of former Peace Corps workers who promoted English language studies, established a program on campus that annually brought in young students from around the world, some of whom matriculated as regular VU students. Such efforts to bring more international students to Valparaiso and incorporate them into campus life, as well as the increasing number of American VU students regularly going abroad, underlined the University's role in building international understanding.

As long-cherished prospects for a new arts center alternately brightened and dimmed, a new organization, Friends of Art, arose in 1986 to promote the museum and support the place of the arts in the curriculum. Conceived and executed by Josephine Ferguson and her husband, Professor Byron Ferguson, the organization united dedicated art lovers from Valparaiso University and the Calumet region into a formidable educational force that eventually succeeded in establishing a new home for the museum.

About the same time, theater professor John Steven Paul created a troupe of players named Soul Purpose. Taking material from biblical stories as well as the provocative narrative sermons of the chapel's associate pastor David Kehret, students and professor turned them into chancel dramas performed at VU and on tour, exploring together new possibilities for a revitalized modern form of the medieval religious drama. The arts were further strengthened by the establishment of the Frederick A. and Mazie N. Reddel Professorship in Music, occupied by Philip Gehring and later by Professors Eldon Balko, Christopher Cock (later the Phyllis and Richard Duesenberg Professor of Music), and Dennis Friesen-Carper.

All the core humanities departments had a strong interest in teacher education. Faculty members supervised teaching in the regional schools, and the English department launched a successful annual conference for area high school teachers. When the National Council for the Accreditation of Teacher Education (NCATE) arrived for an accreditation visit with a new reputation for toughness based on the strong criticism in the early Reagan years of the American school system, the education department, led by chairman Gerald Speckhard, received a ringing endorsement from the agency.

Many of the humanities departments developed lectureships and seminars to enhance their programs. The history department's annual Bauer Award brought leading historians to campus. Through a challenge grant from the National Endowment for the Humanities, VU established a professorship in English literature in honor of Walter Friedrich. The first Friedrich professor was Paul Phipps, followed by Warren Rubel and John

Feaster. An NEH-funded Walter Bauer Professorship in Art History was first held by Nina Corazzo.

In Christ College, the number of Scholars and Associates (the two categories of membership) in the professional colleges increased, but the college maintained its flair for the humanities under Dean Meyer. *Breaking Bread*, Professor Mel Piehl's book on controversial Catholic leader Dorothy Day, was a finalist for the national Robert Kennedy Book Award. Professors Warren Rubel and William Olmsted developed courses on "Word and Image" to link visual arts and literature. Above all, the college worked to intensify its sense of community during years when, for many students, personally and intellectually, the college experience had become subject to vast centrifugal forces.

As students flooded into the nation's business colleges, including Valparaiso, the quest to accredit VU's program with the American Assembly of Collegiate Schools of Business (AACSB) continued, though some questioned whether this approval was necessary for an undergraduate program such as VU's. But the board strongly backed accreditation, which became a major goad toward quality improvement—though it would be costly. Meanwhile, business enrollments boomed. The new business building, Urschel Hall, had barely opened when Dean Richard Laube claimed that it already was too small for the 800 business majors and 400 liberal arts business minors. But quantity was not quality. The underfunded business program was undemanding, and some marginal students gravitated to its classrooms. With Laube, who had served doggedly, cheerfully, and well in an impossible assignment, approaching retirement, VU appointed Associate Dean Barry Haber to restructure the curriculum. The new methods of quantitative analysis that pervaded the curriculum required mathematical and statistical facility, resulting in the loss of 200 majors in a single year. The changes constituted a blow to the University's bottom line but a large step up in quality.

Dean John Miller of the University of Colorado-Colorado Springs followed Dean Haber. Dean Miller intentionally sought faculty who were both competent and understanding of VU's Lutheran traditions. Insisting on a much improved faculty salary scale—made possible by the law school's improved financial footing—Miller began the work of recruitment.

Miller's first year (1986) at Valparaiso turned out to be bizarre. Given the budget limitations, a number of faculty had been appointed with administrative fingers crossed. Less than two weeks after classes began, one professor simply walked away from the job, leaving a note under the dean's door. Another was discovered to have taken, simultaneously, a full-time position at another college. Another quit mid-term. Then, tragically, two colleagues who were not only established VU faculty but qualified with the rare doctorate died suddenly—Professor Robert Listmann in a fatal auto accident, followed by Professor Raymond Buckley of cancer.

Undeterred, Miller proceeded with his mandate to build a quality college practically from scratch. All told, Miller conducted about 75 on-campus interviews with candidates to find 15 new faculty members who were best suited to throw their lot in with this college. Three new endowed professorships helped to attract a core of especially strong faculty. The first, donated by board member Richard Meier, went to Professor William Schlender, a nationally known VU alumnus and former dean at Cleveland State. But money could not buy AACSB accreditation. Once the qualified faculty was assembled, a record of achievement over a reasonable period of time was necessary before the accreditors would accept a self-study and visit the campus. After consultants had pronounced the school extremely well prepared, the accreditors visited in 1993. That spring, they rendered their favorable report. Valparaiso thus joined Notre Dame as the only two private business colleges in Indiana so accredited.

Following Gilbert Lehmann as dean of engineering, James Scroggin single-mindedly initiated the college into cooperative education. Under his prodding, it became a model program. The faculty insisted on a rigorous academic dimension to the co-op program, an emphasis that the college's accreditors eventually praised. The idea spread to other undergraduate programs, where it became a component of Valparaiso's educational possibilities.

Stuart Walesh, a Valparaiso alumnus with extensive academic and professional engineering experience, succeeded Scroggin. Knowing the high quality of faculty, Walesh encouraged them to become more visibly active in professional scholarship. He set an example by delivering papers and writing a book in his own field of water management. The faculty, however, was more responsive to Walesh's vigorous promotion of the computer, including the creation of a computer lab and a computer engineering degree. The Leitha and Willard Richardson Professorship in Engineering, first occupied by Professor Demosthenes Gelopulos, was established under Walesh's deanship.

During the 1980s, the College of Nursing truly transformed itself. As more career opportunities opened to women during the decade, nursing first experienced falling enrollments, then less talented students. The new dean, Freda Scales, who initially held the only Ph.D. on the faculty, persuaded the administration to support the faculty in its desire to acquire doctorates during this period of low enrollment. Lower enrollments were met by flexible programs, appealing to nurses seeking college degrees, and by cooperative and master's degree programs.

During the 1980s, VU faculty across the campus embraced the computer. Aided by a $50,000 donation from the Guild, faculty in all areas, including the humanities and social sciences, were enabled to acquire the latest technology. Faculty computer buffs such as Professors David Truemper and Larry Baas helped their colleagues become comfortable with the new machines. Soon computer literacy spread widely on the campus.

Added impetus came from an active computer committee chaired by Professor Donald Koetke. In January 1983, Koetke and mathematics professor Sorenson, after several appearances before the board, proposed a major expansion of the Computer Center: the acquisition of a Data General Eclipse MV 8000, which was four times as powerful as the current computer, along with advanced computer technology for engineering. It would cost $1 million, which could be paid partly by a special tuition add-on. The board needed no persuasion. It was far ahead of the rest of the University in understanding this technological revolution. Because the expansion could no longer be contained within Gellersen Hall, a new Academic Computer-Communications Center (later Schnabel Hall) was constructed to house computer facilities and the growing Department of Communication.

Moellering Library, already expanded twice, received major endowment support for its humanities collections through a National Endowment for the Humanities match grant and, later, a Lilly grant for automating its holdings. This expansion was guided by head librarian Margaret Perry, who also continued the professionalization of the library staff that had begun decades earlier with the appointment of the first professional head, Carl Sachtleben. Assistant registrar Ann Trost, who later succeeded longtime registrar Paul Thune, also computerized that office, changing advising and registration processes for the better. With Katharine Antommaria's appointment as associate dean of arts and sciences and Dorothy Smith's appointment first as assistant to the president for budget and strategic planning and later as vice president for admissions and financial aid, Schnabel suddenly had a strong cadre of female administrators.

In 1985, for the second time in a decade, VU faculty who were members of Phi Beta Kappa, such as Howard Peters, Sarah DeMaris, and Meredith Berg, took the lead in applying for a chapter on campus. A consultant experienced in such applications visited the campus and gave an optimistic report on the prospects. However, once again, the application failed in the highly competitive race among the many colleges eager for this distinction.

Shortly before the VU board meeting in October 1985, news reached the university that *U.S. News and World Report* had ranked VU second in the West and Midwest combined region in its category of "comprehensive universities," behind only Pepperdine University. These rankings caught the media's attention and were widely disseminated to the U.S. public. Despite skepticism about their validity, and reservations about the process of ranking colleges in this fashion, it was practically impossible to ignore the impact. Shortly afterward, when Valparaiso was also selected for inclusion in two reputable publications—*Peterson's Competitive Colleges* and *New York Times* education editor Edward B. Fiske's *The Best Buys in College Education*—Dorothy Smith's admissions staff produced materials featuring these recognitions. In Schnabel's final year, VU was ranked first in the *U.S. News* midwestern regional category, and it remained highly ranked thereafter.

CRUSADES AND CELEBRATIONS

In 1983, VU launched a major fund-raising drive called the Crusade for Valparaiso University (CFVU). Three capital needs had been clearly identified: an athletics center, a performing arts center, and additional space for the law school. Planning committees met with prospective architects and produced initial drawings for each project. The University also engaged planner Richard Dober, who developed a new campus master plan that identified sites for the major new buildings and other needs.

Vice President Koenig and his fund-raising team were eager to go, though the national economy had entered a recession. The 18-month "silent phase" preceding the launch, with meetings and dinners across the nation, was an exhausting effort. Robert and Ellen Schnabel did the bulk of the work, passing through 43 airports during that period. In April 1983, the campaign was launched officially with a festive dinner and speech by Martin Marty in the Great Hall. Harold Bernthal, who recently had succeeded Robert Moellering as chairman of the board, announced a campaign goal of $50 million. The response was enthusiastic.

Despite the ambitious sum, it turned out that only two of the three proposed major building projects could be undertaken. More space for the law school and its climbing enrollment was a necessity. After considering expansions of Wesemann Hall, the decision was made to construct a new building on the West Campus.

Schnabel's personal preference for the second building was the Performing Arts Center that had been designed by Hammel, Green and Abrahamson of Minneapolis, but some on the board leaned toward an Athletics-Recreation Center (ARC) because they believed the immediate need was greater. This was not a popular priority among the faculty because the University's controversial decision to play big-time basketball had been made without significant faculty discussion. Many thought the arts deserved priority. Powerful board member Ewald Mueller, whose commitment to academics had been demonstrated through his instrumental role in establishing Christ College, emphasized the importance of a good athletics facility for students who, on a residential campus, were physically more active than ever before and needed to let off steam. He noted that VU students were cramming the present inadequate gym until the wee hours of the morning. Furthermore, Mueller believed that a tie-in with big-time basketball, and thus to the unavoidable American popular culture, eventually could bring more attention to the University. While there was disappointment in postponing the longed-for arts center, these arguments proved persuasive. The decision was to build the ARC.

The fund-raising campaign was conducted amid much publicity and fanfare. Events such as the announcement of the building of the computer center (separately funded) and the law school, and the actual groundbreaking for the Athletics-Recreation Center, provided an exhilarating sense of outward progress at the University. *The Torch* carried a wonderful cartoon of Schnabel as Superman pulling VU forward.

Valparaiso University always has enjoyed its anniversaries, and 1984–1985 was a major anniversary year: the 125th anniversary of the founding, the 60th year of Lutheran ownership, the 50th year of the Alumni Association, and the 25th year since the chapel dedication. The anniversary committee, chaired by Dean Arlin Meyer, made it a glorious year of "celebrating our history and welcoming our future." Festivities accompanied the dedication of the Academic Computer and Communications Center (AC-CC) in October 1984, and in December, the new ARC was jammed for the inaugural basketball game between Valparaiso and Notre Dame.

A positive feature of the anniversary year was a reversal of the downward trend in enrollment. Admissions vice president Smith devised new financial aid policies specifically to advance the University's stated priorities, which included increasing the academic quality of the student body along with the number of Lutheran students. A year after her appointment, the president announced to the board that the enrollment goal for the year had been exceeded. Soon he could announce that the percentage of Lutherans in the student body had recovered to the desired level of more than 50 percent and that indices of quality had improved as well.

The 125th anniversary year saw cultural events, convocations, and lectures devoted to the theme. There were lectures and features on VU history throughout the fall, and archivist Daniel Gahl put on a magnificent display of photographs. In February, the Department of Speech and Drama presented *College Hill*, "an anecdotal and slightly musical history of Valpo" written by Sylvia Pick and directed by theater professor Richard Pick, with faculty in the leading roles. The anniversary was a time of remembrance. Old buildings and even older magnificent trees came down on West Campus to make room for the new law school. This was not progress, lamented *The Torch* editor. Many students had loved the old West Campus as a place for quiet walks, rendezvous, and parties. Now it was being "destroyed." Reflecting the sense of transition, *The Torch* from time to time ran articles on the history of the University and its traditions.

Students were conscious of even deeper changes. Marcia Klett, who had been wrestling with difficult moral texts in Professor Dale Lasky's Christian ethics class, wrote a long, thoughtful column for *The Torch* on sexual morality:

> When my grandmother was a college coed, women were escorted to dances and parties by fine, upstanding young gentlemen who, at the appointed hour (perhaps 9 or 10 P.M.) brought their young ladies safely home again before returning to really party with the boys. When my mother was a college coed, no woman of good repute ever accepted an invitation to visit a man's apartment after an evening out. ... Particularly off limits was the bedroom, and even more so, the bed, which was considered the ultimate danger zone.

Klett then described what she saw as the results of the intervening feminist and sexual revolutions, including the Pill:

> Instead of forcing men to assume an equal share of the responsibility, they preferred to cast aside responsibility altogether. ... Obviously I do not advocate a return to my grandmother's or even mother's time. The invaluable strides women have made in emancipation, the more honest acceptance of our sexuality that we have gained, and the healthy overthrow of convention that we have managed should not be wasted, however, by a hasty rejection of Christian values.
>
> What is our course? When it comes to sexual activity, we must choose the path that our faith calls us to choose, the path most natural and consistent with the way God created man and woman to live. ... Concerning moral issues, God calls us to consult His Word, but most importantly He calls us to think for ourselves. ... We must learn to discern the difference between true justification and rationalization. ... There are no longer external restraints to protect us from ourselves. We have welcomed the freedoms of this new era. Are we mature enough to live up to its responsibilities?

The history Klett recounted and the issues she raised struck a chord with more than a few students. On Valparaiso's campus, one could still appeal to the Christian moral tradition and expect to get a hearing.

While the campus took the anniversary opportunity to reflect backward, there was little opportunity for Schnabel to rest or enjoy the year's activity. The fund-raising crusade turned out to be a huge success, and the president reported to the board in April 1985 that the $50 million goal might be achieved by June, well ahead of schedule. Rather than take a breather, the decision was made to push on. A CUPP II Committee was formed to propose new goals. In July, the board announced an expanded campaign to raise an additional $22 million in three years, bringing the grand total to $72 million. Koenig's confident team swung into action and achieved that goal, again ahead of schedule.

RECONSTRUCTING CHURCH RELATIONSHIPS

While VU was making significant academic and financial strides, the wounds from the battles within the Missouri Synod were still open. Longtime friends of Valparaiso had ended up on opposite sides of the bitter and painful conflict. Many other connections and institutional relationships that had once been part of VU's fiber and being had to be reconstituted and new relationships established. As time passed, more people were willing to attempt healing in the new situation. But the process was not easy.

In his first synodical convention as Valparaiso's president, Schnabel was denied a proper hearing regarding the fire then being directed at the VU-based Lutheran Deaconess Association. The Synod moved to establish its own deaconess program at Concordia-River Forest, creating strains within the LDA and raising questions about the ability of Valparaiso and the association to continue to furnish deaconesses to The Lutheran Church—Missouri Synod. By 1981, the LDA completed a thorough self-study and effectively revised its operations. Under the thoughtful leadership of deaconess Louise Williams, it decided to stay at VU, creating a "Center for Diaconal Ministry" to serve both nontraditional and traditional deaconess students. About the same time, the Lutheran Human Relations Association took a different course and decided to move its headquarters to Milwaukee, in line with its new focus on urban problems. Thus, 24 years of close and valuable association with VU came to an end.

Earlier, Schnabel had persuaded former LHRAA executive director Karl Lutze to become director of church relations, and Lutze worked effectively to consolidate the University's relationships with many congregations in and beyond the LCMS. It was in this dense but informal network that Valparaiso's relationships with the church once again flourished, distinct from the Synod's officialdom—a pattern that actually had existed since the beginnings of the University's Lutheran ownership in 1925. Lutze's national reputation also permitted VU to reach out to other Lutherans in search of an expanded constituency, and dozens of congregations entered into partnerships.

Nevertheless, formal relations with Missouri remained important. At the October 1979 board meeting, Synod president J. A. O. Preus appeared at Schnabel's invitation and stated his desire that the relationship between the Synod and the University be strengthened. He expressed "personal embarrassment" over the way Valparaiso had been treated at recent conventions, particularly the difficulties with the LDA, which he blamed on communication problems. He claimed ignorance of the earlier practice of maintaining an official synodical liaison with the VU board and announced that now he would be that representative. Until his retirement in 1982, Preus did appear on the campus in that capacity to meet with the board and to preach in the chapel.

Preus's successor, Ralph Bohlmann, continued the practice of annual visits to the VU campus and of serving the board as an advisory member. When mandated by the synodical convention to conduct a "dialogue" with the University, Bohlmann appointed the highly regarded synodical vice president Dr. Will Hyatt as chairman of a delegation that met in 1983 and 1984 with VU board and faculty leaders. The work of Hyatt and Professor James Nuechterlein laid the basis for a final report for the Synod that was distributed over the signatures of both the synodical and university presidents. Entitled "Valparaiso University and The Lutheran Church—Missouri Synod," it recognized that "unresolved tensions, differences, and perceived unkindnesses have placed something of a wall between these two institutions," but it affirmed that VU and the Synod did not intend to turn away from each other. The report recognized the strong contribution that the University had made to the church and could make in the future. Despite the problems, it saw a situation full of promise.

So did LCMS President Bohlmann. He also saw positive opportunities in the new condition of Lutheranism in America. As the new Evangelical Lutheran Church in America, with its small but influential band of Valparaiso supporters, came into being in 1988, Bohlmann challenged the University to become, as part of its mission, one place where the Missouri Synod and the ELCA could interact creatively for the sake of the future of the church.

Whatever the difficulties with institutional church relations, the "acids of modernity" did not diminish VU campus religious activities during the 1980s. The Catholic population at VU grew from 500 to 800 students in the 10 years after Thunderhouse Newman Center opened in 1973. In the fall of 1987, the center was renamed St. Theresa of Avila after the famous reformer—the first woman "Doctor of the Church." The Catholic diocese of Gary took care to appoint open and engaging priests to its VU campus ministry, including eventually an alumnus, Father Douglas Mayer. A student board kept its program active and alive.

Evangelicals also were prominent on and off the campus. Vans from local churches came on Sunday mornings to take students to services. One in the Spirit continued its lively activities, linking such groups as St. Theresa's, New Testament Fellowship, Intervarsity, Bread for the World, the Student Deaconess Association, Fellowship of Christian Nurses, the Sweet Wine musical group, the chapel's residential ministry, and so on. One fall, an outdoor rock event, "Celebration in the Son," drew 400 students; the next year 850 students attended. Sweet Wine, begun in 1975, made appearances first at northwest Indiana churches and eventually went on spring break concert tours across the country.

The smaller percentage of Lutherans since the beginning of the 1970s meant lower attendance at regular Sunday and weekday services, but the

Chapel of the Resurrection remained a vigorous entity. When chapel dean Norman Nagel left for Concordia Seminary, there was an immediate sense of regret and loss. Departing with Nagel was his wife, Betsy, the energetic and popular executive director of the University Guild. Betsy Nagel had followed Sophia Heidbrink and Bernice Ruprecht in this position. In turn, she was succeeded by Dorothea Nuechterlein, Janie Lichtfuss, Rebecca Balko, and Julie Thomas. This strong tradition of leadership maintained the unique function of the Guild as an independent group of women serving the University in many tangible and intangible ways without being fully incorporated into it.

Replacing Nagel was his assistant dean, Daniel Brockopp, a liturgical expert who proved to be a strong preacher and good pastor. Brockopp and Associate Dean David Kehret, a talented campus pastor from Omaha, Nebraska, continued such programs as the chapel counseling service and the Wednesday night folk mass that attracted hundreds of students. They also multiplied personal approaches to campus ministry and brought even more students into the chapel structure. *The Torch* did an article on the chapel in 1986 that detailed the buzzing infrastructure: Social Concerns Committee, Christian Growth and Witness Committee, Visitation Committee, Worship Planning Committee, Hospitality Committee. The Worship Planning Committee coordinated 17 regular services each week. There were squadrons of acolytes and ushers, the Kantorei Choir, the Matins Choir, and several instrumental groups, with music under the direction of Professor Frederick Telschow.

When the Evangelical Lutheran Church in America was formed in January 1988, many wondered what this would mean for the chapel. As early as 1982, the Chapel Council debated which Lutheran hymnal to use—the blue Missouri Synod *Lutheran Worship* or the green "other Lutheran" *Lutheran Book of Worship*. With donors' help, the chapel ended up with *both* books, along with other excellent worship supplements. More challenging was the issue of the role of women in public worship. Already Walter Keller had published in *The Cresset* an argument for the ordination of women, which was not the practice in the Missouri Synod. Especially under Dean Brockopp, women took a more public role in worship, including assisting in the Eucharist.

EXTRACURRICULAR LIFE

During the 1960s and early 1970s, membership in Greek organizations had declined at VU and elsewhere, and some people thought their demise was imminent. But the Greek tradition on American campuses is nothing if not resilient, and fraternities and sororities regularly have proved able to adapt to major changes in student culture. By the late 1970s, Greek membership nationally began recovering from its slump. By the early 1980s, it was in a full-fledged revival. At Valparaiso, the numbers of students pledging these organizations reached highs reminiscent of the 1950s. But much had changed from the era of coat-and-tie meetings and formal dances. For one thing, the distinction between Greeks and non-Greeks was much softer. Important student leaders were found among the independents in many areas of student life, and many social activities were no longer "closed" to nonmembers.

The results of the national Greek resurgence in this period were by and large not positive. Fraternities in particular seemed to lose the sense of camaraderie that had once sustained them at their best. For more and more people on campuses, fraternities became "the fraternity problem." Drinking, often accompanied by individual or group disturbances, was the largest issue. Pledging was also a problem. Hazing persisted and, in some cases, became worse, with fraternities forcing pledges through various physical ordeals and sororities playing extensive "mind games."

This was also true at VU. Huegli's last year as president had been marred by a "death kegger" held by the bankrupt Phi Kappa Psi fraternity that ended in an enormous bonfire and the appearance of police. Thus, one of the first things Schnabel did after his arrival was to appoint a task force to investigate fraternity life. The task force's devastating report detailed the drastic decline in the character of fraternity life, especially the loss of upperclass leadership in the houses. It made numerous recommendations, including limiting all-campus parties to weekends. The faculty supported tough action. Many would walk from Lembke Hall to the new campus along Mound Street amid the party debris deposited from weekend or Wednesday evening keggers, then they would witness the consequences of such events in their classes.

Despite administrative efforts to address these issues, the essential problems did not go away. Throughout the decade, periodic signs of improvement were undermined by new incidents and the recurring issue of drinking. Crackdowns against particular abuses or new rules to limit the negative impact of parties generally had only temporary effects. In 1987, a series of high-profile negative events led to a temporary moratorium on Greek parties. The worst and most widely publicized incident occurred at the Sigma Phi Epsilon house in the spring of 1988, when a repulsive hot mixture was poured on a student during a lavaliering ritual, inflicting severe burns that required hospitalization. In response, the administration withdrew recognition of the fraternity for three years and instituted a Greek Social Responsibility Committee and tightened monitoring of parties and events.

Throughout all these distressing episodes and their accompanying bad publicity, the Greeks and their defenders continued to present themselves as groups where service and leadership were fostered and campus life enhanced. Certainly there were many leaders and members of the organizations who tried to uphold these principles and ideals. Greek organizations have survived on American campuses because they meet the perpetual needs of young men and women for bonding with their peers, for identity formation, and for a small group of friends who can aid them in the passage from adolescence to young adulthood. For some, this passage includes plenty of rough spots, and the resulting dynamics can easily become reinforced in group settings, as can more healthy responses.

Indeed, it was quite true that not all Greek organizations and members were equally responsible for the serious problems that got out of hand. Within the organizations, many genuine friendships were formed, and there continued to be valuable opportunities for developing organizational skills and leadership experience. Greek members regularly protested the lack of public notice to the other side of their lives: "Both the Pi Kappa Alpha and Phi Kappa Psi Houses volunteer their services annually to the city of Valparaiso." "We have brothers who volunteer to help out at nursing homes in town. ... But that's not news, so no one hears about it." " 'We've adopted a child from Kenya,' said Paul Eichelmann of the Sig Eps." "Lambda Chi Alpha is a local contributor to a scholarship fund." Whether such worthy efforts compensated for the less edifying activities was debatable. But in the 1980s, unfortunately, the balance seemed tipped to the negative side, while Deans Ruosch and Schroer and others struggled to evoke the positive.

A more healthy development on campus was the upsurge in physical recreation and exercise. The student generation of the 1980s was perhaps the most physically active in American history. Public policy since at least the time of President Kennedy's "New Frontier" had been stressing the importance of physical fitness. But in the 1980s, the drive for athletic activity was everywhere.

Most dramatic was the explosion in women's participation in physical recreation and sports. The days when young women who enjoyed sports risked being labeled "tomboys" were over. Title IX changed all that. From the grade school level to the colleges, women became involved in athletics in ever-growing numbers. At VU this upsurge of interest in recreational and competitive sports alike happily coincided with the building of the ARC. Almost immediately, the structure was fully used, and the huge intramural sports program swelled to meet the newly available facilities as well as sustained usage of the old.

Unfortunately, building the ARC did not improve the fortunes of the major intercollegiate teams. As some had predicted, in the highly competitive Division I environment, basketball coaches Kenneth Rochlitz and Thomas Smith—a former VU player—presided over woefully underfinanced teams with losing records and no conference. Transition was in the air. VU became one of the founding members of the Association of Mid-Continent Universities (AMCU), which began play in 1982–83 in all men's sports except football. But the record remained poor and attendance at the home games actually declined; half the seating in the ARC was shut down.

When the NCAA in effect drove the amateur-oriented AIAW out of business in 1985, VU women's athletics also became part of the NCAA. Schnabel upped the women's athletic budget to provide proper coaching, operating support, and some athletic scholarships for basketball. Gender equity was, however, still in the future, though women fought hard for everything they could get. VU women's softball played solid competition and developed winning records. At the end of the decade, a women's soccer club was established, paving the way for intercollegiate competition a few years later. Men's intercollegiate soccer had begun earlier in the decade.

Football, the one sport exempted from playing Division I, competed in Division II under alumnus coach William Koch. By 1985–86, VU was a member of the football-only Heartland Collegiate Conference. At mid-season that year, the team, led by all-American receiver Mike Healey, was ranked 13th nationally in Division II. But that was a rare bright spot. Throughout most of the decade, the football team was undersupported and mismatched, leading to dismal results. Presiding over this difficult decade in athletics was the new director of athletics, alumnus William Steinbrecher.

THE END OF THE 1980S

Toward the end of the 1980s, the relative tranquility that had descended over American campuses ended. The change involved not some new upsurge of 1960s-style student activism, but increasingly intense scrutiny of the whole enterprise of higher education. Public interest in what was going on in American colleges and universities mounted. In 1987, Professor Allan Bloom of the University of Chicago published *The Closing of the American Mind*, a polemic against what he saw as the sharp decline in the general quality of U.S. academe, a development that he blamed squarely on the mentality of the 1960s. To universal astonishment, the book turned into a huge best-seller. Following Bloom's broadside, a host of other writers jumped into the fray in the next few years with titles such as *Profscam* and *Tenured Radicals*. Major newspapers began reporting on the increasingly fierce struggles over the curriculum at leading colleges. Another voice not bashful about speaking up on such matters was U.S. Education Secretary William Bennett. After criticizing public schools, and before taking on the music industry, Bennett leveled sharp criticisms of what he saw as the failures of U.S. undergraduate education.

Most within the academy were quick to reject attacks such as those of "the killer B's," Bloom and Bennett. But developments within the universities themselves soon revealed that there were indeed serious intellectual transformations occurring. At a major Duke University conference in 1988, leading representatives of academic "postmodernism" proclaimed that the purpose of higher education should be understood as the liberation of the American mind, rather than any search for truth and justice. The latter concepts as traditionally understood, they declared, were simply masks for power plays. An outpouring of controversial articles and books on these issues revealed the disarray in American academe, at least in the humanities and social sciences. Even the natural sciences were not immune.

The term "postmodernism" itself was hardly new. O. P. Kretzmann had said in August 1945 that the world had come to "the end of the modern age" with the dropping of the atomic bomb, and in the 1950s and 1960s, he called for a dialogue between what he called, remarkably, "the modern and postmodern minds." As it entered public discourse in the late 1980s, however, the term "postmodernism" turned out to be perpetually elusive, seeming to mean many things to many people. But its general outlines were evident. In the nineteenth century, prophetic foes of modernity such as Nietzsche already had been assaulting the foundations of the Enlightenment, undermining them and preparing for what scholars now call postmodernity. Many of modernity's critics share a deep pessimism about the Enlightenment's confidence in the autonomous, reasoning self.

Rather, it is social location, they declared, sometimes defined in terms of race, gender, or ethnicity, that determines ways of knowing. Forms of rationality were widely seen by such critics as a mask for the will to power. They insisted that knowledge always should be called "knowledge/power."

Such rarefied matters were first debated primarily at professional meetings in the humanities and to some extent among the social science disciplines. But through the circulation of ideas in the academy, as well as the influx of faculty trained in research universities where these assumptions reigned, they eventually filtered into curricular struggles on college campuses, including Valparaiso. Amid all the flurry of indictments and controversies, it was hard to sort out the actual state of affairs, much less make intelligent judgments about the new intellectual directions. Some VU faculty saw the importance of engaging such fundamental questions about the aims of knowledge and learning in the modern world. Writing in *The Cresset*, Professor Mark Schwehn argued that the very purposes of higher education were at issue and began probing more deeply into the nature of the academic vocation itself.

Some Christian scholars saw new openings in postmodernism. Thinkers such as George Marsden suggested that if feminists, for example, can openly proclaim their own ways of knowing within the now-unfettered curriculum, why not the same for Christians and their worldview? Most Christian intellectuals, however, did not think these developments give license to assert any and all truth claims in freedom from a shared reasonable discourse. And many were less enamored of the idea of making Christianity another competitor in the ideological marketplace.

Much more promising and relevant to universities such as Valparaiso was the historical work of scholars such as Marsden, Philip Gleason, and James Burtchaell in probing the paths toward secularization taken by universities that were once firmly church-related. Others were developing a critique of both the Enlightenment and postmodernism, searching for the truth in these perspectives while retrieving and restating the place of the Christian intellectual tradition as a viable option in the modern world. No single thinker did all of this, but there was a developing body of contemporary Christian thought addressing these problems. And Christian scholars of quite different backgrounds benefited from one another's work.

Most people at Valparaiso University could only occasionally turn from heavy teaching assignments and other duties to explore the significance of these contemporary intellectual developments for the Christian university. But some did so in various forums. For example, Christ College dean Arlin Meyer arranged in the late 1980s for a series of meetings among faculty from Notre Dame, Calvin College, and VU. Together they explored not only their own distinctive tradition's approaches to Christian higher education, but also what they saw as the common features of the shared Christian intellectual tradition in the modern world. They also studied the way their institutions functioned, the role of worship in their common life, and the ancient issue of the interaction between faith and learning.

In light of the startling new intellectual situation that called into question the reductive, rationalist university that had long dominated the American academy, it was at least clear that the tradition of Christian higher education had the opportunity to gain a wider hearing in a way that would have been impossible a century before. It is also clear that these issues require fresh consideration. In the VU-Notre Dame-Calvin "trialogues," for instance, James Nuechterlein upheld the traditional Lutheran position of paradox and distinction with respect to the relationships between faith and learning, denying that there is any such thing as "Christian politics," for example. Yet even Nuechterlein had to admit that faith does shed at least shafts of illumination onto subject matters such as his own field of American political thought. Faith is more than knowledge, but it is also knowledge, and it informs the various historical manifestations of the Christian intellectual and artistic traditions.

These trialogues were only one of many events that enlivened the campus in the late 1980s. In 1985, VU brought in a large number of scholars and performing artists to observe the 300th anniversary of the birth of Johann Sebastian Bach. Throughout November, there were art exhibits and films. Beginning on November 10, the birth date of Martin Luther, an intensive week of music and a symposium featuring scholars from across the nation enchanted and uplifted the campus. The programmers had commissioned an original work by Alan Hovhaness, who was present for the world premiere of his "Symphonia Sacra," composed in honor of Bach. Professors Eldon Balko and Robert Bergt, chairman of the music department, conducted the University-Civic Choral Society and the VU Symphony Orchestra in this world premiere performance.

Such events again increased talk of the importance of a center for the performing arts. *Torch* editor Kristin Jass found students and faculty optimistic: the AC-CC was in use; money was flowing into computers; the new law school building was under way. The arts were beloved by many at VU, and a proper venue for them was a strongly felt need.

In the fall of 1985, a stroke forced Robert Schnabel to slow the pace of his activities on campus and off. Nevertheless, he continued to preside over further physical changes. VU completed negotiations with the LDA to acquire its residence hall in the center of the campus. As part of the arrangement, it transferred the former chapel dean's residence on LaPorte Avenue to the deaconesses. As the Center for Diaconal Ministry, it became a lively focal point for students. Deaconess Hall was transformed into Huegli Hall, a home for the College of Arts and Sciences. The departments of English, theology, political science, and history found themselves at the center of campus, near the library. It was soon hard to imagine that these departments had been quartered nearly a mile away from their students and classrooms.

On moving day the new occupants of Huegli Hall saw a strange procession marching toward them from across the campus to the south. Dressed in academic garb, the inhabitants of Christ College, including President Schnabel, were solemnly processing. Entering the building, they found the newly arrived faculty awaiting them. In the ritualistic ceremony that ensued, Schnabel orated, welcoming them to the East Campus. His delivery was a parody of one of his own speeches, consisting of one long tortuous sentence in which numerous "Schnabelisms" abounded. Others gave equally humorous speeches of welcome and admonition, replete with quotations from various out-of-context sources.

About the same time, the law school carried out its move to Wesemann Hall, another piece of complicated logistics masterfully executed by Assistant Dean Curt Cichowski and law librarian Mary Persyn. The building was formally dedicated in spring 1987. The law school now occupied a well-designed, stimulating set of spaces on its own quarter of the campus, spilling over into historic Heritage Hall, which housed the law clinic. The new law school—and the generosity of the Muellers and the Richardsons—made possible the remodeling of the old Wesemann Hall into a new administrative center named Kretzmann Hall. All administrative services thus came under one roof for the first time since the Kinsey Hall fire. In April 1988, family and friends of O. P. Kretzmann came to hear the Rev. Oswald Hoffman, the *Lutheran Hour* speaker and a surviving member of the influential "Forty-Four" that O. P. had sparked, speak at the dedication. The Rev. A. R. Kretzmann, now in a wheelchair because of a stroke, was present as well.

Other changes reflected Schnabel's emphasis on improving the academic quality of VU. Two fully endowed "university professorships" were created with the goal of making imaginative faculty appointments reflective of needs as seen from a broader university-wide perspective. The indefatigable board member Richard Duesenberg was behind the endowment by the Lutheran Charities Association (St. Louis, Missouri) of the Eckrich Chair in Religion and the Healing Arts, whose occupant was Professor James Bachman. The other endowed chair to enhance VU's Christian mission was the gift of Emil Jochum, a German immigrant manufacturer who generously supported Lutheran causes, including VU. Although a holder had not yet been identified, the chair was dedicated during Reformation Day observances at Valparaiso in the setting of Luther's *German Mass*.

Schnabel concluded his administration by dealing with a longstanding organizational matter. Board chairman Harold Bernthal had longed to merge the two nonprofit corporations, the holding company and the operating company, which the Lutheran founders had established as a consequence of the messy legal status of VU at the time they purchased it in 1925. For 60 years, there had been two budgets, two boards of directors, two annual meetings, two general ledgers, two sets of financial statements, two business officers, and two sets of accountants and clerks. They had to deal with each other at arm's length and write checks back and forth, sometimes paying the same vendor with two different checks. The reasons for this convoluted arrangement had long since disappeared, and in the summer of 1988, it was ended. After Schnabel's final board meeting in July, Valparaiso University was solely owned and operated by The Lutheran University Association.

As the 1980s came to a close, Valparaiso University was still not the great Lutheran university of America that its founders had envisioned. But it was also a far cry from the run-down institution they had acquired or even the weak and struggling little campus of the early decades of Lutheran ownership. By the 1980s, VU had a clearly established—if not totally well defined—place as a quality university on the American higher educational scene. Neither a major graduate university nor a liberal arts college, Valparaiso belonged to that class of institutions that the Carnegie Foundation called "comprehensive universities" and later "Master's universities"—places with a liberal arts core and a cluster of professional schools, including nondoctoral graduate programs. Within that category, VU was among the relatively few private universities, and it was one of the very few institutions that defined themselves religiously.

Many of its far-flung alumni were achieving considerable distinction in social service, business, government, academic life, communications, religion, and other fields. VU graduates also were earning an admirable reputation for their success in combining the more visible sort of achievements with equally strong commitments to faith, family, and community.

As Robert Schnabel retired in 1988, the faculty went all out with the biggest and warmest going away party ever seen at the university, including a major academic convocation. The University had perceptibly moved forward under his leadership. The endowment had quadrupled with a financial campaign launched in the teeth of a recession, faculty salaries and quality had improved, the University had been sharply and favorably profiled by national media, and the campus had been reconfigured. Schnabel had expanded the international programs, infused remarkable talent into the faculty, enhanced library resources, recruited more able students, created a modern computer system, and established the first eight endowed professorships and chairs in VU's history. It had been a time of bold moves and growing stature.

13

The 1990s

Postmodern Times

A Widening Whirlwind of Change

While the label "postmodernism" came to be widely applied to the intellectual and cultural developments of the late twentieth century, the terms "postindustrial society" or "the new information age" were most often used to characterize the major social changes of the 1980s and 1990s, especially those connected to the all-pervasive transformations in the economy that shaped much of life in the United States and the rest of the globe. Economically, this period began to seem qualitatively different from the industrial era that went before. As the Cold War ended and the global information revolution took hold, the Internet replaced the Berlin Wall as the dominant symbol of the age.

In the United States, the burgeoning Hispanic and Asian population signaled a new variety in U.S. society, adding their interests to those of other identity and ethnic groups. "Multiculturalism" and "diversity" entered the common vocabulary and mixed explosively with contested and conflict-laden terms such as culture wars, radical left, radical right, radical feminism, political correctness, patriarchy, deconstruction, and hegemony.

Todd Gitlin, a student leader of the left in the 1960s and an enthusiastic early supporter of multiculturalism, by 1997 sadly wrote a book titled *The Twilight of Common Dreams: Why America Is Wracked by Culture Wars.* While Gitlin strongly supported social and economic justice and intercultural understanding, he concluded: "The squandering of energy on identity politics, the hardening of the boundaries between groups, the insistence that individuals are no more than their labels, is an American tragedy."

While most social analysts recognized that America was inevitably adapting to its greater diversity and openness, the fiercely divisive ideas about means and ends made it even more difficult for institutions of all kinds to be effective. Many observers described the 1990s in such terms as hyper-individualistic, eclectic, fragmented, discontinuous, and de-centered. Powerful centrifugal forces everywhere dominated. Social institutions of all types—family, church, school, government, business—no longer held for many people the kinds of values and commitments they once had. It was, increasingly, every man and woman for himself or herself. Some people hailed these developments as "liberation," but it was hardly an accident that isolation, alienation, and various forms of dysfunction increased exponentially as well. If individuals were "freed" from institutions, they also lost the sense of strength and solidarity and meaning that such institutions once offered their members.

Valparaiso University itself was plainly changing in its faculty, its constituent community, and its students. At the beginning of the 1990s, the senior generation of faculty at VU were still those who had been guided by the compelling vision articulated by O. P. Kretzmann and handed down in various ways: the ideal of bringing together, as the University hymn put it, "on one fair campus Athens and Jerusalem." These committed men and women had helped shape the University in difficult times. They were soon to retire.

The middle generation had far fewer seminary graduates or others from synodical schools, but this generation drew its leadership from faculty who had studied at other Protestant or Catholic colleges, as well as some strong alumni from Valparaiso. Theological interest, perhaps even literacy, was high among them. Fewer had any personal memories of the earlier visionaries and pioneers, and they derived their sense of VU and its mission from more varied sources, including the example of their senior colleagues.

The outlooks of the junior faculty were more complex. Some had caught the vision of Valparaiso as an interesting school, a committed but open Christian university. Some were puzzled by the various religious dimensions of the campus; others were unfazed, happy to have a position in a tight job market but with little interest in the institution and its broader traditions. It was among the junior faculty that the graduate school ethos, with its commitment to the discipline and to career, was the strongest. Some who would be tenured during the 1990s were increasingly interested in exploring VU's future. But there was some erosion of social and intellectual cohesion as the hyper-individualism of the times affected many faculty members, junior and senior alike.

In the 1990s, the Lutheran student population of VU declined to less than 40 percent, with the proportions of LCMS and ELCA members nearing parity. Some students were vigorously evangelical; others were poorly educated in Christian doctrine or history. Still others had little interest in religion, attracted to VU by its academic reputation or other factors. Increasingly, all groups—Lutheran students of both denominations, the growing Catholic student population (about 25 percent of the student body), and the variety of students from other religious backgrounds or none at all—came from well-off middle-class families. These families were not immune to the many problems that affected other young people and their parents: divorce, substance abuse, physical and sexual abuse, and so on. Yet most came from families that had helped them develop some kind of moral compass. Many had somehow survived the treacherous passage through adolescence by hanging on to supportive families, church summer camps, youth rallies, the church softball team, junior choir, sensitive pastors, special friends, and other vessels of grace.

Nevertheless, they were very much members of their own generation, carefully studied by scholars such as Arthur Levine, who noticed a sudden change in the 1990s' generation of students. These were young people whose formative public memories were the explosion of the *Challenger*, the *Exxon Valdez* oil disaster, the fall of communism, and the AIDS epidemic. Aware of life's fragility, the new generation was less cynical and more optimistic than the previous cohort. Still career-oriented, they seemed able to look beyond themselves in ways that their immediate predecessors did not. While there was despair at solving the "big problems" of the world, there was a strong interest in working at "little problems" and a belief that this was the way to make a difference. This helps explain the explosion of service activities on American campuses in the 1990s. Socially, these students tended to cluster in small interest or affinity groups. In some respects, they embodied the hyper-individualism of late modernity, prizing personal freedom from all constraints. More open to the broadening influence of higher education, there were still difficulties for many of them in appropriating any serious religious or intellectual tradition or of engaging the widest problems of American and global society in deeper ways.

VU's constituencies were changing too. Lutherans remained the crucial supporters, and the Missouri Synod constituency was still vital for providing good students and financial support. The numbers of confirmands within the LCMS declined, though there were still plenty of able college-going students to draw on, if they could be reached. As in most church bodies, the authority of the Missouri Synod's central bureaucracy declined, while congregations and committed individuals provided encouragement and millions of dollars through campaigns such as the Crusade for Valparaiso University. This would continue so long as these supporters discerned a connection between VU's education and the vital life of the church.

The organization of the Evangelical Lutheran Church in America in 1988 included many friends of VU. A number of board members and leading faculty members were now members of the ELCA. How to relate to this new body, which naturally was protective of its own 28 affiliated colleges, was a major diplomatic challenge. The ELCA connection opened new sources of students but little financial support. Valparaiso alumni, growing in size and prosperity but vastly underdeveloped as a support group, were approaching a time when they could become a main pillar of support for their alma mater.

HARRE TAKES THE REINS

Alan F. Harre became the sixth Lutheran president of Valparaiso University in the summer of 1988. The faculty advisory committee had favored VU alumnus and political science professor David Leege of the University of Notre Dame. Late in the process, President Emeritus Huegli recommended that Harre, then the president of Concordia College-St. Paul, Minnesota, also be considered. When he met with the faculty committee, it knew he was a strong candidate. The faculty committee still recommended Leege, but the board elected Harre.

The new president was born in 1940 in the small southern Illinois farm community of Nashville. After parochial school and two years of public high school, Harre left home for one of the Missouri Synod's "prep schools," St. Paul's College-Concordia, Missouri. From there, he attended Concordia Senior College in Fort Wayne and Concordia Seminary in St. Louis, finishing an additional master's degree at the Presbyterian School of Christian Education. While serving a parish in Grosse Pointe, Michigan, Harre earned a doctorate in the social sciences from Wayne State University. He then taught religion and some social science courses at Concordia-Seward, as well as serving in a number of other posts, including acting president, before becoming president of Concordia-St. Paul.

Unlike all the previous presidents of the Lutheran era, Harre had nothing more than a passing previous acquaintance with VU. Having met and known enthusiastic VU alumni, Harre said that he wanted to find out for himself why so many people thought of Valparaiso University as a special place. His introduction to the campus in the summer of 1988, however, was hardly inspiring. Even before he was officially installed in office, he was forced to deal with the aftermath of the Sigma Phi Epsilon episode that had occurred the previous spring.

Harre called the incident a "watershed happening." It convinced him that one of his major agenda items had to be student life. In an early campus presentation, he said his own personal approach to moral education would be from a "Lutheran Christian" perspective. But he appealed to "an even broader perspective," that of "humaneness," in insisting that all students be held to basic standards of conduct. Harre also spent a lot of time meeting and dining with students, visiting all 18 student residences during the first 12 weeks of the semester. Harre's plunge into the student body won friends. His willingness to talk frankly about issues such as sexuality and drugs was welcome, especially from one who thought and acted like a pastor. In a similar spirit, Diane Harre, the president's wife, soon joined the chapel staff, serving in the residential ministry program. While these kinds of personal exchanges with the president could not continue for long on a campus of more than 3,000 undergraduates, they created a sense that Harre would listen to student concerns, though he decided not to live on campus in the president's house.

At the inaugural event in October, students lined the processional walk from the Union to the chapel, cheering their new president and setting a festive tone for the entire ceremony. In the packed chapel, former Presidents Huegli and Schnabel and LCMS President Bohlmann were in the places of honor, and the crowd heard Professor Kathleen Mullen's poem on "The American Scholar" and Professor Philip Gehring's "Te Deum" cantata, composed for the university choirs. In his inaugural address, Harre identified moral education as the key problem to be addressed by the University, citing the widespread sense of an ethical breakdown in American higher education and in other realms of common life. The task of moral education, he said, is not confined to courses in philosophy or theology, but must occur in every discipline. In literature, we encounter the human condition; in the sciences, we are face-to-face with reflection on our relationship to the physical world; in the social sciences and in law, we deal with such questions as justice, racism, and poverty.

Harre declared that for the University to contribute to a pluralistic society, it must enter into public discussions about the moral health of that society. Christians, he said, bring to such reflections their own unique motivation of gratitude and love, offering optimism and freedom to a skeptical and chaotic world. It was now time for Christians to bear witness to the truth as they know it, he concluded. An inaugural week faculty symposium continued the theme of moral education. It used as a starting point Professor Mark Schwehn's recently published articles that argued that American higher education had taken a wrong turn in focusing on knowledge creation at the expense of what he called the venerable and necessary questions, "Who are we and how can we know and relate to others?"

The spirit of high good cheer during Harre's first semester peaked in the ARC on December 17, 1988, when, before a record crowd of nearly 5,000 fans, Valparaiso's basketball team achieved what newly appointed coach Homer Drew called a "Lutheran miracle" by defeating Notre Dame in overtime, 71–68. The dramatic victory seemed a fitting welcome for the new president and the young coach with the broad smile.

Shortly after arriving on campus, Harre appointed a strategic planning committee led by Professor Albert Trost to examine everything at the University in light of the economic, demographic, religious, and cultural forces bearing down on the institution. Its major achievement, according to Trost, was a strong and influential "mission statement" for VU. Eventually, a revised strategic plan set four "directional themes" for the period 1993–99: Lutheran character, integration of professional studies and the liberal arts, internationalization, and diversity. Meanwhile, the successful fund-raising campaign surpassed $73 million on the way to exceeding its goal by July 1989. Leitha and Willard Richardson provided a large gift for repairs and improvements in the Chapel of the Resurrection.

The happy and successful first year ended on a more ominous note. All semester long, new student applications had been falling. By July, the numbers looked alarming. Reporting to the board, now chaired by alumnus Gerald Pelzer, Harre took responsibility for the problem, citing numerous institutional and environmental factors that might explain the plummet. The unexpected enrollment decline would continue for six more years. This was partially masked by record high enrollments in the law school and larger numbers of part-time students, particularly in nursing. Even if these areas of increase kept overall numbers up, they could not soften the financial blow from falling full-time undergraduate tuition receipts, on which the University's budget was heavily dependent.

DIFFICULT ISSUES

Innumerable hours were given to planning and coping with admissions and budgetary issues. Meanwhile, other events were in the saddle, especially in the areas of gender and race relations. Some were minor, taken alone, but when they multiplied and overlapped, they became unsettling.

At VU, as at many other institutions, the multicultural emphasis helped stimulate a rise of "identity politics" in the early 1990s. Its first manifestations were among black students, linked to general questions of race relations on campus. The phenomenon of dwindling numbers of black students applied to American colleges generally in the 1980s and especially to private, largely white institutions. It was felt acutely at VU, where the Sanders-Spagoletti tragedy had seriously reduced the numbers of African-American students. By 1983, despite the fine mentorship of Professors William Neal and LouJeanne Walton, there were only 37 black students compared to 113 a decade earlier. The Black Student Organization (BSO) and the Black Association of Law Students (BALSA) remained active. But as a sense of stagnation in overall black social progress increased, so did frustration among black students. In 1986, when the Student Senate sought to eliminate its separate seat for the Black Student Organization, minority affairs director Victor Glover pointedly linked it to a resurgence of racism in the country and on campus.

Concerned faculty and students persuaded the University Senate in 1987 to vote that Valparaiso University should officially observe the birthday of Martin Luther King Jr., though Indiana had not yet adopted the federal holiday. In January 1989, Martin Luther King III spoke on campus, and in January 1990, the entire day was dedicated to what would be an annual observance. All classes were canceled and the day devoted to "alternative education." Father George Clements of Chicago addressed a full chapel, and the crowd heard Gospel songs sung by the VU choir and the Gospel Choir. Later that day, smaller sessions on relevant social topics met across campus, and the chapel filled again in the evening to hear Julian Bond. While no one believed that the observance alone was a substitute for other actions, the continuing event did contribute to an improved understanding of racial and social justice. Throughout the 1990s, the annual appearance of MLK Day became a valuable time for education, reflection, and renewed commitment to often-violated ideals on the Valpo campus.

In fall 1991, the College of Arts and Sciences dean Philip Gilbertson, who had succeeded the retiring Forrest Vance, obtained a competitive grant of $250,000 from the Knight Foundation, matched by another $250,000 from the University, to promote cultural and racial diversity on VU's campus. This grant, together with several other significant grant-funded projects spearheaded by Assistant Dean Linda Ferguson, was aimed at improving both academic attention to minority perspectives and the "campus climate" for diversity.

On the weekend of April 3–5, 1992, two high-profile racial incidents—a fight on Mound Street and a fire set at the door of a respected black student in Wehrenberg Hall—brought to a head the issue of racism that had been simmering all year long. Although the fire was quickly doused, emotions flamed high during the following week. Finally, President Harre called a convocation on Friday, April 10, and 2,300 students and faculty filled the chapel. When Harre provided in his address a routine account of what had happened over the weekend, along with a recitation of University policies, a large number of students and some faculty rose and walked out in protest over what they felt was the lack of a sense of outrage.

On Wednesday morning, April 15, the black students held a press conference in which they outlined a list of grievances and charges against the University and demanded a dialogue with the administration on these points. A thousand students met in the chapel, heard brief speeches by Pastor Kehret and BSO president Tony McDonald, then marched to Kretzmann Hall in support of the black negotiators. Harre met them at the door and welcomed them to the administration building, expressing hope that the discussions would go well. Negotiators and administrators met in the Kretzmann Board Room, with supporting students sitting in the hallway, milling in and out. Outside the building, despite bad weather, pizza and soft drinks sustained the crowd.

The black students, including some from the law school, were well organized and well informed. At the end of an afternoon of negotiations, about 150 students still remained outside, huddled against the inclement weather. Aided by the availability of the Knight funds, agreement was reached on goals of increasing the number of black faculty and students, hiring black campus security officers, enhancing the Office of Minority Affairs, and so on. As the victory bell rang in the background, LeTari Thompson, the leading student negotiator, and the individual who had been attacked in the Wehrenberg incident, spoke publicly with evident satisfaction.

Then President Harre addressed the students:

> I denounce the attack on LeTari Thompson, a member of our community, as a racially-motivated personal assault, threatening grievous harm to LeTari. Such behavior is outrageous, and neither I nor the University will tolerate it. So long as even one member of this community lives in fear of others, we will not be worthy of the name community.

That is what the concerned students had wanted to hear—a man speaking from the heart and not simply an administrator intoning cold policy. "I'm going to sleep very well tonight," said Thompson.

While many efforts to address race relations already were under way, these events impressed their urgency on everyone. The promises made in the Kretzmann dialogue in the areas of recruitment, course offerings, and campus climate were kept. VU also joined an overseas program in Namibia in cooperation with Augsburg College. Several new minority faculty joined the university, though their turnover rate was also high. By the end of the 1993–94 year, there were a record 245 people of color enrolled in the law school, the undergraduate colleges, and the part-time graduate program, 134 of them African-American.

But the problems did not go away. A number of people expressed disappointment over what they still saw as the lack of attitudinal progress on campus. "Fear and ignorance will always be there," Dean Gilbertson pointed out but urged no slacking of efforts to drive them back. Others thought that politics was infecting education. A conservative law student wrote a strong article in *The Torch* condemning what he saw as a creeping political correctness vitiating the University's striving for academic excellence. Other students felt that frank dialogue about racial and political questions was still difficult to come by. One thing everyone agreed on was that these issues would not disappear from the campus agenda.

The growing attention to diversity on campus also appeared in the efforts to make a place for homosexuals in VU's public life. In 1990, the Gay and Lesbian Association (GALA) applied for recognition by the Student Senate as an official VU social organization, which would make it one of roughly 50 such groups that could apply to the Senate for program funding, use campus meeting spaces, and so on. The application for recognition was normally a fairly routine act—not in this case. Lively debate and a special student forum preceded the senate's resolution of recognition. The question then became whether Harre would veto it, as he could.

The interest in Harre's decision was intense. Distinguishing between homosexual orientation and practice, he let the senate decision stand. The president was unprepared for the torrent of negative mail that descended upon him, particularly after one publication disseminated a distorted version of the events. Harre was frustrated by the misrepresentations of his views. He personally answered all the letters. Nevertheless, some individuals evidently found a new reason to distance themselves from Valparaiso University. Others, who had tried to deal seriously with homophobia as a pastoral issue in their ministries, took courage from the University's stand, though they made less noise than the critics.

Gender issues also were highly visible in the late 1980s and early 1990s, often linked to "identity politics." The existing women's movement on campus became much more vocal when a highly publicized sexual assault occurred at a Greek party in 1987. Rape became a topic of frank public discussion, together with the general question of trust between young men and women. Victims began speaking openly about their fear of reporting the crime and their frequent mistreatment when they did. The women's movement had made a good deal of progress in explaining rape not as a sexual crime, but as an act of violent power, tied into deep-seated cultural phenomena degrading the status and image of women. But these ideas were slow to gain acceptance.

In the fall of 1991, the growing national discussions of sexual harassment were fully aired in *The Torch*, as well as in the administration, which was required to prepare written policies on this subject for faculty, employees, students. Meanwhile, a vigorous new student group had formed, Feminists Ready for Enlightenment and Equality (FREE). The theme of gender struggle continued that spring of 1992 with an event called "Take Back the Night" that aired the problem of sexual violence, including rape and sexual abuse. It included a chapel "healing service," marches, rallies, and separate gatherings by men and women to address concerns. In the fall of 1992, the intercultural studies committee made presentations regarding gender and racial issues to incoming freshmen. Associate Chapel Dean Kehret stressed the need for each person to battle persistent and powerful attitudes and habits of speech and to respect all members of society.

New efforts in that direction were marred, however, by incidents of alleged date rape in fraternities in 1992 and 1993. In the 1993 incident, the offender was found guilty in campus judicial processes and suspended from the University. He then filed a $12 million lawsuit that attracted media attention until it was dismissed. In August 1993, a faculty workshop was devoted to the subject of sexual violence, and in November, the Sexual Assault Advocacy and Facilitating Education office (SAAFE) opened. Student-operated at first, it became a haven for students in need, providing counseling and referral to support groups, shelters, and legal services.

While these efforts received considerable attention, many women's concerns involved the less visible drama of working for greater equality in various areas of life on and off campus. Gender equity was the watchword, and relevant committees were appointed to study conditions throughout the University. Pressure mounted for a fair allocation of resources for women's athletics. There were efforts to recruit more female faculty and to improve the Gender Studies minor.

An issue of special concern at VU was the role of women in the chapel. This took on new urgency with the formation of the ELCA, which ordained women to the ministry. There were now many ELCA students at VU, adding weight to the request that ordained women participate in chapel services, a view at odds with the public position and practice of the Missouri Synod, which opposed the ordination of women, as did the Catholic and Orthodox Christian traditions represented by large student segments.

For some, the issue was one of simple gender equity, comparable to other similar matters. For others, it was also a serious theological concern. Some women on campus—including pioneering YLTP graduate, sociology instructor, and Guild leader Dorothea (Dot) Allwardt Nuechterlein—were actively involved in the women's movement in the Missouri Synod. Professor Gail McGrew Eifrig, editor of *The Cresset*, connected the issue of women's ordination to the biblical witness, the nature of ministry, and the presentation of the Gospel in the modern world. While the board declined to change existing policy when the matter was first presented in 1993, it was plainly on the campus agenda.

TRANSFORMATION

The host of difficult issues the campus faced in Harre's first years tended to create a sense of frayed direction and unclear focus. The national and local inclinations toward "identity politics" made it more difficult to define and act on a set of shared goals. Harre's initial "open door" approach entangled him in numerous small problems, making it difficult to concentrate on the large ones. The enrollment difficulties created constant administrative anxieties, compounded by turnovers in the areas of admissions and financial aid and difficulties in recruiting administrators.

To free the president to concentrate on fund-raising and other matters, the strategic planners urged the president to get an assistant and to centralize his administration. He appointed William Karpenko as assistant to the president in 1990. After a two-year search and several turndowns, Harre also found a provost who could guide the University's internal affairs: Roy Austensen, a cosmopolitan churchman, historian of modern Europe, and prize-winning specialist on Metternich. Within a year, Austensen accepted the resignations of several recently appointed administrators in admissions, financial aid, and marketing and appointed Katharine Wehling the vice president for admissions and financial aid. At about the same time, vice president Gary Greinke moved elsewhere, and President Harre replaced him with Richard Maddox as vice president for institutional advancement.

Meanwhile, the strategic planners were deciding among several key campus-wide needs: a performing arts center, a new student union, an expanded library, and new space for the psychology department. Lobbyists for each of the four needs made strong cases, but the performing arts developed an edge in the argument. "We must show students that culture is as important as careers," wrote Professor John Steven Paul on behalf of an arts center. The case for the arts center was aided by some existing funds that already had been raised for that purpose and by the long history of promises and delays going back to the Kretzmann administration.

The building planning committee, chaired by Professor Edgar Luecke, followed Harre's farsighted directive to plan a comprehensive building for all the arts, though it cost a $1 million gift for Phase I of the three-phase design proposed in the 1980s. Stressing the imperatives of artistic collaboration, Professor John Steven Paul chaired a newly formed arts division that pledged to work together throughout the time of planning and construction. When it became clear that the $15 million budget limit set by the board would not nearly meet all the needs of the three departments as well as an art museum, the committee overcame its disappointments and made several crucial decisions. It refused either to surrender its grand goals or simply to shrink all the components. Because the building was intended first for teaching purposes, a large concert hall was deferred for a later phase. The bulky art studios also were deferred; painters and sculptors would work elsewhere. But the planners were able to retain space for the burgeoning photographic and design programs.

The board originally had projected a $60 million fund-raising campaign. Vice President Maddox and his staff proposed an immediate $35 million capital campaign for the center and a few other projects and a larger $70 to $100 million dollar campaign later in the decade. Alumni Robert and Lori Duesenberg chaired "Lighting the Way," as the drive was named, leading with a $1 million gift. A $3 million gift from the Urschel family enabled the museum to be "done right," as they insisted. When furnishings and equipment were taken into account, the whole arts center project came to more than $19 million. The success of the campaign led to a celebratory groundbreaking on July 24, 1993. Present for the festive event was the aged, wheelchair-bound Dr. Vera Hahn, one of the pioneers of the arts at Valparaiso, who turned some soil for a building she would unfortunately not live to see.

In 1994, the huge new arts center rising in the center of the campus suggested vigor and growth. Not so visible was the declining number of students in the classrooms and residence halls. Full-time undergraduate enrollment had fallen 20 percent since 1988, creating a growing budgetary problem. Vice President Smith pointed out continually that austerity upon austerity was not only crippling the ability of the University to carry out its work, but reserves were running low. Rising enrollments in the law school, evening division, and part-time nursing students masked the decline but added little to the general coffers.

The University was uncertain how to grapple with the problem. VU was not poor, but no one wanted to travel the road some schools had taken of mortgaging their future by expending the endowment, especially one that had been so carefully built only in recent decades. To cut costs, the Strategic Planning Committee marked decaying Dau-Kreinheder Halls for demolition, and in the summer of 1994, that familiar complex disappeared, leaving only its cafeteria to be converted into the University Book Center. Some proposed also closing Wehrenberg, but Harre resisted. Instead, the University undertook a major $5 million capital renovation, funded by a bond issue, to make Wehrenberg a more attractive and habitable residence.

None of these steps was enough, and by fall 1994, it was plainly no longer possible to do business as usual. The entering freshman undergraduate class was 553, with lower quality indicators and the percentage of Lutherans down to 32 percent. A sudden one-year upsurge in transfers allowed the University to speak of an increase in new students—but budget analysts knew better.

Harre decided it was now time to turn to a consultant, tough-talking Thomas Bakewell of St. Louis. Bakewell presented to the board the goal of saving $5.2 million so, within 30 months, operating expenses would be covered by operating income. There was no time for discussion. Senior administrators were ordered to prepare lists of the people in their area, ranking them according to their importance to the operation, with those on the bottom most liable to dismissal. For faculty, the provost's office offered a highly attractive early retirement plan that was accepted by 18 faculty, nearly all those eligible. Altogether a total of 76 members of the community retired or were terminated. All told, the moves cost the University $1.3 million, but the savings, together with a revised health plan, amounted to approximately $3.5 million annually.

In his announcement of these measures in December 1994, Harre used the term "transformation." The term put a positive spin on what for many was seen as bad news. The president had been for some time unhappy with not only the downslide in enrollment and the constraints this brought, but also the fact that in a time of rapid intellectual and cultural change, many in the academy seemed unresponsive to new conditions. In presentations to the faculty, he contended that the pain of short-term cutbacks would be balanced, in the long run, by a healthier fiscal picture that would enable the University to make forward gains. He called for creating an "extraordinary learning environment," with a focus on more hands-on learning and undergraduate scholarship.

One positive change was a closer alignment of academic and student affairs, a move strongly encouraged by the academic deans. After the retirements of the deans of men and women and the resignation of Vice President Daryll Hersemann, Harre appointed Bonnie Hunter to be the assistant provost for student affairs. She reported directly to the provost and served on the academic council of deans.

Meanwhile, Harre had concluded that, with savings of about $3.5 million having been achieved, no further cuts in operations or academic programs should be undertaken. The negative impact on class sizes and the Freshman Seminar were becoming evident, and morale had suffered correspondingly. Bakewell had targeted even more reductions, but Harre declined to go along. In January 1996, Bakewell was released.

CAMPUS DEVELOPMENTS

By the fall of 1995, there already were signs that this distressed period in the University's history was ending and a new chapter opening.

Enrollment began to turn around and quality indicators resumed their upward climb, remaining as before well above national averages. The Lighting the Way campaign exceeded its goal, ending with a total of $37.5 million. The dedication of the Valparaiso University Center for the Arts (VUCA) drew several thousand guests for a mid-September weekend of festive dedicatory activity.

The VUCA was a major achievement. With its theater, recital hall, dedicated classroom and rehearsal spaces, and spacious, inviting Guild Lobby, the center rapidly established itself as a focal point of activities on campus and a magnet for student recruitment. Students from all departments found themselves involved in the arts, often collaborating across the various arts disciplines. Such facilities and opportunities were rarely found in similar undergraduate institutions. The Brauer Museum, named after Richard Brauer at the request of the major donors from the Urschel family, opened in 1997 and quickly became a venue for major exhibitions. It hosted the Romanian national art collection on its American tour, attracting more than 20,000 visitors and a good deal of national attention to the VUCA. In this show, great masters such as Rembrandt, Tintoretto, and El Greco, hidden during the Cold War, suddenly became available for viewing and study by students and visitors. Lectures by guest experts coincided with the exhibit. An outstanding exhibition of Ansel Adams's photographs attracted a large midwestern audience and critical acclaim. Complementing such exhibits were programs of art education for the children of the schools of Northwest Indiana, which extended programs already in place for the permanent collection of the museum, especially its notable Hudson River collection.

Meanwhile, the president appointed two committees to shape a forward look for the campus. A budget advisory committee included several faculty members. A committee on campus planning and space use decided on the demolition of historic Baldwin and DeMotte Halls and the relocation of the geography and psychology departments to new quarters. Another committee concluded that Moellering Library could not be remodeled. Soon plans were drawn up to construct a new library and information center. The firm of Hammel, Green and Abrahamson developed a new campus master plan that would frame the contemplated major fund drive and define VU's physical development well into the future.

All this time, the wiring of the campus proceeded at a rapid pace, so by 1998 VU provided 1,350 computers and similar devices for students and faculty, with approximately 500 additional student-owned computers in service. A three-year Lilly grant supported training and workshops for faculty members and assisted them in integrating the new technologies into their teaching.

Campus involvement in volunteer activity continued to grow. The former psychology department home, Moody Laboratory, was sold to a neighborhood development group led by retired professors Walter Reiner and Edgar Senne. The group created Hilltop Neighborhood House, an organization providing child and health care for low-income residents in the area near the West Campus. VU students, faculty, and staff were instrumental in the Hilltop effort and related programs. A vigorous campus chapter of Habitat for Humanity built affordable houses. Through a Volunteer Service Center, students gave thousands of hours to volunteer activities of all sorts in Porter County and throughout northwest Indiana. The University became part of the Indiana Campus Compact, a consortium of Indiana colleges that received funding to promote service learning and help incorporate volunteerism into some course work.

Campus governance was another area undergoing revitalization. Since the early 1990s, faculty leaders had contemplated reorganizing the internal governance system that had been virtually unchanged since the original creation of the Instrument for Internal Governance in 1969. The former University Senate became the University Council, incorporating staff as well as faculty and student representatives. A new Faculty Senate assumed many of the duties, including committee supervision, previously lodged in the faculty as a whole. The Student Senate, under presidents such as Amy Flesch, Brad Jessen, and Benjamin Schnakenberg, also reasserted a strong and responsible role on campus.

In student life, professional directors sought to improve the quality of residential living. After the disappearance of three fraternities and the demolition of two of the Mound Street houses, there were signs that the remaining fraternities were attempting to recover some of their ideals. In 1998, the VU sororities ended their longtime local status and affiliated with national organizations.

At the same time, a soaring economy uplifted general U.S. morale and spilled over to campuses as well. The rocketing stock market, which had been on an upward surge since the presidency of Reagan, suddenly climbed exponentially after 1994, more than doubling the Dow average from its 5,000 level in 1995. The University's endowment also doubled during that period, even without a major fund drive. In 1996, it had stood at around $60 million; by 2000 it was $140 million. In this climate, the board authorized Harre to spend several million dollars from endowment earnings and other unanticipated income for unbudgeted projects that would have an immediate impact. These funds went for campus beautification, Union remodeling, new weight-training facilities, and similar projects. Incremental increases through the late 1990s allowed the administration gradually to rebuild the faculty. Associate Provost Renu Juneja led several teams of faculty members in writing proposals that garnered Lilly Endowment funds for a variety of innovative campus programs. The net impact of this spending, along with sharply increased salaries for faculty, staff, and administration, was to create an improved sense of well-being, despite the stresses that a thinly stretched faculty still experienced.

While the new VUCA and the enlargement and remodeling of the Reddel organ focused major attention on the arts, other academic areas also maintained and strengthened their programs in the 1990s. At Valparaiso, as elsewhere in the academy, the sciences and professional schools were much less affected by the unsettling ideological and epistemological currents stirring the humanities and social sciences.

The sciences as a whole were perhaps the academically strongest sector of the College of Arts and Sciences, continuing to require rigor of their students while resisting the grade inflation that afflicted much of higher education. Under Professor Donald Koetke's leadership, the physics department developed a strong faculty research program in subatomic nuclear particles as well as other areas, and the department came to be listed in *The Directory of Research Institutes in High Energy Physics*. Led by the internationally recognized stellar research of Professor Bruce Hrivnak, the department became the Department of Physics and Astronomy.

The research ethos in the biology and chemistry departments was less well funded and less fully developed. New faculty began to change that while strong teaching remained the hallmark of those departments. Faculty scholarship kept the curriculum abreast of the onrushing flood of new scientific knowledge, particularly in such areas as biotechnology and polymer research, as well as the revolutionary developments in instrumentation. In chemistry and biology, too, VU students experienced high success rates in graduate and medical schools, often distinguishing themselves in their careers. Increasingly, good students in all the science departments were involved in undergraduate research, frequently collaborating in sophisticated projects with their professors. VU's psychology department and the rapidly expanding program in meteorology (housed in the Department of Geography) both gained increasing recognition for their active student involvement in innovative research. Perhaps more than any other sector of the campus, too, the sciences have included a number of scholars who are theologically informed members of the Christian community.

Under Dean Ivan Bodensteiner and his successor, Edward Gaffney, the VU law school acquired new resources, increased faculty strength, and won growing recognition through a flurry of fresh initiatives, including a requirement that each graduating law student engage in *pro bono* activities. The scholarship of faculty such as Rosalie Levinson in civil rights liability and Robert Blomquist in environmental law drew attention to VU's program. Students benefited from the endowed Luther Swygert Memorial Moot Court competition and other moot court activities. In 1991, the school began sponsoring summer sessions in Ningbo, China, and Cambridge, England. In 1991–92, the school observed a yearlong bicentennial of the Bill of Rights and designated 1993–94 as a year honoring the role of women in law, climaxing with the appearance of Justice Sandra Day O'Connor before a packed VU chapel. Justice O'Connor was one of five justices of the United States Supreme Court—including chief justice William Rehnquist—who visited VU because of Gaffney's personal efforts. Justices Antonin Scalia, Ruth Bader Ginsberg, and Clarence Thomas also taught in VU's Cambridge summer sessions.

Gaffney, a theologian-lawyer nationally known in the field of church-state relationships, had a deep interest in conducting legal education within the context of an ethically and socially conscious community of law students and professors. While there were other able faculty members who saw a relationship between their faith traditions and lawyering, this important discourse and intellectual work lagged behind other concerns at the law school. The question of how to connect the School of Law and the University's fundamental purposes remained a major issue.

VU's undergraduate professional schools attempted to maintain their academic quality while battling the declining enrollment that affected them all. When Edgar Luecke succeeded Stuart Walesh as dean of engineering, financial reductions forced him to cut back the computer engineering degree, though computer use actually grew across the engineering disciplines, as it did elsewhere on campus. Despite fewer resources, younger replacement appointments brought fresh interdisciplinary approaches to teaching and developed new areas, such as biomedical engineering. The new Frederick F. Jenny Professorship of Emerging Technology, the Alfred W. Sieving Chair of Engineering, and the Paul and

Cleo Brandt Professorship of Engineering fostered innovative engineering through the work of their occupants. Several faculty conducted outstanding research programs that involved students, including Professor Robert Palumbo's studies in solar energy. VU engineering graduates regularly went on to top graduate programs and also were in demand for challenging positions in government and industry.

For the College of Business Administration, the 30-year journey toward accreditation by the AACSB came to a successful conclusion in 1993. The college also participated in Valparaiso's internationalizing theme, creating an International Business major that included a foreign language requirement. Lilly Endowment largesse encouraged the faculty to experiment with collaborative teaching and a new network of internships, together with more interaction with the business community. The new Louis S. and Mary L. Morgal Chair in Business Ethics was first occupied by Professor Michael McCuddy.

Falling enrollment in the 1990s hit the College of Nursing the hardest. Acceptance of marginal students caused a worrisome upward drift in the number of graduates not passing their state board examinations. The college was forced to take measures to turn this around. On the other hand, the new Master of Science in nursing prospered, and Dean Scales sharpened the college's national profile through her activities with the National League of Nursing.

Several new degree programs appeared in the Graduate Studies Division. Dean James W. Albers, succeeding Professor Ferencz Kallay in administering the graduate program, also reached into the northwest Indiana community with vigorous initiatives for adult learners. In 1999, a new College of Adult Scholars was created to serve them, under newly appointed Dean David Rowland.

In contrast to the natural sciences and professional studies, the humanities and social sciences in the 1990s were generally marked nationally by conflict and fragmentation. As scholars in these latter areas surveyed their fields, they acknowledged a sense of disarray. Typical was the observation of David Damrosch, in his book *We Scholars*, on the contemporary state of the humanities: "There has been an increase of factionality and coterie behavior." At Valparaiso such national trends generally were reflected only partially or intermittently, and most work proceeded along relatively traditional lines. In the mid-1990s, all the humanities and social science departments struggled, with varying success, to maintain their numbers of majors and minors in addition to upholding general education and serving various professionally oriented programs. All the humanities reflected a growing recognition of the voice and place of women, as well as of other groups historically marginalized within Western and American culture. The conception of literature and history was broadened to include new genres and voices. In the history department and in Christ College, non-Western traditions enjoyed a greatly increased presence. The International Economics and Cultural Affairs program attracted about 60 majors a year, and eventually a similar International Service major was added. Within both the foreign languages and literatures and the English departments, attention to the great cultures and civilizations that constitute the global context of contemporary life replaced in part the devotion to traditional literary studies alone, though classical works retained a strong place in the VU humanities curriculum.

Attention to newer topics similarly grew in theology. Professors Theodore Ludwig and Edgar Senne made VU a center within Lutheranism for the study of world religions, stimulated in part by new general education requirements in non-Western culture and "U.S. Diversity." Ludwig was honored as the first occupant of a chair in this field created by Dr. Surjit S. Patheja, a distinguished physician in northwest Indiana and a practicing Sikh who was particularly interested in promoting mutual understanding among the world's religions. Under Professor David Truemper, VU became the headquarters of the national Council of Societies for the Study of Religion and its publication. Professor Walter Rast, author, coauthor, and editor of more than a dozen books, concluded his outstanding scholarly career with an appointment as the Annual Professor at the Albright Institute of Archeological Research in Jerusalem. Professor Thomas Droege published highly regarded work on various aspects of faith-formation. Through major Lilly grants, Professor Dorothy Bass led the "Valparaiso Project on the Education and Formation of People in Faith," which brought about, among other things, the publication of a widely praised anthology, *Practicing Our Faith*. Nevertheless, the changes in the theology department were not always smooth. The reservoir of classically trained Lutheran theologians that had traditionally furnished VU's department was greatly diminished by the internal strife within the Missouri Synod. Affected by the prevailing ethos, the department lost some of its focus, though it retained a commitment to being a strong theology department within a Lutheran university. Just how it should be accountable to the church became more problematic.

The philosophy department had been sustained by the shrewd leadership and excellent teaching of Professor Kenneth Klein, even through the wilderness years of the 1980s when its existence seemed threatened. Noting the renewal of Christian thought in professional philosophical circles, the administration in 1989 initiated the rebuilding of a department that could address the major shifts in cultural and intellectual life. Several excellent younger philosophers were appointed and began reviving the department's position as campus intellectual stimulant, a role that it had not played since the 1960s.

In the social sciences, geography continued its strong tradition at VU, sending many majors to graduate school and new professional fields. The political science department was stimulated by the creation of a Community Research and Service Center that involved many students in scholarship and community service in northwest Indiana and elsewhere. The social work department, long led by Professor Walton, remained an important campus voice promoting diversity and service within the context of a Christian university. The physical education department developed several new programs, including one for athletic training.

The arts remained especially strong in levels of teaching, performance, and scholarship, and in their determination to carry on the church-related traditions of Valparaiso University. The fine generation of musicians represented by William Eifrig, Philip Gehring, Eldon Balko, Frederick Telschow, and others was replaced by new talents who were committed both to upholding the University's traditions and to reaching out to embrace the musical traditions of other cultures. The highest level of organ performance in worship and concert was assured by the creation of the Frederick J. Kruse Organ Fellowship, held first by Professor Martin Jean and, after his departure for Yale University, by Professor Lorraine Brugh. The appointments of Linda Ferguson, John Bernthal, and more recently Christopher Cock, Dennis Friesen-Carper, and Jeffrey Doebler, elevated the excellence of the choral and instrumental traditions at VU. Professor David Morgan's work on American religious art and culture, including his *Icons of American Protestantism* and *Visual Culture*, gained national recognition. The theater program led by Professor John Steven Paul experienced a striking growth in sophistication and quality. The many new and gifted faculty and students in all the arts helped to create a remarkably vibrant artistic community—a community that successfully reached out to become a center of life for Valparaiso University and attracted followers in northwest Indiana, Chicago, and beyond.

Special chairs and professorships underscored the importance of the humanities at VU. In 1991, the endowed Jochum Chair was filled by Professor Walter Wangerin Jr., a preacher and speaker and above all a writer of uncommon gifts, whose compelling voice carried the vision and purposes of Valparaiso University far beyond the campus. Students were enriched by his preaching in the chapel and lined up for places in his popular classes. A National Endowment for the Humanities grant and a bequest from Walter Wente created the Richard Baepler Professorship in the Humanities, first occupied by Mel Piehl. In 1997, on Harre's strong initiative, the Phyllis and Richard Duesenberg Chair in Christian Ethics was filled by Professor Gilbert Meilaender, a widely recognized Lutheran theologian and ethicist.

As Christ College matured, some of its earlier experimental flair faded. Keeping its original focus on the integration of fields of learning, it strengthened its work as a humanities honors college and attracted even more talented students. The college also became the seat of a formidable development, the Lilly Fellows Program, brainchild of its new dean, Mark Schwehn. In 1993, Schwehn published *Exiles from Eden*, in which he argued that the prevailing graduate school ethos defining the university almost exclusively by the mastery of specialized knowledge contributed to the current crisis in higher education. As an alternative, he proposed "education for thoughtfulness," in which religion could generate the values needed to sustain academic vocations that would address a broader set of questions. To turn argument into action, Schwehn created a "Lilly Fellows Program in the Humanities and the Arts" that offered young Christian scholars who had just completed their Ph.D.'s a chance to attend VU for two years and there renew their sense of Christian vocation.

The Lilly Fellows Program, under the direction of Arlin Meyer, was launched in 1991 with a national conference of 26 Christian colleges and universities. This evolved into the Lilly Fellows National Network, a coalition that grew to 65 institutions and developed numerous initiatives related to Christian higher education funded through the Lilly Endowment. Thus, Valparaiso became in this area a national leader among a wide range of institutions, from Notre Dame to Baylor University, that sought to embrace high academic quality within their religious mission. The network was not merely an institutional self-help organization, however; it recognized that Christian higher education has major intellectual tasks to perform that must to a great extent be done collaboratively. The annual network conferences produced papers that *Cresset* editor Gail Eifrig regularly turned into memorable special issues for wide dissemination.

Clearly, the Lilly Fellows Program constituted the most dynamic initiative throughout the 1990s at the University. In the same vein, VU's link to the Rhodes College Consultation on the Church-Related College helped produce an anthology of significant articles, *The Lutheran Reader* (1999), edited by David Morgan and Paul Contino. To incorporate such efforts into the entire University would constitute a major challenge for Valparaiso as it worked to transmit its vital traditions to a new generation.

EIGHT DAYS IN MARCH

One unexpected development of the late 1990s was VU's sudden burst of success in athletics. The "Lutheran miracle" of 1988—the surprise defeat of Notre Dame in basketball—proved to be a portent of things to come, though it took a while for the reality to follow the sign. Basketball Coach Homer Drew had immediately appealed to the campus as an attractive person of impeccable character, but the team record, except for that first bright year of 1988–89, was dismal. There was sharp criticism of the program in the press and on campus. Attendance remained disastrous, and questions about the relation of VU's academic and athletic goals grew louder.

Harre finally asked a subcommittee chaired by the highly respected faculty leader Professor Judith Peters to study and make recommendations regarding the University's intercollegiate sports program. The committee's exhaustive report, which appeared in March 1991, provided a detailed and frank account of the problems of VU athletics, including the inferior budgets and equipment for women's athletic teams and the poor condition of sports besides basketball that also had to compete in Division I. Besides its fact-finding, the committee examined the pros and cons of various options and solutions. The implications of remaining Division I, or of moving to Division II or III, were explored. The report made it clear that the present practice of underfunded activities was unacceptable. If the University decided to remain in Division I, it would have to "do it right." That meant much more money at a time when VU was cutting back elsewhere because of falling enrollment.

The report went to the University Senate for debate. Many asked whether the University could retain academic integrity and maintain a "big-time" program. The numerous problems associated with the top levels of college athletics, from pressures on coaches and athletes to outright corruption, were publicly reviewed. The question came down to this: Could Valparaiso become one of the few exceptions in the collegiate world to the evils associated with such approaches? After debate, a motion to move to Division III was defeated. The problems of finding compatible midwestern opponents weighed heavily against Division III and against a Division II solution as well. This was in effect an endorsement of remaining Division I. In April, the board resolved to stay in Division I and to make the necessary financial commitments. The athletics program was permitted to raise money beyond the regular budget for its own purposes.

The impact of the new policies was instant. Female athletes soon were able to get chartered buses, better uniforms and equipment, access to training, and locker and practice facilities on a more equitable basis. When the North Star Conference expired at the end of the 1991–92 season, the women's athletic program joined the men in the Mid-Continent Conference. As women's basketball became more visible nationally and professionally, the Lady Crusaders under coaches David Wolter and Keith Freeman began to create a competitive ethos in women's basketball. Gradually, too, other VU sports began to become competitive against institutionally similar Division I opponents.

Men's football was a different story. The Heartland Conference had merged with a group of largely Michigan state colleges to form a new Division II football conference, the Midwest Intercollegiate Football Conference. This mismatched set of teams produced for Valparaiso football players the agony of a 91–0 loss to Grand Valley State and a record home losing streak that was finally broken by a win against Wayne State. Again the NCAA intervened with new legislation, forcing all teams in Division I basketball to play *all* other sports, now including football, in Division I. But the legislation also, fortunately, allowed schools such as Valparaiso to field football teams in Division I-AA conferences that would not give any athletic grants-in-aid for football—the policy followed by such academically demanding conferences as the Ivy League, the Patriot League, and the Metro Atlantic Athletic Conference. Thus, VU was able to join in the Pioneer Football League, consisting of private schools similar to Valparaiso—Drake, Dayton, Butler, Evansville, and San Diego universities. VU football bounced back to achieve competitive records in the late 1990s. Like VU's other sports, it began to attract more athletes who were solid students as well.

Fortunes for the men's basketball team also began to change in 1992 when two talented former Valparaiso High School players transferred to

Valparaiso University, joining a team with another local star from Michigan City, Indiana. The season of 1994–95 was more notable because it marked the beginning of the collegiate career of Bryce Drew, Homer Drew's son. Heavily recruited, Bryce decided to play for his father and quickly became Valparaiso's most celebrated athlete. The next year, a new source of talent opened up to Valparaiso recruiters: Europe. Seven-foot Tony Vilcinskas from Lithuania and later 6-foot, 11-inch Zoran Viskovic from Croatia gave VU tough and athletic big men in the center post. Around this core, Coach Drew built a winning team that took the conference title in 1995–96 and became the first VU team to go to the modern NCAA tournament. Mismatched with Arizona, they were embarrassed in a 90–51 blowout. The next year, they repeated the conference win, this time fighting Boston College in the first NCAA round all the way to a 73–66 loss.

During these two years, the basketball climate at VU changed. Student interest returned; the pep band and a lively cheering section of noisy, dedicated students entertained the crowds. The Crusader Club, made up of local boosters, started contributing in six figures. Additional NCAA revenue flowed in. Attendance figures climbed.

Favored in the conference, the team won the title again in 1998 and again proceeded to the NCAA "Big Dance." Hundreds of supporters gathered in the ARC to watch the pairings on television and learn that the team, seeded 13, would go to Oklahoma City to play the fourth-seeded University of Mississippi, starring All-American Ansu Sesay, in the first round.

It was a tough nip-and-tuck contest. Two points behind with 95 seconds to play, guard Jamie Sykes, Jared Nuness, the freshman "sixth man," and Drew each narrowly missed three-pointers. With 4.1 seconds remaining, Mississippi's Sesay incredibly missed two free throws. Sykes now stood at the end of the court shouting "Pacer," the name of a well-practiced play designed for exactly this situation. Mississippi players were guarding closely. Pump-faking, Sykes, who was also a star baseball player, threw a long, looping pass to Bill Jenkins. Eluding two close defenders, Jenkins caught the ball in midair and flipped it to Bryce Drew, who sank the winning 23-foot shot. A year later, the shot was still being replayed on television, together with the joyous sequel of VU's team mobbing one another on the basketball floor and the Drews, father and son, in an emotional embrace.

Such is American popular culture that overnight, Valparaiso's team became the darlings of the nation. For the *New York Times* and other newspapers across the country, it was front-page treatment. Two days later, VU (enrollment 3,500) defeated Florida State (enrollment 30,000) in overtime, 83–77, proving that the first win was no fluke.

The next stop a week later would be in the fabled "Sweet Sixteen" in St. Louis. For the entire week leading to the game, Valparaiso University received media treatment unlike any it could have imagined. Networks and writers descended on the campus. What charmed them was not only the Cinderella and David-Goliath stories being reenacted, but the winning articulateness and evident character of the VU players. Pictures showing VU students crowding to welcome the team home exuded wholesomeness. So did Coach Drew. Overlay on this the father-son relationship between Homer and Bryce, plus a similar one between Coach Jim Harrick Sr. of Rhode Island, the team's next opponent in St. Louis, and his son, Jim Jr., who was an assistant coach at VU, and the ingredients were there to challenge the best writers.

Rhode Island defeated VU in St. Louis. But the Valpo team seemed to be the real winners as their supporters called them back to the floor for prolonged applause. Afterward, editorialists tried to make sense of the entire phenomenon the country had experienced. Sports writers remembered, pondered, and didn't want to let go of the magic. Said the editorial writer of the *Indianapolis Star*, "It's funny how success in sports can cause us to take note of an institution that was already distinguished, simply ignored and unappreciated by the secular world. It's funny how national TV exposure can jam the phone lines at a place already deserving of a good reputation." To underline his point, the editorialist noted that nationally known Lutheran theologian Gilbert Meilaender had left Oberlin College to join VU's theology department. Whether Valparaiso could translate these golden moments into something more permanent in the academic realm, the season and the spotlight were unforgettable.

HOLDING THE CENTER

Amid the many centrifugal forces and pressures at work on a modern university, VU has continued to struggle to hold to its center of identity and mission. The general education program, the core of any university curriculum, was a continuing focus of attention. Despite continuing reforms, such as the addition of global and U.S. diversity requirements, budget constraints and the decline in numbers of full-time faculty took a serious toll, especially on the set of required freshman courses, which had prized a common, rigorous approach, particularly in the area of writing.

Under the leadership of Albert Trost, who succeeded Gilbertson as dean of the College of Arts and Sciences virtually by faculty acclamation, faculty leaders boldly attempted to reverse the centrifugal forces by proposing a single university-wide common core course, the "Valpo Core," to be taught by faculty drawn largely from the departments of theology, English, philosophy, and history, but including others as well. Faculty participants voiced optimism in this effort to reclaim a distinctive and relevant intellectual center and to innovate with a variety of cocurricular support activities. This was a daring goal, given the hyper-individualism of the times. The "Valpo Core" was taught for the first time in 1998–99.

"It's time we said that this University stands for something," said the widely respected history professor Meredith Berg after a meeting that debated the central religious, literary, and historical themes and texts to be taken up by the core. Berg is one of many accomplished teachers, too numerous to be named in these pages, who have over the years been the great strength of Valparaiso University. They range from the VU French professor who stood on her desk to make her point while experimenting with new methods of language instruction to the psychologist, political scientist, and economist who together explored "love, power, and money" in an advanced team-taught seminar. They include fine lecturers and imaginative discussion leaders, scholars well grounded in their subject matter but ready to venture into neighboring fields of study or to address difficult religious or political matters to help their students find coherence and meaning for their vocations and their lives. That spirit remained a powerful tradition, carried on from Valparaiso's earliest days as a Lutheran university, that provided one antidote to the many de-centering forces at work in the University and the culture at large.

From the beginning of its work in the early 1990s, the strategic planning committee made the maintenance of the Lutheran character of the University the first of its directional themes. As Lutheran enrollment in the undergraduate schools dipped below 40 percent, and as a number of retiring Lutheran faculty members were replaced by fewer Lutherans, the question became more pressing.

A committee on Lutheran character published a 54-page document in August 1992, perhaps the most complete analysis and imaginative set of recommendations on this subject ever produced at VU. It spawned an interesting year's discussion, resulting in about 25 brief faculty essays on the matter, but much of its effort lay dormant, though still usable. In the mid-1990s, a relatively small group of Lutheran faculty calling themselves "Light Lutherans" began to meet regularly with a view toward making the chapel once again "the heart of the University"—to use the words of the provost in his report to the board—as well as promoting critical faith-formation curricular concerns in teaching theology and in mobilizing VU's outstanding artists for the University's mission. Their efforts were welcomed by a board increasingly worried about the Lutheran character of the University; but the group suddenly dissolved, leaving the problems it addressed unresolved.

One of the more visible points of stress was the decline in attendance at the chapel both on Sunday morning and at Morning Prayer, though a variety of special evening services flourished. Both faculty and student habits of attendance at Morning Prayer declined, as activities crowded into the time set aside, though the University held to its historic policy of offering no courses during the daily chapel time. An issue that put additional stress on the chapel program was the question of women presiding at the Eucharist. Several rounds of student and faculty petitions, at first rejected by the board, led to a committee, including distinguished church leaders, that proposed a larger role for the dean of the chapel and a comprehensive study of women's new role in church and society. The president declined the larger proposals but endorsed the idea of having the ELCA sponsor some chapel services with women presiding. Since the fall of 1997, this has been the practice in the chapel, one more step in the long evolution of chapel practices that constantly respond to new needs in a multifaceted and often experimental ministry.

Other strong forces have worked to counteract the centrifugal pressures of the 1990s. Chief among these has been the board, which has strongly promoted VU's academic improvement but has not been content to see it begin to evolve into "just another Princeton." This is a remarkable fact because, unlike many traditional Catholic and Protestant college boards, the clergy has never played a dominant role on the VU board. The large majority of men and women of the board are committed Christian laity who seek to serve the church through Valparaiso University. The VU Guild is even more tenacious in supporting the deep links between academic and churchly aspects of the University.

The University administration also tried to respond to the threats to VU's religious center. It built into the strategic plan clear goals for increasing the percentage of Lutheran students and the number of Lutheran faculty. When the University Senate voted to include antireligious discrimination clauses in the University's legal statements, Harre vetoed it and thus preserved the University's freedom to keep religious identity as a professional qualification.

Equally powerful in promoting the University's identity have been strong initiatives from its constituency. Longtime supporters Oliver and Emma Allen bequeathed more than $4 million through which the Allen Scholars Program might attract top students to professional church service. The new Kade-Duesenberg German House and Cultural Center includes in its program goals the continuing ecumenical relevance of Luther and Bach. Phyllis and Richard Duesenberg have further targeted their multimillion dollar gifts to enable the University to establish three identity-conferring chairs: one for Christian ethics, one for religion and the visual arts, and one to further the Lutheran heritage of music. Other constituents plan major moves to enhance the university's ability to serve Lutheran parochial schools, especially Lutheran high schools. So while there was reason for concern that "the center will not hold," so long as such strong constituents retain their commitments, there will be countervailing forces as well.

The modernization of Valparaiso University's administration and staff, begun under President Huegli, accelerated in the 1980s and intensified in the 1990s as organizational complexity and government regulations increasingly required more expertise and highly competent middle managers. By the end of the 1990s, the University was better poised to deal with its opportunities. The board adopted a new practice of giving the president specific extensions of his appointment. Harre had become a tireless and effective fund-raiser. In due course, new names appeared among the senior administrators: Charley Gillispie became vice president for administration and finance; new deans included Gerald Seeley (engineering), William Moore (business administration), Jay Conison (law), Joseph Cunningham (chapel), David Rowland (graduate studies and continuing education), and Janet Brown (nursing).

The Office of Institutional Advancement, its quarters and staff once again enlarged, was at long last ready to implement a new campaign for $75 million, beginning with the silent phase in the summer of 1998. Named "Three Goals, One Promise," the campaign, under the chairmanship of alumni Richard and Phyllis Duesenberg, aimed to capitalize on the huge increase in wealth potentially available to the University and featured as its centerpiece a visionary Center for Library and Information

Resources. In little more than two years, the campaign already had exceeded its goal.

Observers and faculty members held several points of view as to where Valparaiso University stood as the twenty-first century began. Most agreed that the University appeared to be stronger than ever. The institution was better funded, better equipped, better marketed, and better known than ever before in its history. The administration kept a cool eye on the bottom line and on public relations. More individual faculty members became well-known scholars and artists; several widely recognized scholars and teachers joined the faculty; others chose to go elsewhere. Students of all or no religious traditions were ardently recruited. They were well counseled, had all the amenities that today's uppermiddle-class students required, including spacious computer labs in their residences and superior cuisine in their dining halls. Valparaiso's graduates continued to win major fellowships, to gain admittance to good graduate schools, and to enter successfully a tremendous variety of professions. There was an emerging, though still spotty, excellence in scholarship, with Valparaiso resembling more than ever the top regional private universities.

Others remembered another vision of Valparaiso University, beholding itself as a Christian community gathered for academic work in the worldwide context of politics and the professions, ideas and the arts, and the life of the church. Welcoming the many improvements in quality and knowing the price of survival, they wondered if that price was too high: the impairment of an effectively Lutheran form of higher education. They remembered a much stronger "culture faculty," as Martin Marty called them—those who showed up at concerts and public lectures and who related their work to that of others in the public dialogue that defines any distinctive institution. They noted that the dwindling numbers of Lutherans among the faculty, administration, and student body are matched by a dramatic reduction of interaction with the churchly constituencies of the University, a distancing from the struggles of the Lutheranism that mothered and sustained VU. They miss the depth of scholarship in areas such as Reformation studies that once marked the Valparaiso tradition. Except for certain islands, such as the chapel program, Christ College, the excellent musical organizations, *The Cresset*, and Soul Purpose, religion was present but no longer central. It appeared to be just one option among many attractive features the University offers in its quest to serve the needs and comforts of middle-class students. In a multicultural world, moreover, it was easy for Christianity to take its place as just one more cultural option, an "add-on" that carefully avoids anything that might give even the appearance of offense to anyone. Thus, it is subtly secularized.

A balanced judgment would reject either an overly simple view of decline from past glories or a complacent satisfaction with present achievements. It is easy to underestimate the power of the postmodern world, with its fragmentation and centrifugal forces. It is easy to underestimate the task of finding faculty and administrative talent with the rare combination of abilities and interests that Valparaiso's vision requires. It is also possible to overlook the rich, informal networks of friendship among students, faculty, and alumni that form a significant component of the Christian quest at VU.

While the Lilly Fellows Program in the Humanities and Arts has certainly taken the intellectual lead at VU in probing the relationship between faith and learning, the current renewal of the arts has, in many ways, set the pace for maintaining and enlarging the Christian and Lutheran heritage while simultaneously elevating the quality of its work. John Steven Paul's work in religious drama now draws support from his occupancy of the newly activated W. C. Dickmeyer Chair in Christian Education. The music department goes from strength to strength. While exploring many different musical traditions, it always provides a rich fare of Lutheran masters. The department is especially committed to promoting the understanding and performance of Johann Sebastian Bach, led by internationally recognized artistic performer and musical conductor Christopher Cock. As part of the music department's program in the spring of 2001, Maestro Helmut Rilling directed the University's musicians—comprised mostly of talented student performers—in a memorable performance of Bach's *St. Matthew Passion.* Bach scholars, students, and ordinary music lovers packed the chapel for this notable event, a fitting conclusion for the year in which the celebration of 75 years of Lutheran ownership sought to renew and revitalize the intellectual and religious heritage of Valparaiso University.

The experience of many visitors is similar to that of the North Central Association examiners in 1998 who were struck by the Lutheran character of the University and expressed their satisfaction in their favorable report. Valparaiso is a leader within that minority of the more than 3,600 American institutions of higher learning that seek to engage the problems of the late twentieth century from a Christian standpoint. As recently as 1999, Professor Alvin Kernan of Princeton observed that among America's elite colleges, as well as many others less favored, the pervasive climate emanating from the humanities and social science departments is one of meaninglessness and breakdown. Such a description cannot be applied to Valparaiso University. It remains an institution where faculty, staff, and students still attempt to see things "in Thy light."

CONCLUSION

INTO THE NEW MILLENNIUM

In the millennial year 2000, Valparaiso University celebrated its 75th year as a Lutheran university. Like all such anniversaries, it was an occasion for both reflection on the past and dedication to the future. Whatever else it may have been, the marking of a significant moment in history is also a part of the process whereby institutions, like individuals, look back to understand and interpret where it has been so it can think more clearly about where it should go in the years ahead.

The fact that the modern Valparaiso University grew up literally on the soil of two earlier higher education ventures—the Valparaiso Male and Female College and the Brown-Kinsey Valparaiso University—makes the history of this University unusual and diverse. Perhaps the affinity for rhetoric and theater that runs throughout VU's history created the taste for dramatic plots, surprising reversals, and colorful characters on the campus. In any case, through its many and various forms, Valparaiso University has incorporated much of the history of what "college" has meant in American society during the previous 140 years.

There were few direct continuities of mission and purpose between the old VU and the Lutheran Valparaiso University that assumed its name and grew up in its place, though some parallel intentions do appear. The emphasis of the Brown-Kinsey institution on providing advanced learning to people of limited economic means was explicit and shaped central features of the enterprise. The Lutheran leaders of VU, though operating from a central religious understanding, also made this university an important vehicle of advancement for the sons and daughters of immigrants who were, until the last quarter century, not particularly well off. There were no multimillionaires at the Lutheran foundation, and it was the contributions of many devout members of the church that kept the institution going for most of the decades of its existence.

Yet if Valparaiso University has never served a particularly elite or wealthy constituency, it has nevertheless been an ambitious institution. In its own way, Brown's "Poor Man's Harvard" operated in a large national arena and in its heyday achieved wide recognition as an extraordinary U.S. institution of its kind. Similarly, the Lutheran founders of VU and their successors were visionaries who planned a university that would, they hoped, take its place among the best universities and make a singular contribution to U.S. society as well as the life of the church. Not content with creating another denominational college, these founders envisioned bringing the particular traditions and accents of Lutheran Christianity onto a wide stage where they could engage the broadest forces of learning, religion, culture, and society. The fact that ambitions always outran resources, pushing lofty goals further into the future, does not alter the importance of visionary thinking in the history of Valparaiso University.

Besides these broad continuities, this account has attempted to locate the story of VU within several important historical contexts. Each context helps to show how the institution unfolded as it did and to explain some of the important forces that affected the leaders and people who have shaped the modern Valparaiso. Perhaps the most important of these contexts is the general course of American history and, in particular, the history of U.S. higher education. VU's history also has been shaped by the changing culture of student life and by the various roles that college has played in the lives of young people. Finally, far more than most institutions, the history of VU has been affected by religious factors, especially by Lutheranism in general and The Lutheran Church—Missouri Synod in particular.

The influence of the general history of the United States on VU is obvious but should not be forgotten. The reader of this account of VU's past can readily discern how events and forces affecting the society as a whole left their mark on this institution. Wars, depressions, technological changes, suburban affluence, cultural rebellions, changes in the family, the women's movement—these and other national developments were important in shaping VU's history. To cite only obvious examples, the crisis of World War I contributed to both the collapse of the old VU and the determination of some German Lutherans to enter into the mainstream of U.S. culture. Similarly, the extraordinary post-World War II affluence, together with government policies, enabled Valparaiso University to build its student body, faculty, and physical plant without a large endowment while the state of the economy beginning in the 1970s forced significant adjustments in institutional priorities and campus character.

This study also has attempted to locate VU's history within the context of the rapidly changing history of U.S. higher education. The mid-nineteenth century world of tiny classical-Christian colleges in which the VMFC was born is incredibly far removed from the dawning twenty-first century environment of mass higher education, encompassing millions of students as part of an enormous "industry," in which Valparaiso University now operates and competes. A college education, once a rare achievement that marked its possessor as an accomplished and socially respected person, is now practically another "consumer good" that the vast U.S. middle class takes as part of its birthright.

The Brown-Kinsey VU was, for a time, a strikingly appealing populist and popular institution of learning before it clearly failed to keep up with changes in the academic world. The immigrant Lutheran VU, whose first president still spoke with a German accent, was initially a vehicle by which a highly distinctive ethnic and religious subculture adapted to the wider culture and its opportunities. Eventually, it would have to face the question of whether it had perhaps over-adapted to certain values of American society and, even more dangerously, to the powerful drift of a particular academic ideology that, for more than a century, has dominated U.S. higher education. Some Lutherans at VU were aware, as many in the wider culture were not, that this academic culture had displaced an older alternative tradition, one that has far more affinities to the Christian intellectual tradition.

As serious flaws in the standard U.S. academic culture have become more apparent, some of that earlier academic tradition's values are being recovered and taken up with a new intellectual rigor and sense of relevance to the modern age. At Valparaiso, this has generated revived attention to issues such as the concept of vocation in relation to liberal and professional education, religious commitment and ecumenical spirit, undergraduate teaching and faculty professionalism, and student life and character formation. It also has generated conversation around broad intellectual issues, such as examining American culture and considering how to expand the ways of knowing to include religious wisdom. The Lutheran Valparaiso University's history of standing somewhat outside the mainstream of the dominant culture, while still attempting to be engaged with it, may help explain why it has presented a fertile ground for such questions to grow.

This study also has paid more attention than is usual in such accounts to the history of student life. Oddly enough, it is easy for administrators and faculty to forget the experience of students on their campuses. There is a difference between what a faculty may propose and how students dispose. This history has shown how U.S. students in general, and VU students in particular, have in effect made the college experience something *they* have shaped for their own purposes and goals. In this complex process, the continuities of "college life" have operated in a complicated interaction with general historical changes of lifestyles, class, culture, religion, and moral values to shape the history of life on the campus. This has been particularly so for women, for whom the changing contexts of college life, from severe constraint to liberation, have been especially important. While Valparaiso University students probably have been somewhere in the "middle" of most such collegiate developments, its particular constituency and character also have given distinctive twists to the general trends in American undergraduate life.

Finally, the history of the post-1925 Valparaiso University is plainly connected with the history of U.S. religion and, in particular, with that of the Lutheran Church. As was noted in chapter 5, the modern Valparaiso was founded as part of a modernizing movement within a large German-immigrant church body, The Lutheran Church—Missouri Synod. In its vision, purposes, and people, the Lutheran VU's history has been closely linked with the history of that church, though in complex ways. As one significant way in which originally immigrant Lutherans opened themselves to wider intellectual and cultural worlds, Valparaiso was an important crucible of both new identities and social change for Lutherans. As a "progressive" institution historically related to a largely conservative denomination, VU has sometimes puzzled and challenged those who try to fit it into ordinary classifications. While open to wider worlds, it has not simply accommodated them but has in its own way attempted to bring values from the Lutheran heritage into deeper engagement within increasingly wider environments.

The larger history of Valparaiso's relations with the Missouri Synod, and with other Lutherans and Christians, remains to be written. Clearly, VU has affected not only thousands of individuals connected with the LCMS, but also its institutions and other church-related efforts as well. This history has shown that, whatever its difficulties, the fact of taking faith seriously as a foundation for higher education, especially at a time when not many looked favorably on such endeavors, has been a source of institutional interest and strength for both the University and the church. From the religious vision comes an academic vocation and a restlessness that seeks nothing less than the highest excellence in scholarship and teaching that an academic community can achieve. Academic excellence, like excellence in any worthy human endeavor, pleases God.

Sixty years ago, President O. P. Kretzmann set before Valparaiso University the task of making the Christian intellectual and moral vision relevant to the life of the whole University and through it to public and personal life. His inaugural address has become a classic expression of the perennial relevance of an impossible educational ideal, one that will never triumph but contains the power of truth and that responds to the longing for such an ideal. It is still relevant because it judges present achievements, points to ever new possibilities, and leads to humility because no generation ever achieves the ideal—though, in retrospect, one can see that it could have come much closer.

Three themes from Kretzmann's address are enduring. The first stresses the pursuit of the whole truth, down many paths and apart from considerations of immediate usefulness. The physicist has his way and the poet hers. Christian higher education finds here one single reality bound into a common truth, the total human drama in its cosmic setting.

The meaning of this drama is given in the Christian creed, which becomes the working hypothesis of the University, giving a shape to the whole enterprise. As a human effort, it is exploratory, partial, pluralistic, and open to correction and new possibilities. The breakdown of various Catholic and Reformed attempts to produce grand syntheses of faith and learning suggests restraint in talking about large totalities of knowledge. Yet thoughtful people find peril in specialists' activities that proceed without regard for the wider community of knowledge, and they question whether one can understand the parts of knowledge—which certainly have their own integrity—apart from some knowledge of the whole. Therefore, the collegial probes and intellectual pilgrimages among the disciplines continue to be a crucial imperative for colleges connected to the Christian church, which must always be oriented to the whole truth.

A second theme of Kretzmann's classic address stresses conflict. The Christian faith sees life as a drama, one that certainly includes intellectual conflict. In the modern world, Christian colleges constitute a partly adversarial subculture within the dominant academic culture, requiring at various times critique, retrieval, transformation, or reappropriation. Christian intellectual leaders today see the realm of culture itself as a field of conflict. A searching critique of much contemporary culture discloses its threats to human dignity—in technology, media, law, politics, education, and elsewhere. These developments have given a new priority to the retrieval of the most humane elements of our civilization, which bears the imprint of biblical tradition in every domain. Cultural creativity is also part of this new mandate. For example, the great Lutheran college choirs have kept alive the culture of faith by presenting the finest from this rich musical tradition, seeking to extend it as well. In the humanities, students struggle to find a true understanding of life's meaning in dialogue with humanity's long reflection on such questions. In science and professional studies, they acquire knowledge to change and improve life. Further, as Jaroslav Pelikan has written, the modern university is in the forefront of the struggle against war, famine, disease, environmental disaster, and ignorance. Truth is not neutral, but it calls forth response and engagement.

Third, there is the focus on students, the bearers of the future. The continuing unraveling of the secular moral consensus confronts Christian campuses with a new cultural task. How can young adults learn to think and live as competent modern Christians? Can an ethos be created through carefully crafted rules, practices, discourse, and example? Can faculty and professionals serving students convey a winning account of the Christian moral ideal, suggesting possibilities rather than prescriptions? Can freedom, civility, service, integrity, campus citizenship, and social life be grounded in the Christian moral tradition rather than in atomistic individualism? Can students come to hold "success" and the use of power and money accountable to purposes higher than mere acquisitiveness?

As Valparaiso enters the global and pluralistic twenty-first century, there is no question of recreating sixteenth-century Wittenberg, the nineteenth-century classical Christian college, or 1950s VU. History cannot be recycled. But a powerful living tradition, such as Lutheran Christianity in a university setting, can continue to engage the church and the wider culture, justifying the hopes of its founders and the community that sustains it.

Perhaps, therefore, the most arduous but promising tasks still lie ahead for those colleges and universities in the Christian intellectual tradition, including Valparaiso University. They can fulfill that promise by collaborating in the service of their nation, the new global society, the worldwide communities of learning and of Christian faith, and by graduating men and women who are faithful members of the Church of Christ, as well as self-critical citizens of the world.

APPENDIX A

Members of the Valparaiso University Board of Directors

Herman A. Duemling 1925–27
John C. Baur 1925–27
W. Charles Dickmeyer 1925–66
Charles J. Scheimann 1925
Martin H. Luecke 1925–32
Paul F. Miller 1925–51
George F. Schutes 1925–26
Herman E. Sievers 1925–26
William D. Holterman 1925–28
H. D. Mensing 1925–27
Martin F. Kretzmann 1926
Harry A. Eberline 1926–44
Louis A. Linn 1926–28
Peter W. Meyn 1926–31
Otto C. Lemke 1926–28
Fred H. Wehrenberg 1926–51
Oscar C. Kreinheder 1926–39, 1929–39*
Ralph E. Richman 1926–32
William H. T. Dau 1926–29*
Henry A. Dahlen 1927–43
Edward W. Jaeger 1927–58
Ludwig Holland-Letz 1927–29
George F. Nolde 1927–33
Henry F. Rohrmann 1927–34
William F. Boeger 1928–43
Herbert H. Hackstedde 1928–34
Louis J. Sieck 1928–38
Henry J. Neils 1928–34
Otto Misch 1929–32
Walter A. Maier 1930–43
George H. Letz 1931–36
G. Christian Barth 1932–48
Ernest J. Gallmeyer 1932–37, 1945–71
Henry F. Moellering 1932–36
Henry L. Ulbrich 1933–41
Louis Nuechterlein 1934–40
John A. Sauerman 1934–66
Otto A. Geiseman 1934–46
William H. Kroeger 1934–36
Charles J. F. Staerker 1936–44
Paul Klitzke 1936–40
Robert C. Moellering 1936–83
Martin A. Salvner 1938–39
Paul A. Amling 1938–67
Edward W. Marquardt 1939–48
Harold F. Lichtsinn 1940–81
Edwin T. Bernthal 1940–50
Werner Duemling 1940–44
O. P. Kretzmann 1940–68*
Paul E. Rupprecht 1942–68
Alex O. Benz 1943–52, 1959–67
Henry W. Graebner 1943–46

Edwin F. Dittmer 1944–60
John A. Fleischli 1945–68
Leo L. Hardt 1946–67
Anton E. Horst 1946–52
Walter H. Gross 1948–70
Fred Strieter 1948–52
Richard E. Meier 1950–80
Anne Hansen 1950–51**
Gilbert W. Krause 1950–51***, 1952–79
Richard A. Jesse 1951–57
Paul H. Brandt 1951–94
Walter R. Schur 1951–53***, 1959***, 1970–99
Viola Birner 1951–54**
Dean A. Arnold 1952–68
Raymond A. Wolff 1953–55***
Louise Drews 1954–57**
Frederick A. Reddel Sr. 1955–77
Herbert E. Steinbach 1955–57***
Bernard H. Hemmeter 1957–78
Mabel Frank 1957–60**
Paul E. Nieter 1958***
Edwin A. Kurtz 1959–66
Leonhard C. Heine 1959–69
Norman F. Luekens 1959–75
Richard C. Oster 1959–90
Harry G. Barr 1960–84
Alfred J. W. LeBien 1960–72
Irma Schmalz 1960–63**
Oscar R. Boock 1960***
Julius W. Acker 1961***
Louis A. Jacobs 1962–63***
Sylvia Wismar 1963–66**
Richard E. Pell 1963–64***
John Bolgert 1965–67***
Clarence A. Kelley 1966–77
Edwin H. Koeneman 1966–84
Ewald H. Mueller 1966–91
William H. Zuehlke Jr. 1966–76
Arnold K. Weber 1966–71
Wilma Jacobs 1966–68**
William R. Tatman 1968–86
James W. Chester 1968–74
Fred L. Kuhlmann 1968–73
Bette A. Froehlich 1968–70**
Arthur T. Wellman 1968–70***
Albert G. Huegli 1968–78*
Alfred E. Jordan 1970–87
Lynn Bahls 1970–72**
Paul G. Fleck 1971–83
John P. Schroeder 1971–73***
Dorothy Schoknecht 1972–78
Beata Madoerin 1972–74**
Willard A. Richardson 1974–94
Douglas R. Seltz 1974–90
L. Jane Lichtfuss 1974–76**
Charles F. Lembke 1974–76***
Joseph W. Bibler 1975–89
Arnold G. Busse 1976–99
Jacqueline S. Jungemann . . .1976–78**
Harold G. Bernthal 1977–89
Richard W. Duesenberg 1977–
Rupert Dunklau 1977–
Edward E. Busse 1977–79***
Otis R. Bowen 1978–84
Eleanora K. Pennekamp 1978–93
Barbara J. Maas 1978–80**
Robert V. Schnabel 1978–88*
Gerhard M. Freche 1979–92
Florence Montz 1979–82

Donald L. Baeder 1980–85
August F. Bernthal 1980–2000
Ruth E. Russler . . . 1980–82**, 1985–96
Peter L. Krentz 1980***, 1983***
Charles H. Foelber 1981–91
Elmer P. Simon 1981–90
Don F. Heckler . . 1981–82***, 1986–93
Virginia E. Amling 1982–84**
Dixon W. Benz 1983–91
Herbert F. Stride III 1983–
William R. Heerman 1984–93
Martha Mattes 1984–86**
Walter J. Kretzmann 1984–85***
Lane B. Hoffman 1985–
Gerald E. Pelzer 1985–99
Caroline M. Collings 1986–93
Frederick G. Kraegel 1986–96, 1997–
Phyllis Schuessler 1986–88**
Arnold A. Hilgenkamp 1986–87***
Victor J. Dankis 1987–
David J. Hessler 1987–
Marilyn L. Krueger 1988–90**
Susan R. Steinbruecker 1988–89***
Alan F. Harre 1988–*
Al A. Meitz 1989–95
Harley W. Snyder 1989–
Richard E. Beumer 1990–
James C. McGill 1990–
Paula A. Sauer 1990–92**
Katharine E. Gerken 1990–91***
Howard J. Claussen 1991–
Charles E. Niemier 1991–
Jon R. Schumacher 1991–
William G. Thompson 1991–
Joel R. Wilson 1991–
Carl A. Brauer Jr. 1992–
Donald V. Fites 1992–
Christa R. Klein 1992–
William B. Wehrenberg 1992–
Barbara E. Riethmeier 1992–94**
Susan P. Rosborough 1992–93***
Charles W. Dull 1993–
Paul R. Manske 1993–
James W. Mueller 1993–
John W. Shelton 1993–
Connie Busse Ashline 1994–
Richard C. Vie 1994–
Jane C. Wittlinger 1994–
Beverly D. Wick 1994–96**
Heather C. McGill 1994–95***
Robert H. Duesenberg 1995–
Paul D. Schrage 1996–
Margaret A. Zobel 1996–98**
Christine M. Zrinsky 1996–97***
Charles S. Mueller Jr. 1997–
Steven M. Hronec 1998–
Lorraine E. Dorough 1998–2000**
R. Razz Jenkins 1998–99***
Jay W. Christopher 1999–
Steven W. Parks 1999–
Susan P. Hooker 2000–
Mark R. Ennes 2000–***
Karl A. Kreft 2000–
Judy F. Mason 2000–**

**Ex officio member as University president*
***Member as Guild president*
****Member as Alumni Association president*

APPENDIX B

ALUMNI ASSOCIATION PRESIDENTS

Leonard Schramm
Class of 1931 (deceased 1986) 1934–35

Walter A. Christopher
Class of 1934 (deceased 1994)
. . . . .1937–38, 1942

Robert C. Moellering
Class of 1933 1939

A. John Briel
Class of 1934 1940–41

Clarence H. Ott
Class of 1940 1943–44

Robert H. Peper
Class of 1937 1945

Herbert H. Freise
Class of 1939, 1941 1946

Vernon W. Reich
Class of 1933 1947–48

Gilbert W. Krause
Class of 1947 1949–50

Walter R. Schur
Class of 1935 . . . . .1951–52, 1959

Raymond A. Wolff
Class of 1935, 1937 1953–54

Herbert E. Steinbach
Class of 1935 1955–57

Paul R. Nieter
Class of 1950 1958

Oscar R. Boock
Class of 1948 1960

Julius W. (J. W.) Acker
Class of 1931 (deceased 1979) 1961

Louis A. Jacobs
Class of 1940 1962

Richard E. Pell
Class of 1950 (deceased 1966) 1963–64

John Bolgert
Class of 1947, 1950 1965–67

Arthur T. Wellman
Class of 1933 (deceased 1996)
. 1968–70

John P. Schroeder
Class of 1952 1971–73

Charles F. Lembke
Class of 1954 1974–76

Edward E. Busse
Class of 1947 1977–79

Peter L. Krentz
Class of 1954, 1956 . . . . .1980, 1983

Don F. Heckler
Class of 1956 1981–82

Walter J. Kretzmann
Class of 1972 1984–85

Arnold A. Hilgenkamp
Class of 1959 1986–87

Susan R. Steinbruecker
Class of 1974 1988–89

Katharine E. Gerken
Class of 1979 1990–91

Susan P. Rosborough
Class of 1978 1992–93

Heather C. McGill
Class of 1981 1994–95

Christine M. Zrinsky
Class of 1986 1996–97

R. Razz Jenkins
Class of 1977 1998–99

Mark Ennes
Class of 1974 2000

Abbreviations

ALC	Associated Lutheran Charities
ALL	American Luther League
CHI	Concordia Historical Institute
CHIQ	*The Concordia Historical Institute Quarterly*
ELCA	Evangelical Lutheran Church in America
LCMS	The Lutheran Church—Missouri Synod
LDA	Lutheran Deaconess Association
LHRAA	Lutheran Human Relations Association of America
LUA	The Lutheran University Association
LW	*The Lutheran Witness*
NINS	Northern Indiana Normal School
NLEA	National Lutheran Education Association
PCV	*The Porter County Vidette*
R.G.	Research Group (VU Archives)
VMFC	Valparaiso Male and Female College
WCA	*Western Christian Advocate*

Notes on Sources

Chapter 1: A Methodist College in the Vale of Paradise

The discussion of society and religion in the early American Republic draws on the work of Nathan Hatch, which has deepened considerably our understanding of the resurgence of evangelicalism after the Revolutionary War. The story of the academy movement in Indiana has been illumined by Albert Mock. George Manhart's history of DePauw University includes material on the Methodist role in education and the competition with the Presbyterians. George Salin's dissertation describes the foundation of academies and colleges in Northwest Indiana by the Methodists, including material on curriculum, governance, and student life. Also useful was Timothy Smith's work on midwestern evangelical colleges and Daniel Boorstin's chapter on "booster" college founding. The first board president of the VMFC, the Rev. John Smith, provided a valuable account of the college's beginnings. On women's education in the nineteenth century, Barbara Solomon is especially insightful. The capstone courses and their ethical and cultural context are covered by Don Meyer. The other sources for this chapter are in the VU Archives, including many reproductions of articles from local newspapers (beginning with the Valparaiso *Republic*) available in microfilm at the Valparaiso Public Library. The archives also include most of the college catalogs and the student-edited *Monitor*. Thomas Harding provided a useful background for understanding the VMFC's literary societies. The quotation on spooning is from Mock, p. 141. Brokner's report is from *WCA*, 24 April 1861. Other reports are in *WCA*, 24 July 1861; 8 January 1862; 20 July 1864; and 17 August 1870. The perspective on evangelical colleges presented here relies on the work of Mark Noll.

Chapter 2: The Firm of Brown and Kinsey

The discussion of American higher education after the Civil War relies on the work of Roger L. Geiger, whose article on multipurpose colleges includes valuable bibliographical references to the other research. The history of the Folsom Business College and its successors is found in the historical commemoration booklet of Dyke College, pp. 7–8, in the VU Brauer Art Museum's reference collection. Research efforts by the staff of the Ohio Historical Society could find no trace of Northwestern Normal at Republic, Ohio. However, Sarah Lehr Kennedy provides information that a group of teachers formed a normal school by renting a local academy building for the few years it existed before moving to Fostoria, then to Ada, Ohio, as part of what eventually became Ohio Northern University. The discussion of the National Normal at Lebanon is based on Karl J. Kay's history, Alfred Holbrooke's memoirs, and several articles in the files of the Lebanon Public Library. Louis Bartelt's unfinished manuscript and notes have enhanced the discussion of the early history of the Valparaiso law school.

The letters of Harvey Hatch, provided by alumnus Attorney Roger Burrus, along with other student correspondence, are in R.G. 1, Old School, Student Correspondence. The Norris quotation on his laundry (pp. 52–53) is from Leif, pp. 37–38. The L.U.N. account is found in Norris's autobiography and several biographies. O. P. Kinsey's political prediction is reported in Neuberger and Kalan, p. 16. In the early 1900s, a 504-page "novel," *East Hall*, written by NINS alumnus J. M. Traughber under the pseudonym Hubert Gar, appeared and provided an account of student life at the college in the 1880s. From this source, Simone Baepler wrote an analysis of student life at NINS which, when corroborated from other sources, has been drawn on for this account. Her extended memo is in the VU Archives. Baldwin's archival file (R.G. 1, Old School, Faculty and Staff) contains some speculative information on her relationship with Brown. John Strietelmeier concurs with the point of view taken here, based on reliable oral tradition. On Brown's business interests, see the Valparaiso *Messenger*, 12 May 1904, the Brown file in the VU Archives, and Strietelmeier, p. 43. The *Messenger* article cited on p. 60 is from 4 November 1897.

CHAPTER 3: VALPARAISO MAKES ITS MARK

The *Chicago Record-Herald* (7 June 1901), the *Boston Evening Transcript* (2 December 1903), the *New York Herald* (8 May 1904), *McLure's Magazine* (March 1908), and *Colliers* (14 March 1914) contain major stories on Valparaiso. The 33rd Annual Catalog (1906) emphasizes the culture and refinement of the student body and, for the first time, lists the faculty with their degrees. Richard Matre's history of Loyola University includes information (not always accurate) about the medical and dental schools acquired from Valparaiso. Most of the archival material on the medical college is in the subject matter file, Chicago College of Medicine and Surgery. This includes a copy of the famous Flexner report, as well as the AMA's own middle ranking of the college. Copies of *The American* and *The Bur*, the medical and dental college papers, are in R.G. 1, Publications, Old School, nos. 1 and 2 respectively. The text of the law catalog reveals faculty disputes regarding the introduction of the case method. This is also the view of historian Robert Stevens, p. 62. Dean Bowman's discussion of the progress of the law school is in the 1916–17 catalog.

The discussion of "college life" draws on the work of Helen Lefkowitz Horowitz in *College Life*. Descriptions of student life at VU are pieced together from archival material, especially the annuals, the *Record*, and *The Torch*. A full account of one violent "rampage" is found in *PCV*, 16 April 1913. See also *The Torch*, April 1915. Copies of the *Socialist Educator* are filed in the folder of alumnus and faculty member Ira Tilton (R.G. 1, Old School, Alumni Biographies). *The Torch*, 21 April 1922, notes the newsreel accounts of the Straw Hat Parade. VU students' teaching of English to immigrants in Gary is reported by the *Gary Post-Tribune*, 5 August 1921. The description of college women in the 1900s is taken from Solomon, p. 94 ff. The story of Petra Dahl, including quotations from Williams and *PCV*, are from Beatty's article, based in part on the Dahl papers. The "I decided ..." quote (pp. 77–78) is found in Christowe, pp. 186–87. Balzekas's story is recounted in Van Reenan, pp. 66–67. The discussion of Borodin, Krasnow, and Bolotin is drawn from Dan N. Jacobs's work, VU archival records on these men, and the Hall study. Stimpson's search for VU alumni in Washington is recounted in his letter (20 April 1922) to Mrs. Roessler, which is found in Roessler's personal papers (R.G. 1, Old School, Faculty and Staff). Material on Lowell Thomas in the archives is voluminous (R.G. 1, Old School, Alumni). Further information is from Thomas's autobiography, pp. 65–66. The best biography of Smith is by Jeansonne. Together with Smith's archival file (R.G. 1, Old School, Alumni), the biography is the major source for this discussion. The Mencken quote is from Brinkley, p. 173.

The discussion of Brown's stormy tenure on the NEA's Board of Trustees is based on the minutes of the NEA's annual meetings; the Butler-Brown correspondence (courtesy of Columbia University Archives), secured by VU Archivist Daniel Gahl; Wesley's history of the NEA; Schmid's dissertation; and Ella Flagg Young's biography by Joan K. Smith. The Haley quotation (pp. 86–87) is from p. 225 of an early draft of Haley's memoirs (26 August 1931), which was found in the Chicago Historical Society, Chicago Teachers Federation Files, Box 34. For Pearse's letter to Haley (14 January 1911), see Chicago Historical Society, Chicago Teachers Federation Files, Box 41. See also Gillan to Haley (17 January 1911), Chicago Historical Society, Chicago Teachers Federation Files, Box 41.

CHAPTER 4: DECLINE AND CRISIS

This account of student life is based on the *Record* and *The Torch*, while *PCV*, 21 March 1917, highlighted the first dance in the gymnasium led by the Kinseys. The relationship between colleges and the war effort has been masterfully studied by Roger Geiger in *To Advance Knowledge*, p. 94 ff. The local newspapers carefully chronicled the activities of soldiers as they filled the residence halls and became part of the town-gown scene. *PCV*, 11 June 1919, published the notice of the dissolution of the Brown-Kinsey firm. The discussion of Keogan and early VU football draws heavily on Murray Sperber's history of Notre Dame football (especially p. 42 ff.), Tim Neely's history of

Notre Dame basketball (especially p. 37 ff), and Neil D. Isaacs's basketball history. Notice of the student Klan organization and its proclivities is in *The Torch*, 14 November 1920. A copy of Judge Rush's judgment, entered 25 June 1920, is in R.G. 1, Old School, Brown-Evans. Details on the Roe trial for violation of Prohibition and the dispute with Brown are in the *Chicago Tribune*, 30 March 1921 and 3 April 1921. The discussion of the Hodgdon year is drawn from the newspapers, *The Torch*, Stimpson, and relevant archives, including the Hodgdon files, R.G. 1, Old School, Brown-Evans. The North Central report is in the same file box. On Roessler's attitude when resigning, see Roessler-Brothers, 21 April 1922 (R.G. 1, Old School, Faculty and Staff). On the postwar period, see Geiger, "The Collegiate Syndrome," in *To Advance Knowledge*, p. 115 ff.

There is a great deal of literature on the Klan of this period. Kathleen Mahoney directed me to Dyer's article on Lanier University. Lance Trusty's article provides a well-researched, well-documented basis for understanding the Klan-VU episode and has guided this discussion. The role of women in the Klan, together with some fresh understandings of the movement in Indiana, has been elaborated recently by Kathleen Bliss. The Evans to Muldoon letter (25 August 1923), seeking to calm the dean, is in R.G. 1, Old School, Brown-Evans. Only four days earlier, a distressed Catherine Corboy had written that Muldoon would be automatically dropped because he was Catholic (Corboy-Grandgeorge, 21 August 1923, R.G. 1, Old School, Brown-Evans). The quotes from the *New Republic* are from the 5 September 1923 issue. The quotation from Governor Blaine is from Blaine-Evans, 4 January 1924 (R.G. 1, Old School, Brown-Evans).

CHAPTER 5: THE VALPARAISO MOVEMENT

The literature on the history of the LCMS is substantial. My discussion depends on writers such as Forster, Mundinger, Lueking, W. Baepler, and Todd but especially on Alan Graebner. Carol Coburn has written a most interesting recent study on one community of Missouri Synod Lutherans seen over several generations. Her work also contains an excellent bibliography. James Albers's article in *CHIQ*, 27 May 1972, demonstrates the communal social care exercised by the immigrant Lutheran churches.

Carl Meyer, p. 63, refers to the original hopes for a university. Jon Pahl provides much information on the history of the Walther League, while Carol Coburn provides fascinating insight into young girls' voting and their lives in the Walther League as significant in their maturation and acculturation. Josie Ax is seen by Ruth Fritz Meyer (p. 56) in light of the (prefeminist) women's movement in the LCMS. Dean Lueking's *Century of Caring* describes the ALC and its efforts, including the referenced picture on p. 136. James Albers's dissertation documents the history of shifting opinions on the morality of life in a capitalist culture, including the issue of Missouri Synod members charging interest on loans. O. H. Pannkoke's opinionated autobiography is a valuable source of information on the quadricentennial and the founding of VU, though it needs corroboration at times from other sources. Richard Solberg's reference to Pannkoke is on p. 289. The impact of Fritz's move to St. Louis, and his collaboration with Graebner in the rejuvenation of Concordia Seminary, is in Carl Meyer, p. 179. Schoenfeld's remarkable paper was published, together with Graebner's response, in the *Theological Quarterly* (July 1919). Holst's article is on p. 298 of *LW* 39 (14 September 1920). The history of ALL is presented by Fred Vonderlage. Gallmeier's recollections are part of the Oral History Program in the VU Archives recorded on 24 July 1975. The quote from J. W. Miller is based on Karl Henrichs's recollection of Miller's pro-Valparaiso speeches; it also comes from the 24 July 1975 recording. The account of the convocation celebrating the Lutheran purchase, including the Holst quotation, is reported in *PCV,* 24 July 1925. The documents relating to the initial campaign are in R.G. 2, Board of Trustees, VUA-LUA, Acquisition of Valparaiso University. Much information on the synodical reaction can be found in CHI, Valparaiso Papers, Box I, especially in the correspondence of the secretary of the Synod's board of directors, the Rev. Martin F. Kretzmann. Much archival information on the beginnings of VU was analyzed by Lois (Sohn) Glock; her analysis is available in the VU Archives. Dau's correspondence in the VU Archives is the basis for the discussion of his reaction to the call. His reports to the board, included in the board's minutes, are the basis for most of his observations and complaints. Fritz's notice is in *LW*, 9 February 1926. On the need for a much larger endowment, see Baur to Eberline, 11 October 1926, "Board University Appeal 1925–26," R.G., Board of Trustees, VUA-LUA, Acquisition of Valparaiso University. The Klan-like club is referred to in *The Torch*, 25 May 1927, and in Strietelmeier, p. 98. Dau's enumeration of rumors and his reply are in *The Torch*, 4 May 1927. The description of Kroencke is from a Walter Buescher letter in the VU Archives. The accreditation report is on file in the archives. *PCV,* 16 April 1929, reports on the congratulatory telegrams. *PCV,* 17 April 1929, gives a detailed account of the celebratory dinner, including Dickmeyer's speech. Disappointment with Dau's administrative ineptitude is voiced in several pieces of correspondence among leading VU supporters. See especially M. F. Kretzmann to Lankenau, 20 March 1928, in CHI, Valparaiso University, Box I.

CHAPTER 6: HOLDING ON IN HARD TIMES

The campaign literature is in the VU Archives. The complaints from the Synod's officials and others are reflected in the M. F. Kretzmann materials, CHI, Valparaiso University, Box I. The record of the Kreinheder inaugural is in R.G. 4, Presidents, Kreinheder Addresses. Faculty publications during the decade are summed up in *The Torch*, 2 March 1939. The Washington committee is discussed in *The Torch*, 20 April 1933. The faculty minutes contain a copy of the letter. Ronald Numbers, pp. 274–75, describes the early developments in A. H. Meyer's life. The Graebner quote is from a letter, Graebner-Leimer, 30 November 1938, in CHI, Graebner Papers, Box VI. Meyer's desire for a unitary focus is expressed in a letter to O. P. Kretzmann quoted in Numbers, p. 275. Meyer's desire for a synthesis is expressed in an article he wrote for college students of the Missouri Synod in the Gamma Delta *Spectator*, undated but probably written in the 1930s. A copy is in A. H. Meyer's file (R.G. 6, Faculty, Biographical). The monographs from the summer workshops in 1933 and 1935 were entitled *Studies in Lutheran Higher Education*, vol. 1, nos. 1 and 2. The discussion of the origins of the women's organizations in the Synod is based on A. Graebner, pp. 138 ff., and Ruth Fritz Meyer, pp. 70 ff. The quotation regarding VU as the "spark" is on p. 97 of Meyer. The account of the 1935 graduation is from Walter Buescher.

"Dancing is a sin per se" is quoted from an executive committee report to VU's board concerning VU-synodical committee meetings, 19 February 1938 and 23 March 1938. Dau's turnaround on the dancing issue is clear in his essay "Concerning Chaperoned or Supervised Dancing at Valparaiso University," which was published in 17 June 1942 and is available in R.G. 11, Student Affairs. By the mid-1940s, the *Lutheran Witness* became silent on the dancing issue. The message for the students is from *The Torch*, September 1934. Buescher's reminiscences are in the VU Archives (W. Buescher to R. Baepler: *PCV*, 8 January 1932). The general account of student culture is derived from *The Torch* and from alumni with long memories of firsthand experience, especially J. Strietelmeier, R. Springsteen, Theodore Schwan, and Betty Kelley Schwan. The discussion of Christiansen owes much to the VU Oral History Program and its interviews with former athletes. The inside story of the *Uhlan* naming is reported in *The Torch*, 23 January 1936, though the change took place much earlier. *The Torch*, 1 December 1927, refers to 40 campus organizations.

CHAPTER 7: A CLEAR, STRONG VISION

Kretzmann's telegram of acceptance is in the board's minutes, July 1940. The account of Kretzmann's life owes much to gracious letters to the author from Martin, Norman, Justus, and Mark Kretzmann; an interview with Betty Kretzmann; and discussions with Carlene Bartelt, Dorothy Herscher, Janie Lichtfuss, and with faculty who worked with him and knew him. Kretzmann's personal reminiscences appeared occasionally in the "Pilgrim" column of *The Cresset*; quotations cited here are from the July 1947 issue. The Perry County Christmas quote is from the *Campus Commentary*, December 1955. The *Proceedings* of the Annual Conferences of the ALC are a rich source of critique of the "semi-pagan social order" and of proposals for revitalizing the church. Lindemann's speech was given in 1935 and Kretzmann's in 1938. Contemporary memories of O. P.'s 1938 funeral oration for Lindemann are reported by Norman Kretzmann to Baepler, 17 November 1995. The text of Kretzmann's inaugural has been frequently republished; it is perhaps most accessible in Strietelmeier's *History*, p. 138. Strietelmeier's account of its reception is on p. 140. Fred Rechlin's reminiscences are part of the Oral History Project in VU's Archives. Roosevelt's "Stay in school" letter is found in *The Torch*, 17 October 1940; O. P.'s comments on the *Beacon* name are in *The Torch*, 6 February 1941. Kretzmann's wartime Christmas message is reported in *The Torch*, 17 December 1941. O. P.'s insistence on a critical evaluation of federal recommendations is found in the faculty minutes, V. II. 287. Scherer's account, "Wool Gathering," is in *The Torch*, 5 February 1942. Schwiebert's *Cresset* article is in the February 1942 issue. Kretzmann's account of departing students was written for the *Walther League Messenger* and reported without citation in *The Torch*, 6 November 1992, by Patrick Feaster, a reliable student historian. Richard Koenig's booklet supplies further information on the "World's Tallest Team." The most thorough study of the "Forty-Four," including interviews with participants, is a doctoral dissertation done at Vanderbilt University by Jack Treon Robinson in 1972. Useful reminiscences are provided in a commemorative article in *CHIQ*, November 1971. Kretzmann's papers on the "Forty-Four" are found in R.G. 4, Presidents, Kretzmann Papers, Boxes 13 and 14. The impact of the GI Bill has been studied often; Keith Olsen's survey is the basis for this discussion.

The history of Christian influence in higher education during this period has been studied recently by Douglas Sloan. In his paper on Christian higher education for the DeKoven group, Kretzmann quoted from the 1933 Studies in Lutheran Higher Education. Addresses to the ALCF and NLEC are in R.G. 4, Presidents, Kretzmann Papers, Box 6.2. Kretzmann's *Cresset* retrospective, from which the quote concerning the unity of religion and culture comes, is in the November 1952 issue. The Pelikan articles on the intellectual agenda are in the June 1947 and January 1948 issues of *The Cresset*. Koenker's "existentialism" article was published in the May 1948 issue of *The Cresset*. Strietelmeier's article appeared in the November 1952 *Cresset*. The story of VU and the LHRAA is told by Andrew Schulze in *Race against Time*, pp. 118 ff. The Lilly Endowment reports are on file in the VU Archives (R.G. 3, Institutional Surveys). O. P.'s comments on quality can be found in many places, for example, in his speech to the NLEC in R.G. 4, Presidents, Kretzmann Papers, Box 6.2. The board's minutes of this period are rich in narrative discussion. The Knopp-Board interchange, for example, is found in the minutes of 2–3 November 1951. The presentation of the report over the names of Gallmeyer, Gross, and Meier, along with President Behnken's reaction, are in the November 1953 board minutes.

CHAPTER 8: A TURNING POINT

Kretzmann's account of the fire appeared in the December 1956 *Campus Commentary*. The description of GG from Xanadu, Nebraska, (p. 233) is a direct quotation from Alan Graebner's *Uncertain Saints*, p. 171. Taylor's article in *Commonweal* is in the 29 January 1960 issue, p. 483 ff. The article on Dean Kell was written by VU professor Carl Galow in the *Walther League Messenger*, October 1959, pp. 18 ff. Kretzmann's address on launching the ICPC is in R.G. 4, Presidents, Kretzmann Papers, Box 6.20. The discussion on student life depends on interviews and conversations with former students, as well as on a research paper by Jody Seville. "Kentuckiana" basketball is discussed by Neil D. Isaacs on p. 109 ff. The VU Oral History Program contains a valuable interview with Emory Bauer on athletics at VU, including Kretzmann's attitudes. The chapel address at the end of the semester (p. 244) is found in R.G. 4, President, Kretzmann Papers, Box 6.6. Feaster's recollection (p. 245) is from *The Torch*, 16 September 1975. Koenker's *Cresset* article appeared in the July 1952 issue; Marty's appeared in December 1954. Miller's quote is on p. 129. The particular joint meeting of the boards of VU and the Synod took place 2 November 1956. Marty's account of the Miss America Pageant is in the *Journal of the Association of Lutheran College Faculties*, December 1959, p. 12 ff. Leege's column is in *The Torch*, 25 September 1958. Kretzmann's reaction to the hazing incident is reported in *The Torch*, 24 September 1959. The Lee quote is from the *Lighter*, Winter 1959. A. R Kretzmann's dedication sermon is quoted in *The Torch*, 26 September 1959. Gail McGrew's letter is in the VU Archives. The Hutchins quotation (p. 253) is reported by witness Richard Scheimann. The Tillich reaction was witnessed personally by the author. The Kretzmann Christmas Vespers sermon is in R.G. 4, President, Kretzmann Papers, Box 6.10.

CHAPTER 9: THE 1960S: EXPANSION AND CHANGE

Kretzmann's reflections were published as "The Idea of a Christian University," in *The Christian Scholar*, Winter 1961. The proceedings of the two Theology and Law conferences are in the VU Archives. Rosenhaupt's speech is reported in the VU News Bureau release, 18 November 1960. After his retirement, Dr. Albert Huegli wrote a brief autobiographical monograph for his family, titled *All My Journey Through*. It is in the VU Archives and is a source for this and subsequent chapters. The account of O. P.'s "takeover" of the Administrative Council are part of the detailed minutes of that body, which furnish rich insight into the VU administration in the 1960s (R.G. 5, Administrative Council). The Rupprecht letter is in the microfilmed Andrew Schulze correspondence in the Moellering Library. Fred Bernthal's piece is in *The Torch*, 1 October 1963. Kretzmann's description of the impact of JFK's death is in his *Campus Commentary*, January 1964. The faculty minutes of the time provide basic information on the faculty's struggle to find and express its voice. The account of the skirmish over evolution draws from Numbers, pp. 301–05, and from Krekeler's personal memoir in his file in the VU Archives (R.G. 6, Faculty and Staff, Biographical). The Hutchinson

Report is in R.G. 3, Institutional Surveys. The general historical literature on the 1960s is vast. I have depended especially on Patterson, Ravitch, and Matusow. The Kretzmann-*The Torch* editor account is from a personal account. The Boyd lecture and Ayres's review is in *The Torch*, 20 September 1962. The Friedrich speech at Kretzmann's 25th anniversary is in the Friedrich file (R.G. 6, Faculty and Staff, Biographical). The Tolle study is in his file (R.G. 6, Faculty and Staff, Biographical). Hesburgh's quotation from his address is in the O'Brien biography, pp. 239–40. O. P.'s performance at the All Campus Congress is reported by Fred Spannaus in *The Torch*, 3 November 1967. Piehl's final editorial is in *The Torch*, 17 January 1968.

CHAPTER 10: THROUGH THE FIRE

The summer task force report is available in R.G. 3, Institutional Surveys. The six requests are reported in *The Torch*, 12 March 1969. Carl Krekeler's speech at Huegli's inauguration is in his papers, R.G. 6, Faculty and Staff, Biographical. The "tone and character" announcement is in *The Torch*, 27 February 1970. Heinemann is the source for much of the background material for this period. For the events leading up to and following the Kinsey fire, the 21 October 1971 Report of the Kinsey Hall Investigating Committee, chaired by Louis Bartelt, is a reliable guide, though it wrongly identifies the date of the Cambodia incursion. Its valuable witness interviews are in the R.G. 6, Faculty, Committees and Reports. The Rubke interview confirms the mind-set and armed preparation of the National Guard, though the actual quotation by Galow is from another interview reported on p. 22 of the Steinke, Scharold, Swanson, Burreson, Wohrley team report. For several years, students in a Christ College course investigated this episode and wrote team papers, often based on interviews, which are also illuminating and are filed in the archives. The discussion in this chapter draws from all these materials, as well as extended conversations with faculty and administrative participants. See also "Kinsey Hall Fire" in R.G. 4, President, Subject File, 1940–78. The senate's deliberations on the independent study projects are accurately reported in *The Torch*, 12 May 1970. The account of the legal outcome is based on discussions with Strietelmeier, Mundinger, and Huegli, though they did not reveal names.

CHAPTER 11: THE 1970S: CONFRONTING CONTEMPORARY CHALLENGES

A basic survey of the 1970s is Peter Carroll's study. Winifred Wandersee's study on American women in the 1970s is also valuable for the whole range of that decade's history. The report of consultants from the Robert Johnston Corporation is available in R.G. 3, Institutional Surveys. Edward Schroeder's comments on theology is part of a lengthy analysis he published in *The Torch*, 29 January 1971. The story of computers at VU is based on an interview with John Sorenson. The history of the Sloan Collection relies on a presentation by John Strietelmeier to "Friends of Art" at the dedication of the VUCA. Professor Jack Hiller supplied me with the Naeve Report, which also found its way into the Faculty Handbook. Gwen Sayler, now a professor at Wartburg Lutheran Seminary, provided much insight into student life of the time in a personal interview. Rubke's reports to the board are professionally done and historically valuable documents. See especially the board's minutes for 27 July 1973 on "Christian bases for decisions." The "tradition of drinking" is discussed in Rubke's report to the board on 20 July 1974. David Hoekema's outstanding work is the basis for the legal and ethical discussion regarding the "silent revolution." The 1979 court ruling is quoted by Hoekema on p. 119. Dean Schroer's remarks were reported in *The Torch*, 8 October 1976.

There is substantial critical literature on the NCAA. This discussion depends on Walter Byers (former executive secretary of the NCAA), Murray Sperber, and John Thelin. The North Central self-study is on file in the archives, as is the report prepared by Arlin Meyer's subcommittee. The Strietelmeier-Luecke pieces are in the *Lighter*, December 1972 and March 1973. Strietelmeier's remarks are in his papers (R.G. 6, Faculty and Staff, John Strietelmeier, Papers and Publications). An account of several schisms in American Christianity in the 1970s, including that of the LCMS, is in the book by Bryan V. Hillis. It must be emphasized that participants in this traumatic event still see and understand the events in differing ways. I consulted several participants and different accounts and have attempted to state issues and describe events cautiously. The protest letter was published in *The Torch*, 5 February 1974. Huegli's position is made clear in his memoirs and confirmed in an interview. Huegli's convocation address, together with presentations by other participants in the symposium, are collected in a booklet, *The Splendid Heritage*, on file in the archives.

CHAPTER 12: THE 1980S: BOLD MOVES AND GROWING STATURE

The discussion on the background of higher education in the 1980s depends especially on Geiger, *Research and Relevant Knowledge*, p. 310 ff. The full text of Strietelmeier's comments are in his papers (R.G. 6, Faculty, Strietelmeier, Papers and Publication). Schnabel's papers are in R.G. 4, President, Schnabel Papers. Siess's *Lighter* article is in the Fall 1979 issue. The records and documents relevant to CUPP are in the VU Archives. Faculty comments on students of the 1980s are in *The Torch*, 20 January 1986. C. Nuechterlein's column is in *The Torch*, 20 October 1982. Yamada's account of the death of Spagoletti is found in *The Torch*, 11 December 1979. Senne's sermon and Schnabel's address are in *The Torch*, 11 December 1979. Montague's column is in *The Torch*, 1 November 1982. Farago's paragraphs are in the law school's *Bulletin*, 1979–80, p. 12. A good retrospective on the Pinto case is found in an interview with Berner, *Forum*, 10 November 1980. Schwehn's *Cresset* articles are in the April and May 1985 issues. Ludwig's article is in the September 1984 *Cresset*. The politics of higher education is described by Constance E. Cook. *The Torch*'s cartoon of Schnabel appeared in *The Torch*, 2 May 1983. Marcia Klett's full column is in *The Torch*, 8 April 1981. "Valparaiso and The Lutheran Church—Missouri Synod" is filed in the board's minutes of January 1988. The editorial on Nagel and his interview with *The Torch* is in 28 February 1983. The chapel activities are described in *The Torch*, 21 October 1986. The discussion on fraternities and sororities in this period has been aided by an excellent honors paper by Wendy Bertva that is on file in the VU Archives. The discussion on the NCAA and the proliferation of new conferences is based partly on Byers, p. 35 ff. The NCAA's "takeover" of the AIAW is described as "predatory" by Sperber, p. 322; Byer's account is more sympathetic to the NCAA. The reference to Schwehn's article is to the pair of *Cresset* pieces mentioned above. Kretzmann's address on the ending of the war is in R.G. 4, President, Kretzmann Papers, Box 8.9. Marsden's views are expressed in his *The Outrageous Idea of Christian Scholarship*; his major historical study is *The Soul of the American University*. Burtchaell's study is *The Dying of Light*. Nuechterlein's paper was published in the *Cresset*, December 1986. Jass's views are in *The Torch*, 13 January 1986.

CHAPTER 13: THE 1990S: POSTMODERN TIMES

The director of church relations during this period, Charles Werth, ably tracked the ecclesiastical trends in the current literature and reported them to the board and the faculty. "Watershed happening" is from Harre's address to the faculty on 30 August 1988. Two other addresses—his remarks to the new faculty and his inaugural address—need to be read together to understand Harre's general views at the beginning of his administration. The huge documentation of the strategic planning committee is in the VU Archives. Harre's address after meeting with black students, together with Thompson's response, is in *The Torch*, 17 April 1992. Gilbertson's evaluation of the multicultural efforts is expressed in *The Torch*, 2 December 1994. Harre summarized his 8 April 1992 meeting with students regarding proposed distribution of condoms in his report to the board at the April meeting. For background on the national mood of the time, see "The Fraying of America," *Time*, 2 February 1992. An example of Smith's frequent reminders is in the board's minutes for October 1993. Harre's concern over an empty Wehrenberg Hall is found in the board's minutes of July 1994. The million-dollar-plus windfall from the Gast Scholarship endowment, also approved for other uses by Walter Gast, is reported in the board's minutes of October 1996. The 2 percent additional earnings from the endowment was approved at the July 1997 board meeting. The "Bill of Rights" lectures were published in *Valparaiso University Law Review* 26, Fall 1991. The Damrosch quotation is on p. 9. The full Peters Report is available in the VU Archives. The senate debate is well reported in *The Torch*, 19 April 1991. The basketball story is told in Malayter and Drew. The editorial excerpts may be found in full context in the *Indianapolis Star*, 20 March 1998. The provost's hope is expressed in his report to the board in the board's minutes of April 1996.

CONCLUSION

Robert Benne first applied Reinhold Niebuhr's famous formulation concerning "the perennial relevance of an impossible ethical ideal" to the aspirations of Christian higher education. Pelikan's views on the University are found in his *The Idea of a University—A Reexamination*. See especially pp. 11–21.

Reference Bibliography

Albers, James W. "Aspects of Social Action in The Lutheran Church—Missouri Synod during the Nineteenth Century." *CHIQ* 45 (May 1972): 107–24.

———. "The History of Attitudes within the Missouri Synod toward Life Insurance." Th.D. diss., Concordia Theological Seminary, 1972.

———. *From Centennial to Golden Anniversary: The History of Valparaiso University from 1959–1975*. Valparaiso, Indiana: Valparaiso University, 1976.

Baepler, Walter A. *A Century of Grace: A History of the Missouri Synod, 1847–1947*. St. Louis: Concordia, 1947.

Beatty, William K. "Petra Marie Dahl—Physician, Social Activist, and Norwegian." *The Proceedings of the Institute of Medicine of Chicago* 43 (January/March 1990): 3–9.

Benne, Robert. "A Lutheran Vision/Version of Christian Humanism." *Lutheran Forum* (Fall 1997): 40–46.

Bennett, William J. *To Reclaim a Legacy: A Report on the Humanities in Higher Education*. Washington, D.C.: National Endowment for the Humanities, 1984.

Bliss, Kathleen M. *Women of the Klan*. Berkeley: University of California Press, 1991.

Bloom, Allan. *The Closing of the American Mind*. New York: Simon and Schuster, 1987.

Brinkley, Alan. *Voices of Protest: Huey Long, Father Coughlin, and the Great Depression*. New York: Random House, 1982.

Burtchaell, James T. *The Dying of the Light: The Disengagement of Colleges and Universities from Their Christian Churches*. Grand Rapids: W. B. Eerdmans, 1998.

Byers, Walter. *Unsportsmanlike Conduct*. Ann Arbor: The University of Michigan Press, 1995.

Carrol, Peter. *It Seemed Like Nothing Happened: The Tragedy and Promise of American Life in the 1970s*. New York: Holt, Rinehart and Winston, 1982.

Christowe, Stoyan. *This Is My Country*. New York: Corrish and Evans, 1938.

Coburn, Carol K. *Life at Four Corners*. Lawrence, Kansas: The University Press of Kansas, 1992.

Cook, Constance E. *Lobbying for Higher Education*. Nashville: Vanderbilt University Press, 1998.

Damrosch, David. *We Scholars: Changing the Culture of the University*. Cambridge: Harvard University Press, 1995.

Dyer, Thomas G. "The Klan on Campus: C. Lewis Fowler and Lanier University." *South Atlantic Quarterly* 77 (1978): 453–69.

Fass, Paula. *The Damned and the Beautiful: American Youth in the 1920s*. New York:

Oxford University Press, 1986.

Forster, Walter O. *Zion on the Mississippi.* St. Louis: Concordia, 1953.

Geiger, Roger L. *To Advance Knowledge: The Growth of American Research Universities 1900–1940.* New York: Oxford University Press, 1986.

———. "The Era of Multipurpose Colleges in American Higher Education, 1850 to 1890." *History of Higher Education Annual* 15 (1995): 51–92.

———. *Research and Relevant Knowledge: American Research Universities Since World War II.* New York: Oxford University Press, 1993.

Galow, Carl. "Big Brave in Wild Tepee." *Walther League Messenger.* (October 1959): 19–21.

Gar, Hubert. *East Hall, A Story of the Northern Indiana Normal School.* Private printing, n.d.

Gleason, Philip. *Contending with Modernity: Catholic Higher Education in the Twentieth Century.* New York: Oxford University Press, 1995.

Graebner, Alan. "Thinking about the Laity in The Lutheran Church—Missouri Synod." *CHIQ* 45, no. 2 (May 1972): 125–39.

———. *Uncertain Saints.* Westport, Connecticut: Greenwood Press, 1975.

Graebner, Theodore. "Our Higher Education." *Theological Quarterly* (July 1919): 171–80.

Gitlin, Todd. *The Twilight of Common Dreams: Why America Is Wracked by Culture Wars.* New York: Metropolitan Books, 1995.

Hall, Thomas R. "The Russian Community of Chicago." *Illinois History and Transactions for the Year 1937.* Illinois State Historical Society 44. Springfield, Illinois, 1938.

Hatch, Nathan O. *The Democratization of American Christianity.* New Haven: Yale University Press, 1989.

Heineman, Kenneth J. *Campus Wars.* New York: New York University Press, 1993.

Hillis, Bryan V. *Can Two Walk Together Unless They Be Agreed? American Religious Schisms in the Seventies.* Brooklyn: Carlson, 1991.

Hoekema, David. *Campus Rules and Moral Community: In Place of* In loco Parentis. Lanham, Maryland: Rowman and Littlefield, 1994.

Holbrook, Alfred. *Reminiscences of the Happy Life of a Teacher.* Cincinnati: Elm Street Printing, 1885.

Holst, Byron. "American Lutheran Educational Association." *LW* 39 (14 September 1920): 298.

Horowitz, Helen Lefkowitz. *Campus Life.* Chicago: The University of Chicago Press, 1987.

Huegli, Albert G. *All My Journey Through.* Private printing, 1995.

Isaacs, Neil D. *All the Moves: A History of College Basketball.* Philadelphia: J. P. Lippincott, 1975.

Jeansonne, Glen. *Gerald L. K. Smith, Minister of Hate.* New Haven: Yale University Press, 1988.

Jacobs, Dan N. *Stalin's Man in China.* Cambridge: Harvard University Press, 1981.

Kay, Karl J. *History of the National Normal University of Lebanon, Ohio.* Wilmington, Ohio: Wilmington College, 1929.

Kennedy, Sarah L. *H. S. Lehr and His School.* Ada, Ohio: The University Press of Ohio Northern University, 1983.

Kernan, Alvin. *In Plato's Cave.* New Haven: Yale University Press, 1999.

Kimball, Roger. *Tenured Radicals.* New York: Harper and Row, 1990.

Koenig, Richard P. *The Crusader: Athletic Yearbook of Valparaiso University.* Private printing, 1948.

Kretzmann, Otto P. *The Road Back to God.* Chicago: The Walther League, 1935.

———. "The State of Visible Christendom." *The American Lutheran* 22/23 (1939/1940): (March) 13–14, (April) 7–8, (May) 6–8, (June) 8–10, (July) 9–10, (September) 9–10, (October) 8–9, (November) 11–12, (January) 10–11, (February) 11–12, (March) 18–19, (May) 7–8, (July) 6–7.

Leif, Alfred. *Democracy's Norris: The Biography of a Lonely Crusader.* New York: Stockpole Sons, 1939.

Levine, Arthur. *When Dreams and Heroes Died.* San Francisco: Jossey-Bass, 1980.

———. *When Hopes and Fears Collide.* San Francisco: Jossey-Bass, 1998.

Levine, David O. *The American College and the Culture of Aspiration.* Ithaca: Cornell University Press, 1986.

Lueking Dean F. *A Century of Caring: The Welfare Ministry among Missouri Synod Lutherans, 1868–1968.* St. Louis: Board of Social Ministry, The Lutheran Church—Missouri Synod, 1968.

Malayter, Shawn, with Homer Drew and Rob Rains. *Find a Way: Valpo's "Sweet" Dream.* South Bend, Indiana: Diamond Communications, 1999.

Manhart, George B. *DePauw through the Years.* Greencastle, Indiana: DePauw University, 1962.

Marsden, George. *The Soul of the American University: From Protestant Establishment to Established Nonbelief.* New York: Oxford University Press, 1994.

———. *The Outrageous Idea of Christian Scholarship.* New York: Oxford University Press, 1997.

Marty, Martin E. "The Lutheran College in the Next Decade." *Journal of the Association of Lutheran College Faculties* 10, no. 1 (December 1959): 11–27.

Matre, Richard A. *Loyola University and Its Medical Center: A Century of Courage and Turmoil.* Chicago: Loyola University, 1995.

Matusow, Allen J. *The Unraveling of America: A History of Liberalism in the 1960s.* New York: Harper and Row, 1984.

Meyer, Carl S. *Log Cabin to Luther Tower.* St. Louis: Concordia, 1965.

Meyer, Don. *The Instructed Conscience: The Shaping of the American National Ethic.* Philadelphia: University of Pennsylvania Press, 1972.

Meyer, Ruth Fritz. *Women on a Mission.* St. Louis: Lutheran Women's Missionary League, 1967.

Miller, William Lee. *Piety on the Potomac.* Boston: Houghton Mifflin, 1964.

Mundinger, Carl S. *Government in the Missouri Synod: The Genesis of Decentralized Government in the Missouri Synod.* St. Louis: Concordia, 1947.

Mock, Albert. *The Midwestern Academy Movement: A Comprehensive Study of Indiana Academies 1810–1900.* Ed.D. diss., Indiana University, 1949.

Neuberger, Richard L., and Stephen B. Kaln. *The Life of George Norris.* New York: Vanguard Press, 1937.

Neely, Tim. *Hooping It Up: The Complete History of Notre Dame Basketball.* Notre Dame, Indiana: n. p., 1985.

Noll, Mark A. *A History of Christianity in the United States and Canada.* Grand Rapids, Michigan: Eerdmans, 1992.

Norris, George. *Fighting Liberal, the Autobiography of George Norris.* New York: The Macmillan Company, 1945.

Nuechterlein, James. "Faith and Learning in the Christian University," *The Cresset* 50 (December 1986): 9–16.

Numbers, Ronald L. *The Creationists.* New York: Alfred A. Knopf, 1992.

O'Brien, Michael. *Hesburgh: A Biography.* Washington, D.C.: Catholic University of America Press, 1998.

Olson, Keith W. *The G.I. Bill, the Veterans, and the Colleges.* Lexington: The University Press of Kentucky, 1974.

Pahl, Jon. *Hopes and Dreams of All.* Chicago: Wheat Ridge Ministries, 1993.

Pannkoke, Otto H. *A Great Church Finds Itself.* Quitman, Georgia: Private printing, 1966.

———. "Shall the Missouri Synod Expand Its Educational System to Serve the Laity?" *The American Lutheran* 22 (September 1939): 7–9; (October): 10–12; (November): 8–10; (December): 12–13.

Patterson, James T. *Grand Expectations: The United States, 1945–1974.* New York: Oxford University Press, 1996.

Pelikan, Jaroslav. *The Idea of the University: A Reexamination.* New Haven: Yale University Press, 1992.

———. *The Vindication of Tradition.* New Haven: Yale University Press, 1984.

———. *From Luther to Kierkegaard.* St. Louis: Concordia, 1950.

Ravitch, Diane. *The Troubled Crusade: American Education 1945–1980.* New York: Basic Books, 1983.

Robinson, Jack T. *The Spirit of Triumphalism in The Lutheran Church—Missouri Synod: The Role of The 'A Statement' of 1945 in the Missouri Synod.* Ph.D.diss., Vanderbilt University, 1972.

Salin, George P. *Methodist Schools in the North West Indiana Conference.* Ed.D. diss., Indiana University, 1952.

Schmid, Ralph D. *A Study of the Organizational Structure of the National Education Association 1884–1921.* Ph.D. diss., Washington University, 1963.

Schwehn, Mark R. *Exiles from Eden: Religion and the Academic Vocation in America.* New York: Oxford University Press, 1983.

———. "Academics as a Vocation." *The Cresset* 48 (April 1985): 4–9.

———. "Academics as a Vocation–II." *The Cresset* 48 (May 1985): 5–10.

Schoenfeld, William. "The Present Urgent Call for Expansion of Synod's System of Higher Education." *Theological Quarterly* (July 1919): 143–70.

Sloan, Douglas. *Faith and Knowledge: Mainline Protestantism and American Higher Education.* Louisville: Westminster John Knox Press, 1994.

Smith, Joan K. *Ella Flagg Young: Portrait of a Leader.* Ames, Iowa: Educational Studies Press, 1976.

Smith, John L. *Indiana Methodism.* Private printing, 1892.

Smith, Timothy L. *The History of Education in the Middle West.* Indianapolis: Indiana Historical Society, 1978.

Solberg, Richard W. *Lutheran Higher Education in North America.* Minneapolis: Augsburg, 1985.

Solomon, Barbara. *In the Company of Educated Women: A History of Women and Higher Education in America.* New Haven: Yale University Press, 1985.

Sperber, Murray. *College Sports, Inc.: The Athletic Department vs. the University.* New York: Henry Holt, 1990.

———. *Shake Down the Thunder: The Creation of Notre Dame Football.* New York: Henry Holt, 1993.

Stevens, Robert. *Law School.* Chapel Hill: The University of North Carolina Press, 1983.

Stimpson, George W. *The Story of Valparaiso University.* Private printing, 1921.

Strietelmeier, John. *Valparaiso's First Century.* Valparaiso, Indiana: Valparaiso University, 1959.

Studies in Lutheran Higher Education. Vol. 1, no. 1. Minneapolis: Augsburg, 1933.

Studies in Lutheran Higher Education. Vol. 1, no. 2. Minneapolis: Augsburg, 1935.

Taylor, Jeremy. "Religion in College." *The Commonweal* 71 no. 18 (29 January 1960).

Thomas, Lowell. *Good Evening Everybody.* New York: Morrow, 1976.

Todd, Mary. *Authority Vested: A Story of Identity and Change in The Lutheran Church—Missouri Synod.* Grand Rapids: W. B. Eerdmans, 2000.

Thelin, John R. *Games Colleges Play.* Baltimore: The Johns Hopkins Press, 1994.

Trusty, Lance. "All Talk and No 'Kash': Valparaiso University and the Ku Klux Klan." *Indiana Magazine of History* 82 (March 1986).

Van Reenan, Antanas J. *Lithuania Diaspora: Koenigsberg to Chicago.* New York:

University Press of America, 1990.

Vonderlage, E. Fred. "The American Luther League: A One-Purpose Organization." *CHIQ* 26, no. 2 (July 1963): 33–42.

———. "The Michigan Storm Center in the School Question." *CHIQ*, 37–45.

Wandersee, Winifred. *On the Move: American Women in the 1970s.* Boston: Twayne Publisher, 1988.

Wesley, Edgar B. *NEA: The First Hundred Years.* New York: Harper, 1957.

Wiebe, Robert H. *The Search for Order.* New York: Hill and Wang, 1967.

INDEX OF NAMES

Brief Index of Subjects